HISTORY OF INTERNATIONAL

FASHION

DIDIER GRUMBACH

First published in 2014 by

INTERLINK BOOKS
An imprint of Interlink Publishing Group, Inc.
46 Crosby Street, Northampton, Massachusetts 01060
www.interlinkbooks.com

Originally published in French as *Histoires de la mode*

Published simultaneously by Roli Books, New Delhi, India. www.rolibooks.com
Published with the support of the Institut Français en Inde/Ambassade de France en Inde and the Fashion Design Council of India (FDCI)

Library of Congress Cataloging-in-Publication Data

Grumbach, Didier.
[Histoires de la mode. English]
History of international fashion / by Didier Grumbach ; photo editor Isabelle d'Hauteville.
pages cm
"Originally published in French as Histoires de la mode."
Includes bibliographical references and index.
ISBN 978-1-56656-976-7
1. Fashion design--History. 2. Fashion--History. 3. Fashion design--France--History--20th century. 4. Fashion--France--History--20th century. I. Title.
TT504.6.F7G7813 2014
746.9'2--dc23

2014004755

ISBN 978-1-56656-976-7

General Editor: Michel Moushabeck
English translation: Katie Weisman and Renuka Anne George
Book production: Pam Fontes-May
Proofreading: Ann Childs and Jennifer Staltare

Printed and bound in China

10 9 8 7 6 5 4 3 2 1

To request our complete 48-page, full-color catalog, please call us toll free at 1-800-238-LINK, visit our website at www.interlinkbooks.com, or send us an e-mail: info@interlinkbooks.com

HISTORY OF INTERNATIONAL

FASHION

DIDIER GRUMBACH

PHOTO EDITOR
ISABELLE D'HAUTEVILLE

An imprint of Interlink Publishing Group, Inc.
Northampton, Massachusetts

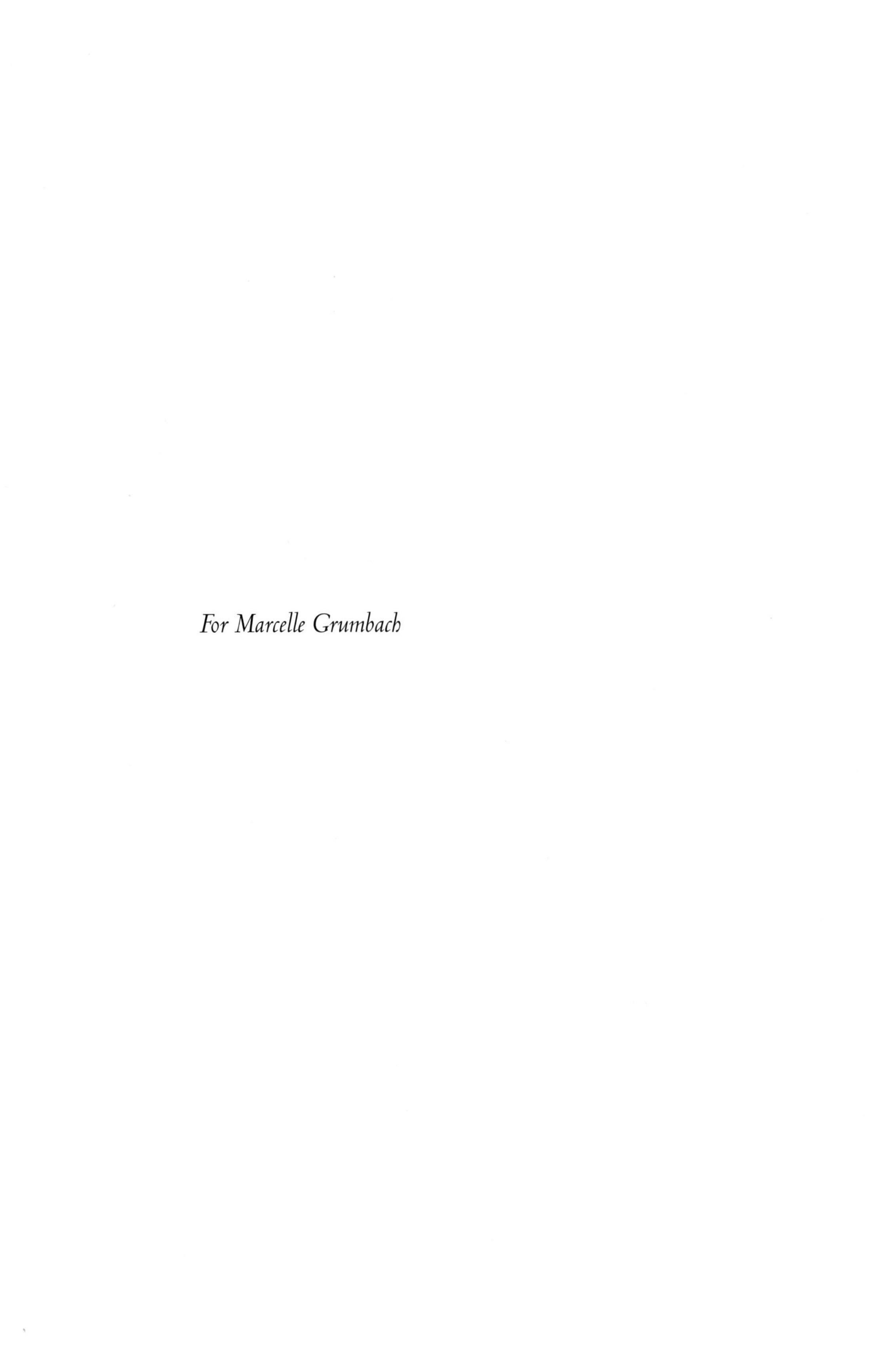

For Marcelle Grumbach

CONTENTS

FOREWORD

Two decades ago the French edition of this book, *Histoires de la Mode,* was published for the first time. Translated since into Brazilian, Korean, Chinese, Romanian, Japanese, it is now making its appearance in English and has a new title—*History of International Fashion.* The change in title echoes the purpose of the book, which explains why our countries' various sources of inspiration are becoming the same.

Written over the years, the book examines the evolution of our profession, the most visible sign of which is the acceleration in the number of foreign brands present during the biannual Paris Fashion Weeks *(Semaine des créateurs de mode).* This cosmopolitanism has always been a part of French tradition. The first few Grand Couturiers were English: Charles Frederick Worth, considered the father of haute couture fashion, and "Lucile" Lucy Duff Gordon, the first guest member of the Paris Couture session. Today, this overture to foreign designers, especially from Asia, exists in all our activities.

The 2013 women's wear calendar featured 23 nationalities. In March, Chinese designer Yang Li was a revelation. From Korea, Wooyoungmi and Juun.J showed immense success with their collections; they are now members of the French Federation, the governing body of French fashion. Japan is also essential to Parisian fashion events. The contribution of Japanese creations to the world of fashion frequently consists of their own interpretation of the European repertory. The first Japanese designer to showcase his collection in Paris was Issey Miyake in 1973. He opened the path to make way for Yohji Yamamoto, Rei Kawakubo for *Comme des Garçons,* Junya Watanabe, and so on, preceding Chitose Abe for *Sacai* and Jun Takahashi for *Undercover.* Even in the haute couture list, usually regarded as a French specialty, Asia is welcome. Yiqing Yin has been elected into the haute couture calendar since 2011. Ma Ke, designer for the Chinese First Lady Peng Liyuan and founder of the label *Wuyong,* was also invited by the Grand Couturiers to the 2008 haute couture calendar.

Said to be fading for decades, haute couture is central once again. Who would have believed that in the twenty-first century, young designers would want to be a part of that venerable institution? After the likes of Chanel, Dior, Valentino, Armani, Jean Paul Gaultier, now emerge young couturiers like Alexandre Vauthier, Bouchra Jarrar, Yiqing Yin, and so on, who like their predecessors will generate global brands until the next generation. As a group, these young couturiers showcased their collections during the Inaugural Singapore Fashion Week 2011 at a special event organized by the French Federation, which was dedicated to French Couturiers and guest members.

Beyond Asia, the Parisian scene sees extremely positive signs from other horizons too. Ralph Lauren's presence is increasing in Paris; he showed his collection in October 2013 at the Ecole des Beaux-Arts (National School of Fine Arts in Paris). Azzedine Alaïa at the same time showcased a retrospective at the Galliera Museum. He also opened a store close to the avenue Montaigne and launched a perfume, like his friend, Thierry Mugler, who created a show in December 2013 called "Mugler's Follies" before initiating a much-expected retrospective.

Numerous fashion weeks attract their respective regional publics but their differentiated collections can only reach the worldwide market that they need from Paris. Rick Owens from Los Angeles or Manish Arora from Delhi would not have been as successful from their own countries. Most of the members of the French Federation who showcase their collections in Paris export about 90 per cent of their sales.

The haute couture committee accepted the return of Schiaparelli in the haute couture schedule in November 2013 after 60 years of absence; it also requested the Ministry of Industry to grant the Frenchwoman Bouchra Jarrar the haute couture appellation and elected two new guest members from Turkey and England. The internationalization of the French Federation has continued from 1998 and has enabled an orderly and constant evolution of each seasonal session.

Finally, can there be another fashion capital? I believe not, as long as Paris remains open to the world.

Didier Grumbach, *January 2014*

INTRODUCTION

Fashion is a complete reflection of society. It does not die on the threshold of its existence as its fleeting nature could suggest. Instead, it works alongside our daily life, infusing it with dreams and passion. This is why the idea of controlling it is so attractive as its influence is closely linked to power. To better understand this, we must examine the changes that affected the industry during the twentieth century that gave rise to the most violent conflicts and assembled the most dogged resistance in a context where the very organization of the fashion trade could only further exacerbate the debate.

French couture distinguishes itself in two ways. Firstly, it enjoys a special status that sets it apart from the apparel sector because of its pricing, technique, clientele, and aura. Secondly, couture stands out from its foreign counterparts because of the unquestionable originality of its developmental path.

For over a century, and until the beginning of the 1960s, haute couture reigned undisputedly over trends and dictated fashion to the world. With such influence, it is easy to understand the desire to keep the cultural and economic heritage of haute couture as a subject of French national interest.

During the twentieth century, three key dates mark the history of couture. In 1910, couture separated from the apparel trade. These two complementary business approaches—often combined within the same company—were split, creating two competing trades that were each represented by their own union. In 1943, under the Vichy regime, the industry saw the introduction of label legislation that divided fashion into several categories, such as couture, couturier, couture-création, and "haute couture." Thirty years later, two industries that had long been considered contradictory assembled—but did not associate—into a new organization: Fédération française de la couture, du prêt-à-porter des couturiers et des créateurs de mode.

This path was chosen for the glory of our industries but nonetheless generated numerous and painful malfunctions. In order to preserve all of its privileges, couture often put business strategies into place that were not supported by other members of the profession. For example, in order to stop the hemorrhaging of revenues it had experienced since 1925, couture increased its sales of the rights for the reproduction of its models exclusively for foreign buyers. This approach stopped making sense in 1950. At that time, couture houses had started to establish their own ready-to-wear lines, thereby competing with themselves, and non-couture manufacturers started to label their collections that had been hitherto anonymous. In its continued fight to stem economic losses, fashion prostituted itself by granting the use of its labels to other industries, a practice that was soon devalued in the 1970s with the emergence of well-established foreign labels and the appearance of fashion creators.

In spite of its desire for independence, couture, by its very nature, cannot be separated from the ready-to-wear industry. Over the years, couture and the apparel trade have lived in relationships of perfect harmony, armed peace, or outright battle, a dynamic inherent to any microcosm.

This book is not a history of fashion, hence the absence of certain key designers. It aspires to be the story of the creation, the evolution, and the implosion of the fashion trade and to offer perspectives on a profession that, like any other social body, defines itself as much by its origins as by its current economic context.

The first part of this work relates the emergence of couture. The second part explains the rise of ready-to-wear in France, from its origins to the moment it was taken over by haute couture, and then by talented designers who till then had kept their distance from the trade.

While it is fairly simple to retrace the history of couture till World War II, when it reflected a society that was used to conventions and that accepted no changes, it is a far more complex affair to explain couture from the 1950s onwards. During the second half of the twentieth century, couture, in its struggle for survival, tried to define itself at both a formal and structural level only to find itself lost in a tangle of plots and proposals.

Thus, in addition to my own memories and in the interest of objectivity, I sought to gather a number of accounts—the excellence of oral tradition—from professionals who played an active part in the history of fashion over the last 65 years.

PART ONE

Haute Couture

Previous page **Jacques Louis David**
Consecration of the Emperor Napoleon and Crowing of the Empress Josephine at Notre Dame, 2 December 1804,
detail. Paris, Musée du Louvre.
Photo RMN / © Hervé Lewandowski.

Elisabeth Vigée-Lebrun
Queen Marie-Antoinette.
Location unknown.
Documentation service painting department, Paris, Musée du Louvre.

Opposite: Rose Bertin, Queen Marie-Antoinette's seamstress.
Rights Reserved.

CHAPTER I
Defending a Tradition

The Origins of Couture

Until the seventeenth century, dressmakers had only a modest place in society. They executed work for tailors and lingerie makers, although some managed to develop their own clientele, of course in the greatest secrecy. In fact, only master tailors were authorized to dress men and women. Dressmakers found guilty of crossing the line into private business were pursued pitilessly. They were the victims of virtual witch-hunts. They were fined, and fabrics and garments found in their homes were seized. It was only in 1675, by order of King Louis XIV, that master dressmakers gained some professional recognition and a share of the "market" on the pretext that it was "suitable and fitting for a woman's and girl's delicacy and modesty, to allow them to be dressed by persons of their own sex, when they considered it appropriate." It was nonetheless forbidden for these dressmakers to keep any lengths of fabric in their boutiques or for them to sell it. The dressmaker's profession was divided into four categories: the garment dressmaker, the children's dressmaker, the underwear dressmaker, and the accessory dressmaker.

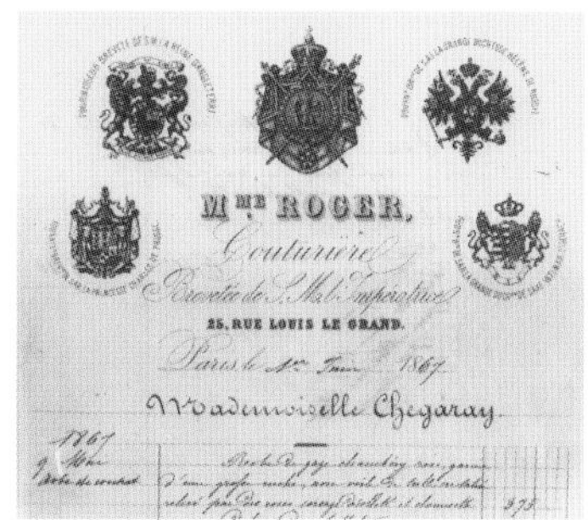
Mme ROGER,
Couturière
25, RUE LOUIS LE GRAND.
Paris le 1er Juin 1867.
Mademoiselle Chegaray.

Bill from the seamstress Madame Roger, 1867. Paris, Musée galliéra, Musée de la mode, Print Collection. © PMVP/Photo Ladet.

In 1782, dressmakers were finally given the right to compete with tailors for making different kinds of corsets, wooden hoops for skirts, men's dressing gowns, and hooded costumes for balls. As a result of this new exposure, some dressmakers became famous. Among those whose names have survived for posterity were Rose Bertin under Louis XVI, Madame Palmyre under Charles X, Mademoiselle Beaudrant under Louis Philippe… However famous they became, their autonomy and scope of business was restricted. Under Louis XIV, when strict rules of etiquette dictated daily life, members of the court and noble families adhered to the rules and obligations imposed by the king.

> Fabric was classified by seasons: in winter, velvets, satins, ratines and wool; in summer, taffetas; in autumn or spring, light wool. Even lace varied according to the season. Point d'Angleterre, that was no warmer than Malines[1], could not be used before the Longchamp parties. Furs were worn from All Saints Day onwards; at Easter, muffs were to be put aside and were not to be seen again, even if it snowed. Once a woman had reached the age of forty, she had to wear a black lace cap to attend court.[2]

In this absence of special dispensation from the fashion norms, the work of the trade groups became significant. Their decisions were paramount and were followed blindly. After long deliberations, annual corporate meetings decided on the changes to bring to fashion. Yet however long they spent in discussing the decrees that were scrupulously followed, their decisions only concerned small details about fashion. Thus, changes in fashion took place slowly. Only an important event, like a sovereign's marriage to a foreign princess, could bring about a sudden change in fashion trends to make them correspond to the habits or tastes of the new queen.

Fashion was primarily a privilege of the court.[3] After all, before she left Austria, Marie-Antoinette received strict instructions from her mother, Empress Marie-Thérèse, to keep full control over it. Once she decided on a model, the notable fashion houses hired specialized personnel for the sewing. Ceremonial clothing, however, was ordered from the tailor or the dressmaker.

The work of a dressmaker, who traditionally worked at home, was to make a dress ordered by a client after the latter had selected the fabric at the draper's. The originality of the dress and its style was not as important as the choice of the fabric. Despite their influence over women's fashion, and however great the notoriety and respect Rose Bertin was awarded by Marie-Antoinette, or that Hippolite Leroy received from Josephine de Beauharnais, they nonetheless remained dressmakers subject to their sovereign's tastes and orders.

Rose Bertin, nicknamed "the fashion minister," who had her establishment at 26 rue de Richelieu, executed the queen's desires once she had inspired them. Madame Bertin took advantage of her influence over the Queen's fashion taste to develop her own business. She enjoyed impressing prospective clients by calling out authoritatively to her saleswomen: "Show Madame the samples of my latest work for Her Majesty."

Hippolite Leroy, who actively served Empress Josephine and Empress Marie Louise, was only able to get his choices of dresses made by means of suggestion and allusion. Empress Marie Louise's dresses were created in his workshops; he or anyone from his establishment never tried them for fittings.

For the Emperor's coronation, Leroy had already thought about the ceremonial costumes, but Napoleon I entrusted Isabey, David's student—while David himself was in charge of directing and staging the ceremony—the job of designing the costumes. Leroy was deeply offended, but he nonetheless executed the designs brilliantly.

When the guilds were done away with, although dressmakers could acquire as much fabric as they wanted, they preferred to do piece work until they abandoned dressmaking for another industry.

> It was a woman's idea and a very simple one—we are very pleased to note that we owe the idea to a woman—that led to the creation of a new industry. Madame Roger was the first to think of stocking the fabric for the dresses she made and selling it to her clients. She could add the cost of dressmaking to that of the fabric itself, and thus double her profit.[4]

Although the means of production evolved with Madame Roger, the design of clothes remained terribly conventional. This lasted until the 1848 Revolution when, with the coming of the Republic, a young Englishman came to Paris. Charles Frédéric Worth, nicknamed by Paul Poiret "the haute couture *Instituteur*," revolutionized the world of fashion design.

Charles Frédéric Worth. Born in Lincolnshire in England, he did his apprenticeship in London from 1838–1845 at Swan and Edgar's, the Piccadilly Circus draper's, before moving on to Lewis & Allenby, the silk merchants on Regent Street. In 1847, at the age of 20, with five pounds in his pocket, he left London for Paris, where he found a job in a novelty shop. He then went on to become an assistant salesman with Gagelin, the famous haberdashery at 83 rue de Richelieu. Worth stayed at Gagelin selling fabric and trinkets, then shawls, short capes, and fashion accessories until 1849. These cashmere shawls and short capes, town clothes for the daytime, came in an infinite choice of cuts: short or mid length, loose or very fitting, etc. They were extremely popular until the end of the Second Empire. He chose a salesgirl, Marie Vernet, who later became his wife, to model them. Vernet inspired Worth to design his first strict and unadorned dresses that his clients greatly admired. Interest in his creations grew and Worth asked his employers to set up a dressmaking workshop inside the store. For Gagelin however, it was out of the question. A luxury haberdasher could not possibly be associated with a "vulgar" dressmaker. It was only in 1850, faced with growing demand by clients for Worth's designs, that Gagelin gave Worth carte blanche to pursue his plans. From 1851 to 1855, his fashions won awards at the World Fairs in Paris and London. "Unused to these innovations, the public was recalcitrant and accepted his new ideas with difficulty. Just recently, one of the members of the jury at the 1851 Exhibition reminded us how his colleagues had strongly criticized the first models, their novelty and originality being totally different to what was considered acceptable at the time."[5] Finally, in 1853 Charles Frédéric Worth became an associate with the Gagelin establishment.

Amidst the wave of foreigners who came to Paris to see the 1855 Exhibition were a large number of buyers, who were intrigued by this nascent industry.

The Gagelin house exhibited a court overcoat, made of antique white moiré and embroidered with gold thread, that was stunning and cut in an innovative way. This item greatly excited a number of buyers who ended up placing big orders. This new industry brought with it the growth of the Lyon, France-based fabric trade.

At the time, Worth was looking for an opportunity to start his own company. He took advantage of a slight disagreement about his wife's maternity leave that brought him into conflict with Gagelin. In 1858, he joined forces with Otto Gustav Bobergh, a young Swede who was also a senior fashion sales clerk. They set up their establishment at 7 rue de la Paix under the sign: Worth & Bobergh—Ready-made Dresses and Coats—Silks—High Novelties.[6] This street was in an area hardly conducive to luxury businesses that were generally located around the Chaussée d'Antin. However, a decision had been made that same year to build a new opera house in the vicinity and this soon turned the rue de la Paix into an ideal location. After Worth's departure, Gagelin, of course, kept its dressmaking department and the outfits were frequently shown in magazines.

Worth transformed the cut of dresses and presented spectacular innovations in fashion. He wanted his designs to come alive and was the first to have the idea of showing them to his clients. Young girls, called "sosies," would model his outfits to his customers. These women were, in a way, the precursors of today's models. Worth called his dresses "ready-to-try-on," and they came in different fabrics. Being a perfectionist, he showed his ball gowns under blazing lights in his salons, lighting the

Franz Xavier Winterhalter *Marie-Amélie de Bourbon, princess of the Two Sicilies, Duchess of Orleans, Queen of the French,* 1830. Versailles and Trianon castles, Versailles. Photo RMN/© Rights Reserved

Franz Xavier Winterhalter *Pauline Sandor, Princess von Metternich,* 1860. Private Collection. Rights Reserved

Lady Duff Gordon founded the Lucile house. Photo Arnold Genthe.

The Lucile couture house's label.

The couturier, Jacques Worth's, salons, 7 rue de la Paix in Paris, 1907. Photos J. Boyer/Agence Roger Viollet.
Charles Frédéric Worth, the first creator couturier. Photo Nadar.

rooms more brightly than necessary, so clients could see how the clothes would look when they would be worn.

"My work is not only to execute but especially to invent," he once said. "My originality is the secret of my success. I don't want people to dictate what they want to buy; if they did I should lose half my trade."

The Second Republic did not last; then came the Second Empire with Napoléon III and his court.

The very elegant Princess Pauline von Metternich, wife of the Austrian Ambassador to France, was held in great esteem at the court. Worth and Bobergh decided to whet her curiosity by having Marie Worth show her a book of drawings. When she realized that a man did them, and moreover an Englishman, her indignation knew no bounds. After a closer look, however, she was captivated by Worth's fashions and immediately decided to order two gowns, one for the day and another for the evening, for a maximum price of 300 francs each, particularly cheap.[7]

Princess Pauline wore the evening gown, white tulle embroidered with silver, at the next Tuileries ball.[8]

While the diplomatic corps was being presented at the ball, Empress Eugénie enquired where the Princess had found a gown of such perfect simplicity. She asked that its designer come to the Louvre at 10:00 AM the following day. For the Empress, Worth chose a floral brocade gown that boasted a French interpretation of ancient Chinese embroidery.

To present a ready-made gown to an Empress was already a crime of lese-majesty. To make it worse, the Empress did not even like brocade! All seemed to be lost, when Napoleon III made his entry. Worth explained in great detail that brocade was a speciality of Lyon and Lyon was a Republican town. He argued that it would be a good idea to promote Lyon fabrics at the court of France. In order to support the French fabric industry, the Emperor requested the Empress to wear the gown once or twice.

Worth could be proud of having doubly influenced the Empress, by selecting her dress and getting her to wear it, even though she didn't like the fabric.

He never took such risks again. In 1864, he became Empress Eugénie's exclusive supplier of official garments and evening gowns. In this position, Worth very rapidly gained an international reputation that indirectly contributed to the wider reputation of French dressmakers.[9] Worth dressed the Tsarina of Russia, the

PAQUIN

Left to right: models by Worth, Jeanne Lanvin, and Worth. Illustration published in *Les Elégances parisiennes*, 1916.

Facing page: Palais des Fils, Tissus, Couture section at the 1900 Universal Exhibition, Paris. Photo Agence Roger Viollet.
The façade of the Paquin couture house, rue de la Paix, is brilliantly lit for King George V's visit to Paris in 1924.
Photo M. Branger/Agence Roger Viollet.

queen of Italy, Empress Elizabeth of Austria, and Queen Victoria, with the same success as the rich singer Mrs. Charles Moulton. The Worth gowns at the Metropolitan Museum of New York, the Victoria and Albert Museum in London, the Hermitage Museum at Saint Petersburg, or the Musée de la mode in Paris are all perfectly adapted to the specific habits and climatic conditions that prevailed in the countries of each of these women.[10]

For the first time, men were creating fashion. By raising the status of the dressmaker, Worth also transformed the way people dressed. Clothing had long been traditional and regional; it became standardized as it evolved. The couturier's role acted upon the most determining and changing element of fashion: finery. All the other professions associated with fashion, from weaving to embroidery, followed suit. Recognized as a creator in his own right, the couturier moved from the status of an anonymous artisan to that of designer, and could now label his creations. The honors the dressmaker now received were not limited to his fashions; his personal company became highly desirable and accelerated the process of social recognition. Princess Mathilda, the Princess von Metternich, and the Ambassador of England became regular guests at Worth's country house in Suresnes. The adulated couturier's time had come.

Within this new fashion phenomenon that Worth remained eternally attached to, a few names appeared after the fall of the Second Empire and it is important for us to mention the most famous of them. Amongst the best, those who really transformed fashion philosophy at the end of the nineteenth century, we can cite Redfern, Jacques Doucet, Rouff, the Callot sisters, Paquin, Paul Poiret, and Madeleine Vionnet, the latter who worked as a designer with Jacques Doucet from 1907 until 1912[11] when she opened her own house.

Charles Poynter Redfern. Despite the rivalry between France and Great Britain, couturiers settled on either side of the Channel. It was even considered in good taste and recommended to open a subsidiary in London if one was Parisian, or vice-versa. Most of the major designers did just that: Worth, Redfern Creed, Lucile, Molyneux, as well as Paquin and Poiret… Redfern, an English tailor established in London and Paris, whose talent ranged from Anglo-Saxon distinction to "Parisian chic," was the first to offer the "skirt suit" in 1885, then the "tailored coat" inspired by the severe cut of gentlemen's clothing. While he excelled at sober,

British-style garments for which he became famous, he was also one of the most sought-after theatrical costume designers. He let his imagination run free when he designed costumes[12] that were greatly admired by spectators and critics, raising him to the status of a dramatic author.

If, quite rightly, we associate Charles Frédéric Worth with high society, as he was the first designer to be admitted to the very closed aristocratic and upper bourgeois circles, we could see Jacques Doucet as the first cultured couturier.

Jacques Doucet. Jacques Doucet was born on 19 February 1853 to a family of upper-bourgeois shopkeepers. Since 1824, the family owned a shop at 17 rue de la Paix that became number 21, called "Doucet Lingerie," before its name was changed to "Doucet et Fils shirt makers." When his grandfather offered him the management of the ladies dressmaking department in 1875, Doucet's vocation as a couturier was settled.

At the outset, Doucet's creations were influenced by the artwork of his friends Degas and Monet. The superimposition and juxtaposition of colors obtained through Doucet's choice of transparent fabrics and floral embroidery—roses, irises, carnations—allowed him to reproduce the shimmering colors and light the Impressionists favored. Then, lace, pearls, and passementerie trim replaced the flowers and decorations on the dresses, while their cut and the pastel silks with which they were made irresistibly brought romantic parties to mind. His creations were unconsciously influenced by his appreciation of the eighteenth century.

After the resounding auction of his collections that he held in 1912, there was little left of his passion for the Enlightenment period, apart from three catalogues and a profit of 20 million gold francs. It was André Suarès, whose work had caught his attention, who helped set up his library that today is one of the most important ones in this field.[13] With the same determination, he entrusted Iribe, Legrain, Csaky, and Poiret with decorating his new apartment, 46 avenue du Bois. André Breton, who became his advisor, initiated him into modernity. In 1925, his studio in rue Saint-James held the best collection of pieces from contemporary artists and furniture designers. Brancusi, Van Gogh, Léger, Miro, and le Douanier Rousseau shared the space with furniture from Legrain, Eileen Gray, and Coard.

Left to right: models by Jeanne Lanvin and Doucet.
Illustration by Jean van Brock published in *Les Elégances parisiennes*, 1916.

Facing page: Jacques Doucet, learned grand couturier, as famous for his library as for his collections, photo Man Ray. © Man Ray Trust/ Adagp, Paris, 2008.

A trial at Jeanne Paquin, c. 1908. Photo A. Harlingue/Agence Roger Viollet.

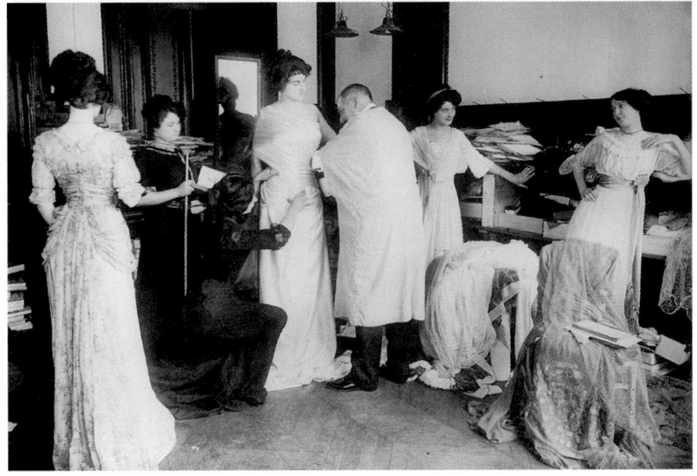

Paul Poiret, 1925.
The first couturier to have diversified his activities beyond fashion, in decoration, etc.

Photo Lipnitzki/Agence Roger Viollet.
Perfume *La Rose* de Rosine, 1912–1916.
Photo Jacques Boulay.

Perfume *Nuit de Chine* de Rosine, c. 1920.
Photo Jacques Boulay.

Facing page:
Poiret's models parade in the garden of his house on the avenue d'Antin.
Taken from *L'Illustration*, 9 July 1910.
Photo Henri Manuel.

Paul Poiret and his tailor Christian adjust a model worn by the model Renée.
Photo Lipnitzki/Agence Roger Viollet.

Martine boutique by Paul Poiret at the 1924 Exhibition at the Grand Palais, Paris.
Photo Lipnitzki/Agence Roger Viollet.

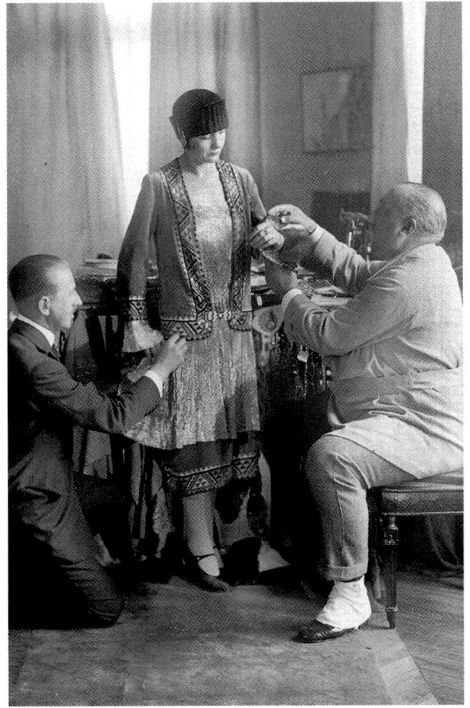

MARTINE
PAUL POIRET

Paul Poiret. After sketching for Doucet and working at Worth, Paul Poiret opened his own fashion house on rue Pasquier in 1904, before moving in 1909 to the magnificent town house on avenue d'Antin, now known as avenue Franklin Roosevelt. He renovated the new space with help from architect Louis Süe.

If Charles Frédéric Worth instituted the rules of haute couture, Paul Poiret fundamentally transformed its scope. Poiret believed that it was not sufficient for a couturier to be an authority on dressing. He thought that since fashion guides society, a couturier's influence can and should extend to all areas of aesthetics.[14]

Poiret, like Doucet, and before Chanel and Schiaparelli, was an ardent promoter of modern art, but most significantly, until the 1925 Exhibition of Decorative Arts, he was the person who gave the applied arts a newfound prestige. "I wanted France to create a parallel movement to that of the Germans in every area of the luxury industry: furnishings, interior decoration, perfume, bottles, drawing, printing, tapestry, furniture, mirror work, tableware, lighting, embroidery, trimming, lace, gowns and coats. I managed to make it happen,"[15] he proudly proclaimed.

The diversification that took place in fashion is incontestably thanks to Paul Poiret's inventions. In 1911, more than 10 years before Chanel and about 15 years before Lanvin, Poiret started producing his own perfume that he named after his first daughter, Rosine. He opened a laboratory in what used to be the outhouses of 39 rue du Colisée, where he lived, and set up a new factory in Courbevoie for glassworks and box-making that employed about 40 people. He soon added eaux de toilette, perfumed soaps, powder, skin creams, lipstick, make up, and nail polish to his stable of goods. He controlled all aspects of production—fragrances, names, bottles—and their distribution, making his products available only at his own shop or his subsidiaries.

That same year, 1911, he founded the decorative arts school, "Martine" in Paris, named after his second daughter. A year later, the Martine school's production was so rich, varied, and original that he decided to open a shop at 107 rue du Faubourg-Saint-Honoré, on the corner of avenue Matignon. Soon, there were nine salesgirls working in the shop. A Martine boutique opened in London and two decoration departments opened in Philadelphia and Berlin. By 1913, the Paul Poiret House had a cumulative turnover of 13 million gold francs, an amount that represented about 300 million francs in 1992.[16]

Paul Poiret,
beige coat with
dark brown motifs
of North African
inspiration,
two blue motifs on the
back, c. 1920.
Colin Poiret collection.
Photo Jacques Boulay

Paul Poiret on the front steps to his house during the 1,002nd Night, one of his sumptuous parties. Rights Reserved

Paul Poiret's letter paper, graphic design by Georges Lepape.

In 1925, following Poiret's model, Jeanne Lanvin opened Lanvin Décoration, under Armand Rateau's artistic direction, at 15 Faubourg-Saint-Honoré. She went on to create her perfume company the following year.

The reign of the Promethean couturier was born with Paul Poiret. He became the catalyst for fashion trends and his philosophy penetrated all the areas in which he extended his influence. The main couturiers followed his lead, and until the 1940s they produced non-fashion products that carried their signature labels. After the war, licensing contracts became the basis for a totally different kind of business growth.

Couture, Apparel Manufacturing, Haute Couture

The distinction between couture and ready-to-wear was very subtle at the outset. After all, both these businesses were part of the same industry and were represented by the same trade union[17] starting in 1868. If we look at the names of both the Worth and Doucet houses, they both contain the word "confection," which can mean anything from "apparel manufacturing" to its current common definition, "ready to wear." But at the turn of the century, these two sectors of the industry were not clearly defined. In fact, there was no hierarchy between the two and the means of production were comparable.[18] Both treated the sale of models for reproduction, unit sales, and mass production the same way. As for the sewing machine, invented by Barthélémy Thimonnier in 1831, it had not yet changed the industry. In a report published for the 1900 World's Fair, Gaston Worth discussed the businesses of 10 high quality fashion houses, 20 honorable houses, and a few others of lesser reputation, making no other distinction between them. Couture had not yet become a "corporation."

In 1850, in Paris, 158 couturiers were listed in the Bottin (telephone directory) and 67 companies listed under "ready-made fashion." In 1872, these numbers increased to 684 for couture and 307 for ready-made fashion. It is, however, impossible to make a real distinction between the two groups because a number of companies were listed under both headings. It is also important to note that a large number of smaller dressmakers, employing between one and three workers, were not listed in the Bottin.

As further proof of this ambiguity between these two branches of fashion, the Chambre syndicale de la confection et de la couture pour dames et fillettes, a trade union for apparel manufacturing and couture for women and young ladies created in 1868, randomly chose a couturier or a manufacturer as president. After the first elected president, Mr. Despaigne (1868–1869), the following people succeeded each other in this position: Mr. Bernard Salle (1870–1877), Mr. Dreyfus (1878–1884), Mr. Gaston Worth (1885–1888), Mr. Marcade (1889–1890), Mr. Brylinski (1890–1892), Mr. Félix (1893–1895), Mr. Perdoux (1896–1900), Mr. Bonhomme (1901–1902), Mr. Pichot (1903–1904), Mr. Storch (1905–1907), and Mr. Réverdot (1908–1911).

It was only in 1910 that the first schism between the two branches of fashion occurred. On 14 December, following the dissolution of the Chambre syndicale de la couture, des confectionneurs et des tailleurs pour dames[19] (a trade group for men's and women's tailors), couture regrouped itself as an autonomous profession. This movement seems to have been encouraged by Jacques Worth, Gaston Worth's son. Léon Réverdot, the only candidate, was elected president at the constitutive assembly. Mr. Doeuillet, Jeanne Paquin, Jacques Worth, Pierre Gerber, and Lucien Lelong succeeded him in this position[20] until the outbreak of World War II.

The Chambre syndicale de couture's first offices were located at 6 rue d'Aboukir.[21] During a meeting on 16 July 1937, Daniel Gorin, the new general secretary, suggested that the headquarters move to its current offices at 102 rue du Faubourg-Saint-Honoré. The committee voted for this proposal. It was only in 1943 that haute couture, as an institution, organized itself into a bona fide trade and defined its member's rights.[22] As soon as the first statutes were established in 1911, requests for membership had to be approved by two committee members in order to be considered (article 4).

At the first union meeting on 15 February 1911, Paul Poiret was concerned about whether the Lucile house from London would be allowed to join. The question of a member's nationality had not been dealt with in the first statutes, but it was addressed in subsequent reviews.[23]

By choosing to dissociate themselves once and for all from apparel manufacturing in 1910, couture houses attempted to establish their own business guidelines. Couture and ready-to-wear were clearly different. The first trade dressed women by making custom-made clothes according to clients' measurements. The second dressed Mrs. Anybody. While apparel makers seemed to be exercising the same profession as the couture houses, the manufacturers—a more dynamic trade—took on the risk of stock since they made models in advance, using average measurements based on experience. Despite the inherent risk in owning stock, apparel makers' garments could be offered at much lower prices.

Very rapidly, each of the professions tried to expand while reinforcing their respective advantages. Couture emphasized the luxury and the skill of its fashion while promoting the creativity of design. By contrast, ready-made fashion became increasingly standardized in order to become even more competitive. As both businesses grew, they easily adapted to the restrictions and demands of a society that became irreversibly divided into two distinct social classes.

After this first transformation, other signs of distinction progressively appeared within the field of couture.

In 1905, a Canadian from London, Lady Duff-Gordon, founded the Lucile house in Hanover Square and went on to open subsidiaries in Paris, New York, and Chicago. On specific dates she organized elaborate presentations of her collections, in a theater-like room designed just for this purpose.[24] At the entrance, a footman handed each client a program that listed the viewing order of the clothes. Then, models walked the fashion show, one after the other, to music. This practice is considered to be the origin of today's fashion shows.

This trend was instantly met with great enthusiasm by the increasingly famous Parisian couture world. The number of foreign buyers and journalists that came to Paris continued to grow. They were eager to celebrate an industry that, in their eyes, represented the best of French creativity and taste. The need to establish a calendar for fashion shows became clear as a means to better welcome this new audience that was fascinated by French fashion. This new organization was done under the auspices of the Chambre syndicale de la couture.

For practical and economic reasons, the norm of 400 models that made up a collection was reduced to about 100. Only the houses listed on the calendar could claim to belong to the world of "haute couture." Those who did not "show," but who, in addition to their private clients, received professional buyers constituted what was called "middle couture." These houses, inspired by haute couture, attracted manufacturers, often British, which were looking to make and sell simplified patterns in their markets. As for the "small couture," it consisted exclusively of traditional, local dressmakers who made clothes to measure for their clients.

Until 1940, it was not very difficult to belong to the world of haute couture. The rules were very adaptable, offered great freedom, and the procedure was quite

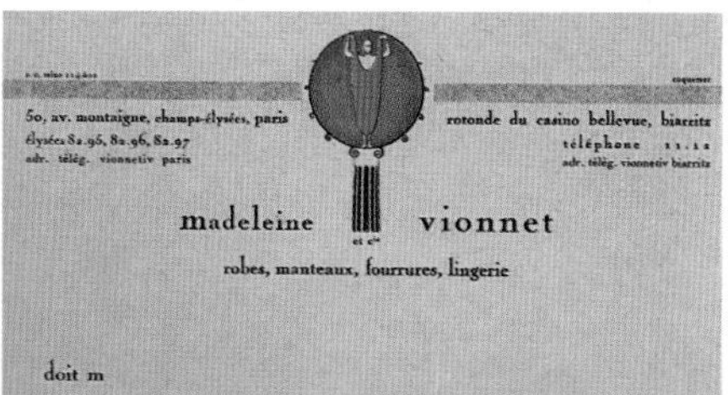

Madeleine Vionnet, inventor of the cross-cut bias with her wooden model. Rights Reserved
Perfume by Madeleine Vionnet, bottle created by Boris Lacroix, c. 1935.
Cards with a graphic design by Madeleine Vionnet, c. 1930.
Madeleine Vionnet's salons at 50 avenue Montaigne en 1923. © BNF. Photo Seeberger, 1936.
Facing page: Model by Madeleine Vionnet, 1931. Photo George Hoyningen-Huene.

simple. Every new French or foreign designer who wanted to open an establishment in Paris had first to make a courtesy visit to the president or the secretary of the Chambre. In addition, if their showrooms were considered of a high enough quality in which to organize shows, the president or general secretary had the authority to include them in the calendar.

Nonetheless, there was a very select group within the realm of haute couture represented by the Association de protection des industries artistiques saisonnières (PAIS), whose offices were located at 50 avenue Montaigne in Madeleine Vionnet's headquarters.

> The PAIS group of couture houses showed their collections over several prestigious days in the middle of the calendar, while the other secondary fashion firms that did not belong to the select group, were reduced to showing their production to the buyers before or afterwards.[25]

The PAIS association was a follow-up to the Association pour la défense des arts plastiques et appliqués created in 1921 by Madeleine Vionnet with the help of her managing director, M. Dangel. The earlier association was located at the same address.

The war blew this wonderful organization apart, sending couturiers and members of Parliament to Bordeaux, where Lucien Vogel, a politically committed journalist and director of *Le Jardin des Modes* fashion magazine at the time, joined them in May 1940. He rented the Chateau de Lavalade, from where he hoped to continue his activity in exile, but the chaos of war meant he quickly left for New York.[26]

Madeleine Godeau[27] recalls that in July 1940 five German officers went to the Chambre syndicale de la couture's office and met President Lucien Lelong and his general secretary, Daniel Gorin. It seemed to be just a courtesy visit. A few days later, though, "– it was a Sunday—the doors were broken open." A quick look around revealed that the files on the professional schools as well as those of foreign buyers had disappeared.

Finally, during a more formal meeting that took place later between Lucien Lelong, Maggy Besançon de Wagner[28] (president of the PAIS), and the Germans in charge of the textile trade, the Germans revealed a project that was incredible, to say the least: haute couture was to be transferred to Vienna and Berlin.

In its French issue of March 1941, *Signal*, the German propaganda newspaper, described the decision in the following terms:

> Until now, Paris has been the center of the fashion world, but the designers along the Seine have had a troubled vision of what is really beautiful, good and suitable... Parisian fashion will henceforth have to be approved by Berlin before a woman of taste can wear it.[29]

In the minutes of the Chambre Syndicale's meeting of 24 September 1940, we read:

> The Ministry for Industrial Production and Labour gave Mr. Lucien Lelong the responsibility to carry out a trade mission in Germany in order to learn about the German fashion industry and study possibilities for an agreement that would allow the activity of French couture and labour to move to Germany...The Chambre syndicale de la couture committee approves Lucien Lelong's trip and places their full trust in him to defend the interests of French couture.[30]

Lucien Lelong went to Berlin, accompanied by Daniel Gorin. Discussions were held, and Lelong, whose sole aim was to gain time, easily showed that couture was a culture of diverse industries and could in no way be transferred to another country on its own.

The couture trade depends on a multitude of small, related artisanal businesses that feed into it. Lelong recommended drawing up an inventory of these industries as a first step. Discussions broke down despite Lucien Lelong's apparent cooperation.[31]

The Germans were surprised by the subtleties of this resistance and they temporarily abandoned the "project of centralising and concentrating the fashion business in Berlin and Vienna. French fashion remained autonomous, in Paris, and was able to retain its specialist workforce."[32] To start with, they thought the rationing of raw materials would dampen the unfailing buoyancy of French fashion. In time, the shortage of raw materials went from bad to worse, creating real sourcing concerns for fashion houses.

The entire trade, with the exception of Jean Patou, faced terrible supply shortages.[33] Patou had the annoying practice of buying up his suppliers' entire production in order to obtain exclusive patterns. This, however, allowed his company to accumulate vast stocks of fabrics that would last through the end of the war.

Under the circumstances, "the directors of the Chambre Syndicale tried to convince the French authorities to make an exception for this prestigious industry that had largely contributed to France's glory... However, Lucien Lelong and

Lucien Lelong's salons at 16 avenue Matignon en 1924. © BNF. Photo Seeberger, 1927.

Lucien Lelong and his model 1937. © Brassaï.

Daniel Gorin's most effective argument was that haute couture production represented a minimum of material for a maximum employment of labour... Thanks to this, some so called 'authorized' haute couture houses were allocated a quota of raw materials set at 60 per cent of the wool consumption of 1938."[34] In fact, although a "clothing card" was enforced in 1941, "couture-création" was given a special dispensation and was allowed to receive supplies from "special" producers.[35]

At the beginning, there were only 30 "authorized" houses. After bitter negotiations, the number of authorized houses increased to 85 in June 1941 but then stabilized at 79 by 1944. It was nonetheless extremely difficult to determine the list of privileged companies and it lead to bitter jealousies. The couturiers located outside of Paris were excluded and were angry. There were, however, no objective criteria that determined the choice of one house over another. The "couture-creation" classification had not yet come into existence. That is why, in 1942, Lucien Lelong sent a questionnaire to the members of the Chambre out of which came the quantitative criteria which have regulated the profession for decades; minimum number of sewers in the workshop, number of designs in the fashion shows, etc.

While it was already a well-organized profession, it was not sufficiently structured to operate in such troubled times. To start with, regulations were required to limit the use of raw materials. Then the objective status of haute couture houses needed to be defined in order to distinguish them from their more modest colleagues. This was the only way to avoid recriminations from the ousted candidates and to please the diktats of the German occupiers.

The regulations regarding the presentation of the 1942 autumn-winter haute couture collections specified, according to a 19 June decision, the composition of the collections and the maximum number of meters of woolen fabric permitted for each category of model. [36] The maximum number of models that could be presented that year was 75. The idea behind the classification was to increase the number of dispensations and to extend dispensations to small couture companies as well as the major ones. Marcel Dhorme, couturier and vice president under Lucien Lelong, was very active and negotiated efficiently with the public authorities.[37]

This extremely complicated dispensation system momentarily saved haute couture and allowed it to retain 97 per cent of its workforce, or about 12,000 workers. On 18 March 1943, a decision taken by Jean Bichelonne,[38] published in the *Journal Officiel de l'Etat Français,* completed the decree of 20 July 1942 by regulating the label "couture" and "couturière" on the one hand, and "haute couture" and "couturier" on the other. It was, however, only upon the Liberation of France that a decree emerged on 29 January 1945, co-signed by Pierre Mendès France and Robert Lacoste, minister for national economy and minister for industrial production, respectively, which annulled preceding legislation. The new decree created a professional office for industries related to the artistic professions and the creation of made-to-measure garments. This organization, under combined public and private governance, was established at the time of the Liberation to replace the organization committees. Its first objective was to serve as a relay to facilitate the distribution of raw materials, mainly fabrics.

The couture companies became subject to certain restrictions. They were forced to declare the title "couture" and "master artisan couturier" or "dressmaker" in their official title, on their signage, labels, and advertising materials. The models they created were to be put into production exclusively by the company, excluding any kind of sub-contracting or mass production. They could produce made-to-measure pieces by fitting clients with muslin, a way to test the pattern of the garment, or the dress patterns could be sold to French or foreign companies to be copied.

Among these companies, the only ones recognized and entitled to the designation of "couturier," "haute couture," and "couture-creation" were the houses whose practices conformed to the decree of 23 January 1945 regarding the classification of "couture" and recognized as creative, in accordance with a later decree published in the *Journal officiel* of 6 April 1945. In the twentieth century, an haute couture trade union, Chambre syndicale de la haute couture, never really existed. What did exist was the Chambre syndicale de la couture parisienne.

A list of haute couture houses, accepted by a regulatory board, was submitted to the Ministry of Industry every year for approval and this procedure still exists nowadays.

Yet none of the haute couture houses followed the rules governing their trade to the letter. How then, was it possible to imagine that new companies would conform to the rules?

Daniel Gorin, who was perfectly aware of the situation, was not overly concerned with knowing whether the regulations were respected or not at the time of the Liberation. Who could worry about counting the number of staff employed by a house that was inaugurating their salons? Balmain employed sixteen people in 1945,

Jean Patou at the races, 1927. © BNF. Photo Seeberger.

Givenchy, eight in 1952, Ungaro, four in 1965... He was, however, very particular about the observance of pre-war practices. Although the obsolescence of the regulations meant they could be ignored, there was something everyone had to conform to: the press-release date, which was the green light for fashion houses to give documents to the press for publication. This regulated the proper functioning of the profession until 1966 when Pierre Cardin transgressed this rule. Upon so doing, he also sent in his letter of resignation that was immediately accepted.[39]

It is easy to imagine that everyone would have found ways to circumvent the empty decrees that regulated the profession if Pierre Bergé, president of Yves Saint Laurent and president of the Chambre syndicale du prêt-à-porter des couturiers et des createurs de mode, had not unequivocally declared that haute couture would not survive the century.

Finally, in 1991, French industry minister Dominique Strauss-Kahn nominated a commission made up of professionals capable of updating couture legislation.[40] The commission members only managed to note the disparity of their interests. Mr. Strauss-Kahn, however, looked at their conclusions[41] and was unable to work with them. It was only 10 years later, in 2001, that regulations dealing with the haute couture sector were modified.

The Business of Couture

Until 1930

In 1873, Worth employed 1,200 workers. An industry had grown out of the foundation he had laid and it began to enjoy a dominant position in the French economy. While it is impossible to establish the exact volume of production, the vitality of couture is evident in the external trade figures that reached their peak, in terms of tonnage, between 1900 and 1905. From then on, export tonnage decreased but its value grew and in 1913 it reached the sum of 160,586,604 francs, which was divided among export markets as follows: Great Britain 35 per cent, Argentina 21.5 per cent, Germany 8.4 per cent, Belgium 8 per cent, Switzerland 6.8 per cent, United States 5.7 per cent, Austria 5 per cent, Brazil 1.6 per cent, Italy 0.6 per cent, colonies 2 per cent, others 5.4 per cent.[42] Great Britain and Argentina were France's best clients at the time while the United States was in sixth position, behind Switzerland.

In 1925, 75 couture houses took part in the Decorative Arts exhibition. The same year, couture represented 15 per cent of global French exports, that is to say 29,592 quintals of garments and a turnover of 2,410 million francs. Garment exports occupied second place in external trade at the time.

The export figures for ready-made apparel were insignificant and impossible to separate from couture.

France's general statistics office, founded in 1921, show the following figures for the years 1926 to 1929:

READY-MADE GARMENTS (in thousands of francs)

Year	Imports (in thousands of francs)	Exports (in thousands of francs)
1926	11,487	1,970,638
1927	8,967	1,771,092
1928	13,129	1,649,596
1929	18,952	1,434,608

In 1929, garment exports ranked eighth place in France's foreign trade.[43] For the country's main clients, it represented over 10 per cent of total sales.[44]

MANUFACTURED GARMENTS (in thousands of francs)

Country	1929	1928	1927	1929 *
Great Britain	787,369	773,078	707,860	7,566,539
United States	339,826	374,544	467,639	3,322,349
Netherlands	62,220	84,799	92,555	1,254,421
Switzerland	61,136	77,599	65,242	3,371,630
Belgium	53,160	63,288	69,652	7,221,252
Italy	33,158	28,705	19,601	2,206,894
Germany	30,895	53,156	55,698	4,732,141
Canada	28,348	60,316	41,578	586,399
Argentina	23,141	25,179	40,435	1,066,754
Spain	10,382	18,661	16,844	1,587,499
Brazil	8,810	9,251	7,544	458,246

*total French exports.

North American consumption of French fashion was rising rapidly, while in South America consumption was declining.

The performance of the couture industry can, of course, be explained by the reputation and the talent of the work force, but it is also largely due to the industry's competitiveness.

We can see this by comparing the cost of a gown made in Paris, in 50 hours, in a couture workshop, with the price of the same gown, made in the same time, in Great Britain or in the United States.[45]

Year	France (£)	Great Britain (£)	Year	France ($)	United States ($)
1920	6.4	7.4	1920	24	62
1923	5.7	7.4	1923	25	62
1926	3	7.4	1926	14	62
1929	5.16	7.1	1929	30	62
1930	6	6.16	1930	29	62
1931	6	6.9	1931	30	59,50
1935	7.11	6.5	1935	43	69
1936	7.13	6.11	1936	48	66
1937	7.15	6.11	1937	38	69

Advertisement for the Chanel couture house. Paris, c. 1930. Photo A. Harlingue/ Agence Roger Viollet.
Jersey suits, models by Gabrielle Chanel.

From these estimates it's clear that French couture was very competitive in the world of free trade that prevailed until the market crash and Depression of 1929–1930.[46] It represented an amazing industry made up of a workforce that employed 350,000 workers directly, and 150,000 artisans in related professions (glove-making, costume jewelry, lace, embroidery, etc.) by 1930.

Economic and social difficulties

The couture world's legitimate hopes for growth were brutally dashed by the prohibitive customs duties and import quotas that were imposed by a number of countries following the 1929 market crash. The Smoot-Hawley Tariff Act[47] was passed in 1930 in the United States to protect American industry and farming from foreign competition. Couture was harshly targeted and got slapped with a 90 per cent tax on articles decorated with embroidery, tulle, lamé, or lace.

This disastrous economic situation, combined with the harm inflicted by counterfeiters, irremediably drove the couture industry into decline. In 1931, in the introduction to his book dedicated to haute couture, Philippe Simon discussed the dramatic change.

> We can see that a kind of anarchy, or rather a huge waste of strength, reigns in this industry that is in the midst of a period of transformation. It seems that French couture is at a turning point in its evolution. Managers' worries reflect the fears everyone shares: does this industry, driven by values of quality, really have a place in a civilisation where quantity is prioritized?[48]

It is disturbing to note to what extent this declaration remains a major concern 80 years later.

There are a number of reasons that explain the decrease in exports from 1925 onwards. To start with, the strength of the franc, between 1925 and 1929, led to haute couture being penalized in foreign markets. This affected the related industries as well as the textile industry in general, leaving them considerably weakened by the 1929 crash. From 1929 to 1935, exports, which represented about three-fifths of all couture sales, saw a drop of over 70 per cent. As for garment exports that were in eighth place in 1929, they fell to twenty-seventh place in 1935.[49] This industry represented over 2 billion francs in 1925, fell to 483,479,000 francs in 1931, and then to 51,224,000 francs in 1936.

The first victims of the economic crisis were, however, the workers. Until this time, the apparel industry was justifiably proud of having no unemployment. By 1931, this was no longer the case. In the department of the Seine alone, 1,266 unemployed were assisted in October 1931; 9,021, in October 1932; and 10,496 in October 1936.[50] It was clear that haute couture was in free fall.[51] In an interview for the magazine *Heim* in 1932, Paul Poiret declared:

Jeanne Lanvin's boudoir designed by Armand Rateau, 1920–1922. DR.
Jeanne Lanvin opened a workshop under her own sign in 1885.
Lanvin is the oldest French fashion brand. Rights Reserved
Logo created by Paul Iribe for Jeanne Lanvin, c. 1920.
Facing page: Dresses by Lanvin, 1934. Photo Hoyningen-Huene.

Gabrielle Chanel and Serge Lifar, 1937. Courtesy Chanel © DR.
Raymond Barbas, Jean Patou's brother-in-law and president of Jean Patou, traveling to the United-States on the liner *France*, c. 1934. Courtesy Jean de Mouy.
Facing page: Gabrielle Chanel, c. 1935. Photo Man Ray. © Man Ray Trust/Adagp, Paris, 2008.

> Couture is dying from having become too ostentatious. The days of gold-laced lackeys at the door are over. Carpets all over the place, tapestries on the walls, sumptuously dressed windows, it's all over. The days of vast numbers of employees are over. No more 400-model collections with captivating furs. No more little suit, copied 1,500 times. No more shops with huge rents on the Champs Elysées.

The workers' life went from very difficult to truly precarious. The instant the collections were shown, workers were laid off. The Patou, Vionnet, and Paquin houses were proud of their employment practices, but after every collection, they were forced to reduce their staff, only retaining 25 per cent of their workforce—about 300 people—until orders had come in. In the absence of the "midinettes" sales girls,[52] senior staff carried out the work assisted by their seconds, preparing "logs"[53] and placing them in bins. In the same way, in 1935, Chanel employed 4,000 workers spread over several buildings on the rue Cambon, where they produced 28,000 models a year.

On 18 June 1936, the Matignon agreement established the compulsory collective labor agreements, paid holidays, and the 40-hour week. The 12 June 1936 issue of *Humanité* announced an agreement between the Syndicat des couturiers et tailleurs pour dames and the Employers union, confirming the decision to do away with piece work; there was a salary increase of about 12 per cent, along with two weeks of paid vacation. The agreement also recognized the right of workers to belong to a trade union. The new costs implied in such legislation were another burden on the already weakened haute couture industry. Fashion exports were further challenged by the resulting increase in prices combined with the social and political crisis France was facing. Fortunately this situation did not tarnish haute couture and it remained a determining influence on the worldwide fashion industry, a privilege it held on to until the 1960s.

Haute Couture after World War II

After a constant decline following the Wall Street crash, paradoxically, haute couture recovered during World War II thanks to skillful negotiations with the German authorities led by Lucien Lelong and Daniel Gorin. The so-called "authorized" houses benefited from raw materials and sold their models freely to clients in possession of a buyers' card:[54] 20,000 cards were issued to haute couture clients in 1941 and 13,629 in 1944.[55] Out of this number, 200 were issued to German clients. Isolated from the international market, but protected from any kind of competition in France, the price of haute couture and its revenues soared. Sales multiplied by five-fold between 1941 and 1943.[56] At the Liberation, there was a slight drop in sales, but they rose again at the beginning of 1945. Nonetheless, after five years of forced isolation, a grand and poetic show brought all the brilliance back to haute couture.

The fashion theater

"In March 1945, the Chambre syndicale de la couture parisienne organised an exhibition at the Paris Musée des Arts Décoratifs. This was not a fashion show, nor was it an exhibit of gowns displayed behind glass cases. Instead, 180 dolls made out of wire and standing 80 cm tall wore gowns, hats, hairstyles, shoes, gloves, bags of couture, but all in miniature. These 180 dolls, or rather characters, were spread around fourteen mini theaters, where the sets had been created by the most famous theater set designers.

"Christian Bérard was the coordinator of this strange show that he called 'Le Théatre de la Mode' ('The fashion theatre'). These dolls were seen as theatre figures, animated by Boris Kochno's skilful hands and they were quite unique. Some 40 couturiers, 36 milliners, and 20 hair stylists took part in the Parisian event.

"We have received invitations from all over the world. We have already been to Barcelona, London, Leeds, Stockholm and Copenhagen. Now we have to go to New York.[57] After New York, the Théâtre de la Mode will visit Boston, Chicago, Los Angeles, Montreal, then Buenos Aires."

Statement by Lucien Lelong, honorary president of the Chambre Syndicale, 1946.[58]

The golden age, just after the war

When the war ended, the habits of the couture profession changed. The reputation that was first attributed to the savoir-faire of the studios slowly shifted to those who created fashion. Couture was no longer just about the workforce. Haute couture became increasingly important because it was fueled by a multitude of young, extremely talented designers whom the media—that is to say the written press—seized upon.

Christian Bérard, program covers of the Théâtre de la mode exhibitions held in Paris and London, 1946.
© Adagp, Paris, 2008.

Jeanne Lanvin and Jean Gaumont-Lanvin at the Théâtre de la mode inauguration, 1946. Rights Reserved.

Poster by Christian Bérard for the Petit théâtre de la mode, 1946.
© Adagp, Paris, 2008.

Facing page:
Robert Ricci and Christian Bérard on the Théâtre de la mode stage, in the background, décor by Jean Cocteau.
Rights Reserved.

REGIME DES CARTES PROVISOIRES
de Vêtements et Articles Textiles

BARÊME GÉNÉRAL
D'EQUIVALENCE

	Woolens	Silks
Lucien Lelong	1,053 m	4,002 m
Jeanne Lanvin a	718 m	3,200 m
Jean Patou	27 m	1,882 m
Nina Ricci	209 m	1,647 m
Schiaparelli	497 m	1,512 m
Robert Piguet	514 m	1,771 m
Gaston	513 m	1,254 m
Maggy Rouff	551 m	1,014 m
Worth	218 m	1,153 m
Bruyère	349 m	1,375 m
Balenciaga	273 m	1,209 m
Marcelle Dormoy	253 m	1,119 m
Marcel Rochas	370 m	896 m
Agnès Drécoll	331 m	1,172 m
Molyneux	743 m	514 m
Jacques Fath	200 m	160 m
Jean Dessès	31 m	85 m

Choosing fabric for Elsa Schiaparelli.
Photo G. Paris/Agence Roger Viollet.
Rationing during World War II, 1939–1945.
Photo Agence Roger Viollet.
Ration cards during World War II, 1939–1945.
Photo Agence Roger Viollet.
Quotas for the month of February 1942, allowed to exempted houses (excerpt from a Chambre syndicale de la couture document).

Facing page: Mr. and Mrs. Marcel Rochas, 1944.
Photo Lee Miller.

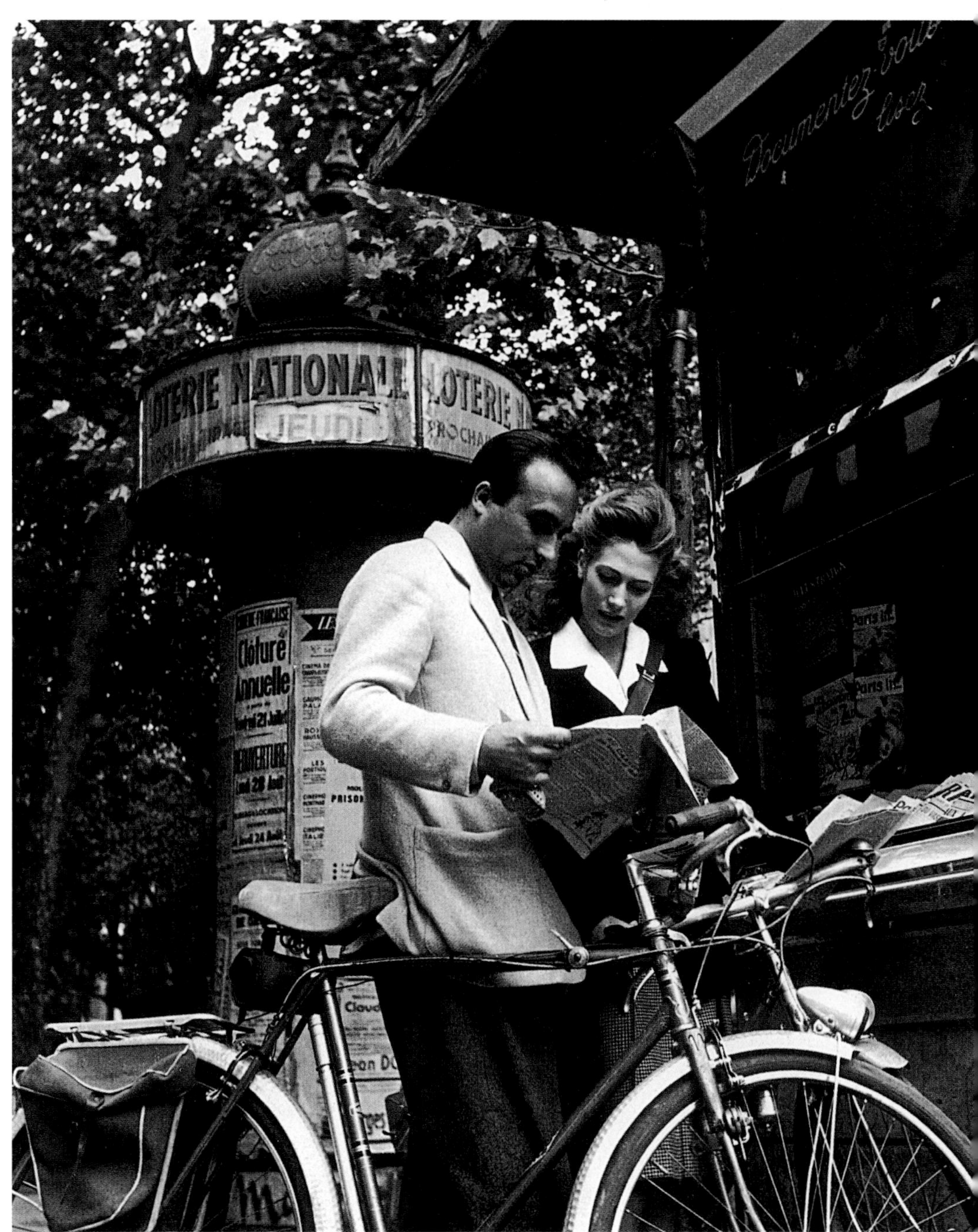
LOTERIE NATIONALE
JEUDI
Clôture
Annuelle
lisez

While he was a student at the Beaux-Arts, Hubert de Givenchy had internships with both Jacques Fath and Robert Piguet. In 1944, he joined the house of Lucien Lelong following the footsteps of Pierre Balmain, Christian Dior, Serge Kogan, and Serge Guérin, who were modelists like him. At the time, the house employed over 1,000 workers. The ritual was invariably the same. At the beginning of the season, each pattern designer presented his sketch pad to Lucien and Nicole Lelong, who were surrounded by their learned group, Raymonde Zehnacker, and the Baroness Genvième Davilliers, the salon manager, who went on to join Pierre Cardin in the same position. Once the sketches had been chosen, each studio independently executed their own muslin samples,[59] proposed their own fabrics, and created their models. Then the general rehearsal took place during which the supreme committee went about the elimination process. This method gave total authority to the couturiers that did not sketch, to the detriment of the creation, and it was abandoned after the war. The head couturiers of each house made way for the creative couturiers: Balmain, Dior, and Givenchy. This new generation of designers prepared their collections themselves under their own names.

Elsa Schiaparelli. Unhappy in his position as modelist, especially as he was the youngest there, Hubert de Givenchy accepted a job as an assistant with Elsa Schiaparelli and refused very attractive positions he was offered by New York-based Hattie Carnegie and Elizabeth Arden. In 1945, Elsa Schiaparelli had just moved back to Paris—after a forced stay in the United States—and she returned to her fashion house at 21 place Vendôme that she had left in the hands of her friend, the Countess Haydn. Hubert de Givenchy spent four years with her, during which he completed his training. He was also delighted to discover a totally free creation process, the opposite of what he had been used to at Lucien Lelong's. Elsa Schiaparelli sought and found her inspiration in the books that she consumed avidly. She found ideas for themes and brought them to the studio heads. And depending on the season, her inspirations included Pharaonic Egypt, the Italian Renaissance, or the circus. She cut out articles, annotated the pages, and colored the illustrations while writing down technical instructions. When she had finished, she sent them on to the workshop, where, in her absence, they made up hundreds of muslins. Then, for about two weeks, in a festive, totally crazy atmosphere, she pulled apart, cut up, tore up, sewed up, and superimposed the different elements, right up to the day the collection was to be shown.

It was here that Hubert de Givenchy met Greta Garbo, the Duchess of Windsor, Patricia Lopez-Wilshaw, Gloria Guinness, the Countess of Bismarck—women who later became his personal clients. The saleswomen, chosen for their beauty, their talent, and of course their elegance, were of different nationalities to satisfy an international clientele: the American Bettina Jones Bergery, the Italian Iridica Gazzoni, and the facetious Countess Maxime de La Falaise (daughter of the official portraitist to the English court), who, when her daughter Loulou was born, sketched little girls' dresses for the boutique, embellished with "poisonous" embroideries. It was also at Schiaparelli's that Givenchy became friends with Françoise de Langlade,[60] the press attaché.

At Lelong's, or "Schiap's" as she was nicknamed, Hubert de Givenchy discovered a joyful, carefree world that had not yet understood that the return of peace did not imply a return to the past.

Reality, however, could not be ignored: for the first time in several centuries, sovereign Europe had become both the instigator and the epicenter of a planetary upheaval. During these years, Europe became erased by an America that had risen to the forefront. Although the US was already the greatest world power, the country never realized it, as they had never had the opportunity to. Europe, nonetheless, still held first place in all areas of creativity and particularly in the fashion world.

The cataclysm that occurred had been more horrific than any before, but it had not decimated the planet, and it was not due to excessive frivolity that, after Hiroshima, couturiers lengthened women's skirts. This fashion revolution was immediately applauded by fashion journalists the world over. The entire luxury business was involved, if not in the reconstruction of the world, at least in its survival, and at a more illusory level, the survival of ideas. The war had marked the dusk of the nineteenth century: the modern world had begun.

This era was organized around new ideas: consumption, technology, new shapes, practicality... and the fashion houses played a role in this renewal, targeting specific clienteles.

Madame Grès. Under the name Alix, Madame Grès (Alice Barton) had dressed a number of famous women before the war: Princess Mathilda of Greece, the Begum, the Baroness de Rothschild, Cécile Sorel, Marlène Dietrich, Edith Piaf, Madeleine

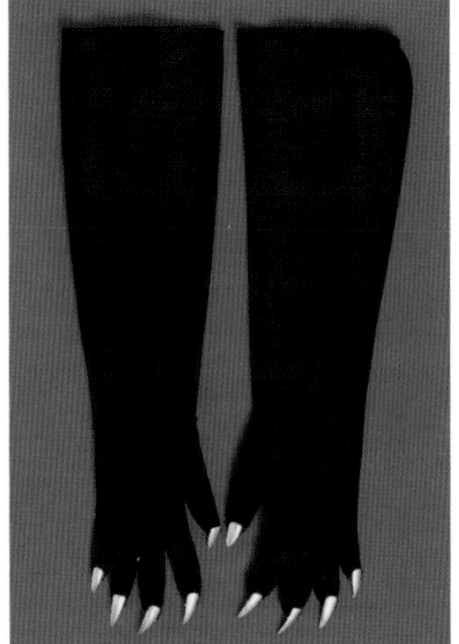

Put "Shocking" in her stocking—
IF you want to knock that Certain Young Woman for a transcontinental goal, we refer to your respectful attention Schiaparelli's *Shocking*. Schiaparelli of Paris, you know. (Anyway—the lady in question knows.)
Shocking is a Creation—Schiaparelli's very *newest*. It's high-fashion French perfume, just off the boat from Paris!
About once in every decade, there appears a perfume that appeals to women like a new fly to hungry trout. *Shocking* is one of those rare perfume occasions. Its scent is strangely spicy but subtly sweet: it combines glamour with gaiety, intrigue with insouciance, romance with reserve...
Schiaparelli says that *Shocking* "brings out your Other Self." It gives women Ideas which they reflect, even if they don't live up to them. (It is not to be given to secretaries or Other Men's Wives except at your own peril.) But as a gift to HER who *does*, or should belong to you, *Shocking* is practically perfect.
Shocking will set you back $27.50 per unit. That it is well worth it—take our word now; and on Christmas, you will get hers!
If the better bazaars in your locale haven't caught up with *Shocking* yet (it comes from France, and there won't be much of it around for a few months), just send your check to us. Or send your card for enclosure as well, and we'll be your Santa Claus.
Gilbert Bundy

Hat created by Elsa Schiaparelli, c. 1937. Photo Agence Roger Viollet.

Black antelope skin gloves, gold metal claws sewn, Elsa Schiaparelli, 1937. Paris, Musée galliéra, Musée de la mode. Photo Jean-Michel Tardy.

Advertisement for *Shocking*, where the bottle has taken on the shape of a woman's body, and for Elsa Schiaparelli's stockings, 1943. Rights Reserved.

Facing page:
Elsa Schiaparelli, c. 1937. Photo Cecil Beaton. Courtesy Sotheby's London.

Draping by Madame Grès. Collection UFAC. DR.
Madame Grès, Paris, 1978. Photo Helmut Newton.
Grès, afternoon dress, c. 1950. DR.

Renaud, or Arletty. On her return to Paris from exile, she learned that her associate had sold her Faubourg-Saint-Honoré company to the investors with whom she did not get along. Having lost her own name, she abridged her husband's to turn it into Grès, and she opened her new company at 1 rue de la Paix.

Madame Grès remained an example amongst the fashion designers for having created and retained her reputation under two successive labels. The fashion press, which became the final authority, worshipped her. *Vogue's* "brain-trust" masterfully managed by Edmonde Charles-Roux; *Elle's* audacious team, Hélène Gordon-Lazareff flanked by Simone Baron and Alice Chavanne before being joined by Françoise Giroud; the almighty Maurice-Augustin Dabadie of the *Figaro;* the omnipresent Carmel Snow, whom all of America bowed to, escorted by her faithful lieutenant Marie-Louise Bousquet from the *Harper's Bazaar* Paris office; the tireless Mme. Castanié from the *Officiel de la couture,* accompanied by her editor, Jalou; and lastly, Mme. Saad, who jealously protected the status that *L'art et la mode* had achieved: all these editors dominated the front row of Grès' shows.

The Baroness Vandeuvre, the war heroine who had accompanied the Marshal de Lattre de Tassigny, reigned over the cosy salons. Everyone whispered or mimed. Mademoiselle hated enthusiasm and the noise that generally goes with it. The atmosphere of her house resembled a convent.

Carven. Mademoiselle Carven owed her label to her music-loving father. She was baptized Carmen, a name she detested, but she changed one letter to transform it into the lovely well-known name. In 1937, her father helped her open a boutique, rue des Pyramides, to sell antiques. However, both she and the clients who visited her shop were hardly interested in objects of the past that were so far removed from the concerns of the early 1940s. She was obsessed with a single idea: creating dresses. She began making pieces for herself from fabric she could get hold of. She had a small frame, only 1m 55cm tall (about 5ft 1in). The fitted two-piece suits she designed, a tight jacket with a bouffant skirt, made her look elegantly taller. She was immediately successful and her target of petite women was clear.

After the end of the war, Carven moved her company to the roundabout of the Champs-Elysées. Cécile Aubry, Pascale Audrey, Martine Carol, Danièle Delorme, and Françoise Arnould... they all trusted her. As her reputation grew, she requested admission to the Chambre Syndicale. The return of peace initiated a good time for weddings and that meant big orders for large, sumptuous wardrobes. Her nephew and manager, Jean Manusardi, said that in 1948 the Carven house produced 18,000 couture items, the equivalent of a luxury ready-to-wear house today. This explains why neither Grès nor Carven needed backers.

Nina Ricci. Nina Ricci was a talented technician. Her salons catered to a bourgeois clientele who wanted to follow the trend of traditional elegance and good taste that were perfectly illustrated by clients like Gaby Morlaix, Micheline Presle, or Danielle Darrieux.

In 1945 the house employed 500 workers for couture. The workshops were spread over three buildings—numbers 18, 20, and 22 rue des Capucines. Robert Ricci worked with his mother, with whom he got on wonderfully. He patiently built up his dream, a family company with an international reputation.

Madeleine de Rauch. Although Madeleine de Rauch's clientele was bourgeois, it was less specifically French. She was the eldest daughter of Mr. Bourgeois, who made pigments for watercolors, and like her sisters, she was a natural sportswoman. On the Biarritz tennis courts, the four sisters were the favorite teammates of the famous "Musketeers," Lacoste, Borotra, Cochet, and Brugnon's. The sisters also played golf, ice-skated, and did horseback riding. Marie Le Quellec was a champion at four different sports. Madeleine de Rauch remained a passionate hunter and continued to hunt with hounds until the end of her life.

In 1927, de Rauch set up her business at 18 rue Croix-des-Petits-Champs in an apartment lent to her by father. She started out dressing women who belonged to sports clubs. It was only later, once she moved to her town house at 37 rue Jean-Goujon that she began to make and show city-wear and evening clothes. In so doing, de Rauch always kept an active touch to her clothes that were perfectly adapted to hunting dinners, along with her sports collection. Between 1951 and 1953, with Marc Bohan's help, she confidently developed a style that combined elegance and an outdoors look that a sporting clientele, not put off by the severity of her cut, enthusiastically adopted.

Jean Dessès. A Greek, educated in Egypt, Jean Dessès' family financed his company and his clientele was drawn mainly from the Greek and Egyptian courts, rich ship

Daniel Gorin, successively general secretary and general delegate of the Chambre syndicale de la couture from 1937–1972.

Nina Ricci with her son Robert, c. 1940.

Right to left: Carmel Snow, editor-in-chief of *Harper's Bazaar*, Richard Avedon, and Marie-Louise Bousquet at a Dior fashion show, c. 1950. Photo Willy Maywald.

Robert Piguet and his assistant, Christian Dior. Photo Willy Maywald.

Portrait of Nina Ricci by Cireuse, 1932, the year she created her couture house.

builders, and their entourages. Hence he specialized in ball gowns, often embellished with pearls and embroideries, and in refined cruise wear with which he was very inventive. His brilliant work marked the 1950s when Dessès, assisted by Guy Laroche and Valentino and supported by Antoine Gridel, an efficient manager, reached his peak. His downfall was certainly linked to the misfortunes the monarchies cited above encountered, as well as the property deals involving the hotel Eiffel on avenue Matignon where he lived and that his backers were interested in.

Lanvin. Even though America had become the land of refuge and the temple for European artists over a very short period of time, they all returned periodically to Europe. Paris was a magnet and an entourage of art lovers, bankers, and industrialists accompanied their wives, who were desirous of acquiring a bit of the savoir-faire that defined Parisian taste.

Lanvin was one of the favorite stops for this foreign clientele who had been deprived of luxury and creativity for five years. The Lanvin workshops operated to capacity. Embroidery regained its original splendor and tens of meters of taffetas and organdie were unrolled to make evening gowns. At the same time, change was in the making, just a few blocks away.

Pierre Balmain, Christian Dior. Of all possible powers, isn't the most stimulating the ability to choose the direction of one's own life? This was certainly what Christian Dior and Pierre Balmain thought in 1944, when together, they thought about leaving Lucien Lelong.

Tired of attending the same castrating ceremony year after year during which their employer generally rejected their suggestions, most often for commercial reasons, Christian Dior and Pierre Balmain decided to create a jointly-owned couture house and establish their business in a town house on avenue Matignon. They did not manage to carry through with their project. After five years of apprenticeship with Molyneux (1934–1939) and six more with Lucien Lelong (1939–1945), Pierre Balmain was the first to decide to set up his own company. Christian Dior could not hold back his tears during the farewell drink.

After having shared some great projects with Christian Dior, Pierre Balmain was faced with the reality of having to raise 600,000 francs in capital. It would be easy for him to find the investors; his mother and two of his friends had spontaneously offered to help him. He would be the majority shareholder with 51 per cent of the capital. On 12 October 1945, at 45 rue François 1er, the first collection consisting of 45 models was shown to the press and clients and it was triumphantly welcomed.[61] In 1948, the house employed 352 workers, 23 heads of services, 12 head saleswomen, 8 second saleswomen, and 20 cabin models.[62] The Balmain company had nine workshops for couture and three for the boutique, all located on avenue George V and rue François 1er.

A public figure who was terrified of the general public, Christian Dior now had to take his turn to open his house in 1947. He offered the world a mythical collection that symbolized French fashion and Parisian elegance for decades to come. As soon as he opened, his production alone generated a profit on a turnover of 1.2 million francs at the end of 1947, 3.6 million in 1948, and 12.7 million in 1949. Licensing contracts were as yet unheard of. Dior's profit margin before taxes ran at 15 per cent. His continued success, from one season to the next, was totally unprecedented.

At each of his two annual shows, the avenue Montaigne salons welcomed 25,000 visitors, personalities, professional buyers, private clients, journalists, and photographers.[63]

Until 1960, sales of patterns, mock-ups, and muslins to buyers alone covered the collection costs. Then there were the sales to private clients. Exports represented 65 per cent of Dior's turnover, 40 per cent of which went to the United States. In 1954 the Dior label alone represented more than half of French couture exports.

By opening their houses within a few months of each other, Pierre Balmain and Christian Dior sounded Lucien Lelong's death knell. Raymonde Zehnacker, the studio manager, followed Christian Dior, while the most experienced saleswomen and the workshop had already left Lelong and divided themselves between the two friends.

Textile aid: couture in the turbulence of a new era

A new fashion inspiration took shape thanks to a new trend followed by hundreds of thousands of individuals who became fervently devoted to taking vacations. This pursuit of leisure gave rise to a new type of apparel, "sportswear," which had never existed before. Although from one end of the planet to the other, luxury and

Queen Frederique of Greece, one of Jean Dessès' clients, 1953. © Rue des Archives/AGIP.
Madame Carven working on the January 1951 collection. © Rue des Archives/AGIP.

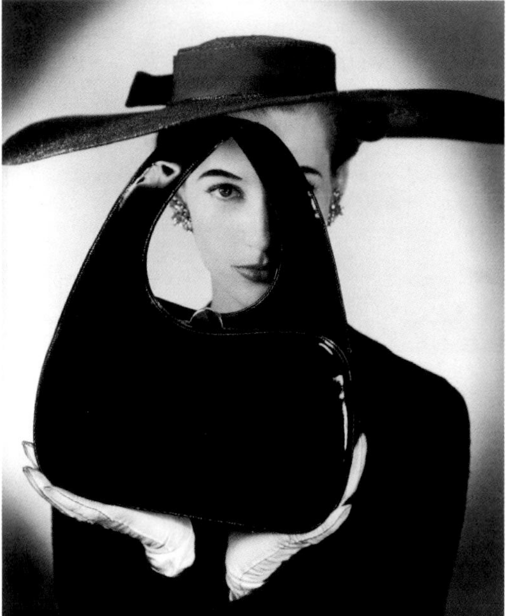

Pierre Balmain and his models, c. 1950. DR.

Karl Lagerfeld joins Pierre Balmain in 1955. Rights Reserved.

Straw hat and patent leather black bag, Pierre Balmain creations, 1961–1962. Balmain archives.

Facing page:
Pierre Balmain, evening dress, 1951. Photo Cecil Beaton. Courtesy Sotheby's London.

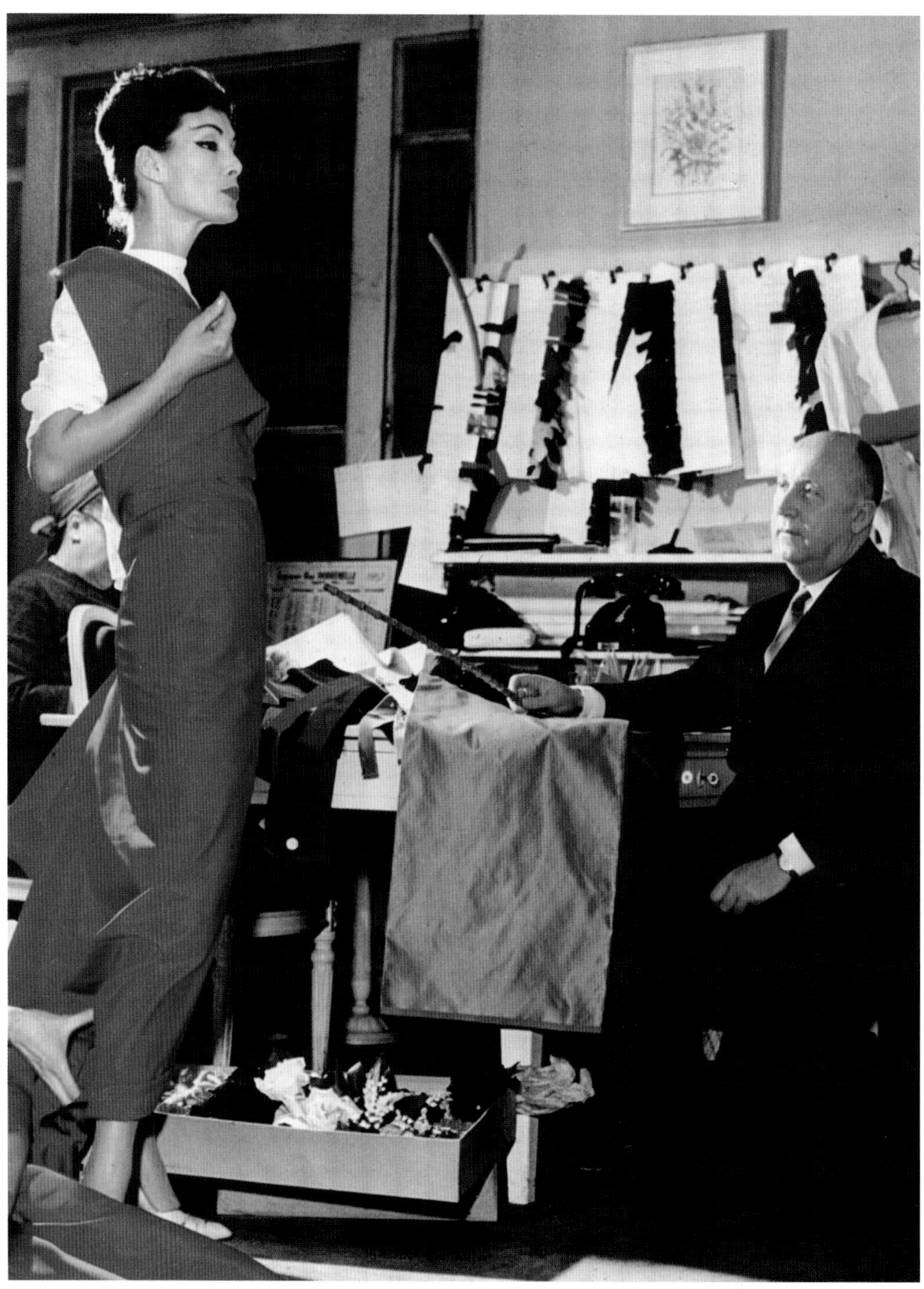

Christian Dior, holding his gold circled reed, working with the model Lucy, c. 1950. Courtesy Christian Dior/Photo Bellini.

beauty were still in demand, couturiers were in search of new stylistic as well as strategic and commercial inspirations.

A large number of old houses disappeared. They began to be ignored by a society that was thirsty for modernity and was ready to welcome talent that stood out. A number of couturiers chose this period of social and aesthetic revolution to attempt to open their own houses. But with habits changing, the economy changed too: it fed greedily off inflation. The timing was bad, particularly in terms of raising the kind of capital required to start a luxury house.

The designer-investor tandems, like Bob Capel and Coco Chanel or Raffin and Nina Ricci, were disappearing. The times when a young girl aged 23, called Jeanne Lanvin, could open her couture house in the attic of 22 rue du Faubourg-Saint-Honoré, with 300 francs lent by her suppliers, were a thing of the past.

So were cases like Madeleine Vionnet's. To establish her business in the sumptuous Hotel Des Ducs de Lariboisière in 1922, she invited her usual investors for tea such as Mr. Martinez de Hoz; Mrs. Lilaz, who owned the Bazar de l'Hotel de Ville; and Théophile Bader, the owner of Galeries Lafayette. At that time, there was a rapid return on investment and the only condition was that the couturiers remained their own bosses. There was only one exception to this rule: the investor Georges Aubert. In the 1930s, after having bought the house of Poiret in 1924, he organized the merger between Doeuillet and Doucet, after the latter's death in 1929. He later set up the merger between Drecoll and Beer, and then founded the Lenief house. The designers were placed under his absolute control.

During the 1950s, however talented they were, young couturiers found it very difficult to establish their own houses.

Towards the end of the war, Jules-François Crahay, in Liège, succeeded his mother at the head of her small family company that catered to a few French clients. One of them, Germaine de Vilmorin, told him of a company that was for sale at a reasonable price, Jane Régny, located at 22 avenue Pierre-1er-de-Serbie. However, the capital she managed to collect, with the help of a few other clients, was not enough to launch an unknown name. Crahay joined Nina Ricci in 1954. Simultaneously, at the beginning of 1953, Marc Bohan, who had just left Madeleine de Rauch, established his house at 7 avenue George V, in association with Raphäel, a renowned tailor.

Unfortunately, with the small amount of capital Marc Bohan had raised, Mr. Tranchant, previously manager of Jacques Heim and future manager of Chanel, was unable to manage the house for more than a season. Marc Bohan joined Jean Patou along with his assistant Gérard Pipart and some members of his workshop. When Gérard Pipart was called up for military duty to serve in Algeria, he continued to send sketches to Raymond Barbas, president of Patou. In 1957, Marc Bohan left Patou; Mad Carpenter replaced him for a short while until Karl Lagerfeld joined Patou in 1958. Guy Douvier also opened his business in 1950 at place de la Madeleine but he closed down and joined Chanel in 1954. 1952 was a bad year for Jeanne Lafaurie, who had just left her assistant André Courrèges when she had to file for bankruptcy. She was forced to leave her town house, 9 rue Quentin-Bauchard, and take refuge with her new company ACP (Associations Clientes Personnel) and her new designer, Michel Goma, in a three room apartment at 12 rue du Faubourg-Saint-Honoré. In 1958, to retain Goma, she added his name to the sign "ACP Michel Goma" to replace "ACP Jeanne Lafaurie." The company's name changed again to "ACP Zabaleta" in 1963 when Michel Goma replaced Karl Lagerfeld at Patou.

However talented the creators were, they were powerless against the financial demands that wiped out companies one after the other. Of the 1959 batch of fashion houses from designers Guy Laroche, Serge Matta, Bob Bugnand, and Capucci, only Guy Laroche survived due to the numerous interventions by the Intra Bank and the Bic group.

The only survivor of this collective shipwreck was, undoubtedly, Hubert de Givenchy. In a note Raymond Barbas, president of the Chambre Syndicale, wrote to the Ministry of Industry in 1956, he predicted a serene future for him.

Always the pragmatist, Christian Dior had seen it coming, and he had no desire to be a partner in his own house. His experience with Piguet, then Lelong, had prepared him sufficiently to apprehend his profession with great lucidity. Without any false modesty, he believed in a strong alliance between capital and talent. It's because of this, when Marcel Boussac suggested he take over the artistic direction of Philippe et Gaston, Dior refused. If he had left Lelong, it was to create a house that bore his name. His new management methods and his firmness convinced Marcel Boussac to invest 60 million francs of the time[64] in Dior. This was a considerable sum if one looks at the amount Pierre Balmain had.

Through the different companies in his group, Marcel Boussac became the sole owner of the company to which Christian Dior gave his name, a company that

Jacques Heim.
Photo André Ostier.

Chambre syndicale de la couture parisienne (Parisian Couture Union) fashion presentation at the Stockholm town hall, 1955. Chambre Syndicale de la couture parisienne archives.

Jules-François Crahay, 1959. Photo Claus Ohm. Marc Bohan, 1959. DR. Gérard Pipart, 1968. Photo Claus Ohm.

Jewelry and accessories at
Jeanne Lanvin,
Paris, 1939.
Photo Lipnitzki/
Agence Roger Viollet.

Choosing accessories
at Jacques Heim, 1939.
Photo Lipnitzki/
Agence Roger Viollet.

Choosing a perfume
at the Worth boutique, 1939.
Photo Lipnitzki/
Agence Roger Viollet.

produced clothing and accessories. Christian Dior remained the manager,[65] a position that gave him real power along with an international veto over the all the accessories businesses. Indexed against that of the most highly qualified staff, his salary, to which a high percentage of the pre-tax and amortization profit was added, was in fact equivalent to a 40 per cent share of the company. Just as he retained a certain power without being a partner, he received benefits without having to invest in the capital. This was a perfect model that led to no major conflict as long as Christian Dior was alive. If it so happened that Christian Dior were opposed to the signature of a girdle or bra license, like the one proposed by the company Scandale, Jacques Rouët, backed by Henri Fayol,[66] promised Dior 40 per cent of the 20 million francs minimum paid by Scandale's parent company, the Pierre Lévy group, to make the deal go through.

The power wielded by a group like Boussac brilliantly demonstrated the sovereignty of finance in a profession that offered few other perspectives.

This cruel situation affected the traditional haute couture suppliers, particularly the weavers organized under the Chambre syndicale des maisons de tissus spéciaux à la couture that were, for the most part, wholesalers.[67] The way the Parisian couture industry worked explained the existence of merchants, intermediaries between industrial weavers, and the designer-couturiers. These people were known as the "Quatre-Septembre" because of the Parisian neighborhood in which they were all located. In 1924, the Labbey house—with combined specialties of velvets and silks—occupied two buildings in la rue de la Banque and employed 900 people. Consumption was so fast at the time, and stocks moved so rapidly, that merchants had a dedicated staff responsible for delivering fabrics to the important houses on rue de la Paix. Fabric dropped off in the morning was gone by evening.

The Quatre-Septembre merchants were different from the Sentier wholesalers (Schmoll, Haas & Lambert, Puppinck, Marcel Blanc, Wurmser, etc) who came together in the context of the Chambre syndicale des tissus. The latter supplied many ready-made apparel makers and were less selective in their choice of suppliers.

Imprisoned in their valleys, the industrialists who supplied the Quatre-Septembre—Viala at Castres, Lasbordes, and Tournier at Mazamet—had no access to the market, apart from the wholesalers.

Direct contact between fabric companies and apparel makers happened at textile trade fairs, the most important of which was Interstoff.[68] But till the 1960s, relations between weavers and garment manufacturers were confidential and considered undesirable.

Three tremors shook the structure to the ground. The first was in 1929, following which Lesur, a rare exception that owned its own production facilities, found itself in debt to the Prouvost textile mills and came under their control. The second was in 1940, when World War II severed couture from its international market. The last tremor was created by the Korean War, which led to a spectacular rise in the price of wool, leaving the most vulnerable fabric houses in a delicate financial situation. Rodier was taken over by Prouvost but Prouvost could not close a merger between Rodier and Lesur in the face of Jacques Lesur's direct opposition. Rodier converted to clothing.

Inseparable, the two professions were in a position of fragility in the 1950s. In order to help them, Raymond Barbas proposed a plan in 1951 that would allow an increase in the number of models Parisian couture could present, while getting support for the French textile industry. He argued the following: every year, the overall number of models the haute couture houses presented was a minimum of 8,000; it cost between 100,000 and 120,000 francs to create a model, so 8,000 models cost about 960 million francs. In order to amortize the amount invested in creation, the profession had to generate a turnover of 9.5 billion francs. The turnover at the time was no more than 4.5 billion. To remedy the excess expenditure (500 million, the cost of design), Raymond Barbas quite logically asked the French government for an annual subsidy of 450 to 500 million francs. Couture would remain in an impasse until free trade really existed and as long as certain countries like Germany, Spain, and the Netherlands maintained their import quotas. In order to ensure the efficiency of this subsidy, Raymond Barbas proposed strict regulation that was adopted by the big fashion houses. Ten years after the classification "couture-creation" that had allowed raw materials to be shared fairly, the regulations this time ensured a fair distribution of the state aid to those who were willing to play the game. The chosen formula was similar to the one that had proved its worth during the war.

Daniel Gorin, who was present at the signature of the first collective agreements of 1936 and was still there for the preservation of haute couture in Paris during the collapse, was a key figure in the new system. He had been a director at Lanvin since 1950, where he had proved his talents as an administrator by hiring Antonio del Castillo as the creative director. His decisions were unanimously respected in the

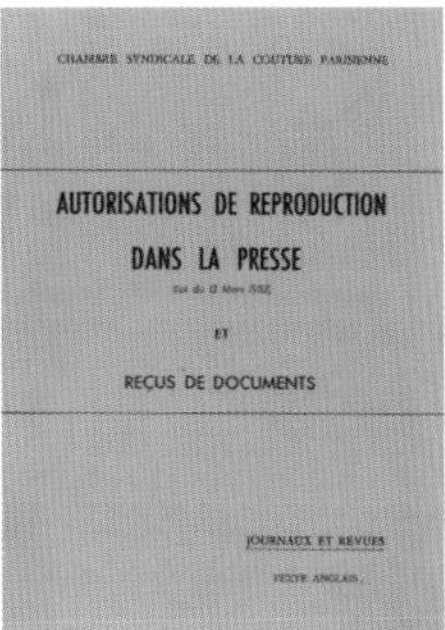

Models appearances, Barbara Hutton and Ginger Rogers' manufacturing notebooks, order books, c. 1967. Balenciaga archives.

Press reproduction authorizations and purchasing commitments. Chambre syndicale de la couture parisienne archives.

Balenciaga workshop, collection preparations, fabric samples, and model chart; 1964–1967. Balenciaga archives.

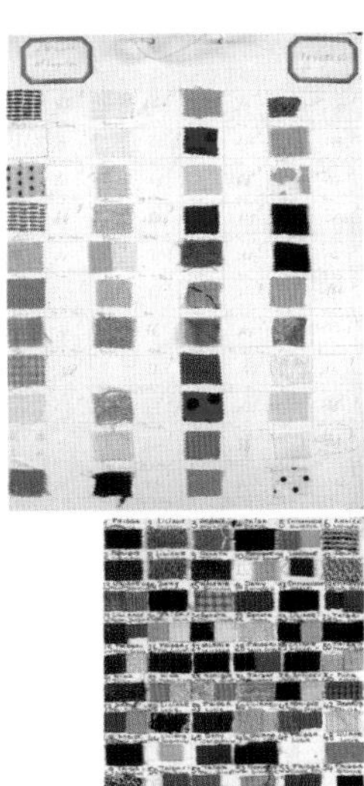

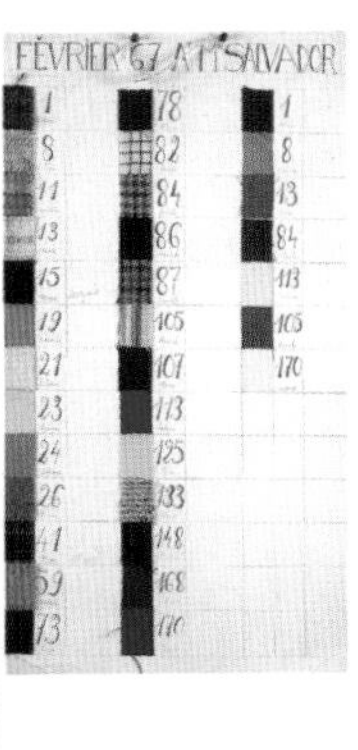

profession. A small man, his stoutness emphasized his good-natured appearance that suited state delegates well. The only sharp angle in the regular features of his face came from his reading glasses that pinched his nose. Jean Manusardi, whom he nominated deputy general delegate in 1958, remembers: "Of all the people I met in this profession, Gorin is the only one—and I am measuring my words—who had an idea of couture... When I think of him, I am tempted to compare him to General de Gaulle who was a remarkable head of state, after having been a mediocre soldier. The great man of couture was born out of a failed couturier..."[69] His death in 1972 coincided with the dusk of haute couture.

Despite the conjugated efforts made by the Chambre Syndicale and the Textile Aid, nothing could stop the slow disappearance of the couture houses whose numbers dropped from 60 to 36 in 1958.

The Textile Aid represented 395 million francs in 1952 and covered 50 per cent of haute couture's expenditure on textiles, before becoming an average of 200 million francs until 1959[70] when it represented only 30 per cent to 40 per cent of textile expenses. It nonetheless allowed the number of models presented to be maintained at about 100 each season and the pieces had to be made up of 90 per cent French fabrics. Every year Raymond Barbas, then Jacques Heim, besieged the ministerial cabinets asking for a renewal of the Textile Aid plan.

When Jacques Heim, who had been elected president of the Chambre Syndicale in 1958, was warned that the subsidy would be interrupted, he set about looking for new ways to replace it. He attempted to interest couturiers in the ready-to-wear sector by creating the Prêt à porter Création, a ready-to-wear group.

The opportunity to reconsider the conditions of a couture-prêt-à-porter agreement came at a time when, for over 30 years, nobody had managed to propose a concrete solution. Heim began discussions with different manufacturing unions, both in France and abroad. His considerations were the following: as counterfeit was becoming a real secondary market that was bleeding haute couture, threatening its very survival, and discouraging the most optimistic buyers, it was urgent to introduce a yearly "fashion passport" that would be delivered personally to every good client who committed to placing a minimum order whose quantity had yet to be defined.

As early as 1958, Jacques Heim spent 10 days in New York with Jean Manusardi. They set out on a real race course—attending over 50 meetings in all—with everybody who was anybody in the press, the department stores, and the Seventh Avenue manufacturers. To start with, the Gotlieb firm, advisor to the Chambre Syndicale in America, developed a fashion passport compatible with American legislation.

Traditionally, America could not tolerate the idea of restrictions or limits in the obstacle course that free trade implied. It was thus necessary to put forward the need to maintain a certain order—the only guarantee of healthy work relationships—so that the project could be accepted. Unfortunately their colleagues in Paris did not see the situation in this light.

The omnipresent Chambre Syndicale, which was the pivotal center of the Textile Aid, had yet again exceeded its rights by inopportunely placing themselves between the top couturiers and their clients across the Atlantic. In addition, Christian Dior, the uncontested master, was against them, followed by Robert Ricci, vice president of the Chambre Syndicale. Their excellent performance did not encourage them, in 1959, to link their fate to that of their less fortunate colleagues. Jacques Heim was unsettled but he saw his efforts compensated by the signature of a contract between the Berlin manufacturers, represented by the IMOS and the Parisian Chambre syndicale de la couture. As a result of his agreement 15 designers—Balmain, Carven, Dior, Dessès, Grès, Laroche, Griffe, Patou, Heim, Lanvin, de Rauch, Rouff, Goma, Ricci, Cardin—agreed to take part in the IMOS show, with about 60 to 70 models. This show was intended to provide the journalists, buyers, and industrialists with the same information, giving them the same directions in order to limit production risks and to encourage coordination between the different sectors of fashion, that is to say fabrics, clothing, and accessories.

The event took place in Berlin and Dusseldorf, six weeks before the major German women's manufacturing houses held their shows. The director of each house that participated in the show was given a personalized fashion passport that included their photograph. It cost 890 deutschmarks, equivalent to 100,000 francs (about 1,400 euros per show), while any other person from the house could acquire one for the sum of 100 deutschmarks.

The IMOS agreement soon gave rise to violent debates, echoed in the eloquent title that appeared in the *Figaro* of 30 April 1959: "Because fashion is made in Paris, the French are at a disadvantage." While Albert Lempereur, president of the Federation de l'industrie du vêtement féminin, was convinced that it was possible to reach an agreement with the couture industry on the main fashion trends, Pierre

Billet, an influential manufacturer associated with the Boussac group, was formal: couture and industry had two irreconcilable vocations; consequently there could be no possible alliance between them. The wise man amongst the presidents, Robert Weill (president of the Chambre syndicale des industries du vêtement féminin) had certain reservations:

> In the month following the couture presentations, the industry is in possession of the range of new models and is able to choose those that can be transposed in the area of manufacturing. However, by assuming that the problem of finance has been resolved by an agreement with couture, the problem will not be resolved at all, as, given the imperative deadlines for the manufacturing of ready made garments, the risk of being confronted with the revelation of whole new couture fashion five months later, will remain unresolved.[71]

What then is the point of collecting tens, even hundreds of millions of francs, for such a risky proposition? It was in this climate of uncertainty that two articles by Jacques Heim, published 10 days apart, one in the *Figaro,* the other in *France Soir,* put an end to the waltz of hesitations.

> The relationship between haute couture and ready-to-wear in France has unfortunately been non-existent until the present. I think that this has been a mistake. Couturiers did not want their models to be democratised immediately. For their part, manufacturers did not react and closed themselves off in a sort of complacency. This resulted in the following consequences: we have lost the opportunity of developing a great apparel manufacturing industry of international quality in France.
>
> During this time, national garment manufacturing industries from foreign countries have developed. They came and bought their models from French couturiers and developed very high quality productions in their respective countries, both in the United States and in Europe. It is thus easier for the women of these countries than it is for French women to buy cheaply made Parisian-style dresses.[72]
>
> Every season an aeroplane carries eight tons of models and mock-ups to New York. Our salons rent their seats to "buyers" from fifty different nations. We had no reason to refuse Parisian fashion to 2,000 German manufacturers who were unable to come here four times a year. The only manufacturers who never came to us were the French. We have created a group of ten couturiers called Prêt-à-porter creation that has managed to do what French manufacturers have not yet managed to do: establish an export line with foreign department stores, both American and European. One of the positive effects of this action has been to stimulate French manufacturing.[73]

The manufacturers saw this apparently innocent remark as a declaration of war. Nonetheless, on 30 April 1959, in a conciliatory letter Albert Lempereur called for calm:

> A few of us are doing our utmost to bring the antagonism between haute couture, in the strict sense, and the ready-made industry, to an end. This declaration of competition that devalues the qualities of our colleagues, to increase the merits of the Prêt-à-porter Création group, has shocked our colleagues. You have misunderstood our industry's accomplishments and successes and you cripple it with weaknesses that it does not suffer from. Do you want to see how you can attenuate my colleagues' frustration? The horizon has cleared to such an extent that I hope to soon be able to suggest ways of reaching agreements that will allow couture-creation to receive some finance from European garment manufacturers.

Jacques Heim replied to him in the following manner:

> I agree that the reminder of certain historical facts in the development of the professions we are concerned with upset certain of your colleagues. One is always very sensitive to this kind of remark coming from outside. In addition, couturiers, and I say this in friendship, have been upset in the same way these last few months, following the repeated criticism expressed in France and abroad, regarding the contract they signed with IMOS.

The desired apologies were considered too casual and the result was immediate; discussions were adjourned *sine die*. "It is not our sensitivity that has been hurt, but Mr Heim has undermined our honour."[74] The Chambre syndicale parisienne du vêtement feminin abandoned the idea of finding an agreement with couture. This was the last attempt at an understanding. There were many consequences, as amongst other hazards. The interruption of the Textile Aid and of these tumultuous negotiations coincided with the development of Italian couture that had gone through its early stages under Mussolini.

The emergence of international competition

Not content with monopolizing the shoe market, in 1932 the Duce entrusted Wladimiro Rossini, a fashion professional, with an ambitious project: he was to find a way to showcase Italian fashion's artistic, artisanal, industrial, and commercial strengths. This meeting led to the creation of the Ente Nazionale Moda that prefigured Italian fashion's irresistible conquest of the internal market. From 1936 onwards, Italian designers were obliged to include at least 25 per cent of Italian-inspired design in their collections. The certificates the pieces earned guaranteed that they were effectively an "ideazione et produzione nazionale," or a national idea and product. The Ethiopian war and the Axis proclamation encouraged this movement and accentuated Rome's isolation.

The major Roman salons that had been used to choosing their models in Paris slowly changed their habits. Those that worked in accordance with the Ente found themselves being patronized by royal princesses, like the Princess of Piémont or dignitaries' wives, like Countess Ciano.

To open a salon in Rome was to gain total recognition. The Fontana sisters from Parma opened a fashion concern there, as did Maria Antonelli, Emilio Shuberth, Irène Galitzine, etc. Ava Gardner and Mrs. Tyrone Power were the flag bearers for this new Roman couture.

Fundamentally, however, these very local initiatives had no international impact. It was only in February 1951, when Count Giovan Battista Giorgini organized the first Italian couture group fashion show in his own palace in Florence with designers like Simonetta, Carosa, and Fontana, that Italian Alta Moda became a reality. The count was familiar with the American market, and he excelled at entertaining. This enabled him to gather the major American buyers and a selection of the international press to the event. The Veneziani and Marucelli houses from Milan joined Emilio Pucci from Capri, in Florence. At the first event, about 15 Italian designers, from Milan, Rome, Florence, and Turin, attracted about 50 buyers. But for the second set of presentations, on 19 July of that same year, 250 buyers and journalists turned up.[75] Henceforth, every season buyers made a detour to Florence where the shows moved from the Giorgini palace to Palazzo Pitti from July 1952 onwards.

The Alta Moda Italiana—Capucci, Simonetta, Fabiani—developed progressively, shifting from Florence to Rome, greatly inspired by the peninsula's textile manufacturers. The latter developed a strategy based on quality and seduction and soon they were in direct contact with all the Italian and Parisian couturiers, to whom they offered their fabric free of cost in the hope of gaining international recognition.

It was at this time, in 1959, that the Textile Aid in France decided to stop its subsidies. French couture became an export market for Italian fabrics. The percentage of French textiles in haute couture collections fell from 90 per cent in 1959 to less than 60 per cent a few years later.

In 1969, a second aid plan was established: "Aide à la creation textile et couture." Based on its principles and its functioning, it was only a revival of the plan that had been interrupted previously in 1959.

This plan guaranteed couturiers free French fabrics for their collections and the Comité interprofessionnel de renovations de l'industrie textile (CIRIT[76]) paid the suppliers directly. The aid represented an amount of 1.5 million francs (about 1.25 million euros) plus another 300,000 francs for advertising costs. The sum allocated was apparently less than under the previous aid plan. Now, it included only 21 couturiers, and the percentage of models that had to be made of French fabric had fallen from 90 per cent to 55 per cent. Concerned about the real efficiency of the aid plan, the CIRIT commissioned the Crédit National bank to carry out a study. It was natural, to say the least, to question the logic of financial support for a profession where everything was condemned to disappearing. This situation was reminiscent of the nineteenth-century subsidy for the sailing Navy versus the steamship Navy.

But a major question arises: in 1970 was haute couture still the leader for the textile and ready-to-wear industries? At the time, 31 wholesalers of luxury fabric for the haute couture industry that sold exclusive designs were still active. Among them, a certain number—Bianchini-Férier, Bucol, Chatillon-Mouly-Roussel, Dormeuil, Léonard, Prudhomme, Racine, Staron—produced their own fabric and sometimes also made apparel. This was the Racine and Léonard's case. Taking their different activities into account, their total turnover represented 300 million francs in 1970. Their wholesale fabric business represented 161 million fabrics of which 69 million came from exports.

In 1970, this figure represented only 4 per cent of total French fabric exports.

In addition, traditional fabric suppliers' sales to haute couture houses began to decline and represented only 5 per cent of the suppliers' revenues. The breakdown of Moreau's turnover, a company presided over by Philippe Rolloy,[77] precisely clarifies this situation: haute couture accounted for 2 per cent of sales; seamstresses and tailors 23 per cent; retailers 30 per cent; and apparel manufacturers 45 per cent. The analysis is simple. Selling to haute couture houses was only done for promotional reasons. The notoriety the fabric companies gained by working with couturiers helped them attract foreign retailers, as well as garment manufacturers, in addition to representatives of the very recent couturier ready-to-wear sector. The

Crédit National study arrived at the same conclusion: "Despite the increasing competition from a feminine, high quality, ready-to-wear industry that challenges haute couture's role as the innovator and inspiration for all fashion, the image couture enjoys is extremely useful in the promotion of French textile sales to foreign markets."[78]

In fact, at the start of the sixties a new phenomenon was taking shape in the geography of international fashion: the Japanese market was opening up to western fashion. This trend enabled large fabric companies like Moreau to sell their production via wholesalers to thousands of small traditional Japanese shops that became stocked with European fabric. Over a period of 10 short years, Japan made the shift from haberdashers to ready-to-wear manufacturers. It took France 100 years to do the same thing. In the same Crédit National report, we read that four "couturiers" from the ready-to-wear sector considered changing their presentation calendar in order to show both aspects of their business-couture and ready-to-wear-in a single venue. Given the importance and seniority of the couturiers concerned—Cardin, Courrèges, Nina Ricci, and Yves Saint Laurent—it was urgent to react because if these companies actually proceeded as planned, the whole future of the profession was at stake.

Yves Saint Laurent soon backed out, but Pierre Cardin and Nina Ricci maintained their position until the 1972 winter season.

Although it seemed that few companies were affected by the influence of haute couture, the Crédit National nonetheless advised maintaining the Aide à la creation. The bank reasoned that the aid would promote the influence of French haute couture and the French textile industries abroad due to the magnificence of the collections. It did not cost very much—1.5 million francs annually, or 3 per cent of the CIRIT's resources. And it was authorized because it was considered an investment in advertising. But because the subsidy could not stop the fall of French fabric sales, the aid was discontinued in 1979, and then re-established in 1980 at the same level, that is to say 2.5 million current francs. It then became the "Aide à la promotion textile" and took the shape of a prestigious subsidy, attributed to the couture and textile unions to allow them to promote French textiles. They bought advertising space that featured the pieces from the 10 creators or couturiers most frequently quoted in the press. It was still in existence in 1993.

Starting in the 1970s, competition from foreign labels became serious and its influence had increased significantly over just a few years. While the Alta Moda Italiana, with couturiers like Valentino, already represented a veritable force within the international market, there were a number of labels appearing in the United States whose reputations were also growing. It was in this context that a society event in Paris had enormous repercussions in New York. On the pretext of an evening organized by the Baronness Marie-Hélène de Rothschild in 1973 to raise funds for the Chateau de Versailles, five American designers—Bill Blass, Oscar de la Renta, Anne Klein, Halston, and Stephen Burrows—were invited to compare their talent to that of five of their French colleagues—Pierre Cardin, Givenchy, Dior, Yves Saint Laurent, and Ungaro. This prestigious group would hold a fashion show at the Theatre Royal, before going on to a gala dinner served at the Galerie des Glaces. As disciplined challengers, the Americans all followed their choreographer Kay Thompson.[79] It was absolutely perfect; the show went off harmoniously, in rhythm, and took 35 minutes. It ended with standing ovations from the enthusiastic supporters, led by Grace Kelly, Josephine Baker, Elsa Peretti, Joe Eula, Liza Minelli, Marisa Berenson…

The French staged their show as the second act after the intermission to their director Jean-Louis Barrault's despair. Each one wanted to steal the show and do his own thing. The effect was disastrous and the show became interminable and chaotic. The brilliance of the fashion was lost in the rivalry of disturbing interventions, leaving the audience surprised and bored.

With the same discipline they demonstrated at the show, American couture organized itself at home. Benjamin Shaw, who was Pierre Balmain's authorized dealer in the United States in 1951, backed new designers like Oscar de la Renta, Geoffrey Beene, or Donald Brooks, then later Stephen Burrows.

Gunther Oppenheim,[80] Pierre Cardin's licensee, went into business with Anne Klein, who died shortly after the Versailles show. Her former assistant, Donna Karan, had exports to Europe in 1991 that were worth 20 million dollars. Maurice Rentner, one of the main French couture buyers in the US, launched Bill Blass; the Jane Derby house became Oscar de la Renta, who, to promote his perfume, presented his collection in Paris every season before he joined Pierre Balmain as artistic director.[81]

There was no way around it. Parisian haute couture was no longer the sole player in the field. Nonetheless, it had reached its peak, so how could it possibly imagine it had a rival? Impossible. It was unique, eternal, successful season after season, and was constantly seeking new inspiration. In fact, for the time being, the competition did not really make itself felt, but a new adventure was clearly taking shape in the fashion world: the American designers launched an aggressive licensing policy that was a frontal attack on second level French couturiers.[82]

Inexorably the business of couture was shrinking.[83] In 1930, the industry employed about 350,000 workers. By 1953, it could only ensure a living for 150,000. Of this number, 6,799 worked for haute couture spread over 59 houses which generated a turnover of 5.5 billion francs (constant francs). The revenues were generated from the direct sales of their clothes, or 90,000 pieces. In 1973, all that was left of the haute couture labor force were 3,120 workers over 25 houses and producing only 30,000 pieces.[84]

As for the turnover, the sum was 508 million francs in 1973, but the breakdown was not the same as in 1953. The 1973 numbers included what Dior called indirect turnover, or revenues generated by the sales of licensed goods:[85] couture creation 18 per cent, women's ready-to-wear 18 per cent, men's ready-to-wear 5 per cent, women's secondary diffusion lines 20 per cent, men's secondary diffusion lines and ready-made men collections 3 per cent, accessories 36 per cent.[86]

In 1990, haute couture only employed 928 workers and the Union artisanale de la couture (Couture Artisans Union) only had 8,000 artisan members.

The Organization of Haute Couture

Haute couture clientele

In order to face problems in the best possible way, problems that everyone knew were almost insolvable, haute couture practiced ritualized work methods with its precious clientele, suppliers, and staff that remained unchanged for decades. The clientele was divided into two categories: individual clients and professional buyers, the latter who, until 1945, were exclusively foreigners.

Yves Saint Laurent, suit, 1979. Photo Helmut Newton for *Vogue.*

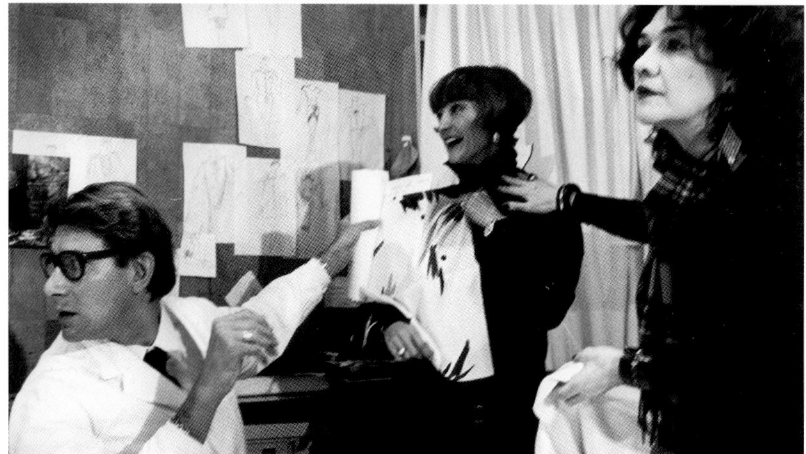

Yves Saint Laurent
and Pierre Bergé
in temporary offices, 1961.

Yves Saint Laurent, 1974.
In the center, Nan Kempner
and Catherine Deneuve.

Yves Saint Laurent,
Loulou de La Falaise,
and Anne-Marie Muñoz.

Photos Pierre Boulat,
courtesy Agence Cosmos.

The individual clientele was international and rich. Until 1914, half of these clients were French. After World War I, the French clients were replaced by those from North and South America, a result of the weakened French economy and the decline of a number of European courts. Then, in the 1970s, the market shifted towards the Emirates, South America, and the Far East.

Over decades, the organization of haute couture sales had followed strict business practices that never changed. Both the production and the sales services functioned as a dictatorial hierarchy. The salon manager gave orders to the head saleswomen, who in turn had a battalion of second saleswomen under their command. The head saleswomen were high society ladies looking for a socially gratifying occupation; they had no fixed remuneration but were paid on a commission basis. They developed and were responsible for a clientele that essentially comprised their business assets and this bound them more closely to the house that employed them.

The departure of a star designer was a major upset to the perfect organization of the couture sales services. Yvonne Minassian, the future Madame de Peyerimhoff, left Dior to follow Yves Saint Laurent, just as a large number of Lucien Lelong's sales staff had left him to follow his assistants, Balmain, Dior, and Kogan, when they opened their own houses. In 1925, Jean Patou employed 100 saleswomen, who used 30 dressing rooms in his buildings at 7-9-11 rue Saint-Florentin. The collection consisted of about 400 models. The shows began in the morning, continued till late afternoon, and sometimes lasted into the night.

When Michel Goma replaced Karl Lagerfeld at Jean Patou in 1963, he enjoyed immediate success. The seventeen saleswomen and the seven atelier heads did not have a minute to spare. The head saleswomen had their clientele and they worked together on the basis of "turns" as they do in boutiques today. Each new client is thus attributed her regular saleswoman.

Their hierarchical superiors paid the second saleswomen. The couture house, however, also paid them a symbolic amount to encourage their work.

Until 1968, the dressing rooms of the company that occupied the town house, at 7 rue Saint-Florentin, were booked hourly. A red velvet ribbon hung down along the length of each of the eight cabins, laid out in a row like confession boxes. Cards were pinned at regular intervals to each ribbon showing the names of the clients and their saleswomen and premières d'atelier. The mornings were relatively calm, but from 3:00 PM onwards, after the collection presentations, the salon came to life. Dressing rooms were places of worship where the client, the head première and two of her apprentices, and the saleswoman and her second gathered. Clients were generally as fond of their head saleswomen as of their première; the latter two had to work in total harmony, as their clients' loyalty depended on their authority and the subtlety of their relationship. For its own production and sales needs, couture had developed an original system with a ritual that conformed to its own idea of what it represented. The industry, however, was blind to the real requirements of a clientele that was visibly disappearing from 1968 onwards.

In 1943, haute couture dressed 20,000 clients;[87] in 1970, 2,000; and in 1990, 200. In 1975, Grès had 80 clients; in 1976, Dior dressed 216 clients, a number that declined to 193 in 1977 and 189 in 1978. This same decline was experienced at Yves Saint Laurent.

The relationship between couture and the retail buyers was more complex. Stores got to see the collections a month before private clients and were billed 40 per cent more for pieces that were never even tried on. This difference in rates was due to the reproduction rights that obligated buyers to sell fabric copies of the couture pieces only, excluding drawings, patterns made from the prototype, rental, transfers, or exchanges. The thought was that this right gave them an exclusive usage and it was reprehensible to transfer it.

In 1947, at Christian Dior's, the most popular model was the "Elle" dress. It was sold at a price of 32,000 old francs to a private client; 10,000 francs for a paper pattern, or pure profit; and at 45,000 francs for a buyer.[88] The differences, however, did not end here. Private clients ordered dresses to their measurements, a service that involved innumerable fittings that could be spread over three weeks and necessitate alterations. Buyers bought models as is, with no changes in fabric or the original shape. Sales to buyers were much more profitable than client sales, but also much fewer. It is believed they made up 20 per cent of the haute couture turnover until 1960. In addition, they represented the twofold, non-negligible advantage of promoting the couturier, because of the publicity the manufacturers and shops created around the designs, which brought in new individual clients to the label. This was all the more important since couturiers did not even consider the idea of investing one *centime* to promote themselves.

How did one access these salons of haute couture houses that were temples of luxury and elegance? It was terribly complicated. A buyer was beset by innumerable restrictions. They first had to make a request to the Chambre syndicale de la couture parisienne, who filled in a form in their name before issuing a buyers' card. The condition was that the buyers had to agree to respect the clauses of what could be called a moral contract. The whole thing was rather like a police investigation. One of the things the buyer promised was not to share the models they had purchased with others, and not to buy from copyists. Any disagreement with a couturier or non-respect of the conditions was carefully noted on the form.

Once they had acquired their card, the professional buyers could register at the couture houses they wanted to visit, where they had to pay an advance on possible future purchases to be able to attend the collection viewings. This "security deposit" had to be paid to the couture house in any event. Each year, and until the 1990s, the Chambre Syndicale drew up a list of prices and security deposits, instituted on the basis of the entry fee applicable in each house. This list was sent to the buyers.[89]

From 1930 until the 1970s, the United States represented couture's main market.[90] In the years around 1925, the most eagerly awaited buyers were the American buying offices. Twice a week at Le Havre, transatlantic ships offloaded their overexcited buyers, who pushed their way into the trains in an attempt to reach the grand couturiers' salons as fast as possible. They ordered a number of models in different sizes that they wanted different copies of. These purchases were meant to fill the luxury departments of America's biggest shops that, in turn, carried out any necessary alterations for their clients. For America, haute couture at the time was only luxury ready-to-wear. It meant that agents had to choose the kinds of garments likely to satisfy a traditional clientele, little inclined to excesses.

The 1929 crash rang in the end of this opulent commerce. America was in crisis. To defend itself, the American government levied a 90 per cent customs tax on imported garments. At the same time, other States imposed draconian quota systems or established controls on exchange rates. All these regulations destroyed the couture industry bit by bit. In order to get around the taxes, buyers imported fewer couture dresses, and instead, more patterns with permission to reproduce the model in large numbers.

Thus, from 1930 onwards, the sale of patterns that had been negligible up until then suddenly became a regular practice. Prices varied depending on the buyers' category and nationality, the elements provided, and the houses, depending on whether they sold models, mock-ups, paper patterns, or the rights to attend a show without buying anything (a category that mainly applied to the affiliated industries, accessories, beauty, etc).

The Chambre Syndicale alone had the right to communicate the collection calendar to buyers and journalists, the first date of the delivery of models to buyers, and the authorized date for the publication of documents in the press. These dates were imperative and the Chambre Syndicale had the means to ensure they were respected.

Amongst the buyers, one could clearly distinguish three specific types:

a) Manufacturers who made mass-produced garments for their own distribution.

b) Shops that were developing an integrated made-to-measure department or providing sub-contractors with patterns and models for mass production.

c) Couturiers working to order.

While French apparel manufacturers had always been refused entry to the grand couturiers' salons because the latter wanted to keep the national market to themselves, foreign manufacturers, on the other hand, had always had access to the creative design laboratory that Paris represented and that allowed them to benefit from the novelty of the models, the patterns, and the prestige associated with the labels. This practice was upheld until 1945, a date at which certain French manufacturers, particularly wholesale couturiers, were admitted to the collections upon paying a "viewing right" that allowed them to use the models as an inspiration, without being allowed to copy them.

Buyers came from all over the world, and amongst them, the most influential Americans, if not the largest numbers, were nicknamed "the Seventh Avenue" after the New York City neighborhood where their businesses were generally established. The Seventh Avenue was often well represented at the same designers; for example, in 1968, Kimberly, Suzy Perette, and Abe Schrader, as well as Adèle Simpson, Ben Zuckerman, and even Norell and Geoffrey Beene, all went to Jean Patou's. It was obvious: industrialists like Jack Lazard from Kimberly were there alongside the upmarket manufacturers like Adèle Simpson and talented designers represented by Geoffrey Beene. To ensure their loyalty, couturiers tried to share the models fairly amongst competing manufacturers, but tension was inevitable. In addition, the few remaining designers who sold their models for ridiculous lump sums saw them reproduced by the thousands. Dissatisfaction was growing on both sides, fed by a system that was perpetuated by tradition.

In some cases and under very restrictive conditions, shops were allowed to associate their names with the couturiers, on the label of the copied garment: "Christian Dior for Saks Fifth Avenue."

All over the world and in different categories of shops, models created by French couturiers were widely commercialized. This trend increased after Poiret, (with the advent of labels like Chanel, Patou, or Molyneux in 1919) as soon as haute couture started creating models destined for a less obviously sophisticated clientele and which stood out by the perfect cut and the quality of the fabric, rather than their boldness or the great originality of their shape.

This phenomenon continued to grow until the 1960s. Harrods of London, Ab Nordiska Kompaniet of Stockholm, or Bon Genie of Geneva attended the shows along with everyone from the department stores on New York's Fifth Avenue. The buyers from Lord & Taylor, Bonwit Teller, B. Altman, Saks Fifth Avenue, and Bergdorf Goodman competed skillfully to obtain the couturiers goodwill. There were two types of buyers. The first owned a couture workshop; the second had "line for line" copies made by sub-contractors.

Marshall Field's in Chicago integrated nine independent workshops into its State Street flagship, and had nine modelists working for the store. The couture salon, the 28th Shop, entirely covered in marble, was far more luxurious than a Parisian salon. Spacious dressing rooms designed with the client's comfort in mind were set in a semi-circle around the main salon. Everything was planned to make a client's afternoon a most pleasurable experience, while the second saleswomen put together the wardrobes.[91]

The jewel in the crown of luxury shops was incontestably Bergdorf Goodman. Hermann Bergdorf was an Alsatian of French origin. He lived above his boutique at the corner of Fifth Avenue and 19th Street when, in 1899, Edwin Goodman came to see him for an apprentice's job. A few years later, the same Goodman set up the company he became an associate of at 616 Fifth Avenue, opposite today's Saks

Fifth Avenue, before they moved to the corner of 58th Street, replacing the Vanderbilt "castle" built in 1928.

In the thirties, Edwin Goodman's son, Andrew, was in charge of the newly created range of ready-to-wear garments, but the "made-to-measure" department was doing much better. Ethel Frankau created Bergdorf Goodman's collection each season, with a subtle mixture of "in house" creations and models that had been chosen in Paris. There were about 150 models in all.[92]

A diplomatic incident can happen anywhere. In 1966, a client was leaving Bergdorf Goodman, carrying her "made-to-measure" suit under her arm. She almost fainted when she saw her suit's "little brother" in a cheaper version on display in the window. The same season and the same day, a saleswoman at Yves Saint Laurent's had mistakenly sold the seven models reserved by Ethel Frankau[93] to Alexander's and Macy's, her irreconcilable competitors.

Little by little and for a variety of reasons, the upmarket stores purchased less, while others, conscious of the publicity they could gain from it, increased their purchasing. Thus, in 1962, about 3,000 Americans were invited to attend a fashion show at Macy's. The models paraded on the runway in pairs. One of the "twins" wore the designer's original piece while the other wore a copy. A Givenchy coat was priced at $1,000.00 while the copy cost $70. Ohrbach's and Alexander's reproduced the event.

Paradoxically, these shops that were unused to showing prestigious labels were the ones who upheld the tradition. Their shows became very popular. At midnight, on the date authorized for the presentation of the models, the crowd rushed to admire the window displays. The whole profession worshipped Sydney Gittler, the coat buyer at Ohrbach's.

Jean Manusardi, delegated president of the Chambre syndicale de la couture who attended a showing at Ohrbach's, remembers having been struck by the elegance of the event and the quality of the local reproductions of Parisian models.

The last category of buyers was made up of foreign couturiers and, from 1945 onwards, the provincial couturiers, or those from outside Paris. In fact, since the founding on 25 February 1945 of the Federation nationale de la couture, an agreement had been signed between Parisian haute couture and provincial couture. It gave provincial couturiers the right to copy models and to use the names of the Parisian couturiers. In exchange, provincial couture had to fight against illegal copies, commit to guaranteeing the high quality of copies for a private clientele, and accept the Chambre Syndicale's monitoring the value of the purchases made by those who were in possession of a green card.[94]

In 1945, the couture houses in France were legion. The Chambre syndicale de la couture parisienne (the Parisian Couture Union) counted 1,100 members (including haute couture): Montluçon 360, Vichy 250, La Loire 169, Nice 125[95]... In 1960, the number of provincial houses that signed an agreement with haute couture, regardless of the type of card, had shrunk: seven in Marseille, six in Lyon, six in Nice, five in Toulouse, and three in both Biarritz and Cannes[96]... On the other hand, there was a plethora of Italian couturiers.

The most famous of them was a strong woman, Enrichetta Pedrini, from Rina Modelli in Milan. Every season a front row seat was reserved for her, and although all the couturiers feared the methods she employed, they were all happy when she ordered a model from them (12 fabric models from Dior every season, far more than what Liétard from Brussels ordered). Once she had made up her collection, she created paper pattern versions that she sold to her Italian colleagues. In 1935 Enrichetta Pedrini had opened a small couture workshop in Milan for a private clientele at 29 via Montenapoleone.

During the 1940s the quality and originality of her creations allowed her to sell her own models to Italian couturiers. After the war, under the name Rina Modelli, she included patterns from French houses including Balenciaga, Dior, Cardin, Balmain, Lanvin, Ricci, Venet, etc. in her collection.

At the beginning of March and of September, a month after the Paris fashion shows, she took a week to show her collections to the Italian workshops: Zecca in Rome, Stassi in Palermo, Calabri in Florence, Trottman in Genoa, Biglia in Venice, etc. These were well-known houses that each had a staff of 20 to 30 people, but these companies disappeared during the mid-sixties. She sold them fabric models, mock-ups, or paper patterns. This is how Gina Lollobrigida bought Dior's dress in Milan, while Elizabeth Taylor, who had bought the same dress from Dior in Paris, was convinced hers was exclusive. The press had a heyday over this fashion mishap and a deeply embarrassed Jacques Rouët, who headed Dior, negotiated compensation with Eddie Fisher, Miss Taylor's husband at that time.

While Mrs. Pedrini still dominated the couture world, her daughter Dogle and her son-in-law Atillio Fare represented Castillo, Madeleine de Rauch, Philippe Venet, and Jean Patou's ready-to-wear collections in Italy starting in 1964—all of which were manufactured in France by C. Mendès. In October and November 1967, they went on to open the first Saint Laurent Rive Gauche boutiques in Milan and Rome. Giancarlo and Maurizio Fare still owned the Italian Saint Laurent Rive Gauche franchises in the 1990s. Mrs. Pedrini had seen her family take an interest in apparel manufacturing, a trade she hated. Nonetheless, for a number of years, her grandsons organized haute couture collection shows in Milan at the beginning of September and the end of February. The paper patterns were entrusted to about 200 small workshops on the peninsula, each of them with two or three employees. The Fares had the exclusive Italian rights over the sale of Guy Laroche, Ungaro, and Yves Saint Laurent haute couture patterns.

In 1992, haute couture could still sell patterns. Philippe Venet provided about 100 patterns for the Italian market and about a dozen for the Swiss market.

Just as the Chambre syndicale de la couture issued buyers' cards, they also issued press cards that were as personal as a passport. They contained a passport photograph, and the signatures of both the publisher and the correspondent of each press agency who committed to respecting the formalities imposed by the profession. In particular, journalists promised not to publish the documents they received by special permission, or that were simply given, before a certain date: the press release date. To guarantee the date was respected, twice a year the Chambre Syndicale set the compulsory deadline calendar: dates for the press fashion show and the buyers' show; the date that couture houses had to hand in the illustrated documents; the date when the newspapers were allowed to publish these documents. There was about a month between the press show and the publication of the photos—the time couturiers required to deliver the models they had ordered to the buyers. Thus publicity arrived at the right time and the buyers were protected from pirated copies for as long as possible.

Haute couture suppliers

The grand couturiers ended up being essentially style offices for foreign buyers, although their label could not be used on the goods made abroad unless the copies of the models conformed exactly to the original. This explains the importance of the reference cards that specified the list of compulsory suppliers and gave the lengths of fabric required.[97]

By being referenced in haute couture, suppliers, whether they were manufacturers or merchants, had the hope, if not the assurance, of an important order and international publicity. In this manner, from Worth onwards, haute couture has been the spearhead of the textile industry. The weavers' desire to be referenced, combined with the couturiers' difficulty in placing firm orders while they were trying out samples, naturally led to a discount that was conditioned on typical cuts shown during the collections. The result was that the amount of fabric required for creating the collection and the first orders was provided free of cost.

Because they wanted to maintain the exclusivity of a pattern[98] they had chosen, couturiers reserved large amounts of fabrics to ensure the availability for copies. The fabric was paid for as it was used, and the remainder was returned to the merchant at the end of the season. The merchant would then try to sell the leftover fabric to dressmakers, discount traders, or the fabric sections of department stores. When they were sure of placing confirmed orders, haute couture sometimes dealt directly with the fabric company. In general though, they worked with the Quatre-Septembre merchants.

Until the 1960s and despite the difficulties, all the textile merchants and the creator-couturiers worked together in perfect harmony. As a production industry, haute couture drew the fabric industry into the export market. However, in the mid-sixties when couture started losing ground to ready-to-wear, and the textile subsidies were withdrawn, the system of conditional fabric orders was abandoned.[99] The weavers naturally replaced the wholesalers, whose intervention now became superfluous.

The battle against copying

It is almost impossible to understand the initiatives Jacques Heim took, or to evaluate the power the Chambre Syndicale possessed, or even to have a judgement upon the way haute couture was organized, without taking into consideration the extent of the damage that counterfeiters have always caused.

Since the dawn of the last century, copies have infected the couture industry. The growth of copies was fairly easy because laws were virtually non-existent in the area of the applied arts.

In 1928, Andrew Goodman,[100] future president of Bergdorf Goodman, who was a trainee with Jean Patou at the time, cooperated with the French police on his employer's request, to catch a gang of counterfeiters. Called "Mister Bosca" and posing as an American buyer, Goodman met the counterfeiters in a room at the Hotel Daunou, opposite Harry's Bar. Three policemen were hiding under the bed and in the bathroom; the presumed copiers introduced themselves, each one carrying a suitcase full of models. Caught red handed, they admitted they worked in collaboration with a female employee of the house. They were handcuffed and taken away.

The situation worsened during the 1930s, when, to fight against the application of quotas and an increase in customs taxes, the haute couture houses increased their sales of patterns and mock-ups. Although they represented fairly substantial sums, these sales were nothing compared to that of ready-made garments. The act of copying was triply "encouraged" by this practice since it is much easier to copy a paper pattern than an actual dress; because the economic crisis had set in; and since haute couture still held sway over fashion.

The couturiers were in a state of total confusion. The large American companies no longer even bothered to attend the Paris fashion shows to gather information. They set up resident buyers' offices in the capital. These became veritable centers of industrial espionage. The American companies were constantly informed of the changes in trends and this allowed them to design their collections in advance, using the shows just to add the final touches. During this period, Macy's and Saks in New York did not hesitate to circulate misleading advertisements in the newspapers. Macy's offered a few "elegant sport suits from the David house in Paris," at a price that was "about half the original price." This disloyal competition (only one of the dresses shown was a David model) meant that David lost several good clients in New York. As for Saks, they were proud to offer their clients bags by Parisian grand couturiers but which had been "copied by small Parisian couturiers" and sent directly to Saks from Paris. An investigation carried out on the basis of this advertisement showed that none of the houses mentioned (Lanvin, Callot, Hermès, Patou, Lelong, Molyneux) recognized these models as being one of their creations. Later, Macy's did it again, advertising copies of knitwear by Jane Regny and Lelong. Jane Regny had sold none of them. The newspaper *Les Echos* carried out an investigation on the subject and concluded on 16 June 1929 that "the American buyer acquired these models by illicit means, in order to have them copied in Vienna and then produced by the hundreds."[101]

At the same time, model rental companies were coming into existence in New York, Berlin, and Frankfurt. The system was simple: for a few dollars or deutschmarks, buyers rented models, mock-ups, or patterns they had acquired in Paris to their couturier or manufacturer clients. Elsie Cobin was the worst and she was much talked about as early as 1933. At each fashion show, she bought about 20 Parisian pieces and took them to the United States where she organized fashion shows with models. For a high price, each spectator could make drawings or rent a model for a few hours, just long enough to copy it. It was only in 1949, during one of Elsie Cobin's stays in Paris, that the police were able to put a stop to her activities.[102]

The buyers had developed a kind of complicity amongst themselves over the years. They created a vast international network to share models, ignoring the commitments they had made to the couture houses. In the 1960s it was easy to procure mock-ups, patterns, and samples for a price in the hall of the Hotel Rosa, behind Le Dôme, the fashionable café on boulevard Montparnasse. The same "dealers" also met in a bar in rue Jean-Goujon, a veritable exchange market. In the same way, in the 1980s, photos of fashion shows were sold on the sly at la Coupole, boulevard de Montparnasse.

Another attack on the system: a habit that was at first frequent but which became routine is when department stores bought patterns or models for the manufacturers or vice-versa.

At another level, the fabric models that were exported using the temporary admission procedure[103] to avoid high customs duties were sometimes returned to France to be discounted there. Very often, however, they were sold to Canadian, Cuban, or South American couturiers that saved themselves a trip to Paris.

From England, the second most important market for haute couture clothes, models found their way to India or South Africa. These practices spread in the 1920s and became more widespread in 1930 with the increase in customs duties. After World War II they were practiced everywhere.

The perversion of the system was the direct consequence of the way it worked: how could one not be copied if the aim of a sale was precisely to be copied? Under these circumstances it was illusory to believe it was possible to control the usage of the models once they reached their destination. The best defense could have been the total prohibition of the sale of patterns, but then companies' losses would have been huge. In fact, at an international level, the legislation regarding fraud or counterfeiting was so lax that it was better to sell whatever one could, rather than being pillaged without having any means of retaliation. The risks the counterfeiters ran were so limited that, until 1952, all the defensive action taken by haute couture remained fruitless. The penalties were not even dissuasive. The highest fine at the time was 2,000 francs for each counterfeit model.[104]

The first serious attempt to fight against copying was taken by Madeleine Vionnet in 1921. With the help of Mr. Dangel, her manager, she created the Association pour la défense des arts plastiques et appliqués (Association for the Defense of Fine and Applied Arts). In 1922, she published a threatening advertisement:

> The Madeleine Vionnet models are registered and published in France. In all other countries Madeleine Vionnet has fulfilled all the formalities prescribed by the laws in force in each State and by international treaties. She will pursue any copy or counterfeit, even partial, made in disregard of her rights. Madeleine Vionnet Creations carry her signature and her fingerprint.[105]

Madeleine Vionnet was determined and she acted upon her words. *Vogue* gave an account of the Vionnet trial in the columns usually reserved for more frivolous subjects:

> The main witness, Jacques Worth [future president of the Chambre Syndicale], underlined the importance of the trial by describing the amount of effort it took to create a new and seductive piece of fashion. An artist declared that couturiers could take their place alongside painters and sculptors, and that, from an artistic point of view, a Madeleine Vionnet dress was certainly worth the Statue of Gambetta that loomed over the Tuileries. After spectacular debates and rich oratorical battles, the law came down on Madeleine Vionnet's side and she obtained the condemnation of the counterfeiters who were copying her models.

The law, however, did not yet situate the major arts and the applied arts at the same level. Because of this, the main business of the Association de protection des industries artistiques saisonnières (PAIS) (Association for the Protection of Seasonal Artistic Industries), set up in Vionnet's headquarters in the 1930s, was to register the models trademarked by couturiers in order to protect their copyright. PAIS soon united the elite couturiers, and photographs of their dresses were published with the mention "PAIS." Company directors created buyers' cards that were issued against the signature of something like a passport application. They also drew up a "black list" of buyers suspected of supplying fashion models to copiers. Nonetheless, "Parisian couture was in such a state of distress, due to the effect of the copying tactics employed by certain American manufacturers, that Mrs. Elsa Schiaparelli insisted that each manufacturer who visited her salon the following season had to buy at least three models."[106]

After World War II, when haute couture regained its role as international arbiter, piracy began again. The Milton affair was the talk of the town. Frédéric Milton sold sketchbooks that were basically a digest of Parisian fashion. He distributed them all over the world, five days after the Parisian collections had been shown.

To have the models sketched clandestinely and to send them to their destinations so rapidly, he used the Belino,[107] a very early precursor to the fax machine. This was a very lucrative business. His thousands of subscribers paid him $1,000 a year in 1956 (350,000 old francs, or 30,000 current francs).

Four couturiers—Lanvin, Dior, Patou, and Fath—who considered themselves particularly hurt by Milton's practices, had him summoned, and moreover, spectacularly, before the United States Supreme Court. They conjointly demanded 50 million francs (1955)—that is to say 4,200,000 current francs. It was only after Jacques Fath's and Christian Dior's deaths that, on 31 March 1962, the case was resolved with a negotiated settlement.

Naturally, all these unsavory events made the grand couturiers very cautious. Photography and sketching in the couture salons was strictly prohibited until the seventies. The risk was being arrested.

To defend themselves against these international gangs, couturiers gave considerable power to the Chambre Syndicale. Daniel Gorin, the president, commented in these terms: "Haute couture is a great wall, protected by one entrance, two towers, machine guns and a till."[108]

It was only on 12 March 1952 that a law was passed to deal with the repression of counterfeiting in the garment and finery industries. This was thanks to an initiative by the attorney Moro Giafferi. Legal registration of a trademark was no longer required. All a couture house had to prove, by any means, was the date of the model's creation. As for all criminal acts, the new law permitted nocturnal raids and could lead to very severe sentences.

After the PAIS was integrated into the Chambre syndicale de la couture's services, a legal position was created in 1943 for a specialist to defend Chambre members' rights over their labels and their models. It was in November 1967 that Françoise Benhamou accepted the title as technical advisor upon request by Daniel Gorin and Chambre attorney Suzanne Dreyfus. Barely two weeks after her nomination, Françoise Benhamou started her war against Belgium, the main kingdom of counterfeiting ahead of Italy. After registering a complaint, the injured parties (at least 18 of them) filed a civil action in a criminal proceeding with an international rogatory commission pronounced by a Parisian magistrate. Benhamou went with the local police to all the searches that were carried out. To her utter amazement she discovered that "small seamstresses" who worked from their charming homes had hundreds of "illegal" paper patterns hidden in their cellars and ran real counterfeiting industries. There were so many items seized and sealed (thousands of them) that it was very difficult to transport them back to Paris. As Belgian law was very similar to French law, young Françoise Benhamou was very successful.

This was not the case in Italy, where in 1970 Yves Saint Laurent's chief executive officer, Pierre Bergé, requested that Françoise Benhamou go to Milan to carry out what is called a foreign attachment in a palace where a fashion show was taking place. Bergé had previously sued and had a rogotory commission carried out. Benhamou had no difficulty in seizing 90 per cent of the models being shown by the counterfeiter. To her amazement, however, an Italian magistrate had the seals broken. The Italian legal approach to these questions was very different to the practices in use in France at the time.

During her first years at the Chambre Syndicale, Françoise Benhamou was constantly on warpath. There were a large number of cases and a number of

The "CHAMBRE SYNDICALE
DE LA COUTURE PARISIENNE"

reminds all concerned that it is forbidden to make sketches or to take photographs of the models presented, unless permission to do so has been formally given.

Unauthorized publicity given to original models makes the offender liable to prosecution.

LA CHAMBRE SYNDICALE
DE LA COUTURE PARISIENNE

rappelle que l'assistance aux collections ne donne aucun droit de reproduction des modèles présentés.

En conséquence, aucun croquis, aucune photographie, ne peuvent être pris ou relevés sans autorisation formelle que ce soit pendant la collection ou après dans les maisons de Couture ou au dehors.

NAME OF COUTURE HOUSE: ....

Name of Publication: (Newspaper, Magazine, Agency) ....

Address: ....

Represented by: ....

Is hereby authorized to publish photographs or sketches, as recorded below, under following conditions, -

Release of photographs: ....

Release of sketches : ....

Tear sheets or clippings of published documents are requested.

Photographs or sketches not published are required to be returned.

Documents are note transferable.

IT IS OBLIGATORY THAT ALL PUBLICATIONS STATE CLEARLY:

Name of Couturier
"Exclusive model — Reproduction forbidden."

NAME OR NUMBER OF DOCUMENTS RELEASED

PHOTOGRAPHS	SKETCHES

IMP. EBT - 21 117

PARIS (date) — Signature of Couture House: — Signature of Journalist accredited by publication:

"Photography prohibited" notices displayed in the couture houses, 1930–1970. Chambre syndicale de la couture parisienne archives.

Marie-Françoise Benhamou, head of Copyright at the Fédération de la couture (Couture Federation) until 2005, c. 1967.

The Belinograph. Rights Reserved.

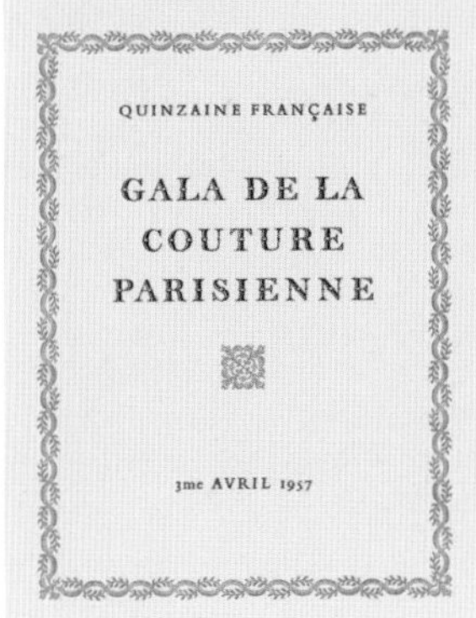

QUINZAINE FRANÇAISE
GALA DE LA
COUTURE
PARISIENNE
3me AVRIL 1957

Program for the Gala de la Couture française, 3 April 1957. Chambre syndicale de la couture parisienne archives.

fruitful raids were carried out. They grew more rare in the 1970s when couture was reproduced in ready-to-wear lines.

When couturiers entered the apparel manufacturers' and designers' calendar with their ready-to-wear lines, they readily adopted the habits the latter had established. The companies believed that, by finally selling their creations themselves, they were more effectively armed against those who could only be inspired by their work after they had benefited from it themselves.

The prohibition to photograph or sketch was lifted. Haute couture that showed its luxury collections three months after the ready-to-wear lines slowly abandoned its methods of secrecy. Even television crews were welcomed to fashion shows. This marked a brutal shift from one extreme to the other.

Piracy that had destabilized couture, while leaving it some profits, attacked the ready-to-wear sector, without having to pay in any way at all. Today, Françoise Benhamou travels to Malaysia, Korea, and South America to find illegal copiers. The problems are similar to those of the past, but the scale of the world has changed.

NOTES

1. Very fine lace produced at Malines.
2. Duchesne the elder, curator of the Mazarine library, quoted by Gaston Worth in *La Couture et la Confection des vêtements de femme,* Paris, Chaix, 1895.
3. "The day a lady is presented at court, in outer wear, the bottom of her dress and her petticoat must be black, but all the embellishments are made of rezeau lace. The whole forearm, apart from the top, towards the tip of the shoulder, where the black of the sleeve appears, is surrounded by two cuffs of white lace, one above the other, up to the elbow. A black bracelet made of pompoms was placed below the lower cuff. The whole upper body was trimmed with a collar of white lace, on which a narrow black stole decorated with pompoms was placed. The pompoms descended from the neck and followed the front of the dress up to the waist. The petticoat and the outer dress were also trimmed with pompoms made of rezeau or gold lace. The outfit that was worn the day after the presentation was the same as the first, except that everything black was replaced by coloured or gold fabric," *Dictionnaire des arts et metiers,* Jaubert, 1773; quoted in *Les Créateurs de la mode,* Editions du Figaro, Ch. Eggimann ed., 1910.
4. *Almanach Bettin,* 1850, p. 693: "Madame Roger & Cie, Women's dressmaker—The only house in Paris where all kinds of women's and children's ready made clothes could be found—26 rue Nationale Saint-Martin." Gaston Worth, *La Couture et la Confection des vêtements de femme, op.cit.*
5. Gaston Worth, *La Couture et la Confection des vêtements de femmes, op.cit.*
6. Otto Gustav Bobergh sold his shares to Worth in 1870. Over a century, the house passed from Charles Frédéric Worth, who died in 1895, to his sons, Gaston and Jean-Philippe, then his grandsons, Jean-Charles and Jacques, and finally to his great-grandsons, Roger then Maurice. Roger Worth was vice-president of the Chambre Syndicale at the Liberation. A Worth's funeral is traditionally an event that brings all the couturiers together.
7. In 1871, Worth considered that a middle level

Parisian could dress herself, quite respectably, for the whole year for 1,500 francs, while this amount was the cost of one of the cheapest day dresses in his establishment. The annual budget spent at Worth's was between 10,000 and 100,000 gold francs.

8. Diane de Marly, *The History of Haute Couture, 1850–1950,* London, Batsford, 1980.

9. The letterhead of Worth & Bobergh's bills read "Special Dressmaking House." The word "couturier" was coined in 1870. Françoise Tétard-Vittu, *Couture et Nouveautés confectionnées,* 1810–1870, Galliéra palace, Au paradis des dames, Paris-Musées, 1993.

10. Worth was already aware of the law of supply and demand. Katell le Bourhis, conference at the Musée de la mode, 21 October 1992.

11. Jacqueline Demornex, *Madeleine Vionnet,* Paris, Editions du Regard, 1991.

12. François Boucher, *Histoire du Costume en Occident,* Paris, Flammarion, 1965.

13. François Chapon, *Mystère et Splendeurs de Jacques Doucet,* Paris, Jean-Claude Lattès, 1984.

14. Yvonne Deslandres, *Paul Poiret,* Paris, Editions du Regard, 1986.

15. Paul Poiret, *Art et Phynance,* Paris, Lutétia, 1934.

16. Jack Palmer White, *Poiret le Magnifique: le Couturier de la Belle Epoque,* Paris, Payot, 1986.

17. Gaston Worth, Charles Frédéric Worth's oldest son, was president of the Chambre syndicale des couturiers et des confectionneurs between 1885 and 1888.

18. "The couture workers who did not belong to a core group, who were sacked by their usual workshop, had no difficulty finding work in an apparel manufacturing workshop, that would have less work when the made-to-measure workshop started working again." In "L'Industrie de la couture et de la confection," *Musée social,* Paris, 30 June 1897.

19. The men's and women's tailors union was created on 15 January 1911. Their main office was located at 8 rue Villedo; today their office is at 8 rue de Montyon.

20. Presidents of the Chambre Syndicale de la couture after it separated from manufacturing: MM. Réverdot (1910–1911), Doeuillet (1912), Aîné (1913–1916), Mrs. Jeanne Paquin (1917–1919), Mr. Clément (1920–1927), J. Worth (1927–1930), P. Gerber (1930–1933), J. Worth (1933–1935), P. Gerber (1935–1937), L. Lelong (1937–1945), J. Gaumont-Lanvin (1945–1950), R. Barbas (1950–1957), J. Heim (1958-1962), R. Ricci (1962–1963), J. Manusardi (1963–1964; vice president), D. Gorin (1964–1972), Mrs A. Grès (1972–1991), J. Mouclier (1991–1998), D. Grumbach (1998–).

21. It was transferred to 8 rue de Montesquieu, in the first arrondissement, and then at the beginning of the 1930s to 27 rue de la Sourdière, where they shared the space with a primary school.

22. Document, *La Couture industrie clef, Propriété artistique et protection des modèles,* Chambre Syndicale archives, 1957.

23. The statutes published in 1928, in the same article 4, specify that apart from wholly French houses, foreign houses could also join the union under the following conditions:
"A) They should not have a manager of German or Austrian nationality unless they had become naturalised French citizens at least twenty years before... B) They should not have received any kind of Austro-German support in terms of their capital or in terms of staff..." These requirements disappeared in the revised 1937 statutes.

24. *Le Jardin des Modes,* Elisabeth de Boucheron, March 1980.

25. In the thirties, the PAIS office was at 10 boulevard Malesherbes. Its president was A. Trouyet, who replaced M. Dangel at Madeleine Vionnet's; it was then presided over by Maggy Besançon de Wagner, founder of Maggy Rouff, before it was integrated into the Chambre syndicale de la couture services. Guillaume Garnier, *Paris-Couture années* 30 Paris, Musée de la mode et du costume, 1987. Chambre Syndicale PAIS documents. Interview with Madeleine Godeau.

26. Interview with Marie-Claude Vaillant-Couturier, Lucien Vogel's daughter.

27. Madeleine Godeau was administrative secretary from 1935 to 1950 and general secretary from 1950 to 1978.

28. On 25 January 1929, Maggy Besançon de Wagner presented her first collection under the name Maggy Rouff, at 136 avenue des Champs-Elysées, in the town house where her parents, Mr. and Mrs. de Wagner, had contributed to the Drecoll house's reputation.

29. Quoted by Dominique Veillon, *La Mode sous l'Occupation,* Paris, Payot, 1990.

30. *Ibid.* Also the archives of the Chambre syndicale de la couture parisienne.

31. Katell Le Bourhis, conference at the Musée de la mode, 21 October 1992.

32. Chambre syndicale de la couture parisienne archives.

33. Interview with Jean de Mouy, President of Jean Patou.

34. Dominique Veillon, *La Mode sous l'Occupation, op. cit.*

35. The meters of fabric allotted to some of the 107 houses, which were able to acquire it in February 1942, was about the same as luxury ready-to-wear companies use today.
36. The terms "model" and "copy of a model" were to be understood as follows: 1 dress (1 piece), 1 coat (1 piece), 1 cape (1 piece), 1 suit: skirt and jacket (1 piece) or skirt, jacket, and blouse (2 pieces), 1 suit: dress and coat (2 pieces) or dress and cape (2 pieces).
37. Inevitably, however, a large number of them were not included in the list and their survival was threatened. They used coupons, the procedure of exchanging two old garments for one new one, points, and the clothing card as well as piece work.
38. Jean Bichelonne, state secretary for industrial production under the Vichy regime.
39. Contrary to the legend, Pierre Cardin was not excluded from the Chambre Syndicale.
40. Members of the commission: Jacques Mouclier (president of the CSCP), Françoise Montenay (couture manager for Chanel), Claude Brouet (Hermès fashion manager), Philippe Vindry (general manager at Christian Dior), François Baufumé (general manager at Kenzo), Angelo Tarlazzi (fashion creator), Emanuel Ungaro (grand couturier), Donald Potard (general manager at Jean Paul Gaultier), Didier Grumbach (general manager at Thierry Mugler and president of the commission), Roland Stutzmann, and Jean-François Derain, representatives from the Industry Ministry.
41. Letter addressed to Dominique Strauss-Kahn, dated 8 October 1992.
42. *Rapport sur l'industrie française, sa situation, son avenir,* Ministry of Commerce 1919.
43. Germaine Deschamps *La Crise dans les industries du vêtement et de la mode à Paris pendant la période de 1930 à 1937,* Paris, Librairie technique et économique, 1938, p. 25.
44. Germaine Deschamps *La Crise dans les industries du vêtement et de la mode à Paris pendant la période de 1930 à 1937, op. cit.*
45. *Ibid.* pp. 64-65
46. *Ibid.* p. 65.
47. Philippe Simon, *La Haute couture, monographie d'une industrie de luxe,* Paris, 1931.
48. *Introduction de la haute couture, monographie d'une industrie de luxe, op. cit.*
49. Germain Deschamps, *La Crise dans les industries du vêtement et de la mode à Paris pendant la période de 1930 à 1937, op.cit.*
50. *Ibid.* p. 89.
51. The export of ready-made silk garments for women that represented 442,851 kilos in 1929 dropped to 23,761 kilos in 1936, and the value dropped from 642,082,000 francs in 1929 to 18,571,000 francs in 1936. The decrease was particularly important in Great Britain and the United States, which were France's best clients. In 1929, Great Britain bought 291,788 kilos of non-silk garments in France; in 1936, it only bought 24,500 kilos. In 1913, in the same category, Great Britain's purchases represented 426,000 kilos.
52. Midinette: "someone who was satisfied with a snack at lunchtime" at the end of the nineteenth century, a young female worker or salesgirl in the couture or fashion industry. Ref. Petit Robert.
53. Log: a bundle of cloth and materials required to make up a model.
54. Interview with Madeleine Godeau.
55. Dominique Veillon, *La Mode sous l'Occupation, op. cit.*
56. *Ibid.*
57. Paris: March 1945—London: September 1945—New York: May 1946.
58. C.S. Archives
59. A sample or toile was the creation of the fashion creator's sketch, made up in white cotton fabric.
60. Françoise de Langlade, who later became editor-in-chief of French *Vogue,* was Oscar de La Renta's wife.
61. The Duchess of Kent, the Duchess of Windsor, Princess Radziwill, Josette Day, Simone Simon, Maria Montez...
62. 40 *Années de création—Pierre Balmain,* Musée de la mode et du costume, Paris, exhibition held on 20 December 1985.
63. Brochure published by the Dior house in 1954.
64. About 16 million francs in 2001 (that is to say over 2 million Euros), less than half had been paid up in 1947 (*France Soir,* 16 February 1947).
65. A manuscript letter Christian Dior addressed to Jacques Rouët in 1946 shows how closely he personally monitored every detail and how dedicated he was to guiding his young and still inexperienced manager, while fully playing his own role as a manager.
66. Henri Fayol, general manager of Marcel Boussac's Comptoir de l'industrie cotonnière.
67. 20 rue des Capucines, at the same address as Nina Ricci.
68. Interstoff: International Textile Fair, created in Frankfurt in October 1958.
69. His wife had opened a couture house in an elegant town house in rue Bayard. Despite his active participation, the house had gone bankrupt. It was on Pierre Gerber's request that she joined the

Chamber Syndicale in 1936, a year after Madeleine Godeau, who went on to become general secretary.

70. About 43 to 21.5 million francs in 2001.

71. Excerpt from the *Cahiers du vêtement féminin*, October 1959.

72. *Le Figaro*, 9 April 1959.

73. *France Soir*, 20 April 1959.

74. Excerpt from *Cahiers du vêtement féminin*, June 1959.

75. American *Vogue*, September 1951, p. 188.

76. CIRIT, Comité interprofessionnel de renovations des structures industrielles et commerciales de l'industrie textile, (Inter-professional Committee for the Renovation of the Commercial and Industrial Structure of the Textile Industry) was created in 1966 to help French textiles compete efficiently against foreign competition. It was replaced by the DEFI in 1984.

77. President of the Chambre syndicale des tissus spéciaux à la couture after Jacques Lesur.

78. In 1970, the Chambre syndicale des tissus spéciaux à la couture that had its head-office at 22 rue des Capucines was renamed Chambre syndicale des maisons de tissus de creation. It was dissolved in 1985.

79. Liza Minelli's godmother. Liza Minelli played Diana Vreeland in Stanley Donen's *Funny Face.*

80. Gunther Oppenheim later financed Jacques Tiffeau who settled in New York, and signed a licensing contract with Christian Aujard.

81. Gérald Shaw, Ben Shaw's son who was Pierre Balmain's first licensee, was president of Oscar de La Renta, Pierre Balmain's new designer.

82. In 1982, Bill Blass and Halston were the most important licensors in the world, *Women's Wear Daily (WWD)*, 9 February 1982.

83. From 1946 to 1967, the number of couture members fell from 106 to 19.

84. The break-up was as follows: 33 apprentices, 1,735 women workers, 118 men and women seconds, 115 men and women cutters, 116 models, 919 various, 64 home workers—a total of 3,120. Fédération française de la couture, note of November 1974.

85. Interview with Jacques Rouët by Catherine Nay, *Paris-Match* 1982: "Since 1971, our direct turnover has been constantly decreasing. By direct, I mean mainly the turnover at avenue Montaigne. In 1971, we made 31 per cent through direct sales, 69 per cent through indirect sales (licenses). In 1981, we only made 9.6 per cent through direct sales. At this rate, in three or four years, we will not be in control of our economic operations. One day we may well find ourselves faced with a licensees union from whom I will have to take orders every day." In 1984, haute couture only represented 1 per cent of the turnover produced by the Christian Dior label.

86. Fédération française de la couture, note of November 1974.

87. "The 106 Parisian couture houses only had 8 359 clients to share amongst themselves. From 3 April to 19 November 1946, 3400 clients requested 'creation couture' buyers cards, indispensable for anyone who wanted to enter or place an order in one of the major houses." *Elle* 3 December 1946.

88. Thirty-two thousand francs in 1947 is equivalent to about 1,300 euros, an amount barely higher than a haute couture ready-to-wear dress today. Costs rose very rapidly; in 1954 the average price of a Dior model was 125,000 old francs, about 2,200 euros.

89. For the 1990–1991 autumn-winter season, Givenchy charged foreign buyers 15,000 francs (about 2,800 euros) for a paper pattern, and French buyers 9,000 francs (about 1,700 euros).

90. The Parisian haute couture/American manufacturing association that made local artisans less attractive were largely responsible in America, a little earlier than elsewhere, for getting rid of dressmakers who took up jobs in workshops attached to shops or industrial production units.

91. In 1966, Miss Scott from Marshall Field again bought 28 original haute couture models in Paris.

92. For the winter of 1954–1955, she chose 68 original haute couture models: Jacques Fath & Cie, 3 models; Hubert de Givenchy, 7; Chanel, 1; Jean Dessès, 2; Christian Dior, 10; Pierre Balmain, 3; Jacques Griffe, 7; Grès, 4; Nina Ricci, 5; Manguin, 4; Jacques Heim, 6; Mad Carpentier, 4; Balenciaga, 10; Jean Patou, 2.

93. Interview with Andrew Goodman.

94. The provincial couturiers had two types of buyers cards: the green card implied an overall financial commitment to the grands couturiers, and the pink card, which did not involve a global purchasing guarantee but involved specific commitments with regard to selected couturiers.

95. History of the Union's foundation, Employment Ministry.

96. Chambre syndicale de la couture (Couture Union) archives.

97. Givenchy evening dress reference: 15 meters of moire, 105 dollars; 9 meters of white faille, 27 dollars; 30 meters of white organdie, 50 dollars; 10 meters of white crêpe de Chine, 15 dollars; 30 meters of white tarlatan, 7 dollars and 50 cents; 1 zip, 40 cents; 1 meter of white flannel, 50 cents; 9 whalebones, 1 dollar and 35 cents; 10 buttons, 50 cents; 6 yards of lace, 3 dollars and 90 cents; silk

thread etc., 5 dollars. Total = 216.15 dollars. *Booton Herndon Bergdorf's on the Plaza,* New York, Editions Alfred. A. Knopf, 1956, p. 149.
98. Here a pattern designates a fabric creation.
99. In 1992, a few houses nonetheless maintained the tradition: Dormeuil, Abraham, (with Gustav Zumsteg as the President)...
100. Andrew Goodman died on 3 April 1993.
101. Quoted by Guillaume Garnier, *Paris-Couture années* 30, *op.cit.*
102. Jean Cartier, *Freddy—Souvenir d'un mannequin vedette. Dans la coulisse de la haute couture parisienne,* Paris, Flammarion, 1956.
103. A procedure that allowed the importer to avoid paying customs duties.
104. Document, *La Couture, industrie clef. Propriété artistique et protection des modèles,* 1957, Chambre syndicale de la couture parisienne (Parisian Couture Union) archives.
105. Jacqueline Demornex, *Madeleine Vionnet, op.cit.*
106. *WWD,* 1 December 1937.
107. A machine invented by Belin in 1907 to transfer drawings or photographs by wire; they were called Belinograms.
108. Quote cited by Jean Manusardi.

Fashion amidst the ruins, 1945. Photo Cecil Beaton. Courtesy Sotheby's London.

Bottom to top, left to right Christian Dior's team: Marguerite Carré, technical director; Christian Dior; Germaine Bricard, inspiration; Jacques Rouët; Raymonde Zehnacker, studio manager; to name a few.

CHAPTER II
THE PROFESSION'S NEW RESOURCES

The Christian Dior Business Model

Neither the March 1952 law that efficiently protected the grand couturiers, nor the Textile Aid that they benefitted from brought any real relief from the natural and cruel tendency towards a decline in business. Garment production alone was no longer a sufficient source of revenue; the couturiers had to find other means of survival. Christian Dior, a pragmatist, moved quickly when he inaugurated the small town house at 30 avenue Montaigne, on 16 December 1946. At the appointed time, five people entered the building with the master: Raymonde Zenhacker, the studio[1] manager with her unquestionable elegance and loyalty; Marguerite Carré, the premier d'atelier who had honed her skills with Patou; Pierre Cardin, head tailor; and Jacques Rouët, manager and future company president, accompanied by his secretary Olga. Jacques Rouët was the son of a court clerk and he had been an unenthusiastic law student until the war brutally interrupted his studies. Following the Liberation, he was given a job at the main civil service offices that were under the secretary general of housing. Rouët was working at the hotel Matignon with Roger Grégoire, state advisor, when the latter's brother-in-law, then financial director with the Boussac group, offered him a job. He was looking for a young manager for a small couture business. Christian Dior, who had mastered his profession perfectly, took an immediate liking to this young, elegant man who knew nothing about the fashion business. Dior skillfully shaped his new manager, who was inexperienced, to say the least, but with whom he shared a taste for great vintages and long simmered dishes.[2]

Three dynamic and creative women managed the studio and embodied the spirit of the "house": Madame Raymonde, Madame Marguerite, and Mizza Bricard, head of millinery, fashion advisor, and confidante and inspiration respectively. These women were a fantastic trinity dedicated to perfection.

Christian Dior, New Look suit, 1947.
Photo Willy Maywald
© Association Willy Maywald/Adagp, Paris, 2008.

The staircase of the Christian Dior boutique
on a first showing day in 1955.
In the front row, Marlene Dietrich.
Photo Willy Maywald
© Association Willy Maywald/Adagp, Paris, 2008.

Facing page:
Christian Dior, formal evening dress, 1950.
Photo Louise Dahl-Wolfe.

All the elements were in place for Christian Dior to achieve the brilliant start that his medium had foretold. The "New Look," an unprecedented sociological, aesthetic, and commercial phenomenon, spread across the world, guaranteeing for all time the reputation of a label whose fame grew incessantly. With success came money, but Christian Dior, a constant worrier, knew how fragile things could be. He realized that only a very wide distribution of the Dior name would ensure his company's long-term survival. Jacques Rouët followed his lead, and the epic fashion story began.

Their first act, at the end of 1947, was Dior's creation of a subsidiary for his perfumes. He entrusted the management to Serge Heftler Louiche, a friend from his joyful childhood days in Granville, Normandy. Heftler was the man for the job. He had worked with Coty and owned a perfume distribution company (SFD) that was headquartered on rue Jean-Mermoz. Marcel Boussac had no contractual rights over the perfumes; however, his general manager, Henri Fayol,[3] convinced him to invest in the capital of the perfume company. Christian Dior took a 25 per cent stake in the company while Serge Heftler took 30 per cent and Marcel Boussac invested in 45 per cent of the capital.

Dior's second collection met with as great a success as the first. The key now was to establish the growth strategy for the company and the business plan was defined by common agreement between Christian Dior, Jacques Rouët, and Henri Fayol. In October 1947, they decided to take advantage of Dior's international reputation to expand the scope of the label, while preserving its level of prestige.

When Christian Dior was founded, the house had 3 workshops and employed a staff of 85 people. By 1956, it employed 1,200 people spread over 22 workshops, housed in 5 buildings.

In 1948, Christian Dior himself made an important sales decision: he opened a luxury ready-to-wear business in New York called "Dior New York" at 730 Fifth Avenue, and it was a subsidiary 100 per cent-owned by Boussac. A grand couturier in Paris, Dior was a manufacturer in New York. The idea was very simple: it consisted of marketing the Dior label in the overcrowded American market by setting up a direct management system that provided stability and freed Dior from the episodic, capricious orders placed by professional buyers. Christian Dior, who spent a few weeks in New York every season accompanied by his triumvirate, designed the collection. The first American collection was shown in November

1948 and its big hit was "Bobby," a suit with a peplum jacket, named after Christian Dior's dog. This suit remained a best seller for eight seasons! This was an interesting lesson for a grand couturier, whose first requirement is to renew his collection every season. Nonetheless, the subsidiary, which saw an increase in the number of authorized retailers from 160 to 250 over a few months, still lost money. Henri Fayol entrusted Jacques Rouët with the delicate task of improving the situation. The trip and travel costs, the rental of a town house, and pocket money were excessive expenses that put a strain on the company. It was decided that, starting in 1952, the American collection would be designed and sewn in Paris. After Christian Dior's death in 1957, Guy Douvier became the designer for Dior New York until that company closed in 1975.

After New York, a subsidiary was established in London in 1952, in a Victorian Gothic townhouse. This building, with its historically protected ceilings, was located in Mayfair.

Mme. Achille from Casablanca ran the company via a licensing contract whereby she received a fee based on turnover. The subsidiary worked with 55 authorized retailers. After suffering losses, the business became a wholly owned subsidiary of Dior Paris in 1954. In 1957, Marc Bohan took over as head designer, followed in 1960 by Philippe Guibourgé and then Frédéric Castet.

Christian Dior London, Ltd. and Christian Dior New York Inc. disappeared with the globalization of fashion, which sounded the death knell for high quality fashions produced exclusively for specific local markets.

In the area of diversification, everything had yet to be invented. In 1950, Jacques Rouët dealt with the core of the Dior business by creating a wholesale division. He asked Hervé du Périer de Larsan to manage it. Stockings, manufactured by Grimonprez, a subsidiary of the Masurel group, were stored with gloves and ties at the Blois warehouse. When they were put on sale at the Parisian department store Galeries Lafayette, clients saw it as a tragedy, and it was even worse for the saleswomen at avenue Montaigne, guardians of a temple whose god, Dior, had incarnated the totally aristocratic idea of supreme elegance.

The very democratic presence of a grand couturier's label in a French department store offended people's sensibilities.

At Christian Dior headquarters on avenue Montaigne, what was called the "boutique" was only a modest counter under the staircase that Christian Bérard had hung with Toile de Jouy. In 1954 Christian Dior, who seemed distracted by these other activities at the time, encouraged Jacques Rouët to transform the "downstairs" boutique that he thought was too cramped into a smaller Bergdorf Goodman. By taking on the building in avenue Montaigne, Christian Dior feared he had been optimistic, but by now, he had already taken over the adjacent stables at 13 rue François 1er, and was soon to move into 28 avenue de Montaigne as well. Inevitably, as the space increased, the number of products multiplied. He expressed his astonishment in his book, *Dior by Dior*[4] (in French, *Christian Dior et Moi*):

> As for the boutique, previously a counter of only a few square metres, it had literally exploded. On an evening in June 1955, the shop at 30, avenue Montaigne shut and it opened the next morning for business at 15, rue François 1er. Marie-Hélène de Ganay,[5] supervised this huge move, akin to a moonlight flit.

There were jerseys, shawls, bags, belts, and all kinds of trinkets from the best creators—who agreed to a six-month exclusivity. They were all chosen by Marie-Hélène de Ganay, assisted by André Levasseur, and supervised by Christian Dior. These carefully chosen gifts filled a void and slowly grew in importance. Perfumed glove bags, pin cushions, velvet frames trimmed with passementerie, fireplace tools, tortoise shell Kleenex box covers, undergarment travel bags, blotters, etc., invaded a space that quickly became too small to hold shawls, simple and affordable summer skirts and dresses, like those found at Chloé, Gaby Aghion's brand new company. With Anne-Marie Muñoz's help, Yves Saint Laurent, a new assistant at Dior, looked after the presentation of the boutique decorated by Victor Grandpierre. On the other side of the alley, another space sold dresses designed by Christian Dior and made up in Madame Yvonne and Madame Jeanne's small workshops or produced by the couture workshops during the slow season. Marie-Hélène de Ganay sold them at unusual prices, to say the least, when one knows that for 30,000 francs (that is to say about 560 euros) a client could expect to have three fittings. Jacques Rouët's logical mind rapidly rationalized production, although he modestly admitted that ready-to-wear couture remained an unprofitable activity until the end of the fifties. Even though the idea of ready-to-wear already existed, its technical production did not allow it to fully profit from the advantages it presented.

The most controversial business measures had to do with the licensing contracts.[6] Schiaparelli had inaugurated the formula during her trip to New York in 1940 when she negotiated a contract for women's stockings with the Kayser company. Everybody remembers the "shocking" pink box that was a huge success.

In 1948, the New York company Prestige offered Christian Dior an annual fee of 10,000 dollars—a considerable sum at that time—to choose the stockings in Prestige's range that he would like to use in his fashion shows. Prestige would acquire the sales rights, and would put Dior's name next to theirs on the packaging. The day before the contract was to be renewed, a puzzled Christian Dior proposed a change in the terms. His idea was a simple one: the specialist hosiery company would pay him a percentage of the turnover. Negotiations with Kayser started immediately. The first Christian Dior stockings appeared on the market at the end of 1949[7] and Kayser replaced Prestige.

At the same time, Benjamin Theise, an American producer of silk twill—a fabric used in couture—suggested that Christian Dior's name appear on ties. It was completely unheard of that a masculine piece of wardrobe would carry the name of a feminine brand. However, the growing reputation Dior had enjoyed since the New Look made Theise optimistic about the success of this new venture. Everything moved with great speed—Christian Dior gave Jacques Rouët permission to negotiate with Theise who introduced him to his biggest tie client: Mr. Lou Mansfield, president of the Stern Merrit company. The collaboration was a huge success. B. Altman, a Fifth Avenue department store, reserved an exclusive space of four separate counters for the Dior ties. Jacques Rouët, who was passing through New York, was given a scathing, slightly malicious answer when he offered to show them to Christian Dior: "Dear Jacques, if I actually see our ties, I fear I will detest them and have to ask you to terminate our contract." In fact, the licensee also designed the ties that were distributed through his network. Jacques Rouët remembers that he once expressed his doubts about a grey spotted tie that he thought was really ordinary, to say the least. "Please don't exclude it," begged the licensee, "it's a model President Eisenhower orders regularly."

These two historical contracts were the prelude to hundreds of others. Dior's colleagues cautiously watched the label's expansion, not really knowing yet what to think, until the day Jacques Rouët signed a licensing contract for costume jewelry with a German house from Pforzheim. This sparked off actual hostility. "You," said Jean Gaumont-Lanvin[8] at a Chambre meeting, "are the wasp who has come to disturb the hard working hive." The press took up the debate. In 1952, Lucien

François, a well-known journalist, went to war against couturiers that vulgarized their labels.[9] Fifty-six years later, his analysis is still worth reading.

> How is it that these grand couturiers do not realise that by speculating, the way they do, on the prestige of their names, they are condemning a secular art, mocking a tradition...? They bow to the prince's habits, they adapt to the lavish doctrines put forward by upstarts who want easy access to everything; they work for mass production, limiting themselves to whatever can be vulgarised and thus collaborate with the systematic suffocation of the concept of elegance in Paris that they are the living heirs to... The haute couture clients will soon abandon the houses whose "devalued names are worth nothing abroad."

The government ministerial cabinets did not remain indifferent to a growing phenomenon. The German Embassy's commercial advisor wrote a report for the Ministry of Industry. Jacques Rouët was summoned to rue de la Boétie and was informed of the official position. As he had come from the civil service, he realized the gravity of the situation but he had not imagined the worst. He was, however, being asked to forego the jewelry contract as the Dior name could in no way be used as a weapon in the hands of German industry. He was terribly upset and requested a meeting with the Finance Ministry. The guaranteed *minima* he received were equivalent to twice the amount that French jewelry exports to Germany produced. The two cabinet attachés he called upon, Valéry Giscard d'Estaing and Michel Poniatowski, assured him of their ministries' support. During his unwavering ascension, Jacques Rouët hired a license manager in 1952 whose job was to develop the worldwide network of licensing contracts for placing the Christian Dior label on clothing and men's and women's accessories. This independent licensing service under the initial management of Christian Legrez was a total novelty in the fashion industry.

As soon as he joined Dior, under general manager Jacques Chastel's supervision, Christian Legrez set about drawing up a standard contract that could serve as a basis for negotiations with all the companies that the house of Dior was in discussions with. He then carried out a market analysis in order to define a rigorous business strategy that would allow him to maintain a very tight control, which had been noticeably absent, over the licensees. Until Legrez' arrival, licensees—not Dior—had the sole responsibility for creation and distribution.

Because the couturier had the possibility to expand the scope of his label and also design his or her models, it became a priority to concentrate on these two areas in the new licensing strategy. The first urgent measure required that the brand's trademark had to be registered all over the world. This would insure that the licensees who bought the concession would be perfectly protected against counterfeiters. This very complex operation required legal assistance from specialized law firms in New York, London, and Paris. Today, the list of trademarks registered by the licensor is merely a routine annex to every license contract.

Another key to a successful licensing strategy is that image of the house had to be preserved. In order to do this, a design studio for licensed products was set up, managed by Marc Bohan and Philippe Guibourgé, in turn.

Little by little, "The Great House" became a complex design company. In addition to the 250 models designed for the Dior collection, there were pieces designed specifically for satellite stores: 50 for Paris, about 90 for London, and 110 for New York. In addition, Dior employed a number of designers in different fields who developed a large number of models or objects that often went no further than the prototype phase. More and more, the couture house proposed the ideas for designs, leaving little room for proposals made by the licensees. In order to better control the domains that were outside of Dior's expertise, such as distribution, production, or promotion, Dior imposed supervisory procedures to limit any kind of abuse. For example, a licensee could no longer place his label next to Dior's, a clause that is currently applied in today's licensing deals. The licensee's name could only appear on the transaction documents. This precautionary measure was established to avoid a dilution of the brand's image that a juxtaposition of two labels inevitably led to. This measure was only put into practice in the women's ready-to-wear sector in the sixties, in order to avoid any kind of possible confusion with haute couture and to better respect the requirements the French government imposed for the aid plan. Distribution for the licensed products was subjected to a common study whereby Dior retained the right to refuse a dealer who had the potential to harm Dior's prestige. Lastly, guaranteed annual *minima* revenues were established, accompanied by advances on quarterly royalties. With these new terms in place, the licensing contract thus took on its definitive shape.

Perfect management of the brand required that the contract include monitoring procedures. These clauses dealt essentially with the licensed product: its quality and conformity, service, distribution, advertising and promotion, verification if necessary of the licensee's accounting records with regard to payment of fees.

When Christian Legrez left Dior for Chanel in 1963, his assistant, Geoffroy de Seynes, who organized the licensing sector brilliantly for 20 years, replaced him until de Seynes moved to Nina Ricci. Dior developed licensing contracts in 70 countries.[10]

In 1990, the number of licenses fell from 184 to 150, but they still represented 95 per cent of the company turnover. They generated 350 million francs of revenue, 45 per cent of which came from Japan. Licensing was the last stage of a rocket that was launched in 1947 (perfumes, ready-to-wear, boutique, licenses) and the licensed products department remained the most profitable division at Dior.

In 1957, the year that Christian Dior died, it was the licenses that ensured the house's "survival" at a time when Marcel Boussac was considering closing down the company. The experience of the Callot[11] sisters—a fashion house created in 1895 at 24 rue Taitbout—had confirmed Boussac's belief that succession in this profession was dangerous, even impossible. If the new designer had a strong personality, he was likely to upset the existing clients; if he continued in the same style, he'd be criticized for a lack of originality. Christian Dior himself had judiciously advised Marcel Boussac on how difficult it was to assume the design of another label when Dior refused to take on the artistic direction at Gaston.

Times, however, had changed. After Dior's funeral, when the licensees from all over the world had gathered in the salons of the avenue Montaigne, their spokesman Grimaldi besieged Jacques Rouët to persuade Marcel Boussac to not close the house. Boussac wanted 10 days to think it over. He wrote the press release himself with, in the order they were cited, Madame Raymonde, Madame Marguerite, Mizza Bricard, and lastly the heir to the Dior design throne, Yves Mathieu Saint-Laurent. Jacques Rouët did not have the time to address the gathering that had literally invaded the building before the flash bulbs were going off in Yves Saint Laurent's direction. Yves Saint Laurent had reached design sainthood even before he had presented his first collection. His first show in 1958 was a triumph, proving that even after his death, Christian Dior had been right. One genius succeeds another; he supplanted the three temple guardians with a mixture of audacity and timidity. The company continued to develop under Marc Bohan, despite the continuous decline of its couture activity.

Christian Dior slowly became institutionalized to the satisfaction of its omnipresent president, Jacques Rouët.

The Purists

Cristobal Balenciaga. Although certain sales methods are subject to systematic controversy, licensing was one of those that met with serious resistance. Cristobal Balenciaga, who was Dior's sole direct competitor,[12] fought determinedly against them. He was born in 1895 in Guetaria, a small fishing village on the Spanish Basque coast. By the time he opened his house in Paris in 1937,[13] Cristobal Balenciaga had already opened two subsidiaries in Spain, one in Madrid (1933), calle Caballero de Gracia, and the other in Barcelona (1935), calle Santa Teresa. After the Great Depression, there was a surplus of creators, ready to fulfill the desires of a society that had watched the world change and which was avid for luxury and beauty. Balenciaga waited for the war to end to reveal the full extent of his exceptional talent. It was as if these years of drama had nourished his style, one that was marked by Iberian austerity. He abolished all artifice and in the 1950s, Balenciaga turned towards a rigorous geometry, an architecture made up of abstract volumes that he attained through a subtle process of elimination. There was no way he could have worked on his "wearable monuments" without a perfect knowledge of fabric. Balenciaga appreciated fabric with as much professionalism as the manufacturers themselves, and he loved them for their weight, texture, and stiffness that he made use of. He went straight to the essential, like a sculptor working on a block of marble.

Balenciaga's fashion mirrored his character: it was concentrated and generous. His designs symbolized the skill of the uncompromising artisan better than anyone else's designs. While he clearly influenced his era and the couturiers of his time, he had an even greater impact on his successors. Balenciaga was uncompromising, even with his foreign buyers to whom he refused to sell his muslins.[14] In this way, he was diametrically opposed to Christian Dior who made his designs very accessible by selling his paper patterns very widely.

Balenciaga only allowed reproductions of his models to be published one month after all the other designers. This practice did not stop magazines from dedicating entire pages to him. Editors had to make a special trip to Paris to see his collections. Buyers were hence unlikely to be influenced by the press he received, a practice that his clients favored, whether they were shops or manufacturers.

Dior's attitude to the press was the exact opposite. Again, Dior fueled the fires of indignation that blew through the Chambre Syndicale when he set a truly original

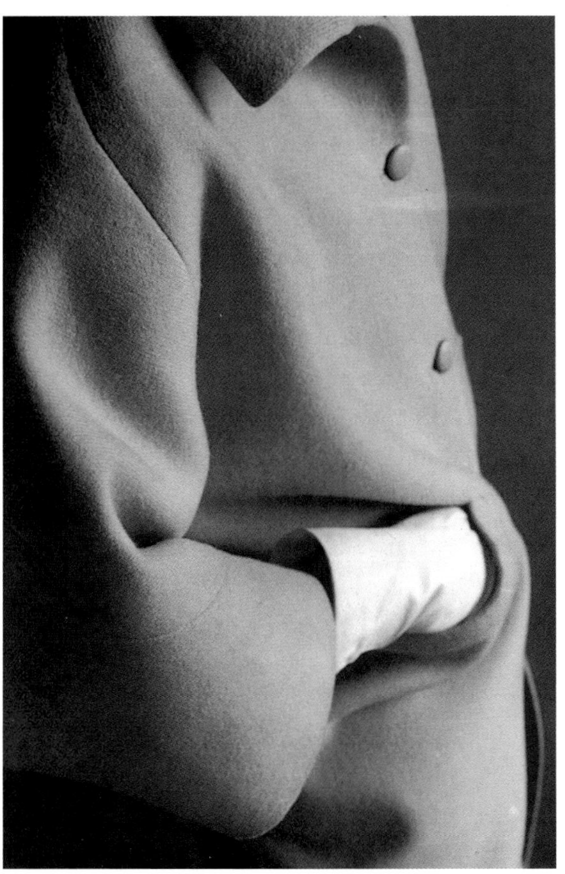

Balenciaga, detail of an overcoat sleeve, 1964.
Courtesy *Vogue New York*, photo Bert Stern.
Balenciaga, 1927. Photo Lipnitzki/ Agence Roger Viollet.

Facing page:
Balenciaga, *Four horn* dress in black gazar, 1967.
Balenciaga archives, Paris.

precedent: transmitting the photographs of a model, via satellite, the day before the show. The profession could not exclude him; he was not a member of the Chambre Syndicale. This was an aberration because, at the same time, Jacques Rouët was on the management committee of the Chambre Syndicale; he paid his dues and often led his colleagues to follow his policies.

Balenciaga firmly resisted the financial attraction of licenses. In the same vein, he turned away industrialists who suggested creating a ready-to-wear line with five words that resounded in the air: "I will not prostitute myself."[15]

It would seem that Balenciaga's only satisfaction came from dressing women to perfection, conferring elegance, goddess-like status, and seduction upon them. "His 1950 winter collection led to Carmel Snow giving him the title of 'the nec plus ultra of fashion.'" Balenciaga created fashion at the same time as Dior, but Dior was the first to bow to the genius of this designer whom he called the "Master of us all."[16] Their relationship was rather like that between two legendary cats, each of them curled up on the most comfortable living room cushions, very close yet very distant, as if separated by an insurmountable barrier that was in fact only a sign of respect and of the affection their solitary natures allowed them to feel for each other. In July 1949, eight days before the collections were to be presented, the CGT and CFTC unions went on strike. Because Dior was not a member of the Chambre Syndicale, he was not affected by collective salary agreements. Dior took the opportunity to show his affection for Balenciaga. He went to see his famous colleague at 10 avenue George V, accompanied by Jacques Rouët, and offered him the use of the Dior workshops. Balenciaga was touched, but chose to decline the offer. Another anecdote recounted by Lucien François is a good illustration of their closeness. An important velvet manufacturer in New York asked Dior and Balenciaga to create a unique model with his latest "velvet." Without any preconceived notions, Balenciaga started work. After three days of fruitless efforts, he picked up his telephone:

"Allo! Christian? This is Cristobal. Have you managed to do anything with this horrible 'fabbrric?'"

"Not yet!"

"Perfect, I get it. Let's 'refouse.'" [17]

Cristobal's fear of crowds kept him away from Christian Dior's funeral, but the most sumptuous garland bore his name.

Hubert de Givenchy. While Givenchy was with Schiaparelli, Jacques Rouët approached him several times in an attempt to "lure him away." Elsa Schiaparelli had a volcanic temper, and in areas that concerned her, she applied the precepts of individualism to the letter, but did not seem very respectful of this quality in others. She had got hold of Hubert de Givenchy and had no intention of letting go of him, even more so because the young man's perfect distinction had made him a regular guest at rue de Berri, where Elsa gave the most amusing baroque dinners in all of Paris. Her latest fancy, her secretary as she called him, nonetheless managed to find a way to leave her, as his greatest desire was to start his own house.

The opportunity came thanks to a close friend of Hubert de Givenchy's, Hélène Bouilloux-Laffond. She was the niece of Pierre Laguionie, the owner of the Printemps' department store. She offered to use her name to raise the necessary capital to start the company. The Americans they had counted on backed down and her uncle desisted. She turned to her brother-in-law, Louis Fontaine, owner of Prisunic stores, and they financed the house together.

Elsa was inconsolable; she threatened, "You will go bankrupt." The always-elegant Givenchy replied: "You will bring me luck, Madame."

With Philippe Venet as his first tailor, Gérard Pipart as assistant, and eight workers, Givenchy took two rooms in the splendid town house owned by Les Chocolats Meunier, at 8 rue Alfred-de-Vigny and opened his business in 1952. Here, Hubert de Givenchy presented a new version of his "separates"[18] that had been the success of the Schiaparelli boutique. His models were naturally suited to boutique sales. They consisted of two or three pieces, more suitable for traveling than Dior's imposing dresses that could only be packed in several cabin trunks. Worn casually by Suzy Parker and Sophie Litvak, the most beautiful models of the time, the collection was a triumph, to the great joy of Bettina[19] who had been named the press attaché for the event. The crowd was so dense that to start they had had to improvise in the main salon, with a screen and a hastily improvised cabin, before taking over several other rooms in the hotel particulier. Three years later, Givenchy opened a hugely successful boutique on the ground floor.

Jean Prouvost was on the lookout for new talent and he wanted to deal directly with the creator. In 1954, he invited Hubert de Givenchy to dinner at rue de Rivoli and he offered him a ready-to-wear contract.

To Hubert de Givenchy's astonishment, Louis Fontaine was offended and refused the idea. Suddenly Hubert de Givenchy realized how insecure his situation was. He was not a partner in his business, could not claim any portion of royalties, and he was paid less than when he had worked with Schiaparelli. This discovery made him very anxious and led him to accept the invitation to the April in Paris Ball in New York.[20] At the dinner preceding the ball, held by *Vogue's* Ivan Patcevitch, Balenciaga was taciturn and not really able to enjoy himself. One of his clients, Patricia Lopez-Willshaw, introduced him to Givenchy. Neither of them spoke English and they took an immediate liking to each other. They planned to lunch together the next day at L'Aiglon, the restaurant in vogue at the time on East 55th Street. Cristobal Balenciaga warmly complimented Givenchy on his designs—he loved their joyful freshness. Hubert de Givenchy was moved and he remembered his unfortunate attempts to show Balenciaga his sketches when he had first arrived in Paris. Mademoiselle Renée had effectively blocked all access to him. The lunch continued, interspersed with bursts of laughter and shared confidences; Balenciaga was happy. On his return to Paris, things were not going well for Hubert de Givenchy. He wanted to call Balenciaga several times, but he could not summon the courage to do so. Maybe he was worried about disturbing him? Finally Marie-Louise Bousquet, a friend of Balenciaga's, convinced Hubert de Givenchy to visit him at his chateau de La Reynerie.

Balenciaga listened attentively to his friend with the clear intention of helping him out: "There is only one thing you can do, have your company valued, buy it, and reimburse your loans with the royalties you will earn from Prouvost." Reassured, Hubert de Givenchy returned to Paris and invited Christian Dior to lunch at the Plaza Athenée. At first amazed that in 1954 anyone would want to "take on a couture house," Dior gave in to Givenchy's wishes and recommended him to his personal lawyer. The valuation almost stunned the young man, but Balenciaga, whom he told, tried to reassure him: "It doesn't matter. I will lend you the money, don't thank me, I trust you."

As soon as he had completed the separation from his business partners, Hubert de Givenchy signed his first ready-to-wear contract with Prouvost.

Everything went the way Balenciaga had expected and the ready-to-wear royalties financed Hubert de Givenchy's acquisition of his own company. Balenciaga soon

Audrey Hepburn, a faithful Givenchy client, in the film *Ariane*, 1957. © RMN, photo Raymond Voinquel.

Hubert de Givenchy, 1978. Photo Alice Springs.

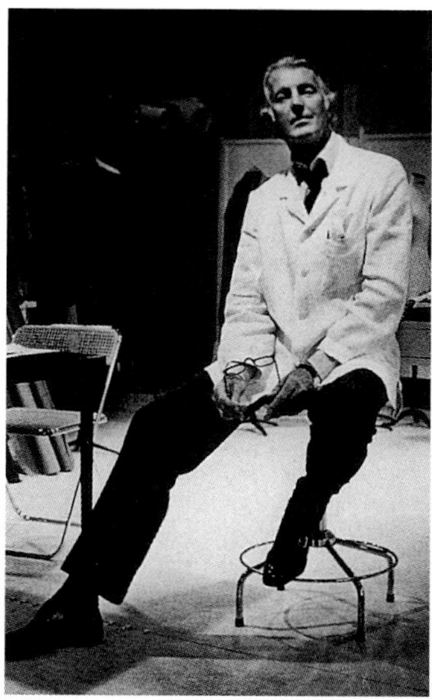

continued in his role as Givenchy's mentor by organizing a visit to the space of tailor Raphaël Lopez, located at 3 avenue George V, just opposite him. Balenciaga was clear: the price was not to be a handicap. On Balenciaga's advice, Givenchy raised the building two floors, and presented a collection of perfumes presided over by his half brother, Jean-Claude de Givenchy. Balenciaga also gave him sound advice about the perfumes, inciting him not to follow Chanel's example: "Royalties of 5 per cent, will not ensure your independence; make sure you own them." To complete his role as benefactor, he gave Hubert de Givenchy the usage of an empty space in his factory at Courbevoie, but refused to become a shareholder in the company. In 1957, Hubert de Givenchy re-enacted Jean Patou's coup of 1925 and simultaneously launched two perfumes, *De* and *L'Interdit.* The American actress Audrey Hepburn was the "face" of *L'Interdit.* Long before Catherine Deneuve, Carole Bouquet, Estelle Halliday, or Inès de La Fressange, Audrey Hepburn was the first star whose image was used to market a perfume.

Balenciaga's gift to Hubert de Givenchy, autonomy, was invaluable. From then on, the student applied his master's teachings, restricting press access to his salons, a prohibition he explained to a journalist from *L'Express:* "Often seventy-five copies of a single coat would be sold just because it was cited in an article... This way, professionals make more balanced choices and I prefer that..."[21]

His completely unaffected friendly relations with his clients[22] guaranteed him a loyalty that allowed him to balance his accounts solely on the basis of his own production.

When Balenciaga closed his couture house in 1968, the press headlines read: "Balenciaga is retiring and fashion will never be the same again." His pride was invincible and he refused to sell his name, thus his designs would cease to exist after closing his company. This attitude was aristocratic to say the least, cost him dearly, and he knew it. He could in fact have saved jobs and sold his assets for an excellent price. "May my experience be a lesson to you," he told Hubert de Givenchy. "When the time comes, if a group wants to buy your business, don't give it away, sell it and sell it well." Hubert de Givenchy followed this advice when Henry Racamier from LVMH made him an offer for his perfumes, before going on to acquire his couture house.

Once the master had gone—should one see a cause and effect relationship? Hubert de Givenchy gave in to following Jacques Rouët's licensing policy at Dior and after having signed a ready-to-wear license contract with C. Mendès in 1968, he slowly gave in to the seduction of licensing.

André Courrèges. Courrèges was not trained as a couturier: after studying at the Ponts et Chaussées, a French university for civil engineering where he had enthusiastically discovered architecture, he joined the Ecole supérieure des industries du vêtement (ESIV) upon his arrival in Paris. When he arrived in the French capital in 1946, André Courrèges had no idea of Balenciaga's existence. It was while looking through a magazine at Jeanne Lafaurie's where he worked as an illustrator, that he discovered his sketches. "He is a genius," confirmed his employer, "his clothes are the most expensive and the most beautiful in the world." Fascinated, Courrèges could only think of one thing: meeting the master. After a first interview, Balenciaga, intrigued, finally showed some interest in him. Six months later, Courrèges showed him his work and he was hired.

Courrèges was highly gifted. In three years he became part of the Balenciaga studio, and four years later he wondered what was left for him to learn. He requested a meeting with the boss, who received him at his home on avenue Marceau. "I am safe under a huge oak tree," he said, "but the sun doesn't shine through the leaves. I feel like an acorn that has fallen at the foot of the tree. You must allow me to leave." It was a delicate situation. Courrèges was lucky enough to belong to Balenciaga's inner circle and in this capacity, he and Ramón Esparza joined in expeditions to the mountains or visits to antique shops. He really could not leave without the master's approval, and this was a long time coming. He had been with Balenciaga for 10 years.

He began to protest, by working very slowly and not taking part in the studio meetings, until Balenciaga asked to see him.

"Let's put an end to it! You can leave. What do you need?"

"Nothing."

"How are you going to live? Where are you going to open your business?"

As a friend he asked to visit the second floor space that Courrèges coveted, but which did not have an elevator, on the avenue Kléber.

"You cannot receive the clients I'm going to send you in a house without an elevator."

"I don't want you to send me any clients; I intend to conquer them myself!"

These two men were very fond of each other, and both had very tough personalities.

Shortly after he opened his house, the Begum came to see Courrèges.

"Forgive me Madame, but I warned Mr. Balenciaga I would not dress any of his clients."

"It doesn't matter!" replied the Begum. "Your agreements with Balenciaga are none of my business."

She was so insistent that Courrèges gave in.

"Very well, but I will not dress you without Mademoiselle Renée's approval."

The Begum disappeared and reappeared a few moments later with a card signed by Mademoiselle Renée: "Permission to dress."

Courrèges' training at ESIV and his time with Balenciaga gave him a certain confidence in his strategy, particularly on two points. Industry could be as qualitatively efficient as craftsmanship, and controlling manufacturing and distribution could ensure a brand's longevity. This kind of control, of course, excluded licensing.

While he was a student, André Courrèges had attended a conference by René Henry in 1946 on the performance of Swedish manufacturing that transformed his idea of clothing. From this day on, he had in fact been convinced that a well-designed and well-made garment could be even more attractive than if it had to be adapted, after several fittings, to an imperfect body. He continually proved this point.

> I felt that I needed to use new technical and aesthetic rules, to invent a modern garment, a garment that one could get into, like getting into a box. A rich American who was passing through Avenue Kléber one day, ordered a dress I had created on a 20-year old model.
> "It needs to be altered," she said, my breasts are ten centimetres lower.
> "No," I said, "from today onwards, you will have the chest of a twenty year old, as I really don't want to create a dress to fit your sixty-year-old breasts into it."
> It was time for the first fitting.
> "You might be right," she said.
> She looked at herself in the mirror
> "Yes, it's wonderful, you're quite right."

Courrèges remained true to his idea. In 1965, he said to his colleague Philippe de Castro, Jean-Claude Weill's brother-in-law and technical manager of the Weill

Courrèges, collection 1965. © Courrèges/photo Willy Rizzo.

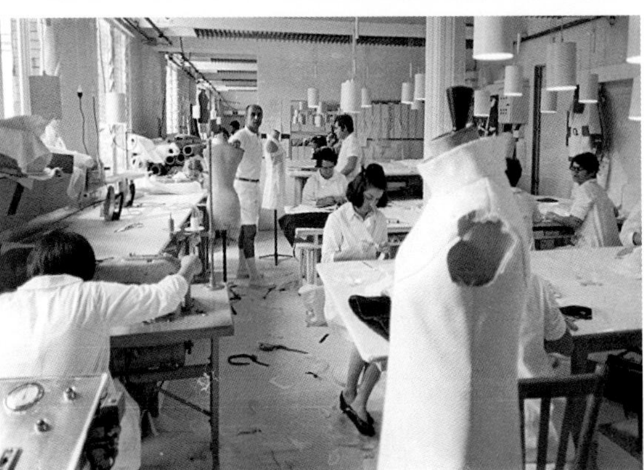

Courrèges and his wife
Coqueline,
Romy Schneider fitting, c. 1969.
Photo Pierre Boulat,
courtesy Agence Cosmos.

The Courrèges factory in Pau
inaugurated in 1972
that employs 600 workers
and the workshop. ©
Courrèges/Rights Reserved.

apparel manufacturing company: "Show me that you can create a dress in your factories that would need forty-five hours of work in haute couture."

He brought him "a charming little double faced frock coat, that was very successful," and he asked him how long it would take to "bring it out." After a careful inspection: "It's difficult to say precisely, but I think I could do it in seven hours."

"My obstinacy had finally paid off! In fact, it only took him five short hours to create a garment that was of higher quality than if it had been made by haute couture."[23]

The following year, Sammy and Maurice Weinberg, well-known industrial manufacturers, invited Courrèges to visit their factory in Bourges. Although he did not manage to poach their technical manager Jean-Claude Zarad, he returned from his expedition convinced he would become an industrialist. At ESIV he had already learnt that overstitching, piping, buttonholes, etc., were better done by a machine than by hand. In addition, every day his experience proved that a certain clientele, the kind he had met at Balenciaga's, was a disappearing social group. Where were the women who used to spend several weeks in the suites of prestigious hotels and whose days were punctuated by fittings? He firmly turned away the American licensees like Puritan Fashion and, to set his mind at rest, visited C. Mendès, where he admired Madame Grès kimono coats. His mind was made up; he wanted to produce everything himself, and distribute everything he designed and branded himself: "My motivation is not earning money. I could have a huge turnover by taking the easy way out, but it would be at the cost of a short term deterioration of my label and a loss of control over my products."[24]

In 1965, everything was ready. Courrèges did not show his couture collection in January as the professional calendar invited him to. In October 1965, for the Spring 1966 season, he inaugurated three collections in one: "Prototype" (haute couture), "Couture future" (ready-to-wear), and "Hyperbole" (inexpensive fashions and knitwear). He was the first to dare to present models sewn by different techniques on the same stage, especially since the trade had isolated the techniques into separate entities.

In order for Courrèges to turn his ideas into a reality, he needed vast financial means and very strong organizational support. The owner of L'Oréal, Liliane Bettencourt, whom he dressed, introduced him to L'Oréal president François Dalle.

The two men took an instant liking to each other; they shared an immense pleasure in power. In 1965, L'Oréal and Courrèges created a common perfume and couture company, shared equally between L'Oréal on the one hand, and André and Coqueline Courrèges[25] on the other. Until the first oil crisis, the Courrèges house grew following a cutting edge strategy, but it grew chaotically.

Courrèges was obsessive and he did not notice that fashion was shifting. He did not know how to delegate power and he did not manage to trust François Dalle, who was unrivaled in the world of perfume. He behaved in the same manner as Pierre Cardin, but with the considerable difference that his colleague had never had the ambition of creating an industrial group, while Courrèges was already the owner of a ready-to-wear factory in Pau that he had started in 1972. In 1976, François Baufumé, export manager, was the first to abandon the ship that had been shaken by successive economic crises. In 1978, the house's policy changed completely.

The first entity to have brought perfumes, couture, ready-to-wear, and accessories under the same brand, and which relied on an exclusive distribution network, was beginning to show signs of weakness. Courrèges was obliged to abandon his concept of total autonomy and offered his manufacturers licensing contracts. The specialist suppliers of the Courrèges boutiques—manufacturers of umbrellas, glasses, and leather goods—obtained the right to sell the products they manufactured through their own sales networks.

L'Oréal took control over the perfumes before Itokin, the fourteenth Japanese licensee acquired 65 per cent of the capital in 1982, including all of L'Oréal's shares. Courrèges retained a veto minority.[26]

Thus the most interesting of commercial efforts of this period came to an end. In 1981, Chanel brought back this formula, placing perfumes, haute couture, ready-to-wear, accessories, and boutiques under the same artistic, sales, and financial management teams.

In 1992, Courrèges defined his profession in the following words:

> The real transformation that has occurred is in communication. The label is mainly an indicator. Courrèges Architecture—Courrèges linen, Courrèges cars… Currently our niche is Courrèges, designer of a modern lifestyle in harmony with nature. If we can evoke a coherent thought expressed by André Courrèges about a way of life, we have developed a niche in terms of life style.

Solidly seconded by Christian Delahaigue, Courrèges had no fear of adventuring into hitherto unexplored areas, like Bordeaux wine, champagne, Armagnac, chocolates... In 1991, his "gourmet" license in Japan alone accounted for seven million francs in sales. His quest for expansion did not stop here: Sorefi (50 per cent Caisse des Dépots, 50 per cent Caisse d'Epargne) proposed "Perspectives Courrèges," that aimed to sell 250 to 400 apartments a year. In order to do this, the Courrèges research office brought together industrialists that specialized in new technology research and who worked under the impetus of integrated architects. Courrèges loved hair styling too and his ambition was to open 50 salons all over France and its territories. Since Courrèges has fallen ill, his wife Coqueline Courrèges carefully controls all the brand's components.

By this time, the field of fashion could be divided into two clans: those for or against licenses; Dior's policy or Balenciaga's attitude. Before they gave in to the temptation of licenses, Hubert de Givenchy and André Courrèges chose the latter path, while Jacques Fath and Pierre Cardin opted for the former.

The Moderns

Jacques Fath. Born at Maisons-Lafitte in 1912, Jacques Fath, whom his parents nicknamed Pommadin because he spent so much time posing in front of mirrors, was already, at the age of 10, consumed by one obsession—to become a broker, or more specifically, to make dresses. He systematically pillaged his mother's and his sister's wardrobes. What mother would not have been worried, watching her son playing dress up with dolls, but using her own clothes?

She was thus fairly relieved when he began work as a messenger boy with broker Paillard-Lacroix. As soon as he had finished his military service, he went to work at the Stock Exchange where, at the age of 21, he distinguished himself by being the youngest to have the best order book at palais Brongniart. Although he carried out these jobs seriously and enthusiastically, he still loved fashion designing and at every opportunity he drew, visited costume museums, or collected books and magazines on fashion. Finally, in December 1936, he opened his house rue de La Boétie, hired

Jacques Fath
evening dress,
1947, drawing by
Bernard Blossac.

five workers, two models, and the irreplaceable Antoinette, who was also a wrapper and cabin manager when required. He presented his first collection in February 1937. His real beginnings, however, were sealed by his marriage, in 1938, to one of the most beautiful models of the time, Geneviève Boucher de La Bruyère, who had been Miss Chanel's secretary. Balls, picnics, collections that were constantly renewed thanks to his wonderful imagination; the Faths rapidly became Paris' most admired couple. In 1947, he was famous. Wherever he went, the most elegant woman in the world accompanied him. They were absolutely irresistible in their kindness and generosity. They conquered all the European capitals and then it was New York's turn, where Jacques Fath became the "fabulous Monsieur Fath."[27]

Lili Pons, Sonje Henley, Paulette Godard, Gene Tierney, Rita Hayworth, and Katharine Hepburn, along with millionaires like Barbara Hutton, Mrs. Vanderbilt, Mrs. Biddles, and Mrs. Vincent Astor became his clients. Most of all, they also became friends who wanted to be one of the idol's favorites. Anyone who had not been to a ball at the Chateau de Corbeville in Seine-et-Oise could not claim to belong to the Parisian set. The brilliance of the balls succeeded one another following a "rhythm of love, drunk on eternity." Each one was more memorable than the last, until the very famous Black and White Ball, where a guest danced all night in a Dior gown worth one million francs. But too much was just too much; a part of the press cried out that decent society could not tolerate this display of opulence during the reconstruction period. Just like Poiret or Boni de Castellane, Jacques Fath was a magician whose talent, combined with his unabashed love of parties, created the kind of magic that was abundantly recounted in the international press, ensuring the influence of French taste and talent throughout the world. After Jacques Fath's death in 1954, followed by Christian Dior's in 1957, haute couture changed forever.

The energy that Jacques Fath brought to everything in life was also evident in the way he ran his business. He used to enjoy saying that his "real success began with Christian Dior."

In reality, Dior did not only have the spotlights of success shine on Paris, he also innovated in a large number of different areas. In 1948, when Jacques Fath was setting up his ready-to-wear subsidiary in New York, he spent three months in America with Geneviève; at the end of this trip, he signed a first ready-to-wear licensing contract with Joseph Halpert, a Seventh Avenue manufacturer. Following Christian Dior's example, Jacques Fath designed clothes specifically for America, but he followed his own methods. Jacques Heim had walked this path before Fath or Dior, although unsuccessfully, with his negotiations for a Heim Jeunes Filles (girls) contract with the Junior League in 1946.

Jacques Fath went to New York every year armed with sketches that he adapted for Joseph Halpert. The 60 models in the collection carried the "Jacques Fath for Joseph Halpert" label and brought in royalties worth 10 per cent of sales, or about 20 million francs annually.

Fath's annual revenues, 55 per cent of which came from the United States, tripled between 1947 and 1949 to 280 million francs. Miraculously, Fath was in solid financial shape[28] in the first year of this deal because one of the greatest advantages of licenses was that they did not require any investment from the licensor. In 1948, he took three million francs from the couture revenues to launch "Jacques Fath Perfumes."

Fath created companies in America, England, and Italy. The firms were to manage sales and send the licensing fees to Paris headquarters. Henri Winter, his manager who had been with Schiaparelli before, confided to Jacques Rouët that every Dior contract was an opportunity for the house of Fath to sign an equivalent contract with a competing licensee. In 1953, the company's turnover was 570 millions francs, not including the royalties from the American collections. In 1954 Fath's prices were as follows: 140,000 francs for a day dress;[29] a suit, between 150,000 and 160,000 francs; an evening gown between 200,000 and 700,000 francs. Still in 1953,[30] a year before he died, he launched Jacques Fath University with Jean Prouvost, predating André Courrèges' adventure with production methods that he had perfected.

In 1989, La Compagnie financière d'Edmond de Rothschild bought the brand that was then sold to Banque Saga in 1991. Soon after, Banque Saga bought the Fath Perfume company from L'Oréal. In 2008, the Lefranc-Ferrant duo was appointed artistic director for the Jacques Fath company, by then a subsidiary of the Dumesnil group.

Pierre Cardin. Pierre Cardin was born to an agricultural family in Sant'Andrea di Barbarana, Italy, near Treviso, that later immigrated in 1926 to the Haute-Loire region. At the age of 14, he became an apprentice at Bonpuis, reputed for being Saint-Etienne's best tailor. When he was 18, he set out to Paris on a bicycle, but as he couldn't cross the war's line of demarcation he stopped in Vichy. Manby, mainly a men's wear tailor who occasionally dressed women, hired him. Manby's manager, Blanche Popinat, taught him the trade.[31]

In 1944, Cardin finally reached the capital where he joined Paquin at 3 rue de la Paix. At its zenith, the house, with Jeanne Paquin as the senior manager, had up to 2,700 employees. To start with, her banker husband—whom Paul Poiret criticized violently—ran the house, followed by Paquin's brother M. Joire. Paquin was considered the best managed house in Paris. It was the first to own foreign subsidiaries. The company, established in Paris in 1891, opened its London branch in 1898, followed by branches in New York, Buenos Aires, and Madrid. In 1954 Paquin merged with Worth. When Pierre Cardin joined Paquin, which was then under Antonio del Castillo's artistic direction, the company had only 270 employees. Luckily, Christian Bérard and Marcel Escoffier had chosen the house of Paquin to create the costume models for Cocteau's *Beauty and the Beast,* and Pierre Cardin enthusiastically helped design the magnificent costumes. Cardin joined Schiaparelli briefly before taking the coveted position of head tailor with Christian Dior, a job he left on a whim three years later in 1949.

Of all his professional experiences, only one seems to have given him pleasure: in association with Marcel Escoffier, he set up a theatrical costume company[32] on the fifth floor of 10 rue Richepanse, previously the Pascaud house. This business allowed Cardin to give his imagination full reign. After a long interruption, the society balls began again, and Pierre Cardin received a large number of orders. For Count Etienne de Beaumont's ball, Christian Dior planned to go as a lion and he asked Cardin to design his costume. For the millionaire Don Carlos de Bestegui's ball in Venice, he created more than 30 disguises. These were followed by the Lopez Wilshaw ball and the Casteja ball for charity that was hosted by Princess Radziwill and Baroness de Cabrol at Prince Czartoryska's former residence, etc. Balls were seasonal; thus Cardin spent the rest of his time creating suits and overcoats, fashions in which he excelled. He was one of the rare couturiers who knew how to draw, cut, and sew. Buyers slowly began to seek out his creations.

Success was not far off. In 1953, he rented the street side apartments of the count of Harcourt's town house located at 118 rue du Faubourg-Saint-Honoré. He set up his business there with a very talented and totally devoted young man, André Olivier.

Pierre Cardin models, 1967. © Cardin/Rights Reserved.
Pierre Cardin models, c. 1980. © Cardin/Rights Reserved.

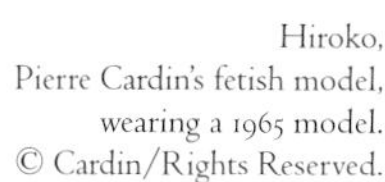

Hiroko,
Pierre Cardin's fetish model,
wearing a 1965 model.
© Cardin/Rights Reserved.

Pierre Cardin "Corner"
in the Printemps department store,
1962. © Cardin/ Rights Reserved.

Pierre Cardin, 1960.
© Cardin/ Rights Reserved.

In July 1957, he presented a complete collection of 120 models and became a member of the Chambre syndicale de la couture the same season as Guy Laroche. The press sang his praises. Three months later, Christian Dior died at Montecatini and on behalf of the International Wool Secretariat,[33] Thelma Sweetinburgh asked Cardin to take his place on the jury that was to deliberate at the theater des Ambassadeurs, the future Espace Pierre Cardin.

At the head of a couture house, at the very time that couture was no longer able to survive by its production alone, Cardin followed in the footsteps of the seniors in his profession, pouring exceptional energy and imagination into all kinds of distribution opportunities. After he opened the Eve boutique, at 118 rue du Faubourg-Saint-Honoré at the end of the fifties, he opened Adam at the Biscottes Heudebert location. In the wake of these store openings, Henry Berghauer orchestrated the launch of Cardin distribution and the expansion of the Cardin brand name.[34] The ties were an immediate, extraordinary success. They were produced in an annex to the house on rue du Colisée and André Oliver, a talented colorist and fabric developer, created most of them. A silk knot with a flannel body as well as the unusual prints lent Cardin ties a particular elegance. In parallel Cardin launched a collection of blazers and Mao suits, produced by the Lyon company, Tatin. The velvet Mao jacket remains a historical classic of the sixties. Fenestrier, also from Lyon, made "cartoufles" a sort of indoor boot, made of very supple kid leather, in a range of unusual colors including prune, bronze, or green for men. The Cardin atelier designed an amazing collection of romantic hats under Madame Nicole's direction. The excellent quality of the work, the elegance of the materials used, and Cardin's original concepts attracted a demanding and sophisticated clientele.

Like his wife, Juliette, Marcel Achard was an unconditional Pierre Cardin fan. He ordered his academician's costume from Cardin, and was soon followed by a number of actor and writer friends. As was the case with Dior and Balmain when they started out, Cardin's own workshops made the Eve boutique collections. The company was growing by the day. The "diffusion" line moved to its own space in an apartment on rue La Boétie, opposite salle Gaveau. Gilio, on boulevard Saint-Michel, became Cardin's exclusive retailer on the left bank more for promotional and image development reasons than for any real profit. Nonetheless, until 1967, licenses were rare. In 1960, under the name Pierre Cardin Sport, Armand Fouks signed a contract for raincoats, but it only lasted a year. In 1961, Pierre Cardin negotiated a license with Georges Bril, the important industrialist from Orleans and Chateaurenard, for men's suits that would be sold in Europe, the Middle East, and North Africa. This contract replaced his manufacturing agreement with Tatin.[35]

It was also in 1961 that Jacqueline Bénard, manager of the Printemps trend forecasting office, introduced Pierre Cardin to Prince Georges Galitzine, the department store's sales manager. The latter ordered a collection of exclusive women's models for Paris that Cardin was, however, allowed to retail in the provinces. The Cardin "corner"[36] (see illus. on page 141) was inaugurated in spring 1962. Since women's wear licenses like the deal Cardin signed with Bril for men's wear did not yet exist, Cardin billed Printemps directly for the women's clothes.

The Printemps clientele, however, scorned the "cosmonaut"-styled fashion that Cardin displayed, resulting in a relative commercial failure.[37] The media success was, however, immediate and far more important than expected. Hélène Lazareff was excited and she coordinated an editorial in *Elle* on the theme of couture's democratization.

Although there was really nothing revolutionary about opening a Cardin shop in Printemps (Jean Dessès had opened a boutique in Galeries Lafayette before him, in 1956), the "hype" was such that the whole profession could no longer contain their irritation.

With this episode Pierre Cardin caught a glimpse of how he could make his label known in a way that nobody had dared to, or had thought of before.

With superb pluck, he declared to his detractors that he loved French women too much to not want to give them the opportunity to wear Cardin at an affordable price, notably when his clothes were available to the British under such conditions at Harrods', or to the Americans at Lord and Taylor's. Moreover, he had realized the importance of a social phenomenon that he involuntarily instigated and he thought about how he could preserve all the advantages of the precedents he created. He needed to repeat the Printemps experience again, rapidly. Cardin "corners" blossomed at stores including Rinascente in Milan, at Hertie's in Germany, Selfridges in London, and Takashimaya in Tokyo. The label was being democratized at top speed.

Meanwhile, Bril's license was growing and it lead to similar contracts for other products including knitwear with Tiberghein, ties with Laffargue, shirts with

Gravereaux, etc. The adventure continued, rebounding to the rhythm of the successive new ventures.

In 1966 Mildred Custin, president of New York's Bonwit Teller, unveiled Pierre Cardin's men's products, manufactured by Bril, in a 25 square meter boutique on the ground floor of the shop. It was so successful that manufacturers of suits, shirts, ties, and accessories all wanted licensing contracts with Cardin.

In 1970, John Kornblith, a men's wear licensee, chose to sub-contract the Pierre Cardin Amérique[38] collection to Maurice Bidermann in France. This decision was a turning point in the Bidermann adventure. Within 20 years Bidermann became the leading men's clothing manufacturer in the world.

Max Bellest, Pierre Cardin's licensing agent in America, dreamt of reproducing the successful operation that had been carried out with men's ready-to-wear for Cardin's women's line. Six months after the men's corner at Bonwits on 57th Street had been inaugurated, he opened an exclusive women's section also at Bonwit Teller. With Nicole Alphand and André Olivier's help he negotiated the production with C. Mendès. A number of American contracts followed, the most important of which was the women's ready-to-wear with Gunther Oppenheim.[39] The same year, they negotiated a Pierre Cardin Jeunesse contract for the French market with the Vaskène company. Although the Printemps Pierre Cardin stand did not reach its expected commercial success, it served as a detonator for a promotional explosion that had inestimable benefits. There wasn't a country in the world that didn't have its "Cardin corner" in a department store. Tatin, the Adam boutique supplier, fueled Bril's desire, who in turn provoked the Bonwit Teller boutique's desire, that in turn stimulated John Kornblith's ambition.

Fifteen years after Cardin opened his house on rue du Faubourg-Saint-Honoré, the Cardin company had established its growth strategy. The company continued to grow until the 1980s[40] and its expansionist policy attained the desired goal. Pierre Cardin, a talented creator, was the monomaniacal head of his own company, its main decision maker, and its unique negotiator.

Firmly and seductively, he had managed to establish his own unique marketing system that could not be infringed upon by the competition. Cardin, greatly inspired by Dior, knew how to establish an original communications policy that created an unbridgeable distance between his company and the competition. At the end of the sixties, he had nothing to fear from either Dior or Balenciaga. Meanwhile, Yves Saint

Laurent and Courrèges were working in a different area, developing their image without resorting to licensing. As for the foreign brands like Calvin Klein, Ralph Lauren, Valentino, Armani, Issey Miyake, or Yohji Yamamoto, they only developed slightly later.

General business practices suggested that strongly personalizing a company seemed to weaken it. This belief, however, was reversed when the main object of the sale was the designer's signature itself. Pierre Cardin was the most prolific licensor in the world, both in terms of the number of license agreements as well as in terms of the volume of revenues the licenses generated. Although it is difficult to know the exact amount (as it was a privately-owned personal business), we can nonetheless go by the 9 February 1982, *WWD* (*The Famous Rich*) estimate: 540 Cardin licensing contracts would have produced a guaranteed *minima* of 50 million dollars.

Before Cardin had perfected his licensing strategy, the licensing system was frequently used as a management regulator, sometimes even seen as a life buoy, but it was never really a big part of a company's growth strategy. The arrogance of Cardin's success was partly related to the expression of a boundless super ego that opportunely found reverberations in a new social trend: communication.

Cardin had sensed an efficient propaganda weapon in this phenomenon and he used it, quite unabashedly, to realize his most cherished goal: to democratize fashion. It was a providential meeting between a myth of modernity and a designer's professional integrity. However, no system is perfect, and Cardin had his avatars. The licensing managers were drunk on their success. They pursued exhausting discussions to negotiate contracts on an object that was as reduced as possible, for a guaranteed minimum that was as high as possible, on the most limited territory possible. But this practice could only lead the label to such large scales of distribution that design inevitably suffered. Pierre Cardin discovered this, at his own expense, fairly quickly. He soon found himself in a situation where his creativity was only visible in his couture, which had become a prestigious expression of his image. Little by little, the cohesion he had sought—between manufacturing, from which the volumes demanded in order to guarantee the *minima* were too high, and couture, the sole aim of which was to uphold the label's image—was diluted. The result was that the quality of the company's image fell due to the rise of its designer's "starisation."

The Last Wave

A rapid analysis shows how the granting of licensing contracts was necessary for the survival of haute couture during the 1960s. It parallels the role that reproduction rights, in the form of paper patterns or muslins, had played in the 1930s. There were no other alternatives at the time. Two major handicaps hindered the modernization of the couture industry: lack of knowledge regarding the new technology coupled with a lack of training for personnel. In 1961, the Jacques Heim commission actively addressed the problem, but was unable to solve it. It was urgent to do so as these weaknesses aggravated a climate of crisis that was already being fueled by the emergence of ready-to-wear in France.

Trendy fashion boutiques like Dorothée, Louis Féraud, Eve, or Laura that appeared at the end of the fifties were another factor in the fashion landscape that couturiers had to fight against for their survival. The press was seduced, along with the starlets and young women who were more comfortable shopping in these stores rather than in the terribly solemn couture houses. Brigitte Bardot's Vichy dress by Jacques Esterel was synonymous with the sixties and with Esterel's success. At that time, production was flexible and the boutiques could obtain some models exclusively and even had their own atelier. Daniel Hechter, who had recently set up a couture workshop, provided Louis Féraud and Jacques Esterel with sketches and finished apparel.

These boutiques were alternative spaces and essential design references. They had a unique role in the world of taste and sensitivity of the time. They were a revealing response to the crisis that had rocked haute couture for half a century and, thanks to their original concepts, these boutiques would decide the profession's future. They simultaneously introduced couture houses and new fashion designer brands.

Louis Féraud and Jacques Esterel. She knew how to hold a pencil, he knew all about color; they opened their first boutique in Cannes in 1950. It was in this town that Zizi and Louis Féraud met an elegant engineer who held a diploma from the Arts and Métiers; he was the poet, guitarist, and songwriter, irresistibly seductive and funny, Jacques Esterel.

Together they decided to conquer the capital. They became associates and under Louis Féraud's name opened two boutiques, 88 rue du Faubourg-Saint-Honoré and

57 rue Pierre Charron. Friendship does not necessarily imply self-denial—this was clearly what Jacques Esterel felt when he decided to break away from his friends. But he had a valid reason: he wanted his name on the storefront.

Esterel was a good sport. He made the boutiques into two separate legal units and divided the bank accounts as equitably as possible before asking his associates to choose which store they wanted. The Férauds kept Faubourg-Saint-Honoré and Jacques Esterel set up his establishment at rue Pierre Charron. In 1958 Leslie Greymour—an American recently settled in Paris who was married to Viviane Greymour, the famous fashion journalist for *Le Figaro*—proposed his services as a licensing agent to Louis Féraud, who was tempted by the idea of capitalizing on his image. Leslie Greymour had barely settled in when he went to visit C. Mendès and, in the course of the discussions, realized that everything would be easier and more efficient if Louis Féraud was a grand couturier.[41] By 1962, it had happened. Féraud had hired then-young designer Jean-Louis Scherrer in 1959. Per Spook replaced Scherrer as studio manager for 15 years. During the same period, Jacques Esterel did the same, hiring Gérard Penneroux, a Balenciaga emulator who in 1960 gave him access to the sacrosanct Chambre Syndicale.

From this time onwards, Louis Féraud managed his house like a "micro-multinational." Féraud established companies in all the industrialized countries. Large companies that sold their own products under the Féraud name in England, Italy, Germany, the United States, and Japan held the shares. "The advantage," he said, "is that we can anticipate—after spending a few days in London—the trend that the English market expects of us." Leslie Greymour efficiently pursued the negotiation of numerous contracts, including the one he signed with Andrew Arkins, president of the Leonard Arkins company in New York.

Louis Féraud had become an international trend forecaster and the company could be proud of having joined the Chambre syndicale de la couture. This gave the firm a status that lent their business strategy a certain credibility. Their business model also made them relatively immune to sudden shifts in fashion; a company cannot both precede the market and follow its dominant trends at the same time.

In 1993 Fink, the German industrial group, was Féraud's only women's ready-to-wear licensee for the whole world, excluding Japan. It was also a 50 per cent shareholder in the brand. Italy's Gruppo GFT made the men's ready-to-wear.

Brigitte Bardot wearing the famous Vichy dress created by Jacques Esterel, 1959. Photo Eyedea/Keystone.

Jacques Esterel and Catherine Deneuve during a fitting, 1960. Photo Agence Roger Viollet.

The collections, manufactured by Fink, were very well distributed throughout the world. Fifteen designers worked in Germany, in perfect harmony with Féraud's Paris studio.[42]

Torrente. Ted Lapidus was a couture tailor with a shop on rue Marbeuf in Paris. His sister Rosette Mett, who was also his assistant, was married to an important manufacturer, solidly established in the German market which was, at the time, the French garment industry's main client. In 1961, Mett felt ready to create her own house. She left her brother's business and instead of searching for a luxurious town house, she set up her company in a 70 square meter shop at the corner of the rue du Faubourg-Saint-Honoré and avenue Matignon. She chose the name Torrente, convinced that the letter "R" was synonymous with success in couture. The basement was turned into a workshop. The 15 models she created each season were shown on live models inside the boutique and she made space for the clients in the windows. Her style flourished; her fluidly structured suits and coats were popular with her demanding clientele. Mett's quality was impeccable; after all, she poached an entire workshop from Balenciaga. Notable women including Marina Vlady, Marlene Dietrich, Natalie Wood, Raquel Welch, and Paulette Godard were among the faithful clients whom she dressed to measure. She employed nine saleswomen at the time. Her fashion was perfect for ready-to-wear; she launched a line in 1969, under the label Miss Torrente, distributed under license by Jean Mett. She was immediately successful, so much so that the huge royalties that poured in represented a sum that the company never achieved again in licensing fees.[43]

To reach her full potential, Mett needed to enter the world of haute couture. She managed to do this in 1971. She asked for membership to the Chambre Syndicale six years after her brother Ted Lapidus did. While the increase in her revenues allowed her to set her sights on this new status, the organization of her house puzzled Jacques Mouclier, the newly appointed delegate of the Chambre Syndicale. The workshop was settled in the boutique basement and he suggested that it should be expanded. As is often the case, the haute couture label had an immediate positive effect on the business's development. One after the other, Torrente signed contracts with Kinetsu in Japan; a perfume contract that was never renewed; as well as a contract for men's suits with Vestra, for which the actor Jean Piat figured the image. In 1992, the ready-to-wear made in France only represented a miniscule proportion of the house's financial stability that was guaranteed by the licenses, an obsolete system. Torrente no longer exists today.

When Torrente moved into haute couture, French brands were evolving freely in a market without any competition and the quantitative selection criteria became inappropriate to say the least. This may be an explanation for the confusion that reigned in the world of haute couture during the seventies. In November 1974 a note written by Jacques Mouclier, the president delegate of the Chambre Syndicales, tried to bring attention to the problem, but it remained unanswered:

> In this respect we are faced with a problem: What policies should professional couture organisations follow in the future, with regard to requests for membership from certain talented manufacturers who exist on the market? Should they limit themselves to a few, very sophisticated, talented houses that they have already taken into their ranks, or go further towards inclusion and accept other houses? This is more a question of general policy than a case-by-case study of each individual company's request. In parallel, we could consider reclassifying some of the couture houses that are on the calendar. Some do not really fulfil the requirements for exercising the profession of couturier and a certain laxity had led us, in the past, to too easily accept the registration of companies classified as "couture-création" on the first page of the calendar.[44]

Brand Management

Was it Christian Dior's unbridled passion for fortune-tellers that gave him such clairvoyance, when at the end of the 1940s he predicted the extraordinary social changes that would take place?

The 1950s came along, ushering in a great appetite for life, in addition to the madness of social recognition, the pleasure of discovering nature, the habit of enjoying weekends and holidays, the passion for country houses, and the euphoria of consumption, all after the difficult years of deprivation... It was vital to take a fresh look at all the problems and amongst them, those at the heart of fashion, and the fashions that emerged such as brand extensions to new products and how that fueled brand growth. This phenomenon of acceleration was furthered by the widespread use of new means of communication. The notoriety that had previously been acquired in private circles or intimate clubs was suddenly intensified and internationalized.

The different types of diversification Paul Poiret had imagined, and that the couture profession slowly adopted, had to conform to the new operating methods in real time, in the form of licensing contracts that Christian Dior had established. A brand's expertise could no longer take over a century to emerge, as in the case of Hermès; this approach took too long, was too expensive, and required too many skills. In the complementary businesses of couture, ready-to-wear, accessories, and perfumes, traditional methods of diversification were no longer the only ones that worked.

Unloved ready-to-wear

In the 1950s ready-to-wear, the ancestor of what is today commonly called the second line, was central to the couturiers' worries, and provoked heated discussions amongst them. All of them tried, more or less confidently, to diversify their companies in this direction. Pierre Balmain and Nina Ricci followed Christian Dior's example. They introduced new secondary collections and fully integrated them into their house's organization, but in the 1960s, apart from Chanel and Balenciaga, there was not a single house that did not have its ready-to-wear line. In the vast majority of cases couturiers, who considered that industrial production was not part of their houses' skill set, chose to subcontract it out to a third party.

The very rapid evolution in habits could not leave the couturiers indifferent, given that their main source of inspiration was to capture change as it was happening. In addition, in the role of disgruntled spectators, they watched the success their models had acquired as they were copied and reproduced more cheaply for years. This had been a warning sign of the dangers in the industry, but it had also aroused their curiosity for the street that had become increasingly demanding. This situation was to have a considerable influence over the future of the profession: while couture had dressed the majority of French women up till now, the social metamorphosis imperceptibly reversed the movement and definitively imposed ready-to-wear in the sixties.

The tidal wave had been coming for a while. As early as 1935, the French Ministry of Foreign Affairs had entrusted Lucien Lelong with the mission of analyzing the production methods of American manufacturers.

In a circular addressed to his "Dear colleagues" dated 13 July 1961 that began with a disrespectful "Mother's couture is dead," Jacques Heim, president of the Chambre Syndicale, warned them of the creation of two committees. One of them, presided over by Jean Howald, manager of Maggy Rouff, suggested establishing norms for the proper management of couture houses. The other would examine and propose reforms to production methods.

> Some will think it absurd... This is not my opinion... it is possible if we acknowledge that in a workshop, work could be more rationally organised. In other words, if one understands that this work is no longer only a question of the workers "magical fingers," but also involves the workshop manager's intelligence and imagination.

In 1965, André Courrèges announced a revolution that he had decided to carry through. He finally didn't succeed.

In 1970, Raymond Barbas inaugurated a factory in Angers exclusively dedicated to manufacturing Jean Patou ready-to-wear. Their business office was centralized on the second floor of rue Saint-Florentin.[45] The factory closed down after two years.

In April 1972, Robert Ricci associated haute couture and ready-to-wear in the same fashion show. The press ignored him and he returned to the usual practices.

All these initiatives went against the establishment's conservatism, with its illusory attraction for policies of choosing the easy way out, and of course, the eternal regulations that really should be qualified as disturbances. In fact, the statutory definition of couture made it impossible to modernize its production. Back to back, couture and ready-to-wear seemed condemned to evolve in totally separate spheres. In addition, the licensing policy allowed couturiers to get around the risks and torments that industrialization threw in fashion's way.

Amongst the earliest trio, only Pierre Balmain and Nina Ricci kept their ready-to-wear on their premises, while Christian Dior mixed his methods: integrated production and granting of licensing contracts. It is clear that the latter could only be harmful to the former. Nonetheless, a few years later Pierre Balmain and Nina Ricci gave in to the idea of granting ready-to-wear[46] licensing contracts.

Even today there are those who affirm that haute couture develops exports for the French textile and garment industries.[47] The opposite viewpoint can be defended.

While one can say that by exporting their ready-to-wear made in France, Chanel and YSL were exemplary, this does not apply to those who exported their branded goods via a multitude of territorial contracts, creating local competition for French exporters. Then there are also those who, by granting ready-to-wear licenses to foreign companies, hurt France's trade balance. This quasi-generalized trend of outsourcing prestigious labels abroad, that took place 20 years before our industries were outsourced, has contributed to weakening the French garment and weaving industries.

Byproducts

At the very heart of couture's savoir-faire is the dress, the mirror that reflects the image of couture. Hence, a label's product range first expanded around the dress, and more specifically into the area of accessories. Schiaparelli's and Dior's stockings, as well as Dior's and Fath's ties, to say nothing of Carven's kisslène,[48] opened up a range of growth opportunities for couture. This strategy has not diminished in the slightest and has largely contributed to the profession's continued existence.

The more specific and complex products that require a specialized expertise in production—like leather products, shoes, hosiery, and jewelry—clearly belong to other professions, each of which are highly specific and use their own production methods and distribution networks. Because of this, few houses branch out into new areas of production. There are, however, exceptions. Chanel and Hermès—long considered outdated—produce their accessories in their own workshops and distribute them through their own boutiques. In the process, they broaden the range of their product lines while preserving their growth potential. Before deciding upon this policy of total control, Chanel had cautiously tested the licensing system. In the seventies, Christian Legrez wanted to draw upon the recipes he had tested with Dior at Chanel. Bags, scarves, ties, shoes, as well as ready-to-wear, were produced and sold under the form of licenses. However, when in 1976 Alain Wertheimer took over the company's reins, he realized that the financial gains from the licenses did not manage to make up for the impoverished brand image that resulted from this policy. He then began to progressively transform his licensing contracts into sub-contracting agreements. Wertheimer broke his contract with Guéné, which held the leather goods license, and in 1981 he reclaimed Chanel's control of its ready-to-wear line after five years of close collaboration with C. Mendès.

The radicalism of his commitment was echoed in the mad and courageous objective he had set for himself: to pass the totality of the Chanel brand to his descendants, just as he had inherited it from his grandfather.

The house of Yves Saint Laurent pursued a strategy that was a mix of Dior's and Chanel's. When Yves Saint-Laurent bought back the direct management of its perfumes, the company successfully pursued the development of licenses. To better appreciate the subtleties, one just has to analyze the group's introductory brochure to the French stock exchange's second market, which precisely describes the company's corporate strategy:

> Three-quarters of the group's profits are from the perfume-beauty product sector and the remaining quarter, from the couture sector. Nonetheless, this observation should be put into perspective. Couture consists of three activities: haute couture, licenses and the boutiques… The licensed businesses are very lucrative and generate all the profits in this sector.

A few years later, PPR condemned the licensing contracts.

The Marriage of Couture and Perfume

From what preceded it is clear that, paradoxically, perfume, the most evanescent product, guarantees a brand's continuous financial health and its survival.

A brand can rely on perfumes' evocative power to attain international fame. However, to reach the target in perfect osmosis, the brand has to pave the way for perfumes. There are two ways to position perfumes: they can be a wholly integrated business and division of a fashion company, or they can be made and sold through licensing contracts. While the first option has real advantages, couturiers[49] rarely had access to the capital and the skills required to develop, launch, and sell a fragrance. The fragility of a couturier, whose only asset is his perfume, doesn't resist the competition for long from new brands launched by his licensee. It can in the medium term exacerbate the divergence of their interests. On the contrary, when perfume and couture are able to combine their activities in a unique structure, the strength of each industry is multiplied.

From Chanel to Yves Saint Laurent, industry experience has clearly shown that only couture houses closely linked to their perfumes could claim to last for eternity.

Chanel. Chanel's *N° 5* was born in 1921. Coco Chanel, like the rest of the cosmopolitan Parisian jet set, had been influenced by the Russian ballet. In 1917, she created the costumes for the ballet *Le Train bleu* for her friend Serge de Diaghilev. The sets for the ballet were done by Henri Laurens, the stage curtain by Picasso, and the music by Darius Milhaud. Her lover at the time, Grand Duke Dimitri Pavlovitch, was the tsar's cousin. Then there was Misia Sert, born in Saint Petersburg, whom Chanel met at Cécile Sorel's and who became a friend. Totally immersed in Russian culture, she met Ernest Beaux who had just been recalled to Moscow[50] by his employers, the Rallet company, essential oil producers. Beaux suggested that Chanel make a signature perfume. He proposed several dozen trials, each of which was numbered, and asked her to choose one. Once she had chosen, he asked her to think of a name and design the bottle and its packaging.

Several years earlier, her enemy Paul Poiret had imagined luxurious names for his Rosine perfumes that evoked the spirit of his dresses and the mood of the period: *Nuit de Chine, Fruit défendu, Minaret, Coupe d'Or, Mea Culpa...* He created highly decorative bottles and boxes in oriental and baroque styles that perfectly matched his aesthetic. As a response to this, Chanel decided to keep the number of her favorite sample, number 5, as the name for her new fragrance and designed a sober, right-angled bottle, on which she stuck a white label, before hiding it inside a white box with the same black contour as the lettering.

Just as the Rosine perfumes were only available at Paul Poiret's stores, *N° 5* was only sold in the Chanel boutiques on rue Cambon, or in Biarritz or Deauville. In 1924, she met Pierre and Paul Wertheimer, owners of the Bourjois perfumes, at the races. At the brink of her brilliant career, Coco Chanel seemed to feel more comfortable leaning on the Bourjois company's financial, industrial, and commercial strength. She brought her name to the "perfume" category and in exchange she received 10 per cent of the shares of Parfums Chanel. It was not yet a licensing contract.

At the outset, she was very happy with the arrangement. As sales for her perfume grew, she realized the deal she signed was to her disadvantage! Convinced she had been cheated, her dislike for Pierre Wertheimer intensified, leading her to use the anti-Jewish laws to regain possession of what, in her blindness, she considered her right. It was a waste of time; she had to wait until 1948 to renegotiate her share in the capital against a fee based on the turnover. In her luxurious retirement in

L'Air du Temps by Nina Ricci, 1948. Photo Patricia Canino.
N° 5 by Chanel, 1921. Rights Reserved.

Vent Vert by Pierre Balmain created in 1947. Photo Patricia Canino.

Joy by Jean Patou, 1930. Rights Reserved.

Calandre by Paco Rabanne, 1969. Rights Reserved.

Lausanne, she nervously watched Christian Dior's success, convinced that she would soon return. Hadn't she already replaced Poiret, the unchallenged master of the time, with Mr. Rodier's jersey? The time had come, she thought, to save the unfortunate women whom this Normand had imprisoned in a straitjacket of interfacings, stays, and corsets. In 1953, at the age of 70, she kept her promise and reopened her house.

Contrary to the legend, Pierre Wertheimer did not have any influence over her return. In fact, at the time, the perfumes were doing much better than anyone had hoped and consequently did not need the support of couture. It was thus her own free will, in the mad hope of a renewed brilliance at the forefront of the fashion world, that on 5 February 1954, after a 15-year absence, she presented her summer collection. She soon realized, however, that times had changed. Managing and financing a house like hers was a drain and she had no intention of drawing upon her personal fortune. She gave Pierre Wertheimer the option of buying her rue Cambon couture house, although she ran the company until her death in January 1971, at the age of 86.

Together, the perfume and couture businesses ran smoothly, supporting each other in a flourishing economic context.[51]

Unlike Coco Chanel, Jeanne Lanvin[52] and Jean Patou tried to hold on to their perfumes, against all odds.

Lanvin. Jeanne Lanvin had set up her fragrance laboratories in the same buildings as her dyeing factory in Nanterre, where fabrics for the collections were finished. Immediately after their respective launches, the perfumes *My-sin* in 1926 and *Arpège* in 1927 were so successful that the factory almost imploded. When Yves Lanvin,[53] Jeanne Lanvin's nephew and a graduate from the Mulhouse chemistry school, was appointed manager of Lanvin Parfums[54] in 1935, the production methods were still old-school. Lanvin used the best quality natural essences and the packaging was discreetly luxurious. Yves Lanvin remembers that during the financial crisis of the 1930s, the perfumes enabled the house to survive the hard times without suffering too much damage. It was also the perfume that contributed to the company's survival after Jeanne Lanvin's death in 1946. In 1950 Antonio Canovas del Castillo became the artistic director of Lanvin, a house that was considered the most respected fashion institution of its time.

In 1936, the same year as Balenciaga, Castillo, aged 23, fled the war in Spain and arrived in Paris. Misia Sert introduced him to Coco Chanel as she had a premonition of his humor, his imagination, and his talent, through his caricatures and his ballet costumes, amidst which were interwoven glimpses of fashion figurines and ornaments. Soon after, he was given his first opportunity: he created a collection for Piguet, who was forced into bed rest. Then during the occupation, he restored Paquin to its previous brilliance, before going on to run Elizabeth Arden's couture house on Fifth Avenue after the Liberation. In 1950 he joined Lanvin which was renamed Lanvin-Castillo, with each name retaining their specific logotypes. This was the beginning of a sumptuous 13-year period during which the house regained its splendor. Castillo, a personality of many contrasts and apparently nonchalant, was caustic and tender, capricious and playful, quick tempered and sentimental, but most of all, unhealthily superstitious. His mood swings were unpredictable and could devastate his victims, and certainly place him in danger. Company president Pierrette Lanvin, nicknamed Madame Yves, was regularly asked to leave the studio. Was it because he had as many quarters of noble heritage as the Duchess of Alba? His time with Lanvin, apart from his undeniable talent, was marked by his authoritarianism. His last feat took place in 1963, when he threatened to resign if the house did not agree to pay his personal taxes. This time, it was fatal.

In 1964 Castillo opened his own couture house on rue du Faubourg-Saint-Honoré, at the angle of the rue de Colisée, having secured financing by the Guinness family. He had been replaced at Lanvin by Jules-François Crahay, who left Nina Ricci for this new post.[55] The same year, Pipart took Crahay's place at Ricci, Goma joined Patou, and Jean-Marie Armand, who was Crahay's assistant, went to Madeleine de Rauch. For a while, all these changes fueled *Women's Wear Daily's*[56] insatiable curiosity and their titles read "Castillo against Lanvin." However, nothing really shook the profession's foundations: the mercenary designers remained, as the haute couture rules stipulate, exclusive to the houses that employed them. Meanwhile, Castillo, whose favorite pastime was to devour his friends with his efficient irony, was in for a shock himself. Loel Guinness was the latest victim of one of his witticisms. But this time Castillo's words were doubly fatal and Guiness decided to totally withdraw his financial support. Everything was collapsing round him. Antonio Canovas del Castillo managed to run his company for a few more years by accepting capital from a real estate financer. Castillo ultimately moved his establishment to the Charpentier Gallery on rue du Faubourg-Saint-Honoré.

At the same time, Elizabeth Arden expressed an interest in Castillo's perfumes. A collaboration was not in the cards because a lady called Mme de La Castillette had registered the name "Castillo" in the "perfume" category, making any deal impossible. She was taken to court by Castillo whose attorney, Maitre Etienne Jaudel, won the case. But the die had been cast. He decided to return to Spain. As for Lanvin, a century-old house, it was bought in 1989 for over 400 million francs, despite accumulated losses of 200 million francs on revenues of 300 million francs. The capital included couture and perfume, which explains the presence of shareholders Orcofi and L'Oréal's, the former presided over by Henry Racamier, the latter by Lindsay Owen-Jones. Today, Lanvin is designed with an amazing savoir faire by Alber Elbaz. The house is owned by Mrs. Wang from Taïwan, who decided unexpectedly in 2007 to sell the Lanvin perfume to Inter Parfums.

Jean Patou. Jean Patou's beginnings go back to the year 1912, when he created the Parry house at 4 rond-point des Champs-Elysées, specializing in fine leather goods and furs.[57] In 1914, he set up an establishment under his own name at 7 rue Saint-Florentin, but the war and his military duties with the Eastern army forced him to delay his first collection until 1919. After these false starts, his talent burst forth, as if it had been held back, and his work was met with immediate success. From his time as an officer with the Dardanelles army, he brought back printed fabric from the Balkans that inspired his first collections. Patou had also become friendly with various members of courts in Eastern Europe thanks to all the embassies where he had stayed. The Queen of Romania and the Princesses of Serbia became his clients.

In 1925, the year of the Great Fair for decorative arts, he simultaneously launched three perfumes. Each one had a fairly philosophical name: *Amour Amour, Que sais-je, Adieu sagesse.* Patou opened an office at place de la Madeleine to run the perfume business. At first, they were sold exclusively in Jean Patou boutiques in Paris, Deauville, and Biarritz.[58] Later, Patou sold them to perfumery shops the same way Chanel had done. Patou then expanded his perfume range by adding a cosmetics collection, like Poiret had done. The beauty range was prosaically called *Sex Appeal* and it consisted of make-up, lipstick, and nail polish. He launched his legendary perfume, *Joy*, in 1930 that continues to be the international symbol of perfumery.

Despite Patou's success, the house, like so many others, suffered from the 1929 Wall Street crash. When Jean Patou died in 1936, the house filed for bankruptcy. Raymond Barbas, his brother-in-law and collaborator since 1922, took over the company's management. He was a shrewd businessman who set up an austerity plan permitted by the severe deflation France was experiencing. Workers' salaries fell by 30 per cent and managers' salaries dropped by 70 per cent. The perfume activity continued growing unhindered although the couture activity suffered and was only able to survive thanks to the buying of sketches from the outside, including those of the young Christian Dior.

Under an unusual management model, the constant changes of designers[59] and the irregularity of their talent did not detract from the label's identity or the client's loyalty. The perfume alone allowed the company to maintain its notoriety. This is a perfect example of a brand continuing to exist through a perfume, especially when one realizes that today, Jean Patou no longer has haute couture or ready-to-wear. When Jean de Mouy attempted to launch another women's wear range, he used the perfume as a basis, as Chanel had done in 1954. Nonetheless, in 1987, when Christian Lacroix left Jean Patou—where he was artistic director—to set up his own brand, he had no successor and the perfumes were sold.

Marcel Rochas. When Marcel Rochas opened his house in 1925, Paul Poiret lent him his first model. Rochas, like his mentor, emphasized femininity in his designs but used pure, simplified lines. Silhouettes became more feminine in his hands, with a surprisingly modern energy. A year before the 1937 World's Fair, Rochas launched his first perfumes including *Avenue Matignon,* named after his new address.[60] It was *Femme,* however, launched in 1944, that brought him real success. When Rochas died in 1955, the house was victim to a period of uncertainty after a very happy life that lasted 30 years, and the house's couture department was closed down.

In 1960, in the absence of couture, Marcel's widow, Hélène Rochas, an archetype of the Parisian woman, created a perfume in her own noble and unchanging image called *Madame Rochas.*

In 1990, Peter o'Brien tried to start up the couture section again,[61] as did Olivier Theyskens who succeeded him in 2003, but the department was shut down again when Olivier Theyskens left to join Nina Ricci. He was replaced by Marco Zanini, who left in 2013 to become the Schiaparelli creative manager.

Nina Ricci. When Mr. Raffin died and the "Raffin et Ricci" store at square Edouard-VII had been closed down, Robert Ricci, aged 26 at the time, after due consideration decided to abandon his profession in advertising. In 1932, he convinced his mother to open her own couture house, Nina Ricci, on rue des Capucines. Robert Ricci was guided by a good dose of common sense and a capacity for analysis enhanced by a certain intelligence. He learned his new profession very quickly. At the end of the war, he understood the limits of a business that had flourished in the hexagonal market. He recognized that Ricci had little chance of growing, especially abroad, without a perfume that alone could guarantee the brand's internationalization.

In December 1945 the first perfume, *Coeur Joie,* was launched, packaged by his friends Marc Lalique and Christian Bérard. It was very successful, particularly with the Americans stationed at the US Army bases in Europe where Robert Ricci had had the good idea of promoting it.[62] While fashion was his mother's domain, he took over the perfumes with surprising authority,[63] rapidly becoming a true perfumer. In 1948, he launched *L'Air du Temps,* "marked with the symbol of peace and eternal youth"[64]: this fragrance had a magnificent flacon made by Lalique with a stopper topped with two flying doves. The bottle only really obtained its rightful recognition in 1956 and reached its summit in 1970 alongside the five greatest successes in perfumery: *Shalimar* by Guerlain (1889), *N° 5* by Chanel (1921), *Arpège* by Lanvin (1927), *Joy* by Patou (1930).[65] In 1953, the perfumes were an essential part of Nina Ricci's financial equilibrium, and in 1963, they ensured its survival. Robert Ricci, who wore his success modestly, began to intervene actively in couture, which had been his mother's domain until then. In 1958, he appointed the designer Jules-Francois Crahay, who vigorously expressed his talent in the 1959 spring collection. The "Crocus" collection was received triumphantly in the international press, placing him on par with Dior and Balenciaga. The bet had paid off, and the creativity that the house had struggled to show off outside France was finally recognized. Perfumes and couture conquered the world in perfect harmony at a frantic pace. It was the first time since its creation that the house of Nina Ricci was in the coveted position of fashion leader, a position it continued to hold with Gérard Pipart after Crahay's departure in 1963.

Now it was time to move headquarters, and in 1979 Nina Ricci shifted to avenue Montaigne, opposite Christian Dior. Robert Ricci, who had been assisted by his son-in-law Gilles Fuchs as co-manager since 1980, and Wladimir de Kousmine, the general manager and one of his earliest collaborators, could be proud of having protected his family's interests within the company. In 1988, he sold some of the Ricci shares to French chemical group Elf-Sanofi, which held 49.9 per cent of Parfums Nina Ricci SA, the couture company's parent company. This outside investment provided the financial guarantee needed to ensure the proper running of an international company. In 1998, *L'Air du Temps* celebrated its fiftieth birthday and Nina Ricci, Couture et Parfums, joined the Spanish family group Puig. Nina Ricci is the best example of the efficiency of a perfume-couture combination. Thanks to the joint efforts of different synergies, this pairing managed to preserve the autonomy of such a large fashion business. It is easy to imagine that Pierre Bergé used this when he bought Charles of the Ritz, the company that owned the Yves Saint Laurent perfume license, for 600 million dollars in 1986.

Yves Saint-Laurent. Mack Robinson, the Texan, had financed the Yves Saint Laurent company until 1965. Through 1973, Yves Saint Laurent belonged to two shareholding structures: Charles of the Ritz with an 80 per cent stake, and the Pierre Bergé-Yves Saint Laurent tandem held the other 20 per cent. Fashion and perfume were subordinate to each other, and both helped maintain couture that showed losses until 1976. This did not worry Richard Salomon, owner of Charles of the Ritz. He understood that the prestige of the perfumes, which already enjoyed a strong position at the time, could grow thanks only to the abundant effects of the couture image. The perfumes were in fact in perfect harmony with Yves Saint Laurent's incredible growth path. Right from the beginning, Saint Laurent had managed to impress his demanding clientele to whom he delivered expressions of his inexhaustible talent every season. He had become the couturier who best expressed the essence of Paris. Saint Laurent's art was a combination of modernity and tradition, drawing on the classic and timeless aspects of each. Yves Saint Laurent incarnated an unprejudiced elegance—indifferent to the current mood.

He was a solitary creator who remained faithful to his own aesthetics and he constantly refined the shapes he had already established. If his first perfume, *Y,* met with a discreet success in 1964, 1971 was a decisive year for him. For the launch of *YSL pour homme,* Yves Saint Laurent was shown as a sports loving student from Oxford who had just returned from Kathmandu, and he posed nude all over the world. But it was *Rive Gauche,* with its insolent fragrance, in which his faithful followers best recognized themselves. In 1977, at the height of his celebrity, he created the most influential perfume since *L'Air du Temps* by Nina Ricci, in terms of its name, its jus, and its packaging: *Opium.* Its image was entrusted to the photographer Helmut Newton, who was the best person to share Yves Saint Laurent's universe. With the launch of *Paris* in 1983, the photographer David Seidner symbolized the myth of eternity; then the same year, the Metropolitan Museum of New York devoted the first personal fashion exhibit dedicated to a living designer to Yves Saint-Laurent.

Pierre Bergé worked alongside Yves Saint Laurent with Promethean ardor, orchestrating the ascension of the house he had co-founded and avoiding each of the traps that inevitably accompany success. Tirelessly trying to attain absolute power, he acted with overwhelming passion and nothing ever left him indifferent. As the director of his own destiny, he could only find real fulfillment in "the extreme experience" echoed here in the inseparable success of a label and its creator. When, in 1973, Richard Salomon of Charles of the Ritz sold his company to the Squibb pharmaceutical group, he made sure that Yves Saint Laurent could buy back all the shares of the couture house while leaving ownership of the brand to Squibb for North America. Pierre Bergé chose this moment to develop his licensing service, managed by André Lévi. Lévi spent two weeks in Japan in 1973 and signed 13 licenses in Tokyo. After the acquisition of the perfumes, Yves Saint Laurent was the sole master of his business. In 1990 his company boasted a magnificent turnover: 2.5 billion francs for the perfumes, 500 million francs for couture.

The demonstration could not have been clearer. After having been developed by the perfumes, his future was totally dependent on them. What then could have been more natural than Elf-Sanofi, a company that held shares in a number of perfume and cosmetic houses, wanting to become the owner, in 1993, of a highly prestigious business whose future depended on its perfumes?

Paco Rabanne. Paco Rabanne's case represents a variation on the same theme but the score was reversed. In his case, it was the perfume that absorbed the couture. When the Spanish group Puig offered Paco Rabanne a perfume contract in 1968, the president Guy Leyssène[66] suggested buying the class 3 rights (perfumes and cosmetics) for a period of 20 years, so that he could develop his concept quite freely. It was thus not really a license.

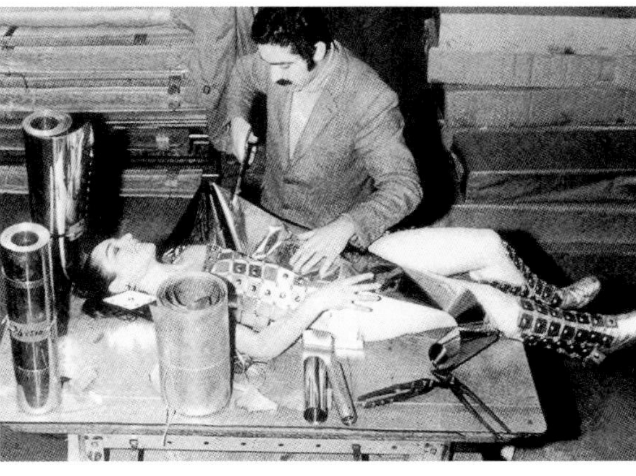

Paco Rabanne, dress and headdress, 1968.
Photo Gunnar Larsen.

Paco Rabanne alters a dress directly on the model.
Rights Reserved.

Along the way Paco Rabanne, the enfant terrible of the 1960s' plastic and metal fashion, financially revived by his perfumes, joined the couture Chambre Syndicale on 25 June 1971. But 20 years goes by quickly! In December 1987, the date when the contract with the Puig group was to end, the perfumer was obliged to buy the brand associated with the couture house in order to better ensure a coherent image and to consolidate its investments. It was a good investment when one knows that structurally associated, each activity enriched the other, while a separation would have weakened them in the long term. For proof of this, one only needs to look at the examples of Pierre Balmain and Jean-Louis Scherrer.[67]

Pierre Balmain. Born at Saint-Jean-de Maurienne in 1914, Pierre Balmain studied at the Beaux Arts, just as Hubert de Givenchy was to do after. This audacious young man lived an unprecedented adventure that lasted 15 years, an adventure that Christian Dior, his colleague and friend when he started out, had judged impossible: to reign single-handedly over his own couture house while retaining ownership of his perfumes. The only ambition he was driven by was an immoderate taste for luxury, the jet set, princely houses, and the opera, all which he consumed as an aesthete, excessively and generously. He never missed a premiere at the Scala and he sent 300 roses to Maria Callas. He had a very good voice and sang Verdi, whom he loved. Helped by Paul Racine,[68] a friend from Paris' Cité Universitaire—an area which housed college students—Balmain launched his first perfume, baptized *Elysée 6483* (his phone number), in 1946, followed by *Vent vert* and *Jolie Madame*. He loved his company and was exalted by what it brought him. Luxury continued to fascinate this overgrown child. In 1960 he started to build his dream house on Elba Island, when Charles Revson, president of Revlon, offered him one million dollars for his perfume company. The dream persisted. He was serene, reassured by the advertising budget that Revlon could conceivably offer, and Balmain began to imagine the dazzling effects it would have on his couture house. The enchantment was short lived. Revlon, which managed a multitude of beauty and fragrance brands, was little interested in creating new perfumes. Plus, the existing ones were excellent and under exploited. *Monsieur Balmain,* launched in 1964, was only a remake of the 1948 *Verveine Citronelle.*

In 1966, the cruel fiasco of an event organized in New York for the launch of *Miss Balmain,* Revlon's first creation, dealt a fatal blow to Pierre Balmain's usual good humor. The haute couture collection show organized to launch *Miss Balmain* took place at the Regency Hotel, but the *New York Herald Tribune*'s all powerful Eugenia Sheppard did not attend; she had better things to do that day. As for Charles Revson, he made a remarkable entrance, an hour after the presentation, a disdainful cigar hanging from his lips. The dream faded, leaving behind the beginnings of nightmare. Pierre Balmain, used to courteous dealings, was deeply shocked by Charles Revson's boorishness. *Ivoire* was created in this climate of indifference. Ill-treated by the perfume business, Pierre Balmain pulled himself together and began to develop his licenses, as his lifestyle left no room for self-pity. Seconded by his director Antoine Gridel, who replaced Emile Hannetel[69] in 1962, he obtained brilliant results that continued to develop until Antoine Gridel left to join Nina Ricci in 1973. To replace him, Pierre Balmain poached Claude Potier, an administrator with Perrier waters, offering him the possibility to be a partner. Potier, who had been a prodigious general manager with Lanvin and missed the fashion world, accepted the offer.

Fast forward to 1974: the first oil crisis shook the international economy. Bayard, Pierre Balmain's most important licensee, owner of six Balmain boutiques, collapsed, followed shortly by several Italian ready-to-wear, knitwear, and accessory licensees. The situation went from bad to worse. The company declared bankruptcy and Jean-Pierre Willot made an offer to Claude Potier to buy Balmain for one symbolic franc, after they had declared bankruptcy. Then it was the president of the Institute for Industrial Development (IDI) Claude Alain Sarre's turn to come to the company's aid, offering to put up the million francs required for the July 1975 deadline, before taking control of the company. The following year, losses reached three million, but in 1977, the company stabilized. The IDI team changed and Pierre Balmain did not hold the same interest for its new management. The company was offered to Leo Gros, president of Montagut, with another business in difficulty, Saint Joseph. In this increasingly depressing context, providence brought Pierre Balmain back into contact with Léo Gros, to whom, with his natural generosity as a young man 25 years earlier, he had lent his waistcoat and his convertible Rolls Royce, for Gros' wedding to the daughter of his first associate, Georges Tinland. This happy coincidence gave Léo Gros a slight advantage when it came to becoming president of the Pierre Balmain Company in 1977.[70] The transaction with IDI took place rapidly: against a loan of three million francs, the royal drapery of Lodève, Teisserenc, and

Harlachol, managed by Léo Gros, bought the Pierre Balmain Company for one million francs. While everything seemed to have worked out, Pierre Balmain meanwhile was forced to abandon his varied international pleasures, selling his house in Marrakech, the villa in Croissy, his pied-a-terre in Florence, and his luxurious apartment Boulevard Suchet in Paris'16th arrondissement, one after another. Eight years later, through Paribas' intermediary, Léo Gros sold the company to Erich Fayer, a Canadian investor, for a sum above 70 million francs. After having bought back the Pierre Balmain perfumes for a little over 100 million francs and having invested funds in the company, Fayer sold it again in 1990, to a bank pool led by Alain Chevalier, previously president of LVMH. After a series of misadventures, the Pierre Balmain Couture et Parfums Company is managed today by Alain Hivelin, its president.

The moral of this story ironically lies in the fact that Pierre Balmain could have done without his house on Elba at a time, in 1960, when he held all the cards for success in his hands. His assistant Erik Mortensen added "If his mother was alive, she would never have allowed him to sell his perfumes."[71]

Perfume had become a highly lucrative industry that excited the desire of couture houses, but since Hubert de Givenchy, no house or designer had dared attempt it alone. Today, it is perfume companies that seek out labels they can capitalize on. Those that appeared in 1962 (an exceptional year—Jean-Louis Scherrer, Oonagh Ferreras, Philippe Venet, André Courrèges, and Yves Saint Laurent) met with varying success, depending on their positioning with regard to perfume.

Jean-Louis Scherrer's journey was far from the most disconcerting.

Jean-Louis Scherrer. Jean-Louis Scherrer joined the profession through the main entrance, Dior. He spent 18 months with Christian Dior, then 18 months with Yves Saint Laurent, before meeting the wife of a real estate promoter, Mme. Chabrol, who owned a boutique at 182 rue du Faubourg-Saint-Honoré. For a salary, Jean-Louis Scherrer offered her a couture collection in her own name. No buyers came to see the first collection, but he worked hard to get Julia Trissel, Bergdorf Goodman's famous buyer, to come to the second collection. She saw it accompanied by Jack Lazard, owner of Kimberly. At that time, that was all it took to launch a house. The couture found a home in the cellar of the shop and the ready-to-wear, manufactured by Maria Carine, on the ground floor. The first floor became opportunely available, but Mr. Chabrol did not want to take this adventure any further. In 1967, he sold the business to a British citizen, Francis Francis, a Standard Oil heir. Although the company bore his name, Jean-Louis Scherrer was not a partner and only received a salary of 6,000 francs a month. This continued until a difference arose between him and his backer regarding a ready-to-wear contract signed with Gaston Jaunet, named Jean-Louis Scherrer Saint-Germain. Like all the French manufacturers of the time, Gaston Jaunet could not produce the level of quality required.

Bergdorf Goodman refused the garments because of their poor quality. Jean-Louis Scherrer was indignant and demanded that Francis Francis terminate the contract with Gaston Jaunet; Francis Francis refused. Scherrer left the company and was replaced by Serge Matta, the painter's brother. Unemployed, Scherrer left the matter in the hands of the lawyer Jean-Denis Bredin and won back his name. As soon as he had got it back, he sold it again to Hubert d'Ornano, who also owned Orlane. This company had been looking for a label for a while in order to launch a new perfume. The house was opened at 51 avenue Montaigne, in what used to be the Charles of the Ritz premises, and the first collection was shown in January 1971.

The combined success of fashion and perfume determined Jean-Louis Scherrer's international fame, and his talent was confirmed with each new collection. However, he was still not an associate of his own house, although his salary was incremented with a substantial interest in the businesses' related activities. Orlane managed the perfumes and couture together until 1976, when the parent company, Morton-Norwitch, expressed their desire to dispose of the subsidiary that had accumulated losses of 14 million francs over six years.

Just like Yves Saint-Laurent, Jean-Louis Scherrer was able to buy the business. He finally became the owner on 31 December 1976, after 14 years of misadventure. As a bonus he received three million francs for taking control. A last handicap persisted: the separation of perfume and couture. He personally took over the couture management and entrusted Béatrice Bongibault[72] with the industrial responsibility for the ready-to-wear line he wanted to develop to compensate for the perfume losses. In 1976, however, the vogue of licensing was over. The perfume belonged to Elizabeth Arden, which had become a Unilever subsidiary.

In 1990, Jean-Louis Scherrer wisely decided to sell his house after he had wonderfully revived and developed it. He handed 87 per cent of his capital over to

Ilona Gestion; 65 per cent of which belonged to Seibu, his licensee in Japan since the label's beginning; 35 per cent was held by Hermès.

In 1992, fate dealt him a harsh blow that took him right back to his beginnings.[73] It was clear: only couture houses that had perfumes to back them up could hope for eternity.

For 60 years, in order to survive, haute couture had sold its models, exploited its perfumes, then gave away rights for its brands. Today couture has run out of options: it cannot live off its creations, nor finance its own perfumes, nor can it live off its licensing contracts. What chance then do the new couture houses have of becoming prosperous, if they do not have a perfume and are, moreover, faced with the greatest difficulty in developing their licenses?

According to Pierre Bergé

"In any event, young people do not want to create haute couture, no one can be enthusiastic about an obsolete profession. If I were to begin again, after Yves Saint-Laurent, we would not create a haute couture house.... In addition, the most important houses no longer have a real existence; they are brands that have mercenaries to create their collections...

However, fashion or luxury ready-to-wear have a long life ahead of them. You can see what's happening in the street with Montana, Gaultier, Mugler, etc..."[74]

Nonetheless, in 1987, a counter example surfaced that confirmed the rule: the Christian Lacroix couture house.

It was only the LVMH group who had the means to relive with Christian Lacroix the experience Marcel Boussac had shared with Christian Dior 40 years earlier. With their excellent financial health and an incomparable international prestige, the group also managed to create synergies between different subsidiaries. For example, to hasten their penetration of the Japanese Eldorado, "Lacroix was supported by Vuitton," said the headline of *Le Journal du textile* on 5 January 1989. On the other hand, in the licensing world, Christian Dior abstained from using their veto right over Optyl to encourage an international contract for Christian Lacroix glasses. Finally, in what concerns perfumes, the Lacroix launch of *C'est la vie* benefited from the financial means of the group that backed it.

Press conference 20 October 1992.
Commission presided over by Didier Grumbach nominated by Dominique Strauss Kahn, minister for industry, to update the couture regulations.

In the first row, the journalists:
Catherine Rousseau *Elle,*
Cathy Horyn *Washington Post,*
Bernadine Morris *New York Times,*
Suzy Menkes *Herald Tribune,*
Simone Baron *France Soir,*
attending the Commission's press conference.

Hubert De Givenchy during his last show in 1995.
The workers parading on the podium.
Photo Guy Marineau.

Yves Saint Laurent surrounded by Catherine Deneuve and Laetitia Casta during the last YSL haute couture show, 21 January 2002, at the Pompidou Centre, Musée national d'art moderne © Fondation Pierre Bergé—Yves Saint Laurent.

We could establish a parallel between Christian Dior and Christian Lacroix. Both had unquestionable talent. When each of them presented their first collection, they had already earned a solid reputation: Dior with Lucien Lelong and Lacroix with Jean Patou.

In 1947, Marcel Boussac[75] had invested the equivalent of one million euros in Christian Dior; in 1987, Bernard Arnault had invested about 11 million euros in Christian Lacroix. In 1947, during the euphoria of Christian Dior's New Look, the house had full orders and positive results. In 1987, buyers had deserted the couture houses (120 pieces in the first collection, 70 in the second[76]) and in 1992 Christian Lacroix announced an accumulated loss of 150 million euros.

Notes

1. In a couture house, the studio is the couturier's, designer's, and assistants' creative nerve center.
2. *La Cuisine cousu-main,* Christian Dior company, 1972.
3. Henri Fayol, general manager of the Boussac group, vice president of the CNPF.
4. Paris, Bibliothèque intercontinentale des nouveautés, 1956.
5. Countess Marie-Hélène de Ganay was a saleswoman with Fath; she joined Christian Dior in February 1951. She managed the boutique until 1956, assisted by Bernadette de Montferrand.
6. Licensing contract: a contract by which the owner of the rights to an industrial property (copyright, brand, drawing, or model) grants the usage of the rights to exploit this property, in full or part, to a third party, free of charge, or on payment of a fee or royalties. *Droit commercial, Lexique des termes juridiques,* Paris, Dalloz.
7. In 1953, this stocking contract was no longer an orphan. Dior Brochure, 1954: "We entered into agreements with the following foreign companies: Germany: Werner Uhlmann (Westphalia); England: Mansfield Hosiery Mills Lts (Mansfield); Spain: F.Y.F. Marimon SA (Tarrasa); United States and Canada: Julius Kayser, 500 Fifth Avenue (New York); Italy: Fama (Milan); Uruguay: Silkor Faname SA (Montevideo); Mexico: Egicia SA (Mexico)." Christian Dior stockings were distributed throughout the world through 2, 500 shops or top of the range "speciality shops."
8. President of the Chambre Syndicale.
9. Lucien François' text is generally addressed to couturiers that sign ready-to-wear licensing contracts. The column was published in the review *Opéra* and reproduced in *L'histoire du vêtement feminine,* 20 January 1952.
10. In 1984, the Christian Dior brand had a turnover of 4,400 million francs, excluding the perfumes. Ninety-three per cent of the turnover was generated by the 184 licensees. The perfumes were sold to a subsidiary of the Moët-Hennessey group in 1970; in 1984, they represented a turnover of 1,420 million francs. As for the remaining 400 million that were produced by direct sales, that came from the boutique and avenue Montaigne (100 million), luxury ready-to-wear (100 million), and the wholesale department that sold accessories in Europe (squares, ties, luggage). High fashion furs and haute couture only represented 1.5 per cent of the turnover the brand generated.
11. Marie Callot-Gerber died in 1927. Pierre Gerber, her son who was both manager and designer, sold the company in 1937 to Marie-Louise Calvet, previously manager of Blanche Lebouvier. These had only been the successive steps towards the final closure of the house in 1952. Marcel Boussac had maintained both a professional and a social relationship with the Callot sisters.
12. Salaries amount in 1964 show that the seven biggest employers are: C. Balenciaga, 4,756,629 francs; C. Dior, 4,724,487 francs; P. Balmain, 3,113,565 francs; H. de Givenchy, 2,998,616 francs; N. Ricci, 2,886,334 francs; J. Heim, 2,834,476 francs; Y. Saint Laurent, 2,298,047 francs after two years of existence.

13. A prosperous time for Parisian fashion, Jacques Fath and Jean Dessès opened their houses that year.
14. "...But once the model had been carefully executed, the reproductions had to copy it exactly, the same fabric, the same lining," Marie-Andrée Jouve and Jacqueline Demornex, *Balenciaga,* Paris, Editions du Regard, 1988.
15. Marie-Andrée Jouve and Jacqueline Demornex, *Balenciaga, op., cit.*
16. *Ibid.*
17. Lucien François, *Comment un nom devient une griffe,* Paris, Gallimard, 1962.
18. Coordinated garments including tops, skirts, or jackets that made up sportswear.
19. Bettina Graziani, the first star model, was first noticed by Jacques Fath and was famous for her relationship with Ali Khan.
20. Annual charity ball co-founded by Claude Philippe.
21. *L'Express,* 15 September 1960.
22. The Mellons, the Witneys, the Duponts, the Paleys, the Kennedys, etc.
23. Interview with André Courrèges.
24. *Depêche Mode,* N° 683, March 1974.
25. On 1 September 1965, L'Oréal gave Courrèges the sum of 11,500,000 francs to finance his establishment at 40 rue François 1er. On 16 November the same year, the capital of the André Courrèges Pvt Limited company increased from 30,000 to 11,520,000 francs; the Private Limited Company Courrèges Parfums was created at the same time.
26. In 1992, the company was structured differently: Epargne Développement 75 per cent, André Courrèges 25 per cent.
27. Merry Bromberger, *Comment ils ont fait fortune,* Paris, Plon, 1954.
28. In 1953, Fath sold about 4,000 dresses in Paris. He designed 200 dresses for the United States, Italy, and Great Britain. He used 19 kilometers of fabric and sold 2,600 hats. Merry Bromberger, *Comment ils ont fait fortune.*
29. *Ibid.*
30. *Ibid.*
31. *Ibid.*
32. Pierre Cardin remained the owner of the unoccupied site.
33. Before her collaboration with the International Wool Secretariat, Thelma Sweetinburgh worked for *Vogue.* Later, and until 1968, she managed the *Women's Wear Daily* Paris editorial offices.
34. Following the model set up at Dior by Hervé du Périer de Larsan.
35. It was not quite a novelty. In the area of men's fashion, Lanvin had preceded Cardin. Lanvin, tailor and shirt-maker, had opened under Maurice Lanvin's management in 1926 at 15 rue du Faubourg-Saint-Honoré. At the time the clothes were made to measure, in the best fabrics, following the traditional methods employed in the Lanvin workshops.
36. A space reserved for a designer or brand within a department store, generally decorated to the namesake's taste.
37. Interviews with Robert Schoettl, Jacques Gourbaud, Henry Berghauer, and Georges Galitzine.
38. Jean Manusardi, *Dix Ans avec Pierre Cardin,* Paris, Editions Fanval, 1986.
39. *Ibid.*
40. Richard Morais, *Pierre Cardin, the Man Who Became a Label,* London, Bantam Press, 1991.
41. Louis Féraud could just as easily have adopted the same approach as his contemporaries, Jacobson and Rykiel, discussed below.
42. Interview with Louis Féraud.
43. Interview with Rosette Mett.
44. Daniel Gorin registered the most important companies on the first page of the calendar.
45. The couture managerial staff who were in control had not yet acquired industrial reflexes that would have allowed the company to develop.
46. In the seventies the Miss Balmain second line, manufactured by Dejac (suits), Ravoux (dresses), and Pierany (jersey), were a first "concession." Robert Neissen was the designer. Miss Balmain did not have a more brilliant fate than Miss Dior, her precursor. A few months before Pierre Balmain's death in 1982, a new contract was signed with the Weinberg company, under the name Pierre Balmain Ivoire. It was not very successful. It was seen as a promotion vector for the perfumes. Nina Ricci's ready-to-wear was also handled internally between 1953 and 1990. It had been licensed out to the company CLNR, in which Nina Ricci held 25 per cent of the shares, but was later taken back and managed in house. *W,* September 1992.
47. Crépuscule des griffes, *Le Nouvel Observateur,* 24 January 1991.
48. First knitwear license.
49. Givenchy is today the last couturier to have initiated his perfumes in 1957. Kenzo is the first fashion creator who integrated his perfume company in 1990.
50. The Bolsheviks did not consider perfume a fundamental necessity.
51. In 1954, Les Parfums Chanel became Chanel SA.
52. Lanvin Parfum SA is set up as a subsidiary of Jeanne Lanvin SA.

53. President of the company Lanvin Parfums from 1958 till 1980, honorary president until his death on 18 November 1989.
54. Interview with Yves Lanvin.
55. Meanwhile, Bernard Devaux created two collections for Lanvin.
56. An American newspaper. The only economic and polemical daily to be devoted to women's fashion.
57. His parents had a high quality tannery and a shop on rue de l'Arbre-Sec. Interview with Jean de Mouy, president of Jean Patou.
58. The five-story Biarritz subsidiary was built on the site of the previous town hall.
59. Marc Bohan (1945-1946), Rosine Delamare (1946-1949), Yves Coutarel (1949-1950), Max Sarian (1950-1952)—who in the sixties became manager of La Toile d'Avion, Julio Laffitte (1952-1953), Marc Bohan (1953-1957), Mad Carpentier (1957-1958), Karl Lagerfeld (1958-1963), Michel Goma (1963-1972), Angelo Tarlazzi (1973-1976), Roy Gonzalès (1976-1980), Christian Lacroix (1981-1987).
60. Marcel Rochas had his establishment at 100 rue du Faubourg-Saint-Honoré until 1931, when he inaugurated his town house, 12 avenue Matignon.
61. Laurent Normand ceased to be president of Rochas in 1993.
62. Camus Cognac also took this fortunate decision.
63. Nina Ricci remained a majority shareholder in couture; however, Robert Ricci held the majority in the perfumes.
64. Marie-France Pochna, *Nina Ricci,* Paris, Editions du Regard, 1992.
65. *Ibid.*
66. General manager of Grès and the person responsible for launching *Cabochard*. President of Parfums Chanel then Parfums Paco Rabanne until 1990.
67. Balmain opened one year before Dior, and Scherrer the same year as Yves Saint Laurent, in 1962.
68. The brother of George Racine, the industrialist in jersey fabric.
69. Manager of Mainbocher before the war; first American couturier to settle in Paris.
70. Claude Potier, who was forced to leave, joined Emanuel Ungaro as general manager in March 1978 before joining the Révillon-Lagerfeld group, five years later.
71. Interviews with Antoine Gridel, Claude Potier, Erik Mortensen, and Léo Gros.
72. Béatrice Bongibault began her career with Jean – Louis Scherrer, then joined Chanel in 1981 to organize the ready-to-wear line, the license for which had been taken away from C. Mendès. She then became general manager of Christian Dior before going on to join Valentino in Rome.
73. In 1993, Jean-Louis Scherrer was involved in a court case against the company that bore his name. Twenty-two years after Serge Matta, Erik Mortensen replaced him in his own house. Gaston Jaunet manufactured his ready-to-wear. Interview with Jean Scherrer.
74. *C.B. News,* 1992.
75. One of the titles in *France Dimanche,* of 16 February 1947, "The new Boussac stable is the most thoroughbred" "To attain this result, Christian Dior who is supposed to be talented, certainly did not lack funds... Marcel Boussac has already spent 25 million francs to set him up (25 million 1947 is equivalent to about 1 million euros)."
76. *Libération,* 27 July 1987.

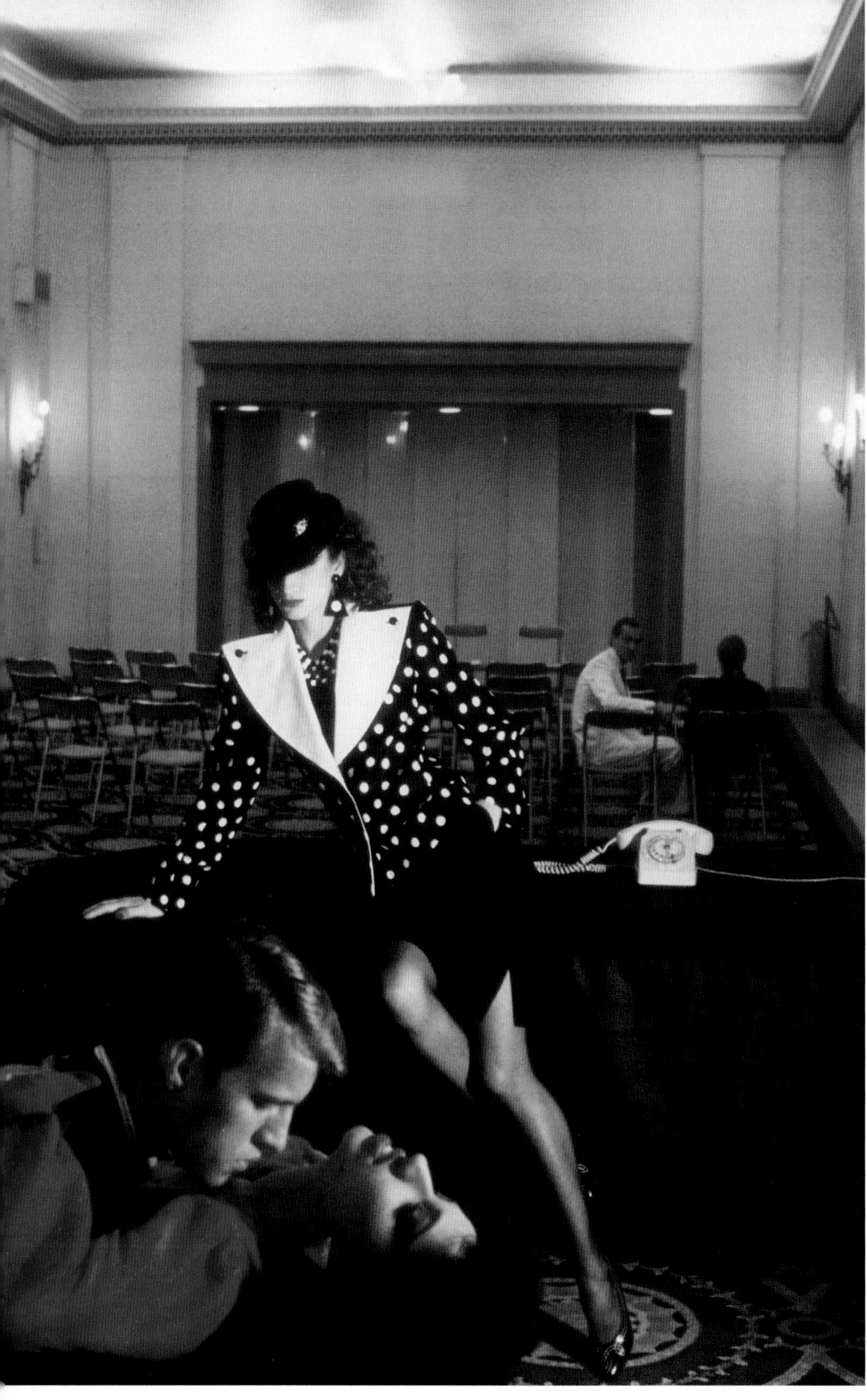

Violeta Sanchez wearing an Yves Saint Laurent suit, 1982. Photo Helmut Newton.

PART II

READY-TO-WEAR

Hall of Galeries Lafayette, founded by Théophile Bader in 1899, renovated in 1912. Its staircase is attributed to Louis Majorelle. Courtesy Galeries Lafayette/ Rights Reserved.

Au Bon Marché in 1878, department store founded by Aristide Boucicaut in 1852. Courtesy Le Bon Marché.

La Belle Jardinière in 1824, the oldest Parisian department store. Paris, Musée carnavalet. © PMVP

CHAPTER I
THE ORIGINS OF THE APPAREL MANUFACTURING INDUSTRY

At the outset, the apparel manufacturing industry made clothes that required mass or assembly production, such as regional or professional clothing. The men's manufactured suit belongs to the latter category; its jackets and trousers were particularly difficult for workers' wives to sew themselves.

In the nineteenth century, workers used to pay their country tailors in kind. They were forced to abandon this practice when they settled in towns where the cost of clothing was much higher. In anticipation of this economic difficulty, manufacturers offered more simplified men's fashion consisting of a straight pair of trousers, a long coat-jacket, and a shirt with a removable collar. It was very much a military style that became the basis for civilian clothing.

Mass manufacturing of women's clothing already existed in 1900. This was due to the interpretation of traditional regional costumes, generally consisting of a long skirt, gathered at the waist and falling in wide round pleats topped with a puffed corsage—generally white—tight at the neck and tucked in at the waist.[1] Workers' lifestyles did not change very much and the result was that mass-manufactured apparel showed little creativity. The garments were of poor quality and made of coarse fabric that was not very attractive. Department stores[2] encouraged new consumer habits and expanded the field of functional clothings, which they helped change by offering more imaginative styles and lower prices than those practiced by local dressmakers. This new kind of clothing that targeted the working class and petit bourgeoisie was represented by the Chambre syndicale de la confection et de la couture française en gros.[3] In 1867, Pierre Parissot, founder of La Belle Jardinière, moved his shop to quai de la Mégisserie; he was the largest French garment manufacturer at the time, employing 1,500 external workers and 50 cutters in his workshop. The demand for his goods was so strong that he was forced to outsource to the mass apparel makers to supplement the usual sub-contracting. Until the 1930s, Robert Weill, who was one of those suppliers, made a quarter of his turnover just from la Belle Jardinière.

The 1929 financial crisis affected all levels of society. In order to survive, haute couture sold its patterns. The apparel manufacturing industry tried to reach a new clientele using a revolutionary sales approach. In 1930 Isidore Berthet, manager of Toutmain, offered dresses, coats, and suits in his Champs-Elysées shop, all for the same price of 150 francs (about 64 euros).[4] French department stores rapidly began opening one-price shops following Berthet's example, and seeing what Woolworths in the US or Marks and Spencer in England were doing.[5]

The business model of these stores was very clear. They targeted a clientele with low buying power and offered mainly utilitarian articles in fixed-price categories of 1, 3, 5, and 10 francs. There were no saleswomen, the stores did not deliver, and no trial or exchange of products was allowed. Théophile Bader, the pragmatic founder of Galeries Lafayette, designed Monoprix in the simplest manner possible to better respond to the different categories of goods and the products he sold were divided as follows: 25 per cent textile and garments, 25 per cent household goods, 25 per cent food, and 25 per cent knick-knacks. In 1934, however, this judicious system began to reveal its limitations. It is difficult to maintain prices when costs tend naturally to rise. In addition, the total absence of any aesthetic style bored the consumers. "Ugliness is difficult to sell," even to poor people.

AU PRINTEMPS
ÉTÉ 1933

Présentation de la première collection de la Saison

Numéros			
1	Trois tailleurs	Le tailleur	350.
1bis	Roland.— Paul Poiret	sur mesure	1.500.
2	Trois robes de sport	La robe	300.
2bis	Saint-Cloud.— Paul Poiret	sur mesure	800.
3	Trois Tailleurs	Le tailleur sur mesure	850.
3bis	Benoiston.— Paul Poiret	sur mesure	1.200.
4	Trois manteaux de sport	Le manteau	350.
4bis	Dactylo.— Paul Poiret	sur mesure	500.
5	Trois manteaux de ville	Le manteau	250.
5bis	Marseille.— Paul Poiret	sur mesure	950.
6	Trois robes d'après-midi	La robe	500.
6bis	Casanova.— Paul Poiret	sur mesure	1.200.
7	Trois robes d'après-midi	La robe sur mesure	700.
7bis	Pan-Pan.— Paul Poiret	sur mesure	900.
8	Deux petites robes	Les deux robes pour	100.
8bis	Paris.— Paul Poiret	sur mesure	800.

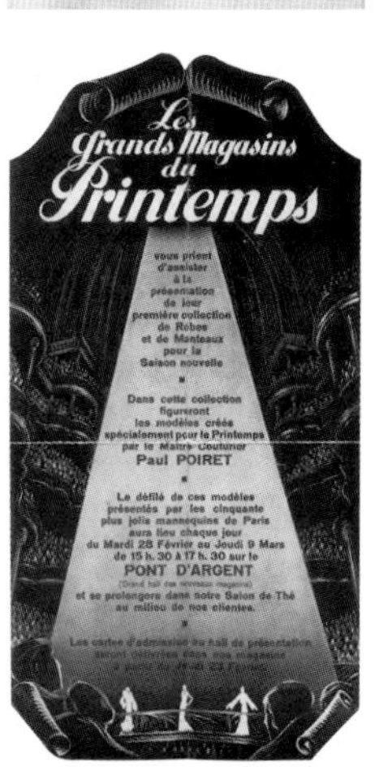

Max Heilbronn, Théophile Bader's son-in-law and future successor, was influenced by his friend Simon Marks of Marks and Spencer whose motto was that a cheap item still had to boast a certain amount of aesthetic criteria. In order to be efficient, the economic theory of Taylorism implied producing these goods in large volumes. Thus, in order to move towards large-scale production, it was necessary to limit the number of designs in each collection. In 1935, Max Heilbronn applied this principle to the letter and began to produce dresses and shirts in series of 100,000 even 150,000 pieces without any hesitation. The quantities of fabric bought in a single design were often as large as 300,000 meters. The manufacture of these goods was contracted to SPC, the Galeries Lafayette production subsidiary, as well as to sub-contractors, a number of which set up factories in the center of France in cities including Vierzon and Montluçon.

Le Printemps, founded in 1865. The floors were accessed by a staircase with four rotations, designed by René Binet, c. 1910. Rights Reserved.

Paul Poiret and his star model. "Le Pont d'argent," ("Silver Bridge") was built for him to present his four yearly collections there. Courtesy Le Printemps.

Left/Facing page: In 1933, Paul Poiret, created a collection for the Printemps department store.
Invitation to master couturier Paul Poiret's fashion show on the Silver Bridge, February–March 1933. Courtesy Le Printemps.

Little by little, the single price shops turned into variety stores at the same time that prices began to rise. The apparel manufacturing industry became very visible in the stores and began to attract clients away from the industrial clothing industry that had produced dull, uniform clothing for workers for over 100 years.

Parallel to the changes in retail, the "working classes" had just won new social rights and they became aware of fashion, in which they developed a growing interest. Access to department stores represented a first step towards luxury for these people.

In the report "Panorama of clothing in France," which was written for the 1937 International Exhibition for Arts and Industry, the importance of the "prèt-à-porter," or ready-to-wear, suit is highlighted. Although couture still remained the most flourishing industry, the women's apparel manufacturing industry dressed no less than 25 per cent of French women. Officially, the women's apparel manufacturing industry produced ready-made undergarments. In this manner it differed from the tailors and dressmakers, shirt and lingerie makers, and knitwear manufacturers. The shirting industry was the first to use the latest management systems in the areas of industrialization of production as well as in its sales methods.[6] There was nothing like it in the women's apparel manufacturing industry. The latter remained much less powerful than the couture industry, in terms of the personnel employed, the turnover generated, and the number of companies involved till the 1950s. Unlike their big sister couture that included large companies and in most cases had huge integrated workshops, the women's apparel makers consisted of small and middle size, little mechanized companies that, for the majority, employed home workers.

In 1938, the apparel manufacturing industry produced 20 million units, a quantity that fell to 5.8 million units in 1943. The shortage of raw materials, the disappearance of labor—often people working from home—consequence of the war measures targeting Jews and foreigners, and the closure of a number of Jewish companies were the main reasons for such a decline. While the apparel manufacturing industry employed 80,000 people in 1938, it could only support 25,000 in 1943. Industrial concentration was little developed if one considers that the 50 most important houses employed only 4,094 people, working mainly in the Paris area, where 86 of the 100 biggest companies were located.[7]

In addition, the most powerful apparel manufacturers were linked to retail chains like those set up by Pierre Parissot at La Belle Jardinière. Independent manufacturers only acquired real power after 1960. The SPC (Société parisienne de confection), a Galeries Lafayette subsidiary, was the foremost French manufacturer; La Toile d'avion, owned by the Boussac group; the SACLEM (Société de confection lingerie-mode), belonged to Printemps; and HVB, le Louvre, Paris-France, Réaumur—four subsidiaries respectively attached to the Bazar de l'Hôtel de Ville, the Louvre department stores, Trois Quartiers, and the Grands Magasins Réaumur. Thus in 1945, Galeries Lafayette and La Toile d'avion produced their own collections using the independent manufacturers as occasional suppliers, just like their direct competitors.

The Apparel Manufacturing Industry after World War II

Max Heilbronn and the Société Parisienne de Confection. Just like Emile Zola's novel *The Ladies Paradise*, Théophile Bader, who was more of an industrialist than a shopkeeper, created the Société parisienne de confection (SPC), an apparel making company. He effectively created his own manufacturing system that would supply his stores and thereby allow him to control his brand. At that time, the apparel manufacturing industry did not really suit Galeries Lafayette's requirements, so each department had its own workshop. At 54 rue de Provence, a menswear workshop made 950 suits a day, while in rue de Courcelles, sheets, bed linen, and lingerie were made; men's shirts came from Nantes, slippers from Strasbourg, and more lingerie from Cholet.

The growing number of industries specializing in manufacturing women's clothes, each more competitive than the other, destabilized the SPC because the company did not have as many assets or as much information to manage their collections. Instead of adapting to the desire of an increasingly demanding clientele, the SPC imposed their models and in this way, the managers of the SPC irreversibly locked their parent company into an industrial straitjacket, depriving it of the reactivity necessary for its survival.

The watchful Max Heilbronn[8] progressively became aware of the inconveniences that impeded the proper running of the company and that would one day place it at serious risk. Worried and seeking solutions that would allow him to improve his productivity, an opportunity arose when one of his collaborators arranged an appointment between his cousin, who was a lingerie maker from Nancy, and Heilbronn.

> I met this gentleman. "Mr Max," he said, "I would like to share my thoughts with you. You manufacture shirts, I do too, but I am 15 per cent cheaper than you because I own specialist workshops, I buy cotton in quantities that are ten times larger than yours, and labour is cheaper in Nancy." My God, he's right, I said to myself, and on top of that, what is true of him is true of others too.

Following this incident, from 1938 onwards Max Heilbronn gradually dismantled the SPC that survived until 1960. Printemps followed his example, abandoning the SACLEM, founded in 1927. By 1952 they only had two workshops, one in Clichy, the other in Auxerre, employing 360 workers, men and women, specializing in men's garments made for the Brummell men's store.

Originally attached to the company Soisson & James,[9] the Auxerre workshop was closed down in 1968.

Marcel Boussac and La Toile d'avion. Marcel Boussac's Le Comptoir de l'industrie cotonnière is another great example of vertical concentration, the opposite of the model of the department stores. In Boussac's case, textiles and the garment industry had come before distribution.

Born in Châteauroux in 1889, Marcel Boussac was the son of a small draper-garment maker whose wife was a poetess who married Catulle Mendès[10] in a second marriage.

At the age of 18, he took over his father's business and he was instinctively aware of the times he lived in. He introduced color into his fabric collections and hoped to make fashion more accessible in variety stores and thus reach millions of women. Châteauroux was soon too small for his ambitions. Only the capital could allow him to attain the goal he had secretly fixed for himself, a goal whose name would take him beyond all limits: "empire." He set up his first company in Paris at square Maubeuge with the 100,000 francs (about 280,000 euros) he received from his father as an advance on his inheritance.

The ascension of the "Chateauroux dictator," as his closest collaborators called him, began. He followed a strategy that made him the Clausewitz of industry. No move that could take his project forward and make him a profit was too audacious for him and he took risks, certain of success. Labor costs were lower in the Vosges, so Boussac chose to have his collections made there. From 1914 onwards, he was immensely successful. With only six employees, he managed to sell 700,000 meters of fabric a month. He then moved to 21 rue Poissonière, in the Sentier, and founded the Comptoir de l'industrie cotonnière (CIC) in 1917. The same year, he bought his first factory that he entirely refurbished at the end of the World War I.

His rendezvous with fortune took the absurd form, to say the least, of several stocks of airplane fabric bought from the allied army for a derisory sum. In 1918, he used it to make shirts and pajamas; their immensely successful sales will always be associated with the most legendary garment products of the century. This unprecedented commercial success allowed him to start his workshops up again, and to acquire others. He only had to develop sales. The first chain of stores he bought was "Le Pauvre Jacques," that he renamed "A la toile d'avion." By 1919, he had made his fortune. He was free to enjoy his passion for horses and he set up a thoroughbred stable. In 1922, he acquired the Rousseau shirt factory. His production had gone up from 7 million meters to 36 million. Boussac was a close friend of Clemenceau and Leon Blum's. As such, he received the world of international finance, ministers, and Parliamentarians in his chateau at Orléans. Nothing that was anything in France's social and political life escaped this wealthy entrepreneur. He advanced, protected from everything, including the 1929 crisis that did not seem to affect the growth of his businesses. Guided by his intuition, he reduced his stocks to the minimum, reduced his sales prices, and consolidated his finances by signing agreements with his banks. Once again, his waiting strategy served him well: between 1933 and 1936, he bought more factories that he integrally modernized, increasing his production in 1939 to 88 million meters.

In 1945, he dumped stocks—accumulated during the war and stored in the CIC basements—on the French market. That year, despite the shortages that paralyzed the economy, his price index rose by 50 per cent. 1946 sealed his meeting with Christian Dior, a historic one, thanks to the latter's *voyante*: "Everything you will be offered later will be nothing compared to the luck you will have today." For once, the luck was shared. Paternalistic and concerned for his workers comfort, Boussac started manufacturing Bendix washing machines under license between 1946 and 1950. These machines were designed to do the washing during work hours, requiring no human intervention; they conquered a brand new market.

In 1950, the Boussac group, at the heart of the profession, went from one success to another. His textile factories were the most modern and efficient in the world. He was the leading French cotton merchant (10 per cent of the market); the leading manufacturer (Toile d'avion, Blizzand, Rousseau...); the leader in haute couture; the leader in washing machines; and, of course, the leader on the race courses of France and England. In 1952, the Boussac production reached 132 million meters. His consolidated turnover was close to 70 billion francs, that is to say, the equivalent of about seven billion francs in 2001 (one billion euros).

Was he truly invincible? Everything seemed to point in that direction. When the Korean War broke out, this subtle strategist held back six months of textile stocks that he started to sell when the rates went up.

At the age of 74, at the height of his success, Marcel Boussac had not realized how much society had evolved. He persisted following the methods he had tested and that had always succeeded until now: production and advertising.

The anecdotes recounted by those who worked with him in different capacities—Max Heilbronn, Léon Cligman, Jacques Rouët, or even Jacques Dransard—clearly show how an apparently infallible management system finally took the group to its death.

The Blizzand raincoat—olive green, American army style, a best-seller at Galeries Lafayette—was an important market. Anticipating the Galeries Lafayette's customers' lassitude, Max Heilbronn wanted it produced in glacial blue. This was an important request that necessitated a visit to Marcel Boussac on rue du Faubourg-Poissonnière. But in the face of the "big boss's" total refusal, Max Heilbronn started looking for another supplier. The following year, Marcel Boussac sent for him:

"Okay, I agree to your glacial blue," said Boussac.

"Too late, glacial blue is outdated!" replied Heilbronn.

In 1958, Marcel Boussac made a tour of his factories: at the Blainville site that produced Blizzand raincoats, work, and sports clothes, he was terrified by the sight of innocent computers that served for market surveys, used to better target advertising. Forty hours later, Boussac decapitated the company management and placed Jacques Dransard at its head.

With Henri Fayol and Jean-Claude Boussac's agreement, Jacques Dransard signed a licensing contract for raincoats with Maggy Rouff. When he approached Marcel Boussac for his signature on the advance check for royalties, Boussac refused with a "I have more than enough with Christian Dior: compensate Maggy Rouff."

Was this behavior that seemed suicidal the sign of old age striking the 74-year-old patriarch? In 1963, when Henri Fayol left, Marcel Boussac turned inwards on himself, destroying all his managers' confidence, as if he was captive to the syllogisms that had earlier traced the path of glory for him. He was a despot and he wanted to maintain sole control of all the companies that were grouped within an anonymous holding, the Comptoir de l'industrie textile de France (CITF). His interventions were increasingly irrational, even destructive. While ready-to-wear was in free fall and Marc Bohan was losing his credibility, Jacques Rouët requested a meeting with Marcel Boussac. But Rouët was sent away with a "Leave for America then by the time you get back I will have solved the problem."

On his return he was welcomed with "There is no more problem! Do away with ready-to-wear! Isn't haute couture the lighthouse that lights up the world when it comes to fashion?" It took all Jacques Rouët's energy and Jean-Claude Boussac's help to avoid the disaster that would have had a negative effect on all the foreign women's wear licenses, and put an end to supplies for wholly-owned or franchised boutiques.

Marcel Boussac was a monomaniac and avoided any idea of a successor. Worse, he continued to manage his empire, as if fascinated by the coincidence of opposites, by making decisions that were contrary to what everyone else suggested. For example, he refused to consider new management systems. Like a stock market player, he stubbornly insisted on retaining and selling his stocks in his usual manner, without understanding that since the 1950s fashion had been changing very rapidly, and his stocks were depreciating as quickly.

Another shock for the old man came with General de Gaulle's first attempt to stop inflation after the Rome treaty had ordered the opening of borders in 1957. Competition was harsh and, to make things worse, Boussac refused to use synthetic and artificial fibers.

Marcel Boussac was the epitome of the powerful man. He forcefully incarnated the ascension of a powerful fashion industry, supported by brilliant management intelligence. But age and lassitude inexorably led to his loss.

Weill, France's oldest independent garment manufacturer. Before 1950, with the exception of the house of Couturier in Fécamp, specialized manufacturers were of little consequence. The Albert Weill factory, founded in 1892, was the doyen of independent apparel manufacturing companies. Like the Worths in couture, the Weills were already in their fourth generation of managers and had all actively participated in the union life of their profession.

Weill was recognized for the high quality of the overcoats the company made. Even with this specialty, they were more diversified than C. Mendès or Weinberg, other Sentier manufacturers that remained "mono-product" for many years and shared similar practices of internal organization for production and sales until the 1960s.

To remain a French citizen, Albert Weill left Alsace when it was attached to Germany. After an apprenticeship with his uncle and thanks to a loan from the Elbeuf, France-based draper Blin & Blin, Weill started his own business in a room on rue d'Aboukir, before expanding and entrusting the management of his collections to his wife.

In 1922 their sons, Robert and Raymond, built the Weill headquarters which still exist today at 8 rue Livingstone, under the sign, "Albert Weill Jeune et Fils." To build a factory specialized in making high-end apparel outside the tutelary Sentier area was a sign of great independence, a trait the family embraced. In September 1944, with the help of his son Jean-Claude, currently president of the company, Robert Weill regained possession of his family's firm that had been confiscated due to the anti-Jewish business laws during the World War II. Faced with difficulties in procuring raw materials, the workshop mainly supplied the American army, which introduced the first notions of industrialization into Weill's factory, allowing the workers to get better use out of the little equipment they possessed. Till this time, manufacturing had always been sub-contracted. Like the commercial representatives, the consignment manufacturers were paid on yield, and received varying expenses. This traditional system worked around a simple structure and benefitted from low overhead because manufacturers were not responsible for their production tools. Its inconvenience was that it was difficult to manage: To ensure their independence, each consignment contractor supplied several companies. While this system made it possible to control costs, quality and delivery deadlines were not well-managed. Certain services were nonetheless integrated: drapery, preparation or handling, reception, pattern making, and cutting. All houses of this size were organized the same way.

The cutters were specialists who worked on the basis of a precise hierarchy and were spread over three categories: "mattress" cutters, "small measurement" cutters, and "large measurement" cutters. Every day the "confectionneurs," those who sewed outside the company, received "special" orders by post. These orders were recorded by the company, then written into a manual bulletin and onto a delivery chart, and given a delivery deadline of a maximum of 15 days. The clients received a price list accompanied by a sample book that allowed them to personalize the model they bought and calculate their articles' prices in the different fabrics. The "small measurement" orders (special lengths) cost 10 per cent extra, and the "large sizes" (more detailed or beyond the usual sizes) cost 20 per cent extra. The making of the goods was outsourced to contractors or home workers. Contractors, who represented a labor force of excellent artisans mainly from Central Europe, could produce 10 to 15 pieces a week.

As for the home workers—generally concierges—they worked alone and could only produce four to five pieces a week. Hundreds of contractors and workers braved the receiving clerks on the due date. The companies recorded the orders before buying the fabric and the slow season was mainly borne by this external network. While the "large retail manufacturers" gradually got rid of their production units, the independent garment makers gained in importance.

Industry Initiatives

Although just after World War II haute couture was at the top of the field, and couture was the leader on the market, the apparel manufacturing industry kept a low profile, as did those responsible for its different professional unions. After the Liberation, however, the situation changed very rapidly.

In 1946, while the paralysis of textile production made it impossible to reactivate the apparel-making industry, the industry rejuvenated itself, changing its name. The very out-dated "Confection pour dames" metamorphosed into the "Industrie du vêtement féminin." This was only the first taste of a profound modernization that took place in parallel to the growth of the ready-to-wear industry, personified by Albert Lempereur, president of the brand new Féderation du vêtement féminin (Women's Clothing Federation). "The apparel manufacturing industry," he said, "must constantly rival couture which knows how to organise its seasonal parties so well."

From 12–21 April 1947, the Lyon Fair hosted two major events. The first showed a selection of fashions produced by 100 manufacturers in a 2,000 square meter space in a newly renovated neighborhood. The second event, under the banner of the

Albert Lempereur, president of the Women's Garment Federation, receiving the Légion d'honneur at the hotel Crillon, in 1955. On the right, his son Pierre. Rights Reserved.

Logo *Lempereur*

"Trois Hirondelles," was an opportunity to showcase wholesale French creations from reputed manufacturing companies whose status was defined by the decree of 1943.

On 18 April, the first convention of the women's clothing industries took place in the large conference hall of the Lyon fair. A banquet for the delegates followed at 8:00 PM in the Berryer-Millet hall, place Bellecour. On 19 April, a fashion show presenting the latest creations by "les maisons de couture en gros," the wholesale couture houses, was held in the salons of the Lyon town hall, in the presence of Edouard Herriot, president of the Assemblée nationale and deputy mayor of Lyon, and Robert Lacoste, minister for industrial production. The speeches followed each other in an atmosphere reminiscent of an electoral campaign.

Maurice Warnery, president of the Association des maisons de couture en gros, a trade group for couture wholesalers, gravely developed the often subsequently repeated argument that the alliance between haute couture and foreign industry was penalizing French manufacturers:

> We must recognise that our export figures in 1939, excluding North Africa, had become derisory... The reasons for this almost total disappearance of the French market for women's manufactured garments on the international markets, were the creation of the Berlin, Vienna, London, New York, Zurich and Amsterdam markets. The splendid success of our powerful foreign competitors was aided by Parisian haute couture which, by selling its own models to our foreign colleagues, allowed them to sell authentic copies on a large scale, thus destroying the French "ready-to-wear" market.[11]

On 12 February 1948, Albert Lempereur organized a big fashion show at the Chaillot palace, under the high patronage of the president of the Republic and Mrs. Vincent and Mrs. Paul Auriol. These events underscored the emergence of a new industry, fully aware of its subjection to haute couture. The beginnings were marked by the intensification of a ferocious competition between two complementary professions that were only calmed by different attempts at a dialogue.

Albert Lempereur's sumptuous parties were the subject of violent controversies, comparable to those his successor Daniel Hechter encountered in 1985, when he organized a gigantic fashion show on avenue Foch. "One of our most important colleagues," complained Albert Lempereur, "sent me a personal note saying that this type of event did not represent, in his opinion, an efficient way to get consumers interested in our production." He went on to add: "Do as I do, sell cheap, and you'll win the day..." Albert Lempereur was used to all kinds of criticism that, as he knew, often turns back upon those who pronounce them. He was not the kind of man to be easily disarmed...

> I always come back to the need for propaganda in favour of ready-to-wear, that is to say the imperious obligation we have to convince French women of the performances of our industry. We must, of course, improve our products and reduce our prices, but spectacular events are also important. I will go even further; a gala like the one at Chaillot made the authorities review certain unfavourable prejudices that we have sometimes had to raise in our official discussions....

Effectively, the "authorities" financed the advertising campaigns, proposed by the federation, that were conducted through the press and posters. In 1948, Albert Lempereur's convincing enthusiasm led him and a few colleagues, quite naturally, to a discovery of the American market.

The 19 missionaries that were to leave on 22 April were to carry out a concrete study of what was called "the American factories" in the framework of the Marshall plan. While Lucien Lelong, who had preceded them in 1935, had returned from his journey rather worried, this was not the case of the apparel industry manufacturers who drew immediately applicable lessons from their visit. Jean-Claude Weill, accompanied by his cousin and production manager Philippe de Castro, made two important discoveries: Weill noticed that American industrialists put their own labels on the models they made while in France, the manufacturers usually only used their clients' labels. De Castro discovered that flexibility was not a synonym for efficiency and that the perforated planning cards that equipped the American companies' production services encouraged a rationalization of sales and production.

In 1955, on the invitation of the American Minister for Commerce, a new study mission led by Albert Lempereur left for a five-week visit to the United States. The itinerary was seductive: New York, San Francisco, Los Angeles, Dallas, and Washington were all a part of it. Journalists from *Elle, France, Soir, Paris-Presse, Femina, Jours de France,* and *Marie France* accompanied the garment manufacturers, and of course the Radio-

Télévision française, Agence France Presse; future fashion advisors like Françoise Vincent-Ricard, and the advertising agencies represented by Neuville and Publicis. *Les Cahiers de l'Industrie du vêtement feminin* described the trip in the following terms:

> The object of the mission will be to study the sales methods in use in America, particularly the active role newspapers and magazines play in promoting "ready-to-wear." The transatlantic press is, in fact, not only a vehicle for selling fashion, but it also acts as an advisor to fabric and apparel manufacturers. ... The coordination that takes place and the enormous means employed (press and advertising) to bring these trends to the consumer, allow manufacturers and retailers to choose their materials more intelligently.

This diverse group returned to France enriched by a wide analysis of the American market. They met at the Mathurins theater, on 23 June, to summarize their journey. In the 25 July issue of *Elle,* Alice Chavanne and Annie Rivemale also shared their impressions in a dithyrambic article: they had in fact discovered marketing, the notion of "separates," and fashion coordination. A few years after Maurice Warnery, they picked up an anomaly:

> Everywhere, particularly in New York, we noticed the absolute hold French haute couture had on fashion; we wondered why it was so willing to allow the American apparel manufacturing industry (that does not always admit to the French influence) to adapt their models. Why doesn't Parisian haute couture have a sort of gentleman's agreement with French apparel makers that allow the latter to see the collections under the same conditions as the American buyers, and would allow them to adapt the best of French fashion, with a certain agreed deadline? It would be a source of profit at a national level.

For their part, the French industrialists were amazed to discover that 80 million American women, or 95 per cent of the female population, wore ready-to-wear clothes, compared with 40 per cent of French women. They also saw that high quality ready-to-wear garments were the norm all over the country, thanks to efficient merchandising which was then relayed by the press, supported by advertising, and offered to the consumer with seductive merchandising: the department store sections are designed to sell luxury and mass products indifferently.

On Albert Lempereur's initiative, the conclusions by those who participated in the second mission led to the creation of the Comité de coordination des industries de mode (CIM) (Committee for the Coordination of Fashion Industries) on 1 December 1955.

The CIM's main goal was to provide each of the different actors in the fashion network—from the textile mills to the professional press—precise and coherent information about "trends." The action committee included chemical fiber producers, textile mills, women's ready-to-wear and accessory manufacturers, and even the central buying offices of department stores. However, the manner in which the meetings were organized did not allow the weavers and manufacturers to determine the trends to be followed despite the help provided by those in the retail sector. While industries were widely represented, stylists were not. The endeavor remained too limited and was not efficient. A change, nonetheless, took place thanks to the impassioned battle led over a period of about 10 years by a coterie of talented professionals, who were convinced of the efficient methods they had discovered during their mission to the United States. The CIM, instituted by Albert Lempereur, was a model for fashion and trend consultants.

The Catalysts of Change

In 1850, Madame Roger invented ready-to-wear couture, and it was Charles Frédéric Worth, registered with the Annuaire de commerce (Business Directory) in 1868 under the heading "Manufactured Novelties," who institutionalized it, setting a serious precedent: offering original shapes in an area of fashion that had hitherto been severely regimented by the court. Control of fashion thus shifted from the empress to an oligarchy that consisted of the grands couturiers. But there would be a reversal of fate: when the latter, a century later and having endured several changes, felt dispossessed of its predominance, its resistance was as strong as that which was exhibited at the London World Fair in 1851. During the twentieth century, society changed rapidly; the news media was not just powerful, it was omnipresent, and foreign influences were widely felt and expressed. This allowed the apparel industry to make its mark more easily than couture had been able to.

The emancipation of the apparel, and more specifically the ready-to-wear manufacturing industry, was decided at the end of the 1950s. Until that time, this industry, was fully aware that it came under haute couture's supervision in terms of creation; it had not envisaged demanding its autonomy. In a document annexed to the request formulated by Raymond Barbas for the aide textile (Textile Aid) in 1956, three short sentences, noted as excerpts and underlined, clearly express the relationship between couture and "confection," or ready-to-wear manufacturing.

> The life of couture, the deep interest it represents for the whole sector, lies in creation. This creation takes place at a rhythm such that, both seasonal and continuous, it excludes any possibility of industrialisation. If creation in terms of fashion could exist in the industry, couture would have changed its production habits a long time ago.

This statement was never contested by the garment manufacturers, or evidently by couturiers. After all, wasn't haute couture's principal role to serve as a laboratory for the whole world, since it had regained its international predominance in 1947? Nonetheless, towards the mid 1950s, the very specific structure of the clothing professions in France led to serious dysfunctions. It was a fact that haute couture was running out of steam, and despite this, there were no other sources of creation recognized outside of it. The press was rather tired of it but nonetheless, despite everything, respected the usages and continued to echo its messages, although without great enthusiasm. The situation soon changed as a result of the combined action led by the "conseillères de mode" (fashion consultants) and a few journalists who happily swapped their professions as the opportunities arose. Thus, on the periphery of a traditional information system which was subject to haute couture's authoritarianism, a resistant communication network came into existence. It was more complex than it had been in the past because the apparel manufacturers did not sell their products directly to their public, and had to respect a longer production process.

The press

Two magazines were to have a determining influence on the future of fashion: *Elle* and *Le Jardin des Modes.*

Elle magazine. Before World War II, at the age of 23, Hélène Lazareff joined *Paris Soir* as an apprentice in a section that covered women and children. In 1940 she went to New York, where she really learned her profession under Carmel Snow and Diana Vreeland, respectively, editor-in-chief and fashion director at *Harper's Bazaar.* At the same time, she worked with the *New York Times* magazine, giving her opinion on the headlines, the captions, the choice of photos, editing as much as she wrote, feeding her appetite for journalism. She was an accomplished professional when she created the magazine *Elle* upon her return to Paris in 1945. She felt the need to reach out to her readers and offer them a magazine that corresponded to their different desires and addressed their concerns. She knew how to make events fascinating and how to create interest. One of her colleagues—the most talented one, Françoise Giroud[12]—spoke enthusiastically of her:

> She came back from the States, freed from the constraints of French taste and quality... She liked things that were colourful, lively, gaudy, shocking. She found the idea of choosing a fabric because it was strong or of good quality obscene. Everything was to be thrown away. Bought quickly, worn quickly, thrown away quickly. Today it seems quite natural, but it was extraordinary in the 1940s and 1950s. She was ahead of the times that were coming. ... Sometimes, Hélène Lazareff wasn't very careful with regard to her audience. The magazine's distribution was always restricted by a certain audacity in its tone that was, in a way, an obstacle in the conservative provinces.

Compared to *Marie France* or *Femme d'aujourd'hui* that sold close to two million copies, *Elle's* circulation was limited to about 600,000 copies. Like her husband Pierre Lazareff at the newspaper *France Soir,* who transformed the daily press, she replaced columns with concrete information, exploited the anecdotal and picturesque aspect of facts, and blew up stories by highlighting the stars in vogue, creating them herself if need be. While *Elle* started off as a monthly, Lazareff became convinced that it wasn't the right rhythm. In 1945, she introduced a weekly formula, bought color photographs in New York (ektachromes) that did not yet exist in France for the cover pages, and made her magazine a lively, attractive object, quite distinct from the usual fashion catalogues. She was also interested in the graphics and the layout. She was the first editor to develop exclusive contracts with photographers.

Peter Knapp, who was art director in 1959, created the definitive look of the magazine. After acquiring *Claudine, Elle* had no other direct competitors in its sector, apart, perhaps, from *Jardin des Modes.*

Hélène Lazareff was a cultured woman. Her talent lay in the way she saw things, and even more in the way she understood how others saw things, and then in the way she entrusted them with all her confidence.

After Simone Baron and Alice Chavanne, Annie Rivemale joined the editorial group in 1946, followed by Claude Brouet in 1953 and Nina Dausset in 1959.

journal du textile
Le Petit Echo de la Mode
EXCELSIOR modes
CITY
MAGAZINE INTERNATIONAL
SPECIAL MODE
ADAM
LA REVUE DE L'HOMME
la femme chic
LE MAITRE TAILLEUR
ABENDMODE
EXTRA
Les Succès d'A. G. B
JOYCE
LES MODES
OFFICIEL
Monsieur
Femina
Les Chapeaux Elégants
Printemps
1931
LA MODE
MYLORD
GLAMOUR
ALAIN BASHUNG PAR LES GUIGNOLS
AVANT LA MODE
depeche mode

In 1946 the magazine's contents were divided between haute couture, to which several pages were dedicated, and practical sections, consisting of cooking recipes and fashion patterns. In the beginning of the 1950s *Elle* showed sportswear, inspired by American fashion, which was non-existent in the ready-to-wear world in France. Every week, two seamstresses created these active lifestyle fashions for the magazine. Faithful to her commitments, Hélène Lazareff imposed an *Elle* style that shattered consumer habits. On 18 February 1952, she published a six and a half page article on ready-to-wear with a terribly explicit title: "Would you like to find your dresses ready-made? A study and investigation." Brigitte Bardot, then an unknown adolescent, posed for this historical editorial. In their issue dated 20 February 1952, *Les Cahiers de l'Industrie du vêtement féminin* voiced their satisfaction:

> This week the press talked about women's ready-to-wear. When one knows that this magazine publishes 600,000 copies, and it is read by over a million and a half women, one can imagine that women will be talking about what we do in the days to come.

It is almost impossible to imagine today the joy this article provoked in the world of French fashion.

Claude Brouet, a young editor who had just spent three years with *Ponchon Editions,*[13] was put in charge of this new section dedicated to ready-to-wear. After her mother Madame Gilberte, couture manager with Schiaparelli then Fath, had introduced her to Hélène Lazareff in 1953, she started her job with an article dedicated to ready-to-wear, and more specifically the "Trois Hirondelles." The models displayed alarm clocks based on the theme "It's ready, it's right now."

At first, Brouet [14] was responsible for producing a ready-to-wear issue each season. But during the 1960s she dedicated almost 52 issues a year to this subject.

Once, when she came out of a Prisunic show held at the Theatre en Rond, Claude Brouet was surprised by what a model was wearing: a skirt worn very low on the hips, a shirt, and a waistcoat.

"Where does the outfit you are wearing come from, Miss?"

Emmanuelle Khanh replied:

"It's one of my creations."

"Come to the magazine tomorrow, we'll make a pattern of it."[15]

At the same time Maïmé Arnodin, editor-in-chief of *Jardin des Modes,* made Gérard Pipart, who had returned from Algeria, a regular contributor.

The two competing magazines no longer contented themselves with presenting fashion or criticizing it. They were the new deciders of fashion and made exclusive fashions in their own workshops. These "trendy" pieces were quickly snapped up by leading retailers like Jean d'Allens, the farsighted purchasing director at Galeries Lafayette, and Fred Salem, the founder of Marie-Martine. This situation implied new sales practices, better adapted to the nature of the products and their target clientele. Annie Rivemale remembers how surprised she was when, during a 1955 trip to the United States, she discovered the bridges that had been built between fashion magazines like *Glamour* and *Mademoiselle*, and shops like Bloomingdales, to ensure the promotion of select fashion items. She suggested that Hélène Lazareff could perhaps create similar relationships with stores in France. The *Elle* style was born first in Galeries Lafayette, and later in Printemps.

The two teams set to work choosing the different types of clothing–overcoats, dresses, sports clothes, knitwear—that would later be accessorized in the *Elle* style and photographed in an *Elle* setting. Twice a year, before the magazine came out, the windows of the two department stores faithfully reproduced the pages of the magazine. On Denise Fayolle's initiative, Prisunic started a similar adventure in 1956, thus widening the field for the development of ready-to-wear.

Shifting between couture and ready-to-wear was in itself a great innovation; handling the sale of mass-market products was a total revolution. Twice a year, *Elle* published eight pages on Prisunic: four were paid for by advertising, the four others were part of the editorial content. Denise Fayolle chose the items in the story. As soon as the magazine came out, the Prisunic stores on rue de Provence, Saint-Augustin, and Passy were raided. At lightning speed, the 2,000 units produced per model were sold out. The number of pieces produced was hardly enough given the clientele's demand and the effect of the promotion. Despite this success, the provincial subsidiaries of Prisunic were sceptical. To encourage the stores to stock the articles chosen by the magazine and protect themselves from complaints from readers who were disappointed not to be able to find the object of their desires, *Elle* developed a new label: heart-embellished *Elle* signboards and hearts for the windows of participating retailers.

In 1959, when Nina Dausset left her job as press attaché with Lempereur to assist Claude Brouet, ready-to-wear had already changed its features as well as its philosophy. Chloé, Germaine, and Jane had given in to the seduction of luxury; C. Mendès

Pierre Lazareff and his wife Hélène Gordon-Lazareff.
On the right, Françoise Giroud, chief editor at *Elle* and future minister for culture, 1954. Photo Agence Roger Viollet.

Hélène Lazareff and Robert Ricci during the Couturama at Maxim's, 1968. Photo Agence Roger Viollet.

In 1968, Hélène Lazareff thought up the Couturama for *Elle*, 12 super Magic Coupons, signed by six grands couturiers: Cardin, Courrèges, Venet, Ricci, Ungaro, Saint Laurent.
The adventure began on 14 March 1968 and continued until the issue dated 14 September 1970. Photo Agence Roger Viollet.

manufactured the couturiers' ready-to-wear; and as for Galeries Lafayette and Prisunic, they were already flirting with a much wider clientele. This did not stop Claude Brouet and Nina Dausset's creativity. This memorable duo of agitators was nicknamed Robespierre and Saint Just. They ardently launched new colors, worked as designers themselves, and prepared a pink and black issue that took the market by surprise.

It was an incredible time for an independent press where editors showed fashion they liked, and created it if it didn't already exist. Yves Saint Laurent and Courrèges were not born yet and the two annual issues reserved for couture were no longer very popular: nonetheless, *Elle* continued to give Chanel and its "darling" Pierre Cardin the lion's share of coverage.

Robespierre and Saint Just managed to create doubt among the citizens; subversion was the tone of the time, the rallying call became a mixture of genres, as was clear from the "Magic Coupon." *Elle's* latest section, born with a Pyrex dish, was edited by Paule Evangélista. Mainly, it was about giving the *Elle* readership a really competitive price on the selected item featured on the coupon. From issue number 1,160, of 14 March 1968, to number 1,291, of 14 September 1970,[16] the adventure culminated in the Couturama—12 super Magic Coupons at a magical price, signed by 6 grands couturiers (Cardin, Courrèges, Ricci, Saint Laurent, Ungaro, and Venet), sparked off a passion. Haute couture was going astray.

The event was celebrated at Maxim's and had the support of the important couturiers as well as attracting new couturiers like Jacques Delahaye for Jacques Heim, and Jules-François Crahay for Lanvin or Cerruti. Chanel was the only one who refused to participate in this "working class party." The obstinate Hélène Lazareff was amused, for the time being.

One day in 1968, she called me at C. Mendès, where I was general manager[17] at the time, and suggested we have lunch the following day.

"I'm busy."

"Cancel, we're having lunch with Coco."

"I accept."

She had maliciously decided she would wangle a Magic Coupon out of Coco Chanel.

I reached the Ritz at 12:30. Chanel's manager, Lilou Grumbach, ran through the usual recommendations: "Don't shake her hand too hard...and never talk to her about Pierre Cardin..."

Made up, wearing a hat, amazingly youthful, and animated by a strange good humor, Miss Chanel talked non-stop from 12:30 to 5:00 PM. Firmly or gently, Hélène Lazareff tried several times to slow down the flood of words, in vain. Miss Chanel knew why we had come and did not want to be disobliging, so she did not allow Lazareff to ask the sacrilegious question. Was this gesture the exemplary expression of a perfect education? Finally Madame Chanel left, and half leaning over the railing, shouted to me: "Young man, we will teach you a lot." Mysterious.

Jardin des Modes. In 1952 Lucien Vogel put a student from the Ecole Centrale, Maïmé Arnodin—who followed the strictest conventions of elegance of the time by wearing Balenciaga—in charge of the *Jardin des Modes* ready-to-wear section. This was an editorial specialty that was expected to have a good future. In order for her to learn about this new profession, Lucien Vogel sent her to British *Vogue* for an internship. She learned quickly, instantly understood the strategic importance of her situation at *Jardin des Modes,* and decided she would not remain a hostage to the establishment. The column was insipid at the time and she devoted a rare energy to transforming it. Gérard Pipart, who was with the French army in Algeria, sent her sketches drawn on his movement orders. She published the renderings after having given them to manufacturers. Under Marie-France de La Villehuchet's direction, the February 1955 issue in which Maïmé Arnodin had an active role announced a surprise: "In this issue, several pages are dedicated to the spring ready-to-wear collections. It is not a new concept, but it's news on an important event in the fashion world that we will henceforth provide to our readers in February and August." As an introduction and to give this new column the weight it deserved, they needed Christian Dior's approval. His recommendations were reproduced immediately by *Les Cahiers de l'industrie du vêtement feminin:*

> . . . We hope that the distribution circuits the apparel makers now have access to will make haute couture adaptations easily and rapidly accessible to everyone, and we hope that thanks to the progress that has been made, the woman in the street will take renewed pleasure in dressing up, because, so often, she makes do with just wearing clothes, and now she will be able to preserve France's reputation for elegance.

The cover showed a Wébé suit, in gentian blue Shetland, with a long fitted jacket (32,000 francs at C. Mirel, about 514 euros), the back cover was a straight Marie Chasseng coat, in red woolen muslin, by Moreau (23,000 francs at Aurore, about 370 euros).[18]

Covers of *Vogue* magazine designed by Georges Lepape, c. 1920. Rights Reserved. Trois Quartiers catalogue c. 1930.

Jardin des Modes February 1955, with a ready-to-wear model on the cover. It was a first. Manufacturer Wébé. © IMEC.

Studio photo session. Carmel Snow, chief editor of *Harper's Bazaar*, preparing a model wearing a Balenciaga suit for the photographer Louise Dahl-Wolfe, c. 1950. © Eyedea/Photo Robert Doisneau.

Finally in August 1956, *Vogue* brought out a special ready-to-wear issue. The cover showed a dress by Lempereur. Marion de Brunhoff, daughter of Michel de Brunhoff, the editor-in-chief, remembers the intense excitement that gripped the editorial staff when the decision was taken. Promoting ready-to-wear in this manner was to sanctify it—and risk being attacked for high treason against couture. Things had reached this point!

It was at the end of the 1950s that ready-to-wear really conquered its own place.

In 1968, the two magazines that set the tone were too far ahead of the market. While their readers followed them blindly, the garment manufacturers, and hence retailers, did not. It was at this time that darkness began to set in. *Elle* became the subject of all kinds of criticisms. Consumers manifested their frustration through an abundance of letters. The manufacturers argued that the magazine was supporting companies that did not produce their designs, and retailers, as usual, complained that they had finished their purchasing before they had received the information from the magazine. At a professional seminar in Brussels, Claude Brouet was harshly attacked. Jean-Claude Weill accused her of promoting products that did not correspond to the reality of the market, and of forgetting those that sold—in particular, the products being advertised when ads were, after all, the magazine's lifeline. A young stringer with *Points de vente,* Ginette Sainderichin, spoke next. "Your profession," she said, in substance to Jean-Claude Weill, "is to make your products, to sell them, and to ensure that they are worn by consumers. *Elle's* profession is to sell its magazine well, so that you want to advertise in it. Each of us has their own role."

Hélène Lazareff was listening from the back of the hall.

A few months had passed since this stormy meeting when Patrick de Genlis and Henri de Legge de Kerlean, the owners of *Points de vente* (*Intelligent Business* magazine), contacted Pierre and Hélène Lazareff to propose a project for a trade magazine that would specialize in fashion and textiles. Its contents would provide retailers with information regarding the choices of different fashion magazines, before the professional salons, in order to encourage the manufacturers to produce the models selected by the press. The Lazareffs were immediately seduced by the project that provided an answer to some of their own concerns. Hélène Lazareff clearly showed her enthusiasm, but on the sole condition that it was managed by Ginette Sainderichin.

GAP (Groupe Avant-Première) came into existence in 1969, bringing together *Elle, Le Jardin des Modes,* and *Mademoiselle Age Tendre.*

Each magazine shared its suggestions with GAP, which borrowed models from the manufacturers. In the *Elle* Club offices, the editors of different magazines came together to attend a fashion show featuring 350 models, of which only 50 were selected. Then Claude Brouet for *Elle* and Catherine Lardeur for *Le Jardin des Modes* classified the selected models in order to identify the main trends of the coming season. All the selected garments were finally drawn with infinite precision.

Soon, they had to make a post-show selection to include the designers who showed their collections outside of the calendar and were not yet ready. Today, that would correspond to the designers issue, and it forced GAP to become a quarterly.

The textile and clothing industrialists and retailers could be proud to have their own fashion information tool. The *Journal du Textile,* GAP's precursor, dealt mainly with economic issues at the time. The professional fashion press established itself in France in response to the model imposed in the United States by *Women's Wear Daily.*

Conseillères de mode

In the 1950s, on their return from the United States, Max Heilbronn and Raoul Meyer were amazed that no elegant French women bought clothes from department stores.

Why not try an experiment in France, and hire a "fashion director" with the task of offering refined fashion for clients of all ages, just like the department stores did in the United States?

In 1952, Max Heilbronn set off in search of a lady from the Parisian jet set that, if possible, had never worked. The perfect "jockey,"[19] Princess Ghislaine de Polignac, niece of Countess Marie-Blanche, of the same name, guardian of the Lanvin house, had all the desired qualities for the job. Distinguished, spiritual, audacious, the grand couturiers fought over her because not an evening passed where she did not triumph, and was constantly quoted in the social columns. Historically, she was France's first fashion stylist, although the word to designate what was such a non-specific occupation at the time only came into existence around 1960.[20]

Ghislaine de Polignac's role consisted of seeing all the ready-to-wear and haute couture collections in order to reveal what, through her choices, would become Galeries Lafayette's selection. Her job was to find a balance between fashion that suited the department store—a subtle blend of boldness and good taste that regular clients would enjoy—while achieving her own goal, which was to attract other generations of consumers to the store. For the moment, however, it was not the right time for her to innovate, if innovation meant questioning sacrosanct haute couture. Nonetheless, it was a period of democratization in fashion as in decoration, a field in which Yvonne de Bremond d'Ars excelled, while Richard Avedon, the American photographer, chose markets and cafés as the backdrops for his photos.

Language was evolving. Used with parsimony, working class vocabulary, even slang, provided a touch of exoticism that suited the very snobbish "Marie-Chantal." She was a character invented in the late 1950s by Jacques Chazot, a dancer and socialite, who penned *Les Carnets de Marie-Chantal.* This character represented the archetype of the young snobbish socialite, and it was a great hit in the posh areas. Ghislaine de Polignac followed her instinct and set to work. She divested clothes of their superfluous ornamentation and decreed, as was her right, that real chic was the simple black jersey sheath dress. She drove both buyers and sellers crazy. Jean d'Allens was the only person who stood firmly by her side. Little by little, pretty, simple outfits, which the princess wore with ballet slippers "to go to work," appeared, becoming all the rage in what is commonly called high society. Unexpectedly meeting her on the Faubourg-Saint-Honoré, the Duchess of Windsor asked the Princess: "Ghislaine, do not tell me your coat comes from Les Galeries Lafayette. . . .— But of course Your Highness!" and she immediately ordered two coats, one pink and the other one blue.

For the Sentier apparel manufacturing industry, this social amusement was a blessing, as the press commented enthusiastically on the event. Given the success of the "chic and inexpensive" operation, the designer service grew. In 1956, Max Heilbronn asked Chloé Huysmans, who became Chloé de Bruneton, to carry out a study on Swedish design in order to assist Ghislaine de Polignac with junior fashion.

Printemps came on board the "fashion train" slightly later, so they had to work even harder. In 1958 Jacqueline Bénard, editor of *Femina* since 1953, left her previous job with *Elle* and became the head of the Printemps style office.[21] For eight years—before she became editor-in-chief of *Marie Claire* in 1966—she

The Duchess of Windsor and Princess Ghislaine de Polignac at the Bal d'Hiver. 1958. Photo André Ostier.

patiently shared her passion with the apparel makers.[22] Under her management, designers were given a special status: they no longer had to clock in. Creation was becoming a plus.

Robert Schoettl, purchasing manager of Printemps before he went on to become general manger of the store in 1970, innovated in every area: gold jewelry sold by weight made the specialists complain; fruit-shaped soaps, sold loose in bins; saw record sales, to the disgust of the perfumers; and Iranian carpets at "souk" prices sold by the thousands in a few days. When he was invited to the Canton fair in 1960, Robert Schoettl quite naturally ordered one billion old francs' worth of different kinds of traditional objects. How could they import goods from Communist China? Pierre Laguionie was in despair. Miraculously, in 1961 General de Gaulle recognized China; the goods could be cleared through customs, and the labels could even be left on.

Competition between the two main department stores was severe, and Robert Schoettl was committed to closing the gap. In February 1961, he created Steve McQueen's Ranch, offering matching clothes, bags, and shoes. In July, *Elle*'s title was "Western fashion invades Paris."[23] At the time when Jacqueline Bénard introduced Pierre Cardin to Prince Galitzine—who went on to become the director of the central buying office—Printemps and Galeries Lafayette were equally innovative and dynamic.

A new fact had been confirmed: fashion was no longer the preserve of haute couture. In 1955, when Claude de Coux heard Albert Lempereur talking about the Comité de la mode (the Fashion Committee) on the radio, she decided to come to Paris to meet him. This new concept fascinated her. In 1957 Relations Textiles, Europe's first independent consultancy and style firm, was born. The clients were Rhône-Poulenc, Les 3 Suisses, Valisère, Caroline Rohmer, and La Mode Côte d'Azur. Designers appeared on the front page of newspapers and remained there for about 10 years. Omnipresent, they had a place in every industry, as suggested by a Prisunic advertisement that combined men's and women's clothes, crockery, table arts, or furniture, in a fairly sober one-page layout. Maryse Belaïsch—France's representative on the Dupont de Nemours Color committee, as well as a textile designer for Cacharel—designed bayadere striped paper that she proposed to the Barnier candy company, and in 1968 created the lipstick and nail varnish range for Christian Dior before going on to create the colors for the first beauty products.

Maïmé Arnodin, who had become the high priestess of style, left *Le Jardin des Modes* in 1958 and started her style firm in 1960, after spending nine months as head of Printemps advertising. She looked for and found "rising talent" like Gérard Pipart, Christiane Bailly, Emmanuelle Khanh, as well as Eric Boman, a fabric designer.

She occupied a position at the crossroads of design, textiles, and the manufacturing industry, and her activities spilled over into pure graphics. Her team created graphics for women's clothing and Peter Knapp directed films for her clients. Designers were the kings of the time; she sanctified them by instituting their predominance, justifying vast salaries. The client-supplier relationship evolved in a mood of loyalty, even affection, inspired by the talent itself, often compensated with gifts. As if she was a diva, Léon Cligman gave Arnodin Cartier jewelry as a gift and, even more unusually, a horse for her daughter.

Not far off, Denise Fayolle saw her choices triumph at Prisunic, where she was in charge of the style office, packaging, and advertising. After 14 years of daily struggle, in 1967 she left Prisunic and joined Arnodin in 1968 to found MAFIA (Maïmé Arnodin Fayolle International Associates)—a style, trend, and advertising agency, which had its offices at rue Ravignan in Montmartre.

Stronger together, they declared war on the establishment with the full support of the left-wing press, Katia Kaupp, then Mariella Righini at the *Nouvel Observateur*, and Christiane Collange and Alice Morgaine at *L'Express*.

It was also at this time that the Center for Industrial Creation, run by François Mathey and François Barré, imposed itself, blowing winds of contestation through the Decorative Arts Museum that had a determining effect on the formal language of a certain modernity.

Then it was May 1968. The profession of designer changed along with the whole society. By returning to the established order, the pioneers made certain concessions to the previously inflexible principles of independence that had been extolled until that time. This opened the door to active competition. History, whichfor a moment saw social revolution and aesthetic necessity meet, withdrew, reducing the power of the leaders of opinion. Encouraged by the inexhaustible demands of the market, certain designers started their own advisory services, following Françoise Vincent-Ricard's example. This defector from Relations Textiles had inaugurated Promostyl in 1965.

Chloé de Bruneton created a company that advised Devanlay, Poron-Guitar, Annick Robelin etc., on clothing, as well as advising four weaving companies.

After she left Printemps, Dominique Peclers opened Peclers Paris in 1970. MAFIA was given its first advertising committee: Dupont de Nemours, with Quiana, Dacron, Lycra; and they inaugurated a lasting relationship with Yves Saint Laurent.

International competition had reshaped the textile industry, leading companies towards an individually pro-active attitude and a constant control over all their activities. From 1980 onwards, their businesses expanded to integrate new professions: artistic direction, communications manager, image manager, and product manager. External offices lost some of their omnipotence and had to specialize. Buyers and the professional press again chose the clothing best adapted to their target clientele from an abundance of styles and products, as they had done at the time when couture was diverse and competitive. After having left the department stores to join the apparel manufacturers, designers—along with fashion journalists and advisors—changed the climate of the 1970s when they all had exercised the same profession for 10 years.

Ready-to-Wear Explodes

In 1950, inspired by their visit to New York, Weill and Lempereur were the first to launch their brands, embark on signature advertising campaigns, and distribute point-of-sale ad cards to their distributors. For the first time, these cards featured the company's labels associated with the term "prêt-à-porter," or "ready-to-wear," which was grammatically incorrect but more prestigious than manufactured apparel. It is important to note that up until then, manufacturers attached their retail clients' labels, which came stapled with the order sheet, to the products they made.

This act was revolutionary, to say the least, if one judges by the difficulties Marie-José Lepicard encountered when, on Maïmé Arnodin's request, she wrote a feature for *Le Jardin des Modes* on French apparel manufacturers. Hostile retailers refused to reveal their suppliers. She remembered the time she had spent at American *Vogue* where Bettina Ballard, fashion director, refused to publish any outfit until she was sure that the retailers had them in stock and she had checked the delivery dates with the manufacturers.

"Advertising was good for soaps and drinks," remembers Jean-Claude Weill, who was the first to sign his ready-to-wear clothing, a century after Worth had signed his couture fashions.

This new practice radically transformed the habits that had developed between producers and distributors. Until then only the retailer was known, leaving the hard-working manufacturer in the background. Imperceptibly, however, the cards changed hands. Manufacturers chose their retail clientele, took control of their image, and imposed their conditions, leading to transformations inside their companies that affected the areas of creation, sales, and production.

The clothing that was now shown and produced under their company brands had to break free of the trends haute couture imposed. Constant control and oversight by the collection design was the first priority.

As they gained confidence, brands imposed new ways of doing business. In the provinces, multi-brand sales representatives became exclusive sales reps for one brand. They were expected to use their local authority to support the imperialist policy of the house that employed them.

Along with the advertising materials that now accompanied deliveries, sales grew. But the vast number of orders submitted left no room for sub-contracting. This led to a reorganization of the profession's archaic production system. Traditions were being lost and the labor force was not being renewed. As society evolved, the sons of tailors had ambitions for other careers. Trade schools for the fashion profession did not exist yet. In addition, retail commerce was becoming more demanding and competition was fierce.

With the changes it brought, the apparel industries' economic geography brought about changes in the profession of designer.

Until 1950, most manufacturers had similar operating structures. They sub-contracted their production, did not impose their brands on labels, and bowed to their clients'—the retailers'—demands. Soon, the economic renewal, combined with the industrial and commercial innovations that followed, brought about differences between the manufacturers, depending on whether they favored industrialization, service, quality, or style.

A report published by the Crédit National in 1971 divided manufacturers into four segments:

Classic: already considerably industrialized, that represented 60 per cent to 65 per cent of the final sales;

Yves Saint Laurent Model, 1967–1968.
Photo Pierre Boulat, courtesy Agence Cosmos.

Luxury ready-to-wear: with 15 per cent of sales that included couturiers ready-to-wear;

Designer: with 15 per cent of sales that had seen a rapid development over the previous five years;

Gadget fashion: that with 5 per cent of sales marked the emergence of a new junior segment of fashion with its production located in Sentier.

Exports represented about 24 per cent of French production. Foreign markets were mainly interested in "creative" articles (luxury and designer ready-to-wear) and accounted for 652 million francs in sales in 1970, an increase of 27.8 per cent compared to 1969. In 1960 French exports were very low, but by 1962 they reached 132 million francs. Exports multiplied five-fold between 1962 and 1970. With a turnover of 170 million francs, the German market alone represented over a quarter of French apparel sales abroad. France's trade balance for apparel was very positive: imports only represented 129 million francs against 652 million worth of exports (in constant francs). According to the Crédit national report published in 1971:

> The companies that export are still very few, but their export figures generally represent at least 50 per cent of their global sales. We could say that it is generally "their name" that they sell abroad, associated with "made in France." Amongst the principal exporters of women's ready-to-wear, we can cite: all the couturiers who have a luxury ready-to-wear department; the luxury ready-to-wear manufacturers like Fouks and Pierre d'Alby; designers like Jean Cacharel and Daniel Hechter.[24]

Unlike the designer businesses, industrial companies, including the biggest firms, exported little: 10 per cent for Weill, 5 per cent for Weinberg.[25]

Weill, Weinberg. For a large number of manufacturers, industrialization represented the only way for their companies to survive. Weill and Weinberg were in this situation. Both gentlemen had been presidents of the Fédération des industries du vetêment féminin, and they transformed their former family sales businesses into industrial companies. The establishment of factories and workshops in the provinces preceded the acquisition of factories in countries further away by about 20 years. The high cost of land and salary levels in the Paris area slowed company growth. This led to vast decentralization that was encouraged by government aid and facilitated by municipal authorities. When Weill inaugurated his first factory in Lens in 1957, he had 200 people working for him in Paris. The second factory opened 10 years later in Provins. In 1962, it was Sammy and Maurice Weinberg who decided to build a factory in Bourges. They worked with a self-taught technician, Jean-Claude Zarad, to manage the project.

To optimize their performance, certain companies industrialized while others tried to "move up in quality" by attempting to copy couture.

After World War II, a semi-traditional production emerged which resulted in better quality clothing than traditional manufacturing.

In the main towns, specialized fashion boutiques appeared where one could buy clothes that cost less than those from a seamstress and the stores were equipped with an alteration workshop. The development of this system encouraged the growth of a group called "les maisons de couture en gros," which brought together wholesale couture houses that were regulated by the decision of 18 March 1943. A jury made up of 10 personalities selected these high-quality manufacturing houses that did not belong to the women's garment industry, but were authorities "in the area of the art of women's clothing or who belonged to the art world." The aim of this competition was to encourage the largest number of companies to improve the quality of their goods and to support the emergence of luxury ready-to-wear houses like those that existed in New York or Berlin.

The number of companies qualified as "wholesale couture" was fixed at a maximum of 50 in 1943. Between 1947 and 1949, 45 houses were given authorizations and, in 1955, Albert Lempereur was elected president. The growth of his house followed that of wholesale couture and its members.

Lempereur. It was not by chance that in their *Histoire de la Mode au XXè Siècle* Yvonne Deslandres and Florence Müller mentioned Albert Lempereur as the only manufacturer amongst the couturiers and creators to have marked the century.

Lempereur was born in 1902. After a three-year apprenticeship with his wife's uncle, who was a children's clothing manufacturer on rue des Petits-Carreaux, Lempereur set up his own company at the age of 27 at 87 rue

Réaumur. He looked after the clients while the administration was managed by his young wife, a graduate from the école normale des institutrices (Teachers Training School) in Saulieu.

From the outset, the company was very successful with its clothing for children aged one to six. Lempereur then opened a department for girls aged six to twelve. He was mainly concerned with creating original designs and his business began to take shape. In order to better manage purchasing and production, he employed representatives. After World War II, a department for 14–17 year-olds was opened, and the company set up new offices across the street at 100 rue Réaumur, in the offices that later became those of *France-Soir*. In 1948, on his return from his visit to the United States, he was convinced of the need to promote his label through advertising, and he spoke to Marcel Bleustein-Blanchet:

"I want to launch my own brand. What do you think of the name L'Aiglon?"

"What is your name, Sir?"

"Lempereur."

"Do you think if I had a name like yours I would have called my company Publicis?"

Lempereur concentrated his activity on the "Young Girls" collection. He opened the Virginie boutique on rue du Faubourg-Saint-Honoré that became the place for the chic bourgeoisie to shop: "Lempereur dresses young girls well."

To better respond to the acceleration in growth, he created four new departments—junior dresses and loose clothing, junior suits, young women's dresses and loose clothing, and young women's suits. A different modelist managed each department. The head office was transferred to the second floor of 5 rue Royale, Molyneux's old offices, above Jacques Griffe. In 1955, Lempereur took the unusual initiative of entrusting his image and public relations to the de Neuville agency. Nina Dausset (future collaborator with the magazine *Elle*) was his account director until 1957, when Albert Lempereur asked her to join his team at rue Royale, where she was communications manager. In this role she also participated, along with the designer Philippe Bodinat, in developing the collection and its accessories as well as its presentation.

Albert Lempereur was convinced that the future lay in ready-to-wear but to excel in this field, he knew he had to apply haute couture norms. What was couture, he wondered? A personality, a label, an image, fame acquired through the press, a perfume…? He unsuccessfully set out to look for a perfume partner.

Lempereur was inflexible and difficult to understand despite his extravagance and his oratory skills. He incarnated the boss by divine right in his company as well as at union events where he appeared as a speaker. After he had been president of the Chambre syndicale de Paris, the Fédération française du vêtement feminine, and the Union européenne des industries de l'habillement (European Union for Apparel Industries); after his retirement; and until his death in 1991, he remained an honorary member of the Paris Federation and participated in all their meetings.

While the move to the rue Royale offices contributed to supporting the house's couture image, it considerably increased overhead particularly because every season Albert Lempereur treated clients and journalists with magnificence. In the summer, his town house on boulevard de la Saussaye in Neuilly was the site of sumptuous candlelit dinners, with about 500 guests over two evenings. Winter dinners were held in a luxurious Parisian hotel.

Costs were increasing while the growth curve was turning downwards. Maurice and Pierre Lempereur knew that production had to be industrialized, and in 1963 they inaugurated a 500 square meter production unit at Bressuire, in the Deux-Sèvres.

It was, however, already too late. The investment in the factory added to the extremely high costs of rue Royale and upset the company's balance sheet. In 1967, Albert Lempereur signed over his company to a financial group led by Mr. Panhard, the automobile man.[26]

A few other houses honored La Couture en Gros, the wholesale couture group: Germaine et Jane, managed by Mr. and Mrs. Deville, Gérard Pipart's first clients; Basta, designed by Graziella Fontana, famous for her elegant sports coats and Franck & Fils' main supplier; Simone Robin, founded by Cassandre's wife Nadine Charteret, recognized by the whole profession for the excellent quality of her production, and managed by Robert Cahier, future manager of *Vogue*; Wébé, famous for his suits; Roga, managed by Jacques Dransard, the man of the first fashion raincoats; and Kazazian, known for his reversible coats.

Under Albert Lempereur's impetus, wholesale couture represented excellence because of the regulatory statues that it operated under and which were similar to those of haute couture. In fact, the admission requirements that companies had to meet corresponded in numerous ways to those demanded by haute couture. Under the label "Les Trois Hirondelles," the wholesale couture houses took part in promotional trips abroad (for example, to the United States in 1953) and undertook advertising campaigns. In addition, every year they organized group shows at the hotel George V, where each member had to present 12 models in four runway passages. Another privilege, in addition to the aura the affiliation provided, those houses with an authorization to use the label "couture en gros" were entitled to automatic entry, to the extent of the space available, to the "Salon du prêt-à-porter français de luxe," a trade show for French luxury ready-to-wear.[27] Nonetheless, all the guarantees that came with belonging to the Trois Hirondelles group did not suffice for it to maintain its equilibrium and its homogeneity, and it disappeared in 1961. The last shows were already tainted by a certain laxity, as this example shows: the Mac Douglas suitcases arrived late and were hastily placed on the podium, but there were several bundles[28] of fabric for making up the clothes amongst them. The shows stopped, but the competition continued. In 1963, there were only 18 companies left that were authorized to use the label "couture en gros."

Jacques Dransard, the president of Roga, began a new initiative and created the Groupement de Paris du prêt-à-porter de luxe (the Paris Luxury Ready-to-Wear Group) with Lempereur's participation. It was stricter than its predecessor and lasted until 1976.

Luxury ready-to-wear was swept aside by the irresistible ascension of couturiers' ready-to-wear.[29] The article, "Chronicle of an awaited death," is a lucid analysis by Claude Berthod that appeared in *Elle*, on 3 March 1969:

> Originally created as a defensive manoeuvre to discourage copies and to make the dying haute couture trade more profitable, (the lowest point was in 1960), "labelled" ready-to-wear has now adopted an offensive approach. "For the moment, its turnover is still modest," says Bruno du Roselle, delegate for the Fédération du vêtement feminin: "10 billion old francs out of the 200 billion for overall ready-to-wear… but this sum will be multiplied by two, three, four, year after year." The first category under threat are the luxury manufacturers, whose survival today is dependent on exports, and who (apart from houses like Chloé, Sonia Rykiel, Fouks, V de V, Charles Maudret, who have nothing to envy anyone) do not benefit from the irreplaceable laboratory of ideas that a couture house represents, or from a comparable prestige.

From the beginning of the sixties, the Trois Hirondelles found it difficult to defend their position. Fashion consultants who had been previously attached to department stores opened their own style consultancies and sold their advice to manufacturers.

Fashion advisors were veritable external creation cells. They were useful to manufacturers because the latters' highly industrialized structures did not lend themselves to the inclusion of an in-house designer. The fashion consultants were also attractive to more traditional companies, whose personality was sometimes acquired through their sensitivity to designers' talents and openness to market needs.

This is how I.D., Nale Junior, Vaskène, Dejac, Pierre d'Alby, Vager, Innoval, Chloé... would create a metamorphosis in the profession in the space of a few years. Amongst the latter, two highly industrialized groups stood out: I.D., subsidiary of the Belleteste group, and Indreco, presided over by Léon Cligman.

I.D. In 1936 Pierre Belleteste,[30] who had been a schoolteacher, created a large women's fashion factory at square des Plantes in Orléans. In the space of 30 years, in association with his brother and with the help of five nephews and sons, he transformed it into an industrial-sized group. The Laval factory, that specialized in shirt making, opened in 1963; the Lorient factory, dedicated to lingerie, in 1968; the Arques factory, devoted to children's clothing, in 1970; and the one in Rennes, that made women's shirts and trousers, in 1976.

In 1960 Pierre Belleteste acquired the company Isidore Dumail, located at 62 rue du Louvre. The sales division was first managed by Jean-Louis Xémard. In 1963, Jean Dieudonné took over the division's leadership and put Maïmé Arnodin in charge of design. She was more specifically responsible for what today might be called artistic direction. Design was more precisely Gérard Pipart's domain, before it became Emmanuelle Khanh's. Fittings were held every week at square Jasmin, in Maïmé Arnodin's offices. The clientele consisted of the most prestigious boutiques: Laura et Dorothée as well as Vog on rue Tronchet, Perry in Toulouse, Aglaé in Aix-en-Provence, l'Oeil in Caen, and Grenadine and Mandarine in Lyons. The success was immediate and grew from one season to the next, until the non-renewal of a contract with Maïmé Arnodin broke the rhythm. The considerable assets that accompany success—like the good will of the press, dynamics of design, an authority over the clients, privileged information from the textile industry—all slowly evaporated, announcing

I.D.'s decline. In 1973, I.D. was signed over to the Prouvost group, along with 10 per cent of Belleteste's overall capital.

Indreco. In the 1920s Serge Cligman set up the workshop on boulevard Sebastopol where he made little dresses, apron blouses, and "back to school" smocks made from Boussac fabric. In 1932, his clients were stores like Monoprix and Prisunic, and the factory he had recently bought in Issoudun grew. In June 1940, concerned with honoring his debt to Boussac, he went to Chateauroux accompanied by his son Léon with a suitcase full of banknotes. Marcel Boussac's appreciation took the form of his supplying cotton to Indreco after the Liberation.

With his American training, even before he took over the management of the business in 1955, Léon Cligman applied the latest production methods within the company starting in the beginning of the 1950s. Jacques Gueden, the head of Prisunic, introduced him to Denise Fayolle, who defined design in the following terms: perfect harmony between the product, its production, and the market needs. Cligman could only agree. The products his clients put on sale, without the help of saleswomen, had to be as well-designed as they were attractive. Unlike I.D., whose clientele consisted of multi-brand boutiques, Indreco mainly sold its goods to the large central buying offices.

After the creation of MAFIA, the collaboration with Fayolle and then Arnodin continued and never really stopped. It was, Léon Cligman explained, a perfect tandem:

> Every season, Maïmé and Denise proposed the concept and developed it with our commercial services. It was the perfect setting for tension, when one knows that the sales representatives were generally looking in the rear-view mirror while they advanced at high speed in the driving seat. How could one address the problem and manage to reach a perfect balance between the novelties proposed and the pieces our services wanted to preserve, particularly as at the time, ideas most often came from the Anglo-Saxon countries, the United States in particular... Our greatest strength until then had lain in our loyalty to Boussac who provided 80 per cent of our fabric, while MAFIA was encouraging us to use other suppliers... and, a new element was that the press honoured us. *Elle*, for example was full of our products.[31]

In fact, the impact of design at Indreco was unbelievable: 10 million pieces a year were manufactured in the factories of Indre and at Tours.[32] In 1968, Indreco bought Newman and Seligman, and then C. Mendès in 1979.

Unlike I.D. and Indreco, which possessed an industrial structure before taking an interest in design, Vaskène and Pierre d'Alby industrialized thanks to the phenomenon of design.

Vaskène. When Georges Vaskène, of Armenian origin, took over from his father at Viroflay, he had 100 people working from home and 18 in the workshop. In order to minimize the dreaded effects of the dead winter season, he thought of offering the large, expanding department stores a shirt-dress, easily marketable in January during the "white" sales. However, to agree to the price the shops imposed, he was forced to industrialize his production. In 1957, for one million old francs borrowed from a friend, he acquired an old nineteenth-century paper factory with an electricity supply, "La Cotonnerie" at Salbris in Sologne, where he made men's day and night shirts. Owning this factory finally enabled him to offer an easily worn poplin dress at the modest price of 120 francs. Every January 100,000 pieces were sold. In 1961, Salbris employed 400 workers. Vaskène then placed the accent on designers. Maxime de La Falaise, who had become one of the foremost mercenary designers after she left Piguet, was the first to take the newly created position. She was soon joined by Renata, whose studies at the Düsseldorf Art School and some work experience with Peter Knapp at *Elle* magazine led her, in order to survive, to sell sketches to manufacturers; Vaskène was one of them. She became Renata Vaskène. Georges Vaskène was the first to marry design and industry within his company, giving design the priority. Born out of the emergence of the design phenomenon, his company very rapidly stood out due to its collection department.

In 1961 he opened a new department, Pariken, for which Maïmé Arnodin designed the label and the logo and for which Gérard Pipart created the first collection. Jacques Delahaye then Karl Lagerfeld, in collaboration with Renata between 1967 and 1969, succeeded Pipart while he was already working for Chloé. When an American engineer joined the company it underwent a technical transformation. Workers had been paid by the hour; they were now paid by piece. Every article was methodically analyzed, and each of the elements that made up a garment were evaluated in terms of time and cost. Work was fragmented into about 20 operations spread over a dozen workstations.[33] The retail prices were competitive, between 30 and 70 dollars in the retail market in New York. After Mercier (the industrialist from Grasse), Vaskène became the second largest French dress manufacturer in terms of turnover. The over-industrialized company was, however, already in stiff competition with the Sentier. The house shut down in 1971, a year after Georges Vaskène died from a fatal fall from a horse.

Pierre d'Alby. Pierre d'Alby was a contemporary of Georges Vaskène. D'Alby excelled at a category of products of higher quality than his colleague, and was less concerned with industrialization.

D'Alby's real name was Zyga Pianko; he was Polish and escaped from the Warsaw ghetto when he was an adolescent. He found refuge in a Russian camp, where the harsh life of a lumberjack awaited him in the Arkhangelsk lands. He ran away, traveled, and after an epic 30-day train journey he reached Tehran, where his first encounter with commerce consisted of selling cloth remnants in the street. Then the camps took him from Pakistan to Uganda, fortuitously leading him to Paris, where he was in transit for Venezuela. In the French capital, he found shelter with a tailor compatriot in Belleville, and in 1951 a chance meeting brought him into contact with someone who owed his father money. He was given the money he needed to start a small reversible gabardine coat manufacturing business. He baptized it Piantex; words ending in "ex" were very much in fashion. Piantex, a name deemed too "Sentier," no longer suited his ready-to-wear that was becoming increasingly famous. He chose Pierre d'Alby for the simplest of reasons: no name sounded as French as d'Alby.

He loved adventure and taking risks. Starting in 1958, he hired designers whose talent surprised him and whose personalities impressed him. He changed them every three years, unless they left before. The first, Daniel Hechter, gained outstanding success with a severe overcoat in a heavy two-sided wool, followed by a series of military style garments. When Hechter created his own company in 1962, Emmanuelle Khanh replaced him. Then in 1967, it was Michèle Rosier's turn to showcase her talent before being replaced by Jacques Delahaye, who passed the torch to Jean-Charles de Castelbajac. The latter left the position to Agnès B, who collaborated with Pierre d'Alby for eight years until 1976. His success was unquestioned. In the sixties he opened a very trendy shop in Les Halles called La Nacelle, which gave birth to Bernard Carasso's famous Maison bleue. His main competitors at the time were Georges Rech, Vager, Nale Junior, and Daniel Hechter—Vaskène was more "distribution," while Dejac was more "boutique."

In 1992, he sold his house and collaborated with Irena Gregory, a compatriot who, like Christina Bukowska, had worked for him a few years earlier, while continuing to spend time and satisfy his curiosity meeting designers.

Chloé. A designer company, Chloé differed from its competitors thanks to its origins, positioning, and evolution within the profession.

In 1945 its founder, Gaby Aghion, arrived from Egypt where she had studied political sciences. She was dazzled by Paris, a city that remained an inaccessible, often dreamt-of place in her Oriental paradise. As a rich heroine, worthy of the characters from *Disenchanted* by Pierre Loti, she attained her dream with maniacal application. She learned from magazines and accounts of a society that had fascinated her since her childhood. Her days followed an unchanging ritual: daily session with her hairdresser Guillaume, lunch in town, couture collections—two a week—to create her wardrobe every season, tea with the right people, a show, supper... every situation punctuated by a change of clothes.

Very soon, however, she realized that this aristocratic lifestyle was not really her own, and in 1952 she summoned a former workshop manager from Lelong's who had often worked for her. She asked him to execute six models, for which she had drawn very rough sketches and chosen the fabric. She made them up with the help of two workers, then laid the clothes in a small trunk and started proposing them to the brand new couturier boutiques that were beginning to take on ready-to-wear. Fath, Dior, Carven, and Schiaparelli bought them. Gaby Aghion never lost her youthful enthusiasm; she still remembers those "charming clothes... that I could still sketch, as if it were just yesterday." She set up her workshop in a maid's room, independent from her vast apartment, and advertised in the press to recruit home-workers. Amongst those who applied, she took on an ex-operetta singer, the wife of a medical student... "who worked admirably." She needed a corporate name for billing purposes. Quite rightly, her own name did not seem suitable to her, so she telephoned her friend Chloé de Bruneton, whose first name she adored: "Will you let me use it?" Chloé immediately agreed; maybe they both thought this affair would be short lived. It was in fact the beginning of one of the most fascinating manufacturing adventures. The boutiques multiplied. Young girls of the time identified with Françoise Sagan, who published *Bonjour Tristesse,* and Chloé's approach fulfilled the expectations of this sector of the market. Simple, well-made products, "prettily sewn" dresses, and most of all, affordable: 20,000 old francs; that is to say, about 320 euros.

In 1953, she became partners with Jacques Lenoir. They got on perfectly. He managed the company; she created the collection from Rome, where she went to live with her husband in 1956.

The Egyptian economy was transformed when Nasser came to power; the vast fortunes were the most affected, and some were totally ruined. For Gaby Aghion, what had been a whim now became a vital necessity. She had Jacques Lenoir's support and he developed the company methodically and efficiently.

In 1957 Aghion's friends—like Hélène Lazareff or Maïmé Arnodin—convinced of her talent, encouraged and supported her, thus contributing to the recognition she received. Christiane Collange[34] suggested organizing a show. It took the form of a breakfast at Café Flore. "The models entered perfectly naturally (there was no podium) as if they were going to sit down at a table." The collection, however, was put together with bits and pieces, and lacked structure. For this reason, Maïmé Arnodin advised her to take on the services of a talented young man who had just been relieved of his military obligations: Gérard Pipart.

This time the shows were held at Brasserie Lipp, the famous Parisian restaurant in Saint Germain des Près. For five years, Gérard Pipart created 50 per cent of the collections with Gaby Aghion. He was paid a fixed rate and, to survive, he was forced to sell his talent to other companies: Côte d'Azur alongside Claude de Coux; Timwear, with Chloé de Bruneton; I.D. with Maïmé Arnodin; Prisunic with Denise Fayolle, etc. When he moved over to haute couture at Nina Ricci in 1963, he was replaced by three designers: Christiane Bailly, Maxime de La Falaise, and a "very scatterbrained" young American whose name Gaby Aghion has forgotten.[35]

As collection manager, Gaby Aghion had to coordinate the designs. The same year, Maxime de La Falaise created the miracle: a navy blue dress with a tie that perfectly incarnated the "Chloé" style and remained an unquestioned commercial success for three years. At the time, designers jumped from house to house. Christiane Bailly joined Nale; she was replaced by Tan Giudicelli and Michèle Rosier. Tan Giudicelli signed a contract with Mic Mac; Graziella Fontana joined Chloé, followed by Karl Lagerfeld.

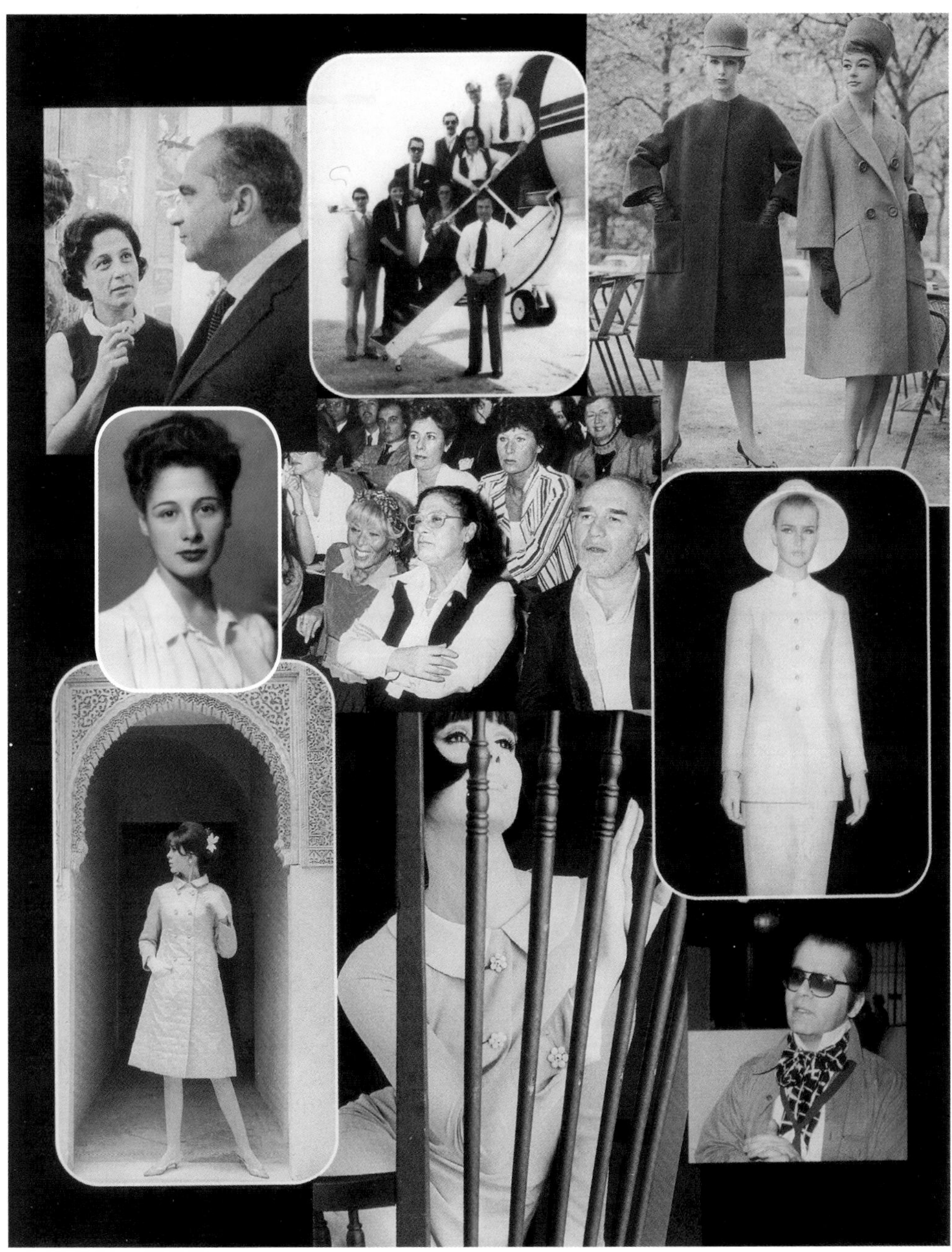

On the left, Gaby Aghion, founder of Chloé in 1952, and her associate Jacques Lenoir.
Medallion: Gaby Aghion, who was from Egypt, on her arrival in Paris. Bottom right: Karl Lagerfeld.

In order to be effective, however, this profusion of styles and ideas needed to be channeled in to bring out a style specific to each house. After having shared the 150 models in the collection with Graziella Fontana, Karl Lagerfeld remained the sole master on board with Gaby Aghion. As a result of their great talent, the Quatre Septembre wool manufacturers and the Lyon or Italian silk manufacturers offered them exclusive patterns in exchange for new ideas, the same terms the weavers practiced with the haute couture houses.

From one collection to the next Karl Lagerfeld, a protean creator, developed stunning creativity and knowledge, which raised the house to the ranks of the greatest. Each collection was an event enthusiastically welcomed by the press; the only one to resist this movement was Yves Saint Laurent.

In addition, the distribution policy introduced by Jacques Lenoir brought Chloé closer to the couture houses like Yves Saint Laurent, with Saint Laurent Rive Gauche; he practiced a selective distribution and kept a close watch over the production quality. Chloé retained its flexibility because the company used sub-contractors and was thus unhindered by any industrial tools, unlike designer industrialists who had built their own factories in the 1960s.

The 1970s were marked by the disappearance of the designer industrialists and the emergence of the créateurs de mode. Some, however, created their own houses, taking their revenge on previous employers who had long opposed their names being recognized.

Finally, the only ones who resisted the storm were the very well managed industrial companies like Weill, who generally maintained a certain reserve, tinged with curiosity, towards style creators. Although their exports were low, they managed to maintain a regular growth.

While the style industrialists and Les Trois Hirondelles were disappearing, new divisions took place. It was no longer the technical aspects of the goods that divided the companies since these were all well controlled; the heart of the matter now was the purpose of the products placed on the market. On the one hand was a group of companies that would adapt to the new trends. These were represented by the very respectable industrial manufacturers and reinforced by a large number of Sentier houses known for their incomparable aptitude to seize upon shifts in fashion. The latter, following the example of Naf Naf, Kookaï, or Chevignon, slowly became more powerful by developing their own concepts. On the other hand, also grouped together, were the labels whose only aim was to cultivate their identity, and who followed other codes. In 1973, Pierre Bergé united them—in a climate that was unfavorable to any kind of calm—in order to create the Chambre syndicale du prêt-à-porter des couturiers et des créateurs de mode.

Notes

1. Yvonne Deslandres, *Le Costume image de l'homme,* Paris, Albin Michel, 1976. Bruno du Roselle, *La Mode,* Paris, Imprimerie nationale, 1980.
2. La Belle Jardinière in 1824, Les Trois Quartiers in 1829, Le Bon Marché in 1852, Printemps in 1865, Galeries Lafayette in 1899.
3. The Chambre syndicale de la confection en gros pour dames et fillettes (Union for the Mass Manufacturing Industry for Women and Young Girls) became the Chambre syndicale de la confection et de la couture en gros (Union for Manufacturing and Wholesale Couture) in 1929.
4. Interview with Max Heilbronn, Guillaume Garnier, *Pars-Couture années 30, op. cit.*
5. In 1930, les Nouvelles Galeries open Uniprix rue du Commerce and avenue d'Orléans. At Christmas 1931, Le Printemps creates Prisunic Caumartin and in January 1932, Les Galeries Lafayette launch Monoprix rue Fontaine.
6. The company Seligmann & Cie is a perfect example of this. This men's and women's shirt and lingerie manufacturing company was founded at Vaucouleurs in 1885. In 1925 they built the building, 35 rue du Louvre, which is on the corner of rue du Louvre and rue d'Aboukir, in Paris for their sales services. In 1930, they controlled 80 per cent of their supply sources. In 1938, they employed 8,000 workers, had a turnover of 120 million francs, and produced 800,000 of dozens of articles in the shirt and lingerie sector. Indreco archives.
7. Monograph on *La Confection féminine,* Centre d'information interprofessionnel, 1944.
8. Interview with Max Heilbronn, Théophile Bader's son-in-law who'll become president of the Galeries Lafayette.
9. The company belonged to the father of the ex-minister Jean-Pierre Soisson.
10. Marie-France Pochna, *Boussac,* Paris, Laffont, 1981.
11. Maurice Warnery, president of the Association des maisons de couture en gros (Association of Wholesale Couture Houses), statement regarding exports, Lyons congress, 18 April 1947. Term "Prêt-à-Porter" in italics, in the summary, *Les Cahiers des industries du vêtement féminin.*
12. Interview with Françoise Giroud, chief editor at *Elle* from 1945 till 1953; later French minister of culture.
13. *Silhouette,* a high quality magazine; *Couture,* which targeted women who had their dresses made up by seamstresses; *Vive la mode,* which Claude Brouet was specifically responsible for, focused on fashion sketches, recipes, and decoration.
14. Claude Brouet, fashion and beauty editor with *Marie-Claire* since 1971, joined Hermès as women's fashion director in 1988.
15. Christiane Bailly and Emmanuelle Khanh regularly provided models for *Elle*'s mini-workshop.
16. The end corresponds to the closing down of the Vaskène factory that manufactured their lines as Salbris; the garments were sold in the *Elle* boutique at 127 avenue des Champs-Elysées.
17. In 1968 C. Mendès manufactured ready-to-wear collections for 12 grands couturiers.
18. A haute couture dress at the time cost about 100,000 old francs. High quality ready-to-wear was thus a quarter of the price.
19. Jockey: an elegant lady, if possible a titled one, who knew how to promote and publicize a house's models. Two famous jockeys were Catherine Deneuve for Saint Laurent and Inès de La Fressange for Chanel.
20. "It is difficult to describe the profession of stylist, quite distinct from that of pattern maker and modelist who translates a sketch into a life size mock-up and creates the pattern for it. The term 'stylist,' today replaced by 'designer' does not only describe someone who creates a garment, but someone who invents shapes that can be used in all the domains that come under the general term of decorative arts, and in all areas of practical life." Yvonne Deslandres, *Le Costume image de l'homme, op. cit.* p. 263.

21. At the same time, Colette Gueden, sister of Jacques Gueden (owner of Prisunic) managed the Primavera table arts section. Jacqueline Bénard hired Primrose Bordier, a defector from Boussac, for the household department. In 1959, with the help of Dominique Bohan, Marc Bohan's wife Jacqueline Bénard created a model workshop, managed by Simone Marbrier; it consisted of 10 mock up people and graduated pattern makers. Five small external, semi-exclusive manufacturers executed the orders taken by affiliates. In May 1968, a strike led to the closure of the workshops. Manufacturing was shifted to India. This was the beginning of outsourced production.

22. She was replaced at Printemps by Micheline Fried, who was in turn replaced by Dominique Peclers before the latter went on to open a style consultancy office in 1979.

23. It was only much later, in the eighties, that concept fashion retailers like Chevignon or Banana Republic appeared.

24. In 1970, Jean Cacharel's export figures were between 30 and 40 million francs and would have represented 60 per cent of his global turnover (source: *Moniteur du commerce international*). At Daniel Hechter it represented 80 per cent of the sales volume (Credit National note).

25. This state of affairs was the same in 1990, where couturiers' and creators' ready-to-wear represented over 70 per cent of exports to the United States and Japan, while the "Caumartin Club" that assembled the most industrialized French manufacturers remained ineffective on international markets.

26. Lempereur's son Pierre remained with the company for two years; he then accepted a managerial job with Guy Laroche, where he remained until he retired.

27. The latter was organized by the Federation at the same time as the international women's ready-to-wear salon that had begun in 1957. Seventeen manufacturers set up their stands in the context of the Association de l'amicale de la confection (Friends of Manufacturers Association) in what used to be the teatime dance hall, an annex of the Ambassadors Theater, currently the Espace Cardin. From then on, every November from 1957 to 1962, the exhibition took place once a year, in buildings belonging to what used to be the Réaumur department store. It was in 1963 that Bruno du Roselle, newly appointed general delegate to the Women's Garment Federation, shifted the event to Porte de Versailles.

28. Cf. note 53 p. 106

29. On the evening of 14 November, the following houses held a group fashion show in the hotel Crillon salons: Algo, Casalino, Chloé, Fouks, Germaine et Jane, Lempereur, Mac Douglas, Peroche, Roga, and Wébé. On 4 October 1961, in Wébé's introduction to its constituent General Assembly under the presidency of Mr. Louis Wolf (Mr. Harry Algo and Mr. Armand Fouks were designated as scrutineers), it was indicated that the new members had the intention of creating an organization whose international reputation would be similar to that of haute couture. "French haute couture has acquired an unequalled reputation throughout the world. It is a source of employment and it brings in large sums of foreign exchange." During the last General Assembly, held on 20 February 1976, there were only three members of the Groupement de Paris (the Paris Group) left: Mr. Weissenstein, manager of the public company Jeannette; Mr. Harry Algo, manager of the Private Limited company, Algo; and Mr. Jacques Dransard, president and general manager of the public company Roga. The organization thus decided to dissolve itself.

30. Future honorary president of the Fédération nationale des industries de lingerie (National Federation of Lingerie Industries).

31. Interview with Léon Cligman.

32. In 1950, Indreco had 1,000 employees, and in 1990, they had 3,000 with a production that was three to four times higher.

33. In 1967, Pariken opened a showroom in New York. *Women's Wear Daily*, of 18 October 1967, titled: "French ready-to-wear crosses the seas." Pariken, the second largest French ready-to-wear house, inaugurated their New York office, its eighth in the world (Renata Vaskène was the designer), with Jeanne Essig, previously vice president of Majestic Sportswear, who managed the American company. The installation of a Telex machine reduced the problems generally associated with importing. The deliveries were sent by air and the replenishments were guaranteed within 10 days.

34. "Madame Express" at the time—Jean-Jacques, Servan Schreiber's sister.

35. Interview with Gaby Aghion.

LE PRÊT A PORTER
A LA PORTÉE DE TOUTES.
PARTOUT
vous regardez,
vous choisissez,
vous essayez,
vous emportez!
LACKMAN
"CONTACT"
ET VOUS VOILA DE SUITE ÉLÉGANTE A PEU DE FRAIS.

Entreprises autorisées à porter le titre de
"MAISON DE COUTURE EN GROS"
POUR L'ANNÉE 1955

Alayne, 22, rue d'Algérie, Lyon.
Algo, 50, rue de Paradis, Paris.
Arkel, 8, rue de la Michodière, Paris.
Basta, 5, cité Paradis, Paris.
Billet, 20, rue Bachaumont, Paris.
Boss et Fils, 17, rue Richer, Paris.
Cisèle – BVR, 13, rue Bachaumont, Paris.
Drea, 23, boulevard Bonne-Nouvelle, Paris.
Esser, 81, boulevard du Montparnasse, Paris.
François Gil, 1, rue Ambroise-Thomas, Paris.
Gattegno, 115, rue du Faubourg-Poissonnière, Paris.
Geo Boutet, 15, rue Saint-Marc, Paris.
Germaine et Jane, 15, rue Feydeau, Paris.
Guy André, 50, rue de Paradis, Paris.
Hemcey, 4, rue de la Paix, Paris.
Henry Oours, 21, rue Georges-Boisseau, Clichy (Seine).
Jacqueline Monnin, 9, boulevard des Capucines, Paris.
Kazazian, 40, rue des Jeûneurs, Paris.
Laurès, 65, avenue du Président-Wilson, Béziers (Hérault).
Lempereur, 102, rue Réaumur, Paris.
Louise, 40, rue Notre-Dame-des-Victoires, Paris.
Max Meyer, 352, rue Saint-Honoré, Paris.
Max Mozes, 6, rue du Sentier, Paris.
P.A. Ber, 34, rue de Paradis, Paris.
Roga, 6, rue Beaubourg, Paris.
Roger Jean-Claude, 2, rue de la Paix, Paris.
S.E.C – Madeleine Casalino, 12, rue de la Chaussée-d'Antin, Paris.
Toby, 33, rue Vivienne, Paris.
Vêtements Sport, 11, rue des Clercs, Grenoble (Isère).
Warnery, 36, rue Saint-Marc, Paris.
Waser, 32, rue du Sentier, Paris.
Webe, 42, rue du Faubourg-Poissonnière, Paris.

LE PRÊT A PORTER
A LA PORTÉE DE TOUTES
PARTOUT
Invitée ce matin,
Déjà prête pour ce soir,
Tel est le miracle...
CONTACT
LACKMAN
Que vous pouvez aussi réaliser :
Grâce aux spécialistes du prêt-à-porter.
Vous voilà de suite élégante à peu de frais.

Women's Garment Federation advertising campaign, 1954.

Companies permitted to use the title "wholesale couture house" for the year 1955.

Yves Saint-Laurent poses in front of the first Saint Laurent Rive Gauche boutique, rue de Tournon, in 1967.

CHAPTER II
COUTURIERS' READY-TO-WEAR

The Forerunners

At the end of the 1950s haute couture, whose financial results were decreasing season after season, once again saw the limits of its growth. This bitter realization had the effect of stimulating the couturiers who, encouraged by Jacques Heim and his professional association, decided to innovate in a hitherto unexploited field: couturiers' ready-to-wear.

Jacques Heim, who had been elected president of the trade union in 1958, seized the sales opportunity ready-to-wear offered and threw himself into the adventure with extraordinary energy and a true fighting spirit.

However, we must step back once again to properly understand a situation that had tormented couturiers since the 1930s. Their concern can be put quite simply: how could they make a profit from their designs and avoid being copied?

In the 1920s, Madeleine Vionnet was furious at the number of her models that were being copied. She signed an agreement with the Eva Boex workshop, 14 rue Castiglione, permitting them to reproduce her dresses. Voinnet's only condition was that Boex had to sell at least three copies.[1] These measures were an attempt to avoid counterfeit copies and were part of the natural process of selling the existing couture line.

In another context, in 1933 Pierre Laguionie invited Paul Poiret to create a ready-to-wear collection for the Printemps department store. The "Silver Bridge" (illus. p.179) was built for the occasion and allowed Paul Poiret to present the four yearly shows he had committed to under contract for a monthly salary of 20,000 francs at the time.

This was a totally new experience for Poiret, who had hit financial ruin again; his house had closed down permanently in 1930. It was an unexpected opportunity to recreate himself, or quite simply, the opportunity for him to continue to express himself. However, Poiret was fiercely individualistic and very temperamental; his unacceptable demands[2] brought this new experience to a close.

Lucien Lelong's pro-active attitude was much more meaningful. In the 1910s, Lucien Lelong was trained in his parents' small couture house: A.E. Lelong, 18 place de la Madeleine. He took over his family's business, just as his colleagues Jacques Heim, Pierre Gerber, Jacques Worth, Raymond Barbas, and Robert Ricci[3] did with their respective family companies. He was not a creator himself, but he had a fashion sense that allowed him to capably manage the house's collections that he went on to develop brilliantly. In 1919, Lelong had only 20 employees, but by 1926, when he moved the house to a magnificent eighteenth-century town house at 16 avenue Matignon, the company employed 1,200 people. The Paris jet set worshipped the couple he formed with his second wife, Princess Nathalie Paley, the last tsar's niece.

Lelong was never short on ideas. In 1934, he published a brochure entitled *La Robe de l'époque* to cope with the economic crisis haute couture was going through. In this document Lelong clearly expressed his desire to create an autonomous collection whose style and construction was a mix of mechanized manufacturing and couture, "so that women could dress themselves under the price constraints of our times." He wanted to act "against banality, against the false luxury of mass manufacturing..." The limited edition dress was made in Lelong's workshop, avenue Matignon. Specially selected workers—as opposed to the relying on repetitive, mechanical, and lifeless piecework—executed it in the most beautiful fabrics.

In 1936, Ghislaine de Polignac bought her first evening dress from Lelong[4] to celebrate her eighteenth birthday. It was in white satin decorated with brown lace and cost 1,800 francs, or about 975 euros. Her mother considered it very expensive for a young girl who had always bought her clothes from Old England before.

In 1939 two designers replaced Lelong's then-designer Jean Ebel. One came from Piguet, the other from Molyneux: Christian Dior and Pierre Balmain. When they had established their own businesses, both Lucien Lelong's previous assistants started the same process where models from the couture workshops were sold directly to a private clientele.

At Pierre Balmain's, the small collection—60 models in all, consisting of coats, dresses, and suits—was shown every morning at 11:00 AM They were not pre-made and were executed in fabrics that were more classic and less luxurious than those used in haute couture. And clients ordered what they wanted from the collection, just as they did at Lelong's. After two years of existence, it was baptized Pierre Balmain Florilège.

Placed under Mme. Hannetel's management, this was a very high-quality collection. Until the arrival of licenses, its selective international distribution contributed to the label's fame. However, the graduations were approximate and it was a costly collection to produce.

As was the case for Dior's first boutique, the workforce Balmain used was the couture workforce, and they used similar methods on this collection that they used in couture, including in-house alterations, basting, or fittings. Whether it was Eaton's in Canada, Cormerais and Marcel in Nantes, or Courtois Soeurs in Montpellier, those who bought the Florilège line were couture clients and were consequently equipped with an alteration workshop. Nonetheless, this false ready-to-wear suffered from being inappropriate for couture techniques. It lacked precision in the use of materials and the way they were cut. The production workshops were set up at rue François 1er, opposite the parent house. Pierre Balmain was responsible for design, assisted by Erik Mortensen from 1948 onwards, and then by Karl Lagerfeld in 1955.

In most cases, couturiers did not think of opening a department for more reasonably priced clothes since the issue of meeting the demands of a new market was not yet a big concern. There was even less question of following the example set by Lucien Lelong and his two ex-assistants, who developed a homogenous line.

In the same vein as Jacques Heim with his Actualité collection inaugurated on avenue Matignon in 1933, Rochas Frivolités and Jean Dessès Bazaar had more modest ambitions. These two lines were introduced to make the ground floor space profitable by offering accessories and small items to complement the clothes being sold in the main department.

Occasionally, clients no longer agreed to pay the haute couture prices for coats or sports jackets that did not require fittings. Thus, couturiers entrusted the execution of these models to certain artisans or good paper pattern manufacturers, along with the orders. This was how C. Mendès was offered the contract to copy jackets and coats for Jacques Heim and Marcel Rochas starting in 1949.

Manufacturing furtively opened its doors to couture before collaborating brilliantly with it for a historical experiment: "Les Couturiers Associés."

Jean Gaumont-Lanvin and Les Couturiers Associés. Director of Lanvin since 1942, Jean Gaumont-Lanvin in 1945 succeeded Lucien Lelong as president of the Chambre syndicale de la couture, of which Daniel Gorin was the general secretary. He was the son of Jeanne Lanvin's youngest sister, Marie-Louise Lanvin, whose married name was Gaumont. At the time, Lanvin family members held the main management positions in the couture house. It was Jeanne Lanvin's daughter, Marie-Blanche de Polignac, who, on her mothers's death in 1946, inherited the position of president. A lady of the most aristocratic restraint in every detail, even down to the feather pinned to her hats, Marie-Blanche reacted badly to her cousin Jean Gaumont's caustic personality. It was true—his son remembers—that nothing enlivened his days better than a well-placed witticism that always hit the target.

Jean Gaumont-Lanvin was elegant, spiritual, and a socialite but he was also imaginative. His lively and creative mind was constantly busy—after all he chose the name *Arpège* for Lanvin's famous perfume. Although he had been able to win over his aunt with his charm and intelligence, this was not the case for his cousin Marie-Blanche, who did not appreciate his brilliant insolence and was always wary of him. On a whim that can only be explained by his unpredictable nature, he left Lanvin on 10 March 1950, and on 16 March terminated his functions at the Chambre Syndicale. To replace him at Lanvin, Mme. de Polignac chose his right-hand man and friend, Daniel Gorin. Undoubtedly it was the best choice, but it was difficult for Jean Gaumont-Lanvin, who was struck a painful blow by one of the little arrows that was shot back at him. He did not remain inactive for long, and soon he embarked upon an adventure that marked the origin of ready-to-wear licenses and was constantly written about between 1950 and 1953.

In 1950 he created a company, Les Couturiers Associés, at 52 rue de la Boétie, in equal partnership with Marcel Dhorme. Jean Gaumont-Lanvin was a good strategist and possessed a real fashion sense. Marcel Dhorme was a reputed tailor and an excellent technician who was well established on avenue Franklin Roosevelt near the Champs-Elysées roundabout. He had been vice president of the Chambre Syndicale under Lucien Lelong for many years.

It was very simple. Couturiers granted the new company exclusive models that would carry their brand, followed by the "Couturiers Associés" label, and in return would receive royalties. These models could be distributed in the provinces. Jean

Gaumont-Lanvin signed with Jacques Fath, Robert Piguet, Paquin, Carven, and Jean Dessès, who were seduced by the novelty of his proposal. This idea was evidently not all that new. Already, under the Marshall Plan, Daniel Gorin (general secretary of the Chambre Syndicale at the time) already had proposals to build apparel-manufacturing factories in Brittany—a disaster area—where they would manufacture then export clothes carrying the grand couturiers' labels to the United States.

This business idea was perplexing. It was not only a question of affixing his label to stockings and ties, as Dior did, or creating simplified models in his workshops. This time, it was a question of manufacturing couturiers garments in France... Unthinkable! However, it was the same idea that Jean Gaumont-Lanvin was selling as his own, although he had neither the financial means, nor the appropriate training to undertake such an adventure.

"Ministerial crisis in haute couture" ran the headline in the 24 June 1950 issue of *Paris Match*:

> Under the banner of "Couturiers Associés," five high level dressers—Jacques Fath, Jean Dessès, Piguet, Paquin and Carven—are each going to create seven models (dresses, suits, coats) that will be mass produced by garment manufacturers and sold for a price between 15,000 to 30,000 old francs (about 310 to 620 euros). Each model will carry a double label, that of "Couturiers Associés" and that of the creators.[5]

In important provincial towns, the selected dealers were the only ones who could centralize orders. The announcement of the first show was awaited with great nervousness. It took place on 8 August 1950 in the Printemps department store, on the Silver Bridge that had been created for Poiret in 1933. The 35 models were presented to the press in advance, on 18 July, thus preceding the haute couture collections by a few days.

For economic reasons, the offices of Couturiers Associés on rue de la Boétie were shared parsimoniously. There was a showroom, a workshop, and an office for each of the directors. Each couturier created seven mock-ups, made on site. The copies would then be made by sub-contracting manufacturers, the most appreciated of whom were Weill for the coats and Lempereur for the dresses.

At that time, selective distribution did not exist in France, and retailers who received regular visits from sales representatives were not subject to the calendars that are in place today. Provincial couture houses made garments to order; as for the boutiques, they stocked supplier's samples. Jean Gaumont-Lanvin thought this organization had to be shaken up a bit; he organized tours where models presented his collection. The shows or presentations took place in the department stores: Dames de France in Bordeaux, Nouvelles Galeries at Saint Etienne, La Belle Jardinière at Lyon... Jean Gaumont-Lanvin's great idea was to go to the clients, to seduce them, entertain them, just as in Paris. The shows, times, and venues—often casinos, if it was a spa town—were announced in the local press.

The authorized agents, who collected and deposited the payments that were then transmitted to Couturiers Associés, took individual orders. Boutiques were not yet used to keeping advance stocks. The following year, in order to better develop the provincial operation, Les Couturiers Associés chose to organize real fashion shows, paid events that were held in casinos, luxury hotels, or department store's tea rooms. The tour started in Cherbourg and lasted three months. It traveled to 100 towns in France, covering two towns a day. It was an ambitious program and although Jean Gaumont-Lanvin was not put off by the costs, they were disproportionate to the turnover produced (5,000 copies the first season). It was clear that the enterprise was already doomed by the mishaps that were to lead to its downfall. François Gaumont, Jean Gaumont-Lanvin's son, remembers a sumptuous dinner at his father's attended by models and Carven's staff that preceded a spectacular show at Ibis, on a small island at Vésinet.

Although this new concept was fairly successful with the clients in Lille, Alger, Angers, and Oran, this was not true of all the other towns. In fact, the managers of Couturiers Associés rapidly realized that taste differed greatly between the rich clients from Melbourne or Buenos Aires who frequented the salons at rue de la Paix, and those from Cambrai or Brive-la-Gaillarde, whom they were reaching out to. The cost of the clothes was not the main selection criteria. Once they had realized this, they drew up a questionnaire—dealing with the collection calendar and deliveries, the categories of models, the price range—for their dealers. It was the first sophisticated market survey carried out in this field. The answers were very instructive, but it was too late to take advantage of them. One learned, for example, that very exceptionally, a provincial lady was willing to spend 30,000 to 40,000 francs for a "dressy" outfit, but never for daywear, a suit, or a coat. The company desperately lacked capital; individual orders were thus accepted in an attempt to make the workshop profitable. The equal shares of the capital, the lack of precision in the definition of each party's responsibilities, the choice of models, the attribution of expenses: there were so many points of discord with which the company could not cope. Mrs. Carven judged Jean Gaumont-Lanvin's management severely because he had not given the company time to generate its cash flow.

Couturiers Associés' failure in the context of the 1950s was almost inevitable and it was widely commented upon in the couture houses and the press. Within the profession, the experience remained one of the most audacious attempts at development. The principle was simple: allowing a couturier to make a garment in the form of a mock up or a sketch and sign the approval slip without any further intervention, dealing with fashion in the same way as an author with his publisher. The last advertisement for Couturiers Associés appeared in *Vogue* in October 1953; only Marcel Dhorme's name was mentioned as manager.

Jacques Heim and the "Prêt-à-Porter Création." There were an increasing number of new experiments, provoking prodigious inventions among couturiers and certain industrialists. Jacques Heim and Marcel Rochas, who had entrusted C. Mendès with the manufacturing of a few models beginning in 1949, thought the next year that it would be better if C. Mendès also distributed them in the best provincial shops. C. Mendès was taken with the idea, as it could have a positive impact on the reputation of its own collection. The year Couturiers Associés was created, André Lévi, marketing manager of C. Mendès—a modest family business, but with a very good reputation—showed his agents the somewhat limited collections that corresponded to a market that was still in its infancy. For the company, the step C. Mendès took that year was a turning point in terms of its marketing practices, which continued to develop and diversify. While the Rochas' experience was short lived,[6] Jacques Heim, on the other hand, worked tirelessly towards developing ready-to-wear, until he died in 1967. He had an energy and a conviction that motivated him several times to try to modify haute couture practices that were outdated, to say the least, if not inadequate.

Jacques Heim was a tall man, made even taller by a receding hairline. He progressed in the haute couture world with the ease and confidence that comes from a good knowledge of the field. When he was born in 1900, his family's fur business had been in existence for two years. This gave him the sense of always being connected to his activity, as he had grown up in this profession and saw all its contours with innate foresight: anticipating orders, raising questions, and being the first to answer them when the winds of change began to blow. His apparent calm attitude was accentuated by his gently twisted expression, but in reality, he was a man of great determination and driven by an imposing intelligence when dreams were to be made reality.

The Heim house, founded by his father Isidore, was located on rue Laffitte, next to the Lion's antique shop that specialized in eighteenth-century articles. It was here that Jacques Heim met Simone Lion, whom he married in 1926.

In 1930, he created a couture department under his own name that he moved to avenue Matignon in 1936. The most cultured of couturiers, Jacques Heim collected paintings by the masters from 1927 onwards. Picasso, Max Ernst, Gleize, Modigliani, the Delaunays, Arp, Marie Laurencin... all shared his walls. Some of these artists became regular visitors to the house, particularly the Delaunays. Robert made a series of portraits of Simone Heim. As for Sonia, she designed a number of prints for the couture house. His curiosity did not end there. In the thirties, he began to write and he created the *Revue Heim*, published twice a year in collaboration with Marcel Zahar, the art critic. Other couturiers had already published luxurious reviews—there was Poiret's *Rosine*, with Iribe's collaboration—but it was the first time that a review of this kind proposed a real cultural content. Leaving aside the *Gazette du bon ton* by Lucien Vogel in 1912, we can see this as the first real connection between art and fashion. Heim's love for publishing went even further; after the war, he launched *La Gazette Matignon*, which was actually the house's press tool; in 1961 he published *Le Traité des visages* with Julliard, an essay on physiognomy that gained recognition as a reference work as soon as it appeared.

The architect Guévrékian was also a friend of his with whom he built his Neuilly town house in 1927, villa Madrid, along the rue de la Folie-Saint-James. This house, with its radical design, remains one of the jewels of 1930s architecture. Guévrékian organized the gardens in his own way, in a series of terraces, pools, and rectangles of earth where he planted rhododendrons.

A few lines in *La Gerbe* of December 1940 mention that Jacques Heim's house was no longer a Jewish house. Following the wartime rules on Aryanization, Jacques Heim had to relinquish his house to a provisional administrator. The article ended: "Madame Jacques Heim has a very Aryan profile. She is charming, as well."[7] Jacques Heim was under very strict German surveillance. "This shopkeeper works very hard against the occupation army and moves around freely."[8] While trying to return to free France in 1942, hidden in a train's water reservoir, he met Pierre Balmain, who was on his way to see his mother at Aix-les-Bains.[9] All journeys, however, did not go so well. In 1943, while Jacques Heim was trying to cross the Pyrénées in the night on the advice of a resistance leader in Lyon, he was arrested and was only saved *in extremis* from the concentration camps by the concern of a few illustrious Spanish clients who interceded in his favor. His following journeys were professional: to South America in 1956, where he opened a haute couture salon under the label JH in Rio de Janeiro; it occupied a floor of the Mesbla department store. On his initiative, two Parisian haute couture shows followed, in Sao Paulo and Rio de Janeiro, while he was president of the Chambre syndicale de la couture parisienne.

On his return to Paris, he had a meeting with his colleagues to inform them that the Brazilian audience was far more elegant than the models who had paraded before them.

Once again, Jacques Heim, the enterprising president of the Chambre Syndicale (1958–1962), provoked a revolt within the profession. His most ferocious detractor was none other than the conservative and purist Raymond Barbas, Jean Patou's brother-in-law, president of the Patou company, and honorary president of the Chambre Syndicale. Heim's quite innocuous, but in fact salutary cyclone of an idea was named "Prêt-à-Porter Création." It had been set up as a defense and coordination group on Jacques Heim's initiative within the Chambre Syndicale. Nine couturiers were involved: Carven, Grès, Madeleine de Rauch, Nina Ricci, Maggy Rouff, Lanvin, Jean Dessès, Jacques Griffe, and Jacques Heim. Guy Laroche, who opened his house in 1957, joined them the following season. The clothes presented by Prêt-à-Porter Création had to legibly mention the name of the manufacturer—Madeleine de Rauch Boutique edited by Mendès—by special authorization, so that the Chambre Syndicale's requirements were respected. It went without saying that the couturier's creative image would be preserved.

In the 1960s the manufacturer's name was removed from the labels of the clothes they made on the distributors request. Little by little, it became prohibited to cite the maker's name in licensing contracts or for any documents other than purely commercial ones. Until that time, the name of the manufacturer had been a kind of guarantee, but starting in 1965 both retailers and consumers preferred not to know where the garment came from and were concerned only with the designer's name. The textile aid subsidy was no longer an argument that induced couturiers to oppose this demand. In addition, after a trial period during which they worried that the exported ready-to-wear would provoke the corruption of their image, the burgeoning success encouraged them to be more visible. The ethical problems that had paralyzed them 15 years earlier had vanished. The taboo had been lifted and these companies had no qualms about affixing labels to clothes that did not come out of their workshops. Imperceptibly, they had gone from the status of excellent maker to creator.

Prêt-à-Porter Création also fulfilled the function of promotion tool. Most of the shows took place in one of the basement salons of the hotel George V, except for a few rare exceptions that took them to the salons of the Hotel d'Orsay. Protocol was very strict. Couturiers were called by alphabetical order and fashion theme; this meant their names came up 10 times. The 10 house managers were in the front row, parsimoniously applauding their colleagues. The favorites were invariably Madeleine de Rauch and Nina Ricci, whose pattern-maker was Jules François Crahay at the time; in addition to the applause, they also took the largest number of orders. The ceremony was directly inspired by the practices that wholesale couture had followed for a few years when they showed in the same salons.

In retrospect, the success of these seasonal events that brought up to 500 buyers and journalists together was surprising. The divergences that a multitude of misunderstandings threw up, however, brought this happy initiative to a close. At the dawn of the 1960s, the group went their separate ways. This was understandable: by this time, almost all the couturiers had their own ready-to-wear lines. In 1964, the indomitable Raymond Barbas signed a contract with C. Mendès.

Jacques Fath University/Givenchy University. The couturiers' idea was highly innovative. Different attempts of the same kind were made over the decade, with the aim of bringing two industries with "irreconcilable" techniques but converging design to live together without binding them in a common commercial and industrial structure. Having learnt from his unhappy experience with Couturiers Associés, Jacques Fath now knew that to succeed in such an adventure, it was first necessary to ensure that the financial and human means existed, at a very different level to what Jean Gaumont-Lanvin had had at his disposal. In 1954, he took up the challenge again and created "Jacques Fath Université."

On 15 June 1953, he registered the name "Jacques Fath Université" with the commercial court in the categories 3, 23, 25, 26, and 28, in the name of the company Jacques Fath & Cie, 39 avenue Pierre-1er-de-Serbie. His experience in America with Joseph Halpert had permanently convinced him of the numerous opportunities that existed for ready-to-wear.

In fact, since 1948—as the first grand couturier to "express himself" outside his workshop—he spent one month every season in New York with a workshop manager and his secretary Charlotte to finalize at least 40 coats, suits, and dresses with Joseph Halpert on Seventh Avenue. He wanted to repeat this experience in France. Fath associated with the Prouvost group to pursue this undertaking. He believed that the association between a renowned couturier and a very influential French textile group had every chance of succeeding. The hazards of life are rarely innocent. The time he had unwillingly spent at the Valenciennes school of commerce and then at the Stock Exchange no longer seemed wasted to him. He evolved with the same ease in the workshops of his couture house as in the world of high finance. The clarity of his proposals, underpinned by a perfect knowledge of the field, soon convinced Prouvost that this was a good idea.

Couturiers Associés, label, model created by Jacques Fath, c. 1950. Musée galliera, Musée de la mode et du Costume de la Ville de Paris. © PMVP/Ladet.

L'Express picked up the news on 27 March 1954: "In a few days, Jean Prouvost (*Paris Match,* Les Laines Pingouin, *Marie Claire,* etc.), is going to launch a ready-to-wear collection designed by Jacques Fath." As a textile and financial group, Prouvost did not have manufacturing factories at its disposal. For this reason, Jacques Fath brought over pattern makers and other technicians from the United States that France did not yet have. Nothing was easier for him than to apply the same formula that had already made him famous in the United States with Joseph Halpert in his own country. He received 10 per cent royalties from Prouvost. The collection consisted of skirts and dresses. The Fred Roy boutique offered him a permanent window on avenue Victor Hugo, in the sixteenth arrondissement. Jacques Fath's death interrupted this wonderful experience that had only lasted two seasons—winter 1954 and summer 1955. A similar contract was drawn up with Hubert de Givenchy, for Givenchy Université.

Hubert de Givenchy remembers Jean Prouvost's request: "'You know, Hubert,

I would like you to make clothes for the young women who ride Vespas.' And I immediately imagined jeans and tee shirts. This concept was so far removed from my world that I could not agree to it. Nonetheless, Prouvost's idea was wonderful, but premature." To renew the agreement, Hubert de Givenchy requested changes that Jean Prouvost refused. The experiment stopped there.[10]

Edition Couture

"The association between a couture and a ready-to-wear house can be compared to a publishing contract. The couturier designs the work, makes his mock-ups, chooses the materials; the editor creates the layout following the couturier's instructions, takes responsibility for having the copies made, and is responsible for their distribution." (Introduction to C. Mendès' catalogue. Didier Grumbach—Winter 1965–1966).

C.Mendès, Maria Carine: edition manufacturers

In 1957, while Prêt-à-Porter Création was beginning to organize itself, two manufacturers, C. Mendès and Maria Carine, manufactured and distributed clothes for the majority of the participating couturiers. C. Mendès had a worldwide exclusivity over the production and distribution of the Carven-Junior, Grès-Spécial, and Madeleine de Rauch Boutique lines, while Lanvin Castillo-Boutique, Jacques Heim-Vedette, Jean Dessès-Bazaar, and Guy Laroche-Boutique were under contract to Maria Carine; Jacques Griffe-Evolution[11] and Maggy Rouff-Extension were contractually committed to other organizations, one with the Henri house, the other with Bon Marché. Nina Ricci's Boutique department remained within the parent company. Created slightly earlier, Pierre Balmain-Florilège remained outside the group, produced and distributed by Pierre Balmain himself.

Like Weill, Weinberg, or Indreco, C. Mendès was a family business. It was founded in 1902 at rue Etienne Marcel by Cerf Mendès France, Pierre Mendès France's father, before it moved in 1909 to 38 rue Léopold-Bellan, where it remained until 1982. At the time, the company was recognized for their coats and jackets, in classic styles, of excellent quality, and at reasonable prices. As a coat manufacturer, C. Mendès did not want to diversify his company's production, and the same was true of his colleagues Weill and Weinberg. Dresses, Mendès believed, were a totally different profession. This forced Jacques Heim to produce his own dresses by creating Maria Carine in 1950. For seven years, C. Mendès and Maria Carine shared all their couturiers: one company made suits and coats, the other, dresses. The structure of C. Mendès, identical to Weill's, emphasized a management based on economics and profitability. All the production was sub-contracted until 1965.

Parallel to this, in 1950 Jacques Heim set up an establishment at rue Pierret in Neuilly, where he saw the possibility of making his dresses himself. The workshop was surrounded by greenery at the end of an alley; it was fairly rudimentary, but handled the subsidiary's production. Maria Moutet, who had joined the couture house to assist Philippe Heim, became the workshop manager.

Maria Moutet, manager, and Carine de La Plenière, a shareholder in the Jacques Heim company, invented the name of the workshop "Maria Carine" from a combination of both their names. Madame Moutet, an emblematic personality in the fashion world, with her husky voice and silver hair, gathered a battalion of women around her. They all revered her as the image of the warehousewoman nicknamed "Aunt Hélène," who turned purple while shouting out bawdy songs on Saint Catherine's day. She never revealed her Russian royal title—the said title was only disclosed after her death, in the obituary column of the daily press.

Both at C. Mendès and at Maria Carine, the sub-contracted production considerably reduced investments, reinforcing the companies' instant financial success. With perfect coordination, André Lévi, manager of C. Mendès, and Maria Moutet easily developed their commercial activities.

Jacques Heim's ingenious policy should have allowed him to progressively integrate the different activities involved in garment manufacturing and distribution within his company. This new formula, perfectly adapted and organized, would have guaranteed his supremacy over his colleagues, giving him an original position and protecting him from the dysfunctions inherent to the changes in manufacturing techniques that upset the whole profession. Maria Moutet's ambitions, however, were of a very different nature; like C. Mendès, Maria Carine proposed its services to other couturiers. Madeleine de Rauch and Jean Dessès were the first to go to rue Pierret. Owned by Heim, Maria Carine was no longer an entity in Jacques Heim's service. Unlike C. Mendès, Maria Carine did not come from a manufacturing background. In the effervescence that accompanies any enterprise during its growth phase, rue Pierret very rapidly reached its limits and created multiple inconveniences for its clients, couturiers, or suppliers. In 1956 Maria Carine made a bid for Spitzer, a coat and suit manufacturing business at rue Réamur. With this, C. Mendès and Maria Carine inevitably became competitors.

The first disagreements appeared when dresses with matching jackets came into fashion. How would the two companies share production of the two elements with the same reference? The rupture became final when Maria Moutet signed an exclusive contract with Lanvin-Castillo in 1957 for all their ready-to-wear. In 1961 they had outgrown rue Réamur, and Maria Carine moved to 5 rue d'Uzès, a 1930s building with an intelligent architecture that made it easy to organize more rational and bright work spaces thanks to a façade filled with bay windows.[12]

C. Mendès and Maria Carine were now enemies. They readied their weapons for a merciless competition, and the couturiers were the actors in this battle. Carven and Madeleine de Rauch, followed by Grès, chose C. Mendès' camp, while Lanvin and Dessès, followed by Guy Laroche and then the very young Jean-Louis Scherrer, went over to the adversary. C. Mendès now had to produce its own dresses and Maria Carine had to make its own coats. These two companies had a quasi-monopoly over ready-to-wear. Nothing could stop their ascension. Refusing the guaranteed *minima*, demanding the world as their territory, and paying 10 per cent royalties for exclusive contracts to be renewed every three years, they authoritatively carried out the long awaited development of couturiers' ready-to-wear.

In 1963, when I took over the management of C. Mendès, the house only had 39 full-time employees. First equipped with a suit workshop, then a loose wear studio, it was enriched over the years by highly qualified personnel drawn from haute couture that contributed to its prestige. Nonetheless, there was an aura of unease: the couturiers suspected C. Mendès of voluntarily or involuntarily using their pattern cuttings in a simplified form for C. Mendès' own production. It is true that the "in-betweens" were inherent to the profession. In 1964, in order to avoid any conflict, I decided to do away with the C. Mendès collection, which nonetheless represented the highest turnover. The same year, I signed two exclusive contracts with Castillo and Jean Patou, whose international fame favorably

C. Mendès' buildings,
38 rue Léopold Bellan
and 26 rue d'Aboukir, Paris.

Return from the Geneva
conference on peace in Indochina.
Left to right:
Palmyre Mendès France,
Marcelle Grumbach,
Cerf Mendès France,
Pierre Mendès France,
and Pierre Grumbach, July 1954.

At C. Mendès' they celebrated
Saint Catherine's day.
Didier Grumbach, 1st row left,
took over the general
management in 1963.
Photo in Madame Germaine's
workshop, 1962.

counter-balanced the loss, thus ensuring a high turnover and allowing the company to flourish. A new kind of company was born.

The two companies ran smoothly for a decade thanks to the public's enthusiasm for fashion. Nothing seemed to worry the sister enemies, C. Mendès and Maria Carine, until 1967 when Jacques Heim Couture, rocked by a financial crisis, took Maria Carine down in its fall. For the first time, the unrivaled manager Jacques Heim's composure was shaken; Maria Moutet resigned, and the banks were looking for a buyer. The quarrels were now forgotten. In all the bitterness of competition, Jacques Heim had always maintained extremely courteous relations with C. Mendès. I took over the management of Maria Carine. They were associates despite being competitors, and they were links in the same chain, but the two companies never merged.[13]

"Edited by C. Mendès." My grandfather, Cerf Mendès France, was born in Limoges in 1874 into a Jewish family that had settled in Bordeaux since the seventeenth century. A free thinker and a militant supporter of Dreyfus, he chose to create his own textile company in Paris rather than take over the family business. The company had been first established on rue de Cléry. It then moved successfully to rue Réamur, then rue Etienne-Marcel and rue de Turbigo, where the family lived for several years, before moving to rue de la Pompe in the inter-war period. During a 1905 trip to Strasbourg, Cerf Mendès met his future wife, Palmyre Cahn, daughter of a shopkeeper specializing in shoes. In 1909, in association with his brother-in-law Joseph Stam, Alice Cahn's husband, he set up the company Mendès & Stam at 38 rue Léopold-Bellan. At the end of World War I, they parted company. Joseph took over his father-in-law's business in Strasbourg, while Cerf, under the name C. Mendès, remained the only director of the company until he entrusted it to Henri Mathonet when World War II forced him to leave. When he took over again in 1945, he was over 70 and, given that neither of his children, Pierre and Marcelle, were interested in taking over the business, he sold 49 per cent of his shares to the Naggar family.

For 10 years he did not miss a day's work. The seven metro stations between Villiers and Sentier ensured a punctuality that made him the first to arrive at the office every morning. The lungs of the house were the cutting studio on the sixth floor: its breath was an indicator of the company's health, so that was his first stop every day. Mounting the stairs four at a time, he was never out of breath when he reached the workshop. He would kiss his niece, Mademoiselle Marthe, head of the cutting section; charm Madame Léone, who cut the large sizes; and tease Mr. Henri, the draper, an eternal pessimist. The cruel absence of a telephone—there was only one in the sales services office on the first floor—forced him to move around the house to gather information. Exactly at 12:00 PM, he took the metro home to 4 avenue de Villiers. The afternoon was divided between the third floor where the receivers, Madame Hass and Mademoiselle Morris, checked the deliveries sent by Mr. Bernard, and the first floor where clients placed their orders. Cerf Mendès maintained a warm, personal relationship with the entrepreneurs, most of whom were Polish, Czech, or Hungarian.

Mendès was neither tall nor short. His slim build was in harmony with his incredible energy that made him absolutely seductive. His thick, black, bushy eyebrows accentuated the malicious vivacity of his eyes. An aggressive nose balanced the lower part of his face with his long, bald head. His slight silhouette, emphasized by his frail limbs, gave an impression of fragility that, combined with his strong sense of humor and unpredictable irony, protected him from all external aggression. He loved and knew his business thoroughly, and nobody ever dared go against any of his decisions. In 1957, on the day of his funeral, the cortege stopped for a long moment in front of 38 rue Léopold-Bellan, where all his employees paid him a last homage. Upon his death, his two children inherited the company. My uncle, who was naturally averse to any kind of compromise, suggested that the Naggar family buy his father's shares, or that they sell theirs to the company that now consisted of him and his sister. Albert and Félix Naggar opted for the latter solution. In 1958, the company thus belonged equally to Marcelle Grumbach and Pierre Mendès France. It functioned in a traditional manner with 28 salaried employees, and provided work for a large number of entrepreneurs and home-workers.

I joined C. Mendès in December 1954 while continuing my law studies. I occupied certain temporary functions, including the very paradoxical position of export representative, although we had no exports. In the face of this apparent anomaly, I thought of trying my luck for the first time by making a business trip to the Benelux countries. To facilitate my journey and mainly to make it more productive, Jacques Heim, for whom C. Mendès manufactured coats, opened his address book to me and shared his best clients. At the time, the big houses that

Valentino in Rome in 1968. Photo Pierre Boulat, courtesy Agence Cosmos.

Madeleine de Rauch, c. 1965. Photo Willy Maywald © Association Willy Maywald/ Adagp, Paris, 2008.

Antonio del Castillo, c. 1965. Rights Reserved.

Philippe Venet, c. 1965. Rights Reserved.

Michel Goma, artistic director at Jean Patou, c. 1965. Rights Reserved.

Guy Laroche surrounded by his models, c. 1968. Photo Pierre Boulat, courtesy Agence Cosmos.

bought mock-ups and haute couture patterns were not yet used to ready-to-wear. At Gand, Bruges, and Ostend, the fear that ready-to-wear instilled was evident despite the warm welcome I received. However, Anna David Marber in Brussels and Jeanne-Cécile in Luxembourg started to become acquainted with this new phenomenon that was slowly transforming the habits of their profession, following the example of their colleagues Cylba in Toulouse and Courtois Soeurs in Montpellier. These provincial couture houses that had been in existence for decades were imperceptibly turning into boutiques.

The following year, I undertook my first tour in Germany, helped yet again by Jacques Heim. Then it was Italy and the whole of Europe.

While Europe eventually opened up to ready-to-wear despite a slight initial resistance, the United States was hardly receptive to this new concept coming from France.

C. Mendès' first American client was the Lili Ann manufacture from San Francisco. A visit from its director in 1955 threw the house into great excitement. Curious or impressed, a throng of employees gathered at the doors to the salon to catch a glimpse of Mendès. He was tall, and fulfilled all the criteria of Anglo-Saxon elegance that the San Francisco Californians are proud of surpassing. A single false note betrayed him: a crested emerald worthy of the Great Duchess Vladimir, worn on his ring finger, with ingenuous ostentation. The effervescence that surrounded his visit illustrated the importance of the American myth that, at the time, held the admiration of a number of industrialists.

Taking C. Mendès' destiny in hand, I planned a trip to New York following the advice Kay Ingliss-Jones, Madame Grès' American press attaché at the time, had given me when we signed the contract with Grès in 1957. I executed my plan in 1961. Wearing a hat bought at the airport that was too small for me, balanced on my head, I visited a large number of clients and journalists—including Jean Rosenberg from Bendel, Madge Caroll from Bloomingdale's, June Weir from *Women's Wear Daily*—to reach the conclusion that we were not ready to pursue ready-to-wear. Nor were our competitors. During those years, we were all in the same boat. American ready-to-wear was clearly superior. It had better finishing, enjoyed a homogenous production, and produced clothes that were easy to "live in." In 1964, during my second trip, Ruth Hammer—American press attaché for Philippe Venet, Balenciaga, Givenchy, and Courrèges—organized a fashion show for the press in the Plaza Hotel's ballroom. My presentation of the Carven, Madeleine de Rauch, Castillo, and Philippe Venet collections in a suite of the same hotel followed. The top American stores, I. Magnin, Neiman-Marcus, Marshall Field's, Lord and Taylor, De Pinna, etc., placed a few trial orders.[14]

With its usual lucid propensity when welcoming new projects, Seventh Avenue could not help compare the fairly mediocre quality of French ready-to-wear with the far superior products made by our American counterparts. For the time being, there was no question of doubting the supremacy of French creativity and design, but the "fit" was American.[15] In addition, the garments had to be adapted to the American morphology. American measurements were different than those of the Europeans—Americans had a long torso, slight hips, and a sporty musculature. C. Mendès cut their first orders to the American norms, on Wolf models (Harvey Berin measurements). There were not many orders and the 10 per cent commission that was to finance the operation did not cover my costs. The company was too small and it was not financially viable enough to bear such investments for long. Nonetheless, it was a good idea and one worth pursuing. The haute couture houses were the first to appreciate the numerous advantages they could benefit from at their true value: finally obtaining a return on the success of their creations.

After Philippe Venet and Castillo, Jean Patou—whose designer in 1964 was Michel Goma, soon assisted by Angelo Tarlazzi—went into association with C. Mendès.

In October 1965, I made my third journey to the United States. Following the same ritual as before, I settled into the Plaza in suite 921 accompanied by five Parisian models, one per house represented and one from C. Mendès. At that time, professional models were not yet essentially American products. Confined to the suite, anxiously awaiting requests for appointments, the naturally lazy young girls often spent interminably difficult, exhausting days irritating each other. Finally the bell rang. Five people had come. "I am Elizabeth Arden,[16] I have come to see the Castillo collection." After the war, taking over from Charles James,[17] Castillo had managed the Arden studio while she still had 22 couture salons spread over the main American towns. She reigned tyrannically over an empire and tolerated neither comments nor weakness from her collaborators, exercising a veritable terror over them that was reinforced by her

Valentino model, c. 1968. Photo Pierre Boulat, courtesy Agence Cosmos.

Excerpt from a C. Mendès catalogue, spring–summer 1966 collection: layout and execution Tiennot; creations by Madeleine de Rauch; creations by Philippe Venet; creations by Michel Goma for Jean Patou; sketches by Angelo Tarlazzi.

Advertisement in *WWD*, 8 November 1967. Ten couturiers present their ready-to-wear, manufactured by C. Mendès, *Paris Collections Inc.* offices, 1 East 54th, Elizabeth Arden's building in New York.

legendary moods. Hated, adored, and solitary in equal measure, she was touched only by her horses, her veritable passion.

Elizabeth Arden sat like a ladybird, wearing a shell of pink, at the very edge of the sofa. Her escort watched from behind, in absolute silence. As each model went past, two words slipped out of her lips: "Twenty-four." I couldn't believe my ears. Twenty-four pieces of each model! That same afternoon, dress, suit, and coat buyers from Lord and Taylor[18] invested their winter budget based on the previous year's results. Separately, all three wrote down their orders in front of me: 4,6,6,4,... These were quantities from each line that we would never have sold in Europe. The next day it was I. Magnin's turn, followed by Neiman-Marcus.[19] We had won. This time ready-to-wear, which had always followed in haute couture's wake, had begun its ascension that would lead it to the position it occupies today in the fashion universe and its economy. The actors who fostered the development of the couture manufacturing industry 50 years earlier repeated their endeavor with as much importance this time on ready-to-wear.

Elizabeth Arden was full of good will and became a client whose importance, along with the regularity of her orders, contributed to our development in New York in 1967. It was in fact on her suggestion that we first established ourselves in her building on Fifth Avenue, at 1 E. 54th suite 601. Once the permanent office had been created, the management was delegated to a young 25-year-old woman, Ariane Brener, who had been a sales director with Courrèges, then Ungaro. Mark Hampton, a young decorator unknown at the time, handled the décor and installation of the offices.

The company, Paris Collections Inc., needed larger premises very quickly, so it moved to 543 Madison Avenue. The unexpected manner in which C. Mendès developed at the time forced us into a kind of real estate expansion. In Paris, the business progressively expanded into two contiguous buildings at the Montmartre–Louvre Léopold-Bellan crossroads, and Paris Collections Inc. (Parco) gradually took over the small five-story building where it had settled the second time. The growing number of brands produced and distributed transformed the decoration and installation of the buildings as well as C. Mendès' history. Over the years, Ungaro, Yves Saint Laurent, Givenchy, Issey Miyake, Emanuelle Khanh, Chanel, Valentino, Jean-Charles de Castelbajac, Christiane Bailly, and many others offered their collections to the North American ready-to-wear markets through Paris Collection Inc. showrooms. Between 1975 and 1980, the three upper floors of 543 Madison Avenue were entirely occupied by Saint Laurent Rive Gauche Ltd, Valentino Boutique Ltd, and Chanel ready-to-wear.

Irreversibly, "couturier ready-to-wear" became "prêt-à-porter" after having displaced Les Trois Hirondelles, whose reputation was much lower. The importance of the American market was proven. The widely appreciated brands received a constantly increasing number of orders that required a better-adapted management. Production had to have consistent quality and deliveries had to be made at unusually early dates. Our tailoring system consisted mainly of Polish and Hungarian tailors—who were getting older—and could no longer satisfy the demand. We now had to set up workshops that soon occupied several floors of rue Mandar, rue Bachaumont, and rue Etienne Marcel. Soon, however, even these workshops did not suffice and the first factory was opened at Chalonnes-sur-Loire in 1966 under Nicole Benquet's management; she was barely 25 at the time and she later became production manager with Thierry Mugler. Situated at the heart of the small town, the factory that had previously manufactured shoes had a rural and almost family-like atmosphere. Workers were recruited through the town hall, where they were registered for jobs.

They first learned to make buttonholes, and very soon the quality was excellent. Two years later, the workshop worked exclusively for Yves Saint Laurent Rive Gauche. As my goal was to create ready-to-wear that had the same quality manufacturing as haute couture, I tirelessly pursued my research to reach a level of technical perfection. It was with this objective in mind that I accepted Sammy Weinberg's invitation to visit his factory in Bourges. He wanted to show me that technical methods could handle all the difficulties couture could possibly invent. I arrived at the meeting with a coat and the pattern for it. Amazingly modern, the factory was already equipped with vertical conveyors. The coats were moved from one worker to another without any handling. Once they were completed, they followed the chain that took them finished to the packing station. I was astounded. The copy of the coat was not perfect, but it could easily be done. This visit was capital for me; it proved that it was possible to produce large numbers of garments and maintain consistent quality at competitive prices.

On my return from Bourges, my only priority was to industrialize C. Mendès.

I did not have to wait long for my wish to be granted. That same year, 1967, "La Cotonnière de Saint Quentin" was in difficulty and wanted to sell its factory in Angers, Cotariel, that employed 450 people. It was a vast nineteenth-century building right in the center of the town that had frequently changed hands. The atmosphere was stifling and strangely resembled that of a primary school—an impression that was accentuated by the playground and the inner courtyard. The real owners were unquestionably the female CGT (union) workers from the workers council. As the only permanent staff, they authoritatively brandished not only their skills, but also their aristocratic adherence to the industrial world that made them untouchable. What surprised me the most was, however, the noise of a heavy, mechanized industry that immediately reminded me of Bourges. My mind was made up; I only had to execute my plan. This was not a simple task: my uncle Pierre Mendès France immediately opposed the project.

During a lunch at Brasserie Lipp on boulevard Saint Germain he lashed out with unwavering determination that if I persisted in what he considered the foolishness I was guilty of, he would give me three months to buy his shares. Sticking to my guns, I signed, knowing full well that the countdown had begun and I had no leeway to transgress the conditions we had agreed to. My salvation came in 1968 in the form of the CEGOS,[20] to whom I had opportunely entrusted a diagnosis of the company. The business' growth curve, if it was auto-financed, surprised the analysts who concluded their study with a glowing report. After looking at it, my uncle frowned and the only words he spoke in congratulation were: "These people are irresponsible, they are just fuelling your bad instincts. If they find the business so attractive, they can buy my shares." Which they did. Noël Pouderoux and Claude Charmont, respectively president and financial director of CEGOS, created a shareholders syndicate that a Swiss group and Balamundi, the Belgian floor-covering king, invested in. The family no longer held 50 per cent of the company's shares. In my uncle's defense, his usual foresight allowed him to evaluate the financial means that were required to bring a factory of this size up to the required quality production, and the kinds of modifications that were necessary to do so. He considered the investment disproportionate given the family resources. In addition, the status of industrialist could only hinder his political career, weakening him with his enemies. We all still remember the huge letters "Go and get dressed by Mendès" written across the Trocadero cemetery wall, as well as the increasing attacks in the press, insisting on his association with a manufacturing business, focusing on a company little known to the public and for whom too much publicity could be dangerous. The family was not rich. The banks could refuse credit and put Pierre Mendès France as an administrator in a difficult position. And, in fact, it ultimately happened.

Although his wisdom was irritating in these decisive moments, it worked once again to his advantage. The investment required to modernize the factories forced us to increase the capital. In 1972, the Grumbach family's participation in C. Mendès fell from 50 per cent to 35 per cent.

We were learning a new profession. Manufacturing had never before tried to make clothing whose quality in cut and finish would so closely resemble that of haute couture. It took three years for the Angers factory to fulfill the quality criteria established by C. Mendès, and the costs involved led to inevitable losses. As for the couturiers, who knew nothing of technical feats, they had not yet learned to use such a wonderful tool; this is clear from the two following anecdotes.

In 1968, Air France proposed that Balenciaga design the airhostess's uniforms. Hubert de Givenchy, who just began working with C. Mendès, suggested to Cristobal Balenciaga that our factories should handle this fabulous order. In all there were 19,000 pieces (suits, coats, raincoats, shirts) that, in 1969, were a test for our new structure.

A few months later when he closed down his business, Cristobal Balenciaga asked me to visit him at avenue George V, accompanied by a model and a première. The quasi-religious ambiance that surrounded the idol was accentuated on this occasion by the funereal atmosphere of the deserted salons where just a few saleswomen dressed in black appeared, only to disappear immediately. We entered a large rectangular room on the third floor where, on the left, were racks holding the Air France uniforms. At the back, behind a diagonally placed desk, sat Cristobal Balenciaga. The usual greetings over, he advanced slowly towards the young woman who had accompanied me, helped her into a jacket, and moved away again, after having placed a few pins at shoulder level. I said timidly:

"Monsieur, it's a size 38; that is not Mademoiselle's size."

He came back, took out the pins and asked me:

"How do you make pockets with piping?"

I tried my best to explain the drill.

"How do you stitch the internal lining?"

I described the shell stitching "bagueuse," then the button-hole machine, then… he went back to his desk and, after a long silence, he placed his joined hands under his chin, and spoke to his assistant Ramón Esparza with a strong Spanish accent:

"Ramón, did you see? We will just have to start everything all over again."

Two months after this visit to Balenciaga, Raymond Barbas, president of Patou, expressed his desire to visit our factories. We were to meet early in the morning at his house, situated on the edge of the Saint Cloud golf course of which he was president. In front of the gates, a fleet of Mercedes was placed at the disposal of Michel Goma and the elegant managers who accompanied him, and they all followed us on this country outing. The incident took place at Angers. As soon as Michel Goma entered the first workshop, at the sight of the frame machine, he felt unwell. He had to be guided to the courtyard where he rested for a moment on a bench.

Raymond Barbas was reaching the end of a highly successful career, at the highest level of his profession. He incarnated a certain sense of permanence. That day he had a sudden vision of the future, reminding me of my fascination when I first discovered Weinberg's factory. The success of his ready-to-wear, licensed to C. Mendès for the last five years, was only the corollary of the inevitable change in his haute couture. With his grandson Jean de Mouy in mind, he decided to regain control of the house, and more specifically over the whole range of women's fashion. He had always retained control of the perfumes. In his renovating mood, he discreetly decided to have a factory built in Angers, where C. Mendès had its largest production units. He poached our Chalonnes-sur-Loire factory director to run it along with several purchasing and production managers from the Mendès Paris office.

This had the effect of a bomb at C. Mendès. I made a legal complaint against the Patou house for disloyal competition, but lost the case after two years of procedure. A poor consolation was that the Jean Patou factory was never profitable, and after two years of conjugated efforts under Michel Goma's artistic direction until 1972, then Angelo Tarlazzi's until 1976, the factory closed down, putting an end to Jean Patou ready-to-wear.

There were two reasons for this failure: the first was the lack of a specialized management team, and the second was the merciless competition from 1966 to 1968 between the four major couture houses that simultaneously launched their ready-to-wear. In fact, Courrèges Couture Future, Saint Laurent Rive Gauche, Miss Dior, and Givenchy Nouvelle Boutique triumphed with ready-to-wear collections that the public adopted from the get-go thanks to their high aesthetic and technical quality. With this radical position, couturiers themselves announced that couture was not alone in knowing the art of dressing women elegantly.

While haute couture still possessed a prestigious savoir-faire, it was, in any case, no longer a trade.

Couture Turns to Ready-to-Wear

By reaching a certain level of perfection, the fashion industry learned to produce efficiently; this time, Courrèges, Saint Laurent, Dior, and Givenchy recognized this and turned it to their advantage. The first collections sold under their control were very successful with foreign buyers and, most of all, won total credibility.

The exacerbated competition left no room for "make-do." The game became a cruel one; certain haute couture ready-to-wear lines had to reconsider their positioning to avoid being completely cut out of the game.

Between 1968 and 1971, C. Mendès terminated most of its contracts, maintaining only Saint Laurent Rive Gauche and Givenchy Nouvelle Boutique. The huge change in consumer and retail habits, however, went far beyond all expectations. In 1968, for the very first time, Saks and Bergdorf Goodman did not send their buyers to Paris for the haute couture presentations. Following a contract that Jean-Louis Scherrer had signed with Bergdorf Goodman for haute couture, another agreement was signed for his ready-to-wear. Prior to this deal, Scherrer's models had been copied and produced in America. For Bergdorf Goodman, the Scherrer fashions were manufactured by Maria Carine and imported from France for Julia Trissel's famous "Third Floor." As for the "Second Floor" couture department, it was soon offered to Givenchy Nouvelle Boutique.[21] C. Mendès manufactured the collection, and the Givenchy space at

Bergdorf's was decorated in the spirit of the Givenchy boutique on avenue Victor Hugo in Paris.

The couturiers almost ceased to sell their models to buyers, choosing instead to earn money from the sale of their ready-to-wear lines, which included more exclusive items that became all the more attractive to stores. Stores now had a wide variety of fashion articles being sold, which created curiosity and desire among consumers. The intrigue was stirred up by the press and slowly transformed consumer habits. This, in turn, over-stimulated the couturiers whose creativity, borne by the general enthusiasm, climaxed. Who does not remember the excitement and curiosity that preceded each of Yves Saint Laurent's ready-to-wear shows, with his wealth of invention that was unanimously appreciated, before being pillaged by all the Sentier manufacturers?

Between 1966 and 1967, the number of haute couture houses registered with the Chambre Syndicale fell from 39 to 17. Since this date, the revenues generated by haute couture of the most famous houses declined regularly and irreversibly.

Courrèges Couture Future. André Courrèges was the first couturier to have expressed the simple idea that with the evolution of technology, the industry would find solutions that would make couture production obsolete. He was determined to master both techniques simultaneously. Thus, he went even further than Jacques Heim who, in 1950, separated his activities into two independent companies. Courrèges presented both of his collections in the same fashion show. There was no rule prohibiting this, and Courrèges quite naturally saw his ready-to-wear succeed, driven by the fame of his couture.

The Courrèges satellite was in orbit. In 1966 he opened his first ready-to-wear boutiques in Paris at rue François 1er, and then in 1967 in Houston at Sakowitz and in New York at Bonwit Teller. Business was slow at first but before long it quickly accelerated. Almost 28 boutiques opened in the United States under the direction provided by François Baufumé, the export manager from March 1970 to December 1976. It seemed that nothing could stop Courrèges' ascension: the turnover was 17 million francs in 1970 and it rose to 68 million in 1973.[22] The production work was carried out by subcontractors in Béarn, where Courrèges had been born. But he soon decided to carefully build his own factory there.

"I designed my Pau factory with the hope of immersing the workers in an aesthetic universe that was as close as possible to my concept, space, nature, time/weather. The alternating concrete and glass domes opened on to corn fields or gardens full of rose bushes, while in the sky, the drifting clouds, the rain or the sun, regulated the days and the seasons," remembers André Courrèges. Managing a factory at a time when prices were blocked (1972–1973) was not a designer's talent. The overhead from such a factory and production was exorbitant: 600 people, 300 of them in Pau and 50 in Tarbes.[23] In addition to the 28 American boutiques, there were 17 in Japan as well as 35 "corners" in department stores; there were 3 stores in Hong Kong and about 20 in Germany.

The 1974 oil crisis cracked the edifice. Strikes delayed deliveries. Christian Delahaigue, the company's president, admitted: "The group had set up a very heavy production system. Our sub-contractors, weavers, dyers and knitters, were organised as if they were in a single factory. Imagine our distress when the dyers began to close down. We needed about ten or fifteen contractors to satisfy their demands and succeed..."

Unfortunately by this time, only André Courrèges and Nina Ricci's house still had total control over their ready-to-wear.

Saint Laurent Rive Gauche. Pierre Bergé was the manager of Yves Saint Laurent, the most envied young couture house, when I invited him to the C. Mendès presentations. Edouard Boyadjean, whom I had met at Madeleine de Rauch, was the director of couture at Yves Saint Laurent and played the role of intermediary. In 1966, Pierre Bergé offered me the opportunity to produce a collection that Yves Saint Laurent intended for a boutique the company was hoping to set up on Paris' Rive Gauche. Although I was very interested and curious to discover Yves Saint Laurent's talent, I sent him a letter of refusal, explaining the dangers a manufacturer ran by making a collection intended for a single boutique. At the same time, I warned him of the dangers for a boutique if they were at the mercy of a single supplier.

In fact, Yves Saint Laurent really wanted to open just one boutique. I received his answer from an almost indignant Raymond Barbas—his relationship with Pierre Bergé was very conflicted—who showed me *France Soir* where an article said that Yves Saint Laurent was going to have its ready-to-wear made by C. Mendès. Surprise!

I telephoned Pierre Bergé. His only answer was: "You'll just have to manage." Something I would have found very difficult to do if the very same evening a dinner at a great uncle's[24] had not brought me into contact with Mr. and Mrs. Hanoka, owners of Prémaman. They had opened a fashion boutique for pregnant women, and two Parisian retailers had shown an interest in this new concept. The way they explained the system they had developed for "franchise" boutiques, allowed me to envisage a multitude of opportunities as yet unexplored in our profession. The same week at another dinner—at Calvet's this time, boulevard Saint-Germain—Richard Salomon, president of Charles of the Ritz, who owned 80 per cent of the Yves Saint Laurent Company at the time, had invited Claude Bernheim (license manager), Yves Saint Laurent, Pierre Bergé, and myself. Full of my subject, I spoke about franchises with such conviction that, although my dinner partners were astounded at first, they all adopted my idea.

Richard Salomon imagined an American style structure. C. Mendès and Yves Saint Laurent would become partners each owning 50 per cent of Saint Laurent Rive Gauche; C. Mendès and myself would each have a quarter of the shares. Pierre Bergé and Yves Saint Laurent would do the same with their 50 per cent. Out of the 12 per cent royalties Saint Laurent Rive Gauche received, 5 per cent would be paid back to Yves Saint Laurent and Pierre Bergé. For a long time 7 per cent was enough for Saint Laurent Rive Gauche to be a profitable company. In 1968, André Levi, C. Mendès' sales director, was appointed manager of Saint Laurent Rive Gauche.

Dinner Jacket. Yves Saint Laurent Photo Helmut Newton from *Vogue*, 1975.

In order to justify his nickname "King Salomon," as he was called by the Seventh Avenue, Richard Salomon held on to two shares that would allow him, if need be, to play the arbiter. It was never necessary.

Unlike André Courrèges, Yves Saint Laurent was trained at the Chambre syndicale de la couture school, rue Saint-Roch, and not the Ecole supérieure de l'industrie du vêtement. Their motivations and interests were thus different. André Courrèges considered couture and manufacturing inseparable; to Yves Saint Laurent, they seemed incompatible.

Yves Saint Laurent, the heir to Christian Dior, believed the couturiers' status lay mainly in their total freedom. He demonstrated this authoritatively while affirming his talent and constantly surpassing himself with each collection that he renewed continually.

He gave a new meaning to ready-to-wear. He discovered that solitary couture work, a constant search for immediately consumable perfection, was finally less creative than ready-to-wear, a profession that was closer to divining the future, predicting women's desires, and anticipating what they might like. He thus had no qualms about exchanging his role as a couturier for that of a stylist.

During the first season he preceded couture with his ready-to-wear, demonstrating sheer brilliance, mastery, and invention, imposing his fashion on the whole world. The meaning behind his approach and the originality of his imagination echoed the breadth of his talent season after season. About every three years he revolutionized his own fashion without contradicting himself, imposing his volumes, his rhythms, his proportions, and his colors. No fashion creator before him had ever achieved this dual control, benefiting from a devoted and captive distribution system like Saint Laurent Rive Gauche.

For the first set of fittings, I accompanied Madame Germaine and Madame Aline[25] to the rue Spontini studio. Slightly tense, Yves Saint Laurent received us, and warned us that in the future the "Rive Gauche" prototypes would be designed, stitched, and adjusted in his couture workshops, under the infallible supervision of the person who had always been his most trusted assistant, Anne-Marie Munoz. Ready-to-wear was finally being paid as much attention as couture.

The number of boutiques multiplied,[26] following the rhythm with the seasons, leading the franchisees to travel abroad for openings. The "Rive Gauche" adventure was exemplary; the concept traveled efficiently from Rome to London, from Brussels to Munich... Store openings were also an excuse to meet again and get to know each other better. Every collection was followed by a lunch at Maxim's or at the Crillon to which all the franchisees were invited. Microphones were placed on the tables. We complimented and congratulated each other; we were exultant with pleasure, until finally the same microphone only transmitted suggestions, complaints, some judicious reasoning, maybe too much. Then, we boycotted the inaugurations—there were too many of them; soon that's all we would have time for; the noise was unbearable, the lunches stopped. The last party was held at Jean-Marie Rivière's Alcazar.

In addition to the guarantee of manufacturing at least half of each season's models, C. Mendès received a share of the profits on what it did not manufacture since it was a partner in Saint Laurent Rive Gauche.

This arrangement had a number of advantages, and of course, a few weaknesses. By offering boutiques the necessary flexibility, by maintaining a constant competition between the complementary manufacturers, and by putting strong pressure on the prices, it encouraged Rive Gauche's[27] exponential growth. The boutiques grew richer: in 1972 the Saint Laurent Rive Gauche boutique at rue du Faubourg-Saint-Honoré, a franchise at the time, achieved a turnover of 15 million francs[28] in a space no larger than 50 square meters. Highly efficient on a small scale, this formula was unmanageable when 70 boutiques had to be supplied properly. The risks C. Mendès took on purchasing, without having any control over the sales, became worrisome. The danger was too great. In 1973 I had to make up my mind to ask Pierre Bergé and Jean-Claude de Givenchy, president and Hubert de Givenchy's half brother, to choose between two solutions.

Option number one: Pierre Bergé could buy our factories. Second option: we buy Saint Laurent Rive Gauche. In 1973, Yves Saint Laurent had just bought the whole of his company from the Squibb group that had become the parent company of Charles of the Ritz. Subsequently, Saint Laurent was no longer interested in his Rive Gauche shares and chose to sell them to C. Mendès. Givenchy took over the management of his ready-to-wear. Saint Laurent Rive Gauche thus became a subsidiary of C. Mendès, and Yves Saint Laurent's most lucrative license in its classic form, along with the license for menswear held by the Bidermann group. C. Mendès held the worldwide exclusivity for Yves Saint Laurent labeled women's wear. This more orthodox formula permitted C. Mendès to better manage its expansion by only allowing those products outside its competencies or that did not correspond to its needs to be produced externally. With greater autonomy, C. Mendès could increase its profits more rapidly. Between 1973 and 1979, under Jean-Sébastien Szwarc as general manager, Yves Saint Laurent twice had the opportunity to buy the industrial organization that produced his ready-to-wear. Neither Pierre Bergé nor Jean Sébastien Szwarc envisioned this option, as it was so ingrained into the way of thinking of the time that couture and manufacturing were incompatible.

The company's situation changed again. A year after I sold my shares in C. Mendès and Saint Laurent Rive Gauche, Pierre Bergé bought C. Mendès on 18 January 1978 in partnership with Léon Cligman, president of Indreco, in order to block a takeover bid launched by Maurice Bidermann against Saint Laurent Rive Gauche. Pierre Bergé thus remained president of Saint Laurent Rive Gauche, an associate holding 34 per cent of the shares in C. Mendès. This was an intermediary option for licensing, between the classical license of the Ungaro/GFT type and the model Chanel developed later that is cited below.

The C. Mendès' licenses signed with Saint Laurent Rive Gauche in 1966 did not include the United States. Despite C. Mendès' early success on the American market in the 1960s, it was accepted at the time that French ready-to-wear could not compete with its American counterpart. Justin Lipman, an American manufacturer and president of Cuddlecoat, 512 Seventh Avenue, took the Rive Gauche business for the US. Nonetheless, after three years of working together, the association was interrupted for a very simple reason: consumers wanted "Made in France." In 1975, the American subsidiary of Saint Laurent Rive Gauche, Rive Gauche Apparel Distribution, alone sold 48,000 pieces of ready-to-wear in the United States, at 30 sales points spread over the country. C. Mendès remained the only manufacturer of Saint Laurent Rive Gauche. In less than 10 years, the French ready-to-wear industry had imposed itself forcefully by becoming truly efficient.

Miss Dior. The "expression" ready-to-wear line, as it was called at Dior, was born with the house and was first managed by Christian Dior, then by Marc Bohan. Twenty yeas later, in 1967, a secondary ready-to-wear line was launched—Miss Dior. In parallel, there were local collections in Japan with Kanebo and, soon after, in the United States with Jones, a license that was subsequent to the closing of Christain Dior New York Inc. in 1978.

In order to ensure Miss Dior's success, Jacques Rouët acquired the company Simone Robin, renowned for their highly sophisticated work. To start with, fittings took place at the head office, rue Saint-Florentin, supervised by Nadine Charteret, manager of Simone Robin. The design then moved to avenue Montaigne, under Philippe Guibourgé's control, assisted by Adeline André.

Situated between the more selective boutique line and the national Japanese or American licenses, Miss Dior reached the top very quickly. After a spectacular ascension, certainly helped by the label's fame, the turnover collapsed after the first three seasons. In fact, in 1967, like all of Dior ready-to-wear, Miss Dior was an unprofitable activity. The workshops that were under-utilized soon accepted external sub-contracting work.

Unlike Courrèges and Yves Saint Laurent who entered the market 15 years after Dior, and who developed ready-to-wear even before they thought of licenses, Dior was captive to his proliferating licensing policy. The company could no longer return to an exclusive distribution system.

Yves Saint Laurent and Courrèges had both developed their turnover through a network of boutiques in their own names that allowed sales to increase at the same rhythm as the network expanded, while protecting them from any kind of competition. In addition, after being in existence for 20 years, Dior was less attractive than its younger competitors. This explains why, in 1974, Miss Dior sales (including the avenue Montaigne boutique) did not exceed 9,500 pieces. Philippe Guibourgé, the designer, whose talent was not called into question, left Dior the following year for Chanel where, for seven years, he created the ready-to-wear line until Karl Lagerfeld took over. Under Marc Bohan's management, Miss Dior continued to accrue losses that between 1975 and 1983 reached 45 million francs. Orders were decreasing every year by over 20 per cent, falling from 30,000 to less than 10,000 pieces.

Givenchy Nouvelle Boutique. In 1955, with his "University" collection Hubert de Givenchy was one of the first to have signed a contract for an industrially made collection. Nonetheless, the failure of this experiment on the one hand, and the success of his couture on the other hand, did not encourage him to attempt a new adventure. In addition, the examples that Courrèges and Yves Saint Laurent set were very seductive, and Philippe Venet, who had signed a licensing contract himself with C. Mendès in 1963, strongly encouraged Givenchy to develop his own ready-to-wear. This was the association, cited earlier, between Givenchy and C. Mendès that lasted five years—from 1968 to 1973. The collection was called Givenchy Nouvelle Boutique, and the Saint Laurent Rive Gauche business model inspired it. Givenchy Nouvelle Boutique enjoyed immense success in the United States, where, under Ariane Brener's impetus, the collection was offered the best spaces in the good stores in the biggest towns. Stores including Bergdorf

Goodman, Neiman-Marcus, John Wanamaker, I. Magnin, Rich's, Stix Baer and Fuller, Swanson, Frederick & Nelson, etc. placed a beige and white space at Givenchy's disposal.

Despite his "University" experience, Hubert de Givenchy had mixed feelings about ready-to-wear. The prices always seemed too low to him. A skirt at a public price of 500 francs (about 350 euros) seemed an anomaly compared to those he created and sold successfully in couture. To actually make up his mind on the subject, he expressed the desire to visit our factories, but he kept his conclusions to himself.

A shy man, despite the ease his elegant silhouette lent him, Hubert de Givenchy was the incarnation of urbanity. The five years our collaboration lasted were light and warm, filled with the enthusiasm for a courteous relationship, exempt from any kind of moodiness.

The Italian competition. In 1970, when C. Mendès decided to concentrate its activities on the most successful lines, there were no factories in France or Italy likely to take over the technical and commercial management of the haute couture labels, which had been orphaned by ready-to-wear.

There were different examples: Jean-Louis Scherrer, in order to reach a lower market with his "Saint Germain" collection, signed a contract with Gaston Jaunet, shortly before Guy Laroche. Jean Patou built his own factory, and Emanuel Ungaro turned to Italy. When Ungaro opened his boutique in 1967 on avenue Montaigne, his supplier was a traditional company: Jeannette, reputed for their reversible coats. He later collaborated with C. Mendès. The first "Ungaro Parallel" collection, manufactured by C. Mendès, was shown in Paris in October and in New York in November 1967, and the second in April 1968.

Nonetheless, the climate was morose. C. Mendès continued forward in a vague uneasiness that was the result of several things. The difficult merger with Maria Carine was one of them. There was also the turmoil that spread from one couture house to another, as they closed their doors, transferring their problem to their main "edition manufacturer." Buyers turned away from haute couture, more interested in ready-to-wear, and the haute couture clients hurried to the Saint Laurent Rive Gauche and Courrèges boutiques to buy more attractive dresses that were ready to be bought and worn.

At the same time C. Mendès, which I have always considered a public institution, was forced to turn itself into an industrial company. The CEGOS engineers arrived and their theoretical analyses worried the company, factory, and workshop managers. Seen as a great success, the Saint Laurent Rive Gauche experience was not, it seemed, something that could be done with other designers.

Dizzy with anxiety, Emanuel Ungaro went to Barfil in Turin on the advice of Vittorio Azzario from Nattier, his main fabric supplier. Ungaro had tested raincoats and sportswear with Barfil a year earlier in 1968. To Emanuel Ungaro's despair, the trial was not conclusive.

In 1970, Barfil put him in contact with an industrial group that mainly worked with men's clothing, GFT (Gruppo Financiaro Tessile de Turin). Although haute couture was not their field, they were fascinated by it. Pier Girogio Rivetti watched Emanuel Ungaro with benevolent curiosity, considering that while they were totally different, their professions could nonetheless find a meeting point that would enable them to forge a new path to take the business forward. He made his decision and he offered Emanuel Ungaro a factory, a manager, and 200 people, through the CIDAT (Compani Italiana Di Abbigliamento Torino).

Quite rightly, Ungaro considered that the workshops so generously placed at his disposal were under his direct responsibility; in fact for about 10 years, CIDAT worked only for him and GFT had no other couturiers under contract.

Until 1980, orders were taken in the avenue Montaigne salons and handled by GFT, which, through its subsidiary, only had a manufacturing license.

Accompanied by Henry Berghauer, Emanuel Ungaro criss-crossed the United States, visiting his clients. GFT paid him 20 per cent of the turnover he generated. The sole guarantee of stability for Ungaro and the future of GFT lay in the relationship of mutual trust between Emanuel Ungaro and Marco Rivetti.

In January 1977, François Baufumé left Courrèges to take up the position of export manager of the Donna division of the GFT group. The latter had a turnover of about 40 billion lira, 600 million of which were from exports. It was still a small business. Although the women's labels GFT distributed—Cori Lady, Marc Tilby, Mix and Match—were famous in Italy, these had little impact abroad.

François Baufumé set up his offices in Paris and proposed a short-term action plan that appealed to Marco Rivetti.

The first phase consisted of recruiting a woman who would fulfill the position of production manager. The lucky candidate, Rosanna Oddone, who would be the future Madame Baufumé, considered that there was only one stylist who would fit into the newly elaborated project: Giorgio Armani. In July 1977, they contacted Sergio Galleotti, president and business partner of Giorgio Armani, located on corso Venezia in Milan, who agreed to a deal in September. The arrival of the new recruit provoked a mini cultural revolution within GFT. Armani was known in the United States, where he had successfully introduced a women's collection. He had presented his first 1978–1979 winter collection in New York; it took place under excellent conditions and it was a triumph. While GFT learned its new profession, in 1974 C. Mendès signed an agreement with Valentino, before signing a licensing contract with Chanel in 1976.

In 1974, no Italian structure was capable of efficiently fulfilling the technical and commercial requirements of Giancarlo Giammetti, Valentino's president. The contract with C. Mendès was finally signed in Rome, via Gregoriana, on 11 December 1974 at 5:00 AM, after a marathon session attended by C. Mendès' and Valentino's American lawyers. Five years of stormy and passionate collaboration resulted in a negotiated rupture in 1979.

Meanwhile, GFT's financial and technical structure had been reinforced, surpassing C. Mendès. Valentino's manufacturing was taken over by the CIDAT. François Baufumé left GFT on 30 March 1980 to become president of Kenzo. Armani and Valentino were internationally well established and GFT negotiated a distribution license with Emanuel Ungaro. The financial structure a company like GFT possessed allowed them to set up sales offices in Paris, New York, and Milan. Their profitability was guaranteed by the Ungaro, Armani, Valentino and Montana collections in 1987, and lastly the Christian Dior collections. Italian ready-to-wear was gaining ground. In the eighties, GFT which was the originator of "made in Italy" fashion, synonymous with high quality and a European style, was worth one billion dollars. Sixty per cent of its sales were coming from outside of Italy, and the United States accounted for 26 per cent of total exports.

Almost single-handedly GFT created the American market for Italian fashion brands. In the early 1990s, it represented at least 10,000 employees, spread over 45

Facing page: Emanuel Ungaro, spring–summer 1986. Rights Reserved.

small companies and 18 factories united under the emblem Gruppo GFT. It distributed and sold 60 branded collections in 70 countries.[29] In fact, in 1992, the group earned 50 per cent of its turnover, some 6.5 billion francs, on labeled couture licenses.

Nonetheless, over a period of 20 years, the system became more complicated. GFT began to produce and market its own brands; Valentino produced its Olivier line itself; and Armani progressively became an autonomous industrial and financial group. The superposition of structures involved a series of costs and margins, weighing heavily on prices and profits. In April 1993, the Rivetti family put up 60 per cent of their shares in GFT for sale.

Another significant Italian company, Genny, was only a small boutique in Ancône in 1966. In 1968, Arnoldo Girombelli (deceased in 1983) built a workshop on the model of the French companies of the time. This was the starting point for an ambitious and brilliant diversification policy.

While GFT had a vast licensing policy, after an attempt at obtaining a Christian Lacroix license, Donatella Girombelli decided to follow the model developed by Gaby Aghion, with the slight, but major, difference that under her management she multiplied companies like Chloé.

Genny, Pierre d'Alby, or Chloé, on the one hand, and GFT or C. Mendès on the other represented two types of companies, each having their own qualities. Genny's tactic was to renew her style by changing designers, like Pierre d'Alby or Chloé. GFT, however, developed their market by multiplying licenses and, to a lesser extent, their own lines. Their success, like C. Mendès', only depended on a creative label's inability to integrate their industrial activity into their own houses.

Chanel ready-to-wear. Couturiers and manufacturers did not manage to coordinate their professions with the same ease. While certain manufacturers like C. Mendès and GFT distributed the clothes they made for grand couturiers successfully, the situation remained more conflicted for the grand couturiers who did not manage to have their manufacturing and couture activities operate harmoniously under the same label.

Courrèges and Jean Patou learned this at their expense. When it was Chanel's turn to grant C. Mendès a ready-to-wear license, it seemed that the couturiers had come to terms with it. In 1975, C. Mendès decided to diversify because the company realized the dangers that a subservience to Yves Saint Laurent, their unique and omnipresent client, represented. In addition, the relationship between Pierre Bergé and the new C. Mendès majority group was lacking in warmth; as for the relationship with Giancarlo Giammetti, Valentino's president, it was disintegrating by the day.

Having entered the couture world with certain modesty, my associates were growing bolder, even claiming an opinion on fashion. The creators I introduced them to with a view to a collaboration—Issey Miyake, Jean-Charles de Castelbajac, Claude Montana, or Thierry Mugler—were refused on the grounds that they lacked credibility. I employed miraculous inventions, cunning even, to extol their merits; it was of no use. Their fashion was considered vulgar, brash, and in the best case, unsellable. Tired of these refusals, I resigned myself to contacting Chanel.

Of all the couturiers that still existed in the sixties, Chanel and Balenciaga were the only brands that decided not to create a ready-to-wear line, along with franchises and licenses, a system that was the basis for the couture's prestige and future.

Accompanied by André Grézaud, new president of C. Mendès, I made an appointment, somewhat half-heartedly, with Christian Legrez, who, to my great surprise, actually showed an interest. Very quickly, Alain Wertheimer and his lawyer—who happened to be his mother Mrs. Liliane Heilbronn—intervened in the negotiations. To start with, the contract was only for the United States. I provided Alain Wertheimer with an exhaustive list of clients where I thought Chanel could have a place. The agreement finally came, but with a request: the client list had to be part of the contract. A written agreement would be demanded for any new decision on the choice of a client. This was an intolerable request as a regular practice, but we agreed to it because the quality of the work relationship between the two houses was so good.

The first collection, designed by Philippe Guibourgé, was a success.[30] About 20 "corners" arranged by Chanel were planned and executed.

In 1981 Alain Wertheimer interrupted his licensing contract with C. Mendès, and Béatrice Bongibault took over production of Chanel ready-to-wear. Thus Chanel, like Poiret in 1913, controlled the production and sales of all its products:

perfumes, accessories, couture, and ready-to-wear. In 1992 Françoise Montenay, couture manager, ran about 70 subsidiary boutiques in the world. In this way, Chanel returned to the practice of absolute control over all the elements involved in the management of their products. This was the specificity of the luxury companies, along the same lines as Paquin, Lucile, or Poiret; they were sole producers of their creations and sole distributors of their products through their subsidiaries.

In 1983, against all expectations, going against all the traditions and rules in application at the time, Chanel did not renew the contract of their exclusive designer Philippe Guibourgé. Instead, they gave the artistic direction of their collections to a man who claimed the status of free designer: Karl Lagerfeld. Setting a precedent, the most famous of mercenary stylists had the most mythical couture house amongst his clients.

By accepting Chanel's artistic direction, he raised the status of the designer to that of grand couturier. Without being bound by any restrictions of exclusivity, Gianfranco Ferré, Angelo Tarlazzi, and Claude Montana also created collections for couture houses that were in competition with their own brands.[31]

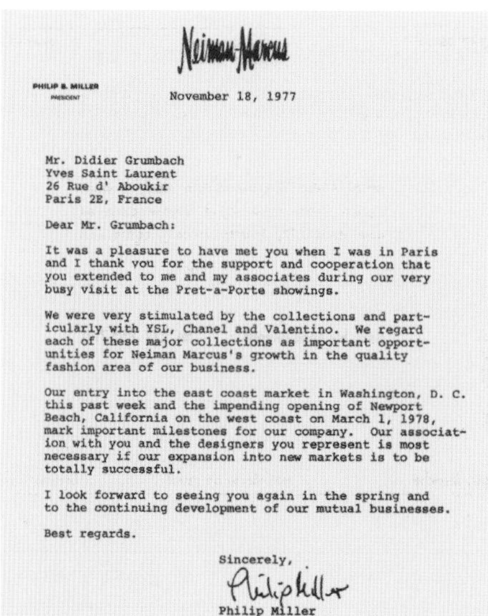

Neiman-Marcus

PHILIP B. MILLER
PRESIDENT

November 18, 1977

Mr. Didier Grumbach
Yves Saint Laurent
26 Rue d' Aboukir
Paris 2E, France

Dear Mr. Grumbach:

It was a pleasure to have met you when I was in Paris and I thank you for the support and cooperation that you extended to me and my associates during our very busy visit at the Pret-a-Porte showings.

We were very stimulated by the collections and particularly with YSL, Chanel and Valentino. We regard each of these major collections as important opportunities for Neiman Marcus's growth in the quality fashion area of our business.

Our entry into the east coast market in Washington, D. C. this past week and the impending opening of Newport Beach, California on the west coast on March 1, 1978, mark important milestones for our company. Our association with you and the designers you represent is most necessary if our expansion into new markets is to be totally successful.

I look forward to seeing you again in the spring and to the continuing development of our mutual businesses.

Best regards.

Sincerely,

Philip Miller

Letter from Philip Miller, president of Neiman-Marcus, addressed to C. Mendès, 1977.

Notes

1. Jacqueline Demornex, *Madeleine Vionnet, op. cit.*
2. Yvonne Deslandres, *Poiret, op. cit.*
3. His predecessors or successors as president of the union/Chambre Syndicale.
4. On the cover of *Marie-Claire* of 21 January 1938, Geneviève Boucher, future Geneviève Fath, wore a Lucien Lelong Edition dress.
5. The UFAC has a copy of Jean Dessès Couturiers Assoicés; the Galliéra Museum a model of Jacques Fath Couturiers Associés.
6. "Marcel Rochas joins Couturiers Associés," *Paris Match*, 9 February 1952.
7. Quoted by D. Veillon, *La Mode sous l'Occupation, op. cit.*
8. Note of July 1941, preserved in the Majestic files. Quoted by D. Veillon, *La Mode sous l'Occupation, op. cit.*
9. Interview with Philippe Heim.
10. Interviews with Hubert de Givenchy and Philippe Venet.
11. In 1963, Jacques Griffe produced his ready-to-wear himself. Armand Léon, interview with the *Figaro*, 23 January 1963.
12. *WWD*, 9 October 1961.
13. C. Mendès became the only organization specializing in haute couture ready-to-wear, with 12 licensing contracts: Castillo, Jean Dessès, Givenchy, Jacques Heim, Jeanne Lanvin, Guy Laroche, Jean Patou, Madeleine de Rauch, Yves Saint Laurent, Jean-Louis Scherrer, Emanuel Ungaro, and Philippe Venet.
14. Bernadine Morris, *New York Times*, 23 May 1964.
15. "Fit" signifying the way the garment fell.
16. Elizabeth Arden—*buyer*: Tania Shaïn.
17. When he opened his house in New York, at 63 E 57th Street, Charles James worked for Elizabeth Arden's fashion department.
18. Lord & Taylor: GMM John Schumaker, DMM Kat Ruttenstein—*buyers*; Bill Shedleski, M. Bradley, M. Larrimer.
19. I. Magnin: VP Russel Carpenter—*buyers*: Jack Miles, Imogene Schubert, Neiman Marcus: VP Kay Kerr.
20. CEGOS: General Scientific Commission, founded in 1926. Training, organization, and recruitment consultancy firm. Honorary president: Octave Gélinier.
21. Eliette Roux, manager of Bergdorf Goodman's haute couture department, became sales and purchasing manager for the Givenchy boutique, located in the same space.
22. About 44 million euros.
23. In 1975, André Courrèges produced 500,000 pullovers in France (compare to the 800,000 produced by Vitos) and manufactured 60,000 pieces of assembly line woven fabric.
24. Joseph Stam, an associate with C. Mendès in 1909.
25. Germaine Guénifet (suits) and Aline Bouet (loose wear).
26. One boutique in 1967, 500 pieces; 20 boutiques in 1969, 20,000 pieces; 50 in 1971; 70 in 1979; 150 in 1980, 160,000 pieces.
27. Previously cabinet manager for Pierre Messmer, Maurice Cau replaced André Lévi as manager of Saint Laurent Rive Gauche. André Lévi's task had mainly consisted of developing Yves Saint Laurent licenses.
28. 15 million francs, 1972; that is to say, 8.8 million euros.
29. *Harvard—L'Expansion*, spring 1992.
30. *New York Times* and *WWD* of 31 March 1977.
31. Gianfranco Ferré for Dior, Angelo Tarlazzi for Guy Laroche, Claude Montana for Lanvin.

CHAPTER III
STYLISTS—THE NEW FASHION CREATORS

In 1952 two young beginners, Ghislaine de Polignac and Maïmé Arnodin, ardently brandished the standard of couture's eternal value. This enthusiasm got them their first jobs. As a connoisseur, Ghislaine de Polignac expounded the rules of good taste at Galeries Lafayette; Maïmé Arnodin went even further and revealed new trends from beyond the mainstream. In the span of a century, they replicated the respective roles played by Madame Roger and Charles Frédéric Worth.

In the chaos that followed May 1968, couturiers had no qualms about granting their brands to those who offered the most money while they adventured down the more seductive and lucrative ready-to-wear path. Maïmé Arnodin and the fashion consultants were worn out by power and gave it up to their favored designers who challenged the premise that haute couture was the sole source of creativity.

During this great upheaval Sonia Rykiel opened her boutique, Karl Lagerfeld made an impact on Chloé, and Yves Saint Laurent triumphed with Rive Gauche... This was a most troubling coincidence, when one considers that the leading self-proclaimed independent stylist, Karl Lagerfeld, and the last of the self-crowned grand couturiers, Yves Saint Laurent, had entered the universe of couture together in November 1954. They had both won a competition organized by Thelma Sweetinburgh[1] for the International Wool Secretariat and were shown on the cover of *Paris-Presse* as the Goncourt of fashion design. The jury consisted of Christian Dior, Jacques Fath, Hubert de Givenchy, Jacqueline Delubac, Gruau, Jean Oberlé, Hélène Lazareff, Michel de Brunhoff, Simone Baron, Andrée Castanié, and Marguerite de Souza.[2] Karl Lagerfeld won the prize for the best coat and joined the house of Pierre Balmain. Yves Saint Laurent won for the best dress and he joined Christian Dior. A young journalism trainee Janie Samet[3] wrote her first article for the *Echo d'Oran*, dedicated to Yves Saint Laurent. Henceforth, couture designers with the same training and, perhaps one could conclude, the same level of talent, used their skills fluently in either couture or ready-to-wear while the stylists—those who designed for others—started to look out for their own interests to become veritable fashion créateurs.

Thierry Mugler. "Les Fourmis," le défilé des 20 ans, Cirque d'Hiver, 1995. Photo Patrice Stable.

The First Stylists

Alain Lalonde. In the 1950s fabric dealers had very close relationships with their clients' manufacturers and weavers. This led to friendships that encouraged healthy business collaborations. Amongst them, Alain Lalonde[4] was the most progressive in terms of the evolution of the fashion trade. He was the first to see how to lead the profession towards those who would soon bring about its transformation: fashion stylists.

At the time I often lunched with him at Louis XIV, place des Victoires, or at Georges, rue du Mail, where he had a standing table. Everything about fabric design fueled his imagination and stimulated his insatiable curiosity. His love of adventure and the solid training he had received at the prestigious Ecole Centrale led him quite naturally to place his talent and his money behind other talents. As the head of an important company—he was the heir in a line of textile industrialists—he could only consider accomplishing his personal ambitions by giving of himself, and this was evident in his passion for discovery. The founder of the family company, Raphaël Lévy, was his ancestor. He was a teacher and mayor of Schirrofen, a small town near Bischwiller in Alsace. Before the 1870 war, Raphaël had several children, including Achille, Alain Lalonde's great grandfather; Paul, André Maurois' grandfather; and Rosine, who married Maurice Blin. That is where everything began. Maurice Blin (Blin & Blin) inherited a fairly prosperous textile company from his grandfather that had been established in Elbeuf after the 1870 defeat and the Prussian annexation of Alsace. As for Achille Lévy and his brothers, they started a fabric business and opened their establishment at rue Etienne Marcel, in the offices that are today occupied by Zadig & Voltaire.

Lalonde and Blin got on famously and united their efforts in a judicious collaboration. While Achille Lévy became a fabric designer and wholesaler, Blin & Blin became industrial weavers. Lalonde, who was a partner with this company, distributed his exclusive designs as well as those he represented from Blin & Blin, a company famous for its soft satin finished *drap amazon*, a special high-quality woven wool serge that came in a variety of colors and was a reference for the whole industry. Alain Lalonde, the grandson of the dealership's founder, was first and foremost an aesthete whose ambition was to pursue his artistic commitment as wholeheartedly as he pursued business. This was his state of mind when he took over the management of the family business after much hesitation. Knowing how difficult it would be to reconcile his passionately romantic aspirations with the seriousness that business demanded, he worked at coordinating his skills throughout his career, making them a second nature; plurality soon became his brand. He had known the horror of the Nazi camps; he managed to escape these before joining the resistance in London. His activity within the resistance was not enough for him. He became editor of *Cadran,* a propaganda paper that he scattered all over the French countryside from an airplane accompanied by the woman who soon became his second wife. It was clear that for Lalonde any undertaking had to be lived as an exalted action. Women, whom he loved as sensual images full of elegance and harmony, occupied a unique position in his life. Weren't the Braques, Picassos, Légers, Giacomettis, Constantin Guys that made up his collection, along with other artists, an acknowledgement of his admiration for the beautiful women that surrounded him, as well as nod to the pleasure he took in creating his fabric collection? In fact, whether it was a piece of art by a master, a hairstyle, or a beautiful fabric, the pleasure of aesthetic emotion was the same for him. Lalonde was raised in the tradition of the old wool weavers, and he maintained the trade's obsession for tactile sensations along with the love for pure materials and beautiful combed fabric. He wanted to share his passion and knowledge, and this time he began a dialogue with the young stylists who visited rue Etienne Marcel.

Christiane Bailly and Emmanuelle Khanh. A tall, elegant, brown-haired young woman often went to Lalonde to choose fabric for her clients: Chloé, Nale, Lempereur, Dejac, Marie Chasseng, Gattegno. Alain Lalonde was convinced of her talent and was captivated by the flexibility with which she moved between the rows of fabric from which she confidently made her choices. He often was the first to see her sketches and one day he suggested that she open her own house. The woman's name was Christiane Bailly, and she became the first stylist not trained in haute couture. Bailly was unsure of herself; the idea of starting her own business frightened her and she declined. It seemed audacious to create a label outside of the haute couture circle. Nonetheless, she had a lot of talent and the idea followed its course. One day Emmanuelle Khanh, who was also a cabin model with Balenciaga, showed Bailly a shirt with a very pointed collar that she had just sold to Cacharel. Christiane Bailly admired the model and immediately suggested she become a partner in her company, following Alain Lalonde's suggestion. This was the birth of Emma-Christie. Gil

"Fashion burst out of the windows." Fashion show for the beginning of the 1963 school year (September) The glass was removed from the windows of Les Galeries Lafayette; concept Emmanuelle Khanh and Quasar. © Archives Galeries Lafayette/ Rights Reserved.

Emmanuelle Khanh and her husband, the designer Quasar, in 1962. Photo Pierre Boulat, courtesy Agence Cosmos.

In 1967, the 20-year-old department, inaugurated in 1959, was displayed in the Galeries Lafayette windows with brands like Pierre d'Alby, Georges Rech…
© Archives Galeries Lafayette/ Rights Reserved.

Christiane Bailly and her husband Antoine Stinco.
Courtesy Antoine Stinco.

Coutin manufactured and distributed the collection, for which Lalonde was the main fabric supplier and financial backer.

The first Emma-Christie collection was shown in 1962 at Pharamond, a restaurant in rue de la Grande-Truanderie; the next was in a Saint Germain bistro, rue du Sabot. Although the women were united under the same label, each stylist showed their models in turn to protect their creative integrity. These very distinct talents evolved quite freely. The events were nearly sacrilegious: no one had ever presented fashion for the street, in the street, under a stylist's name. *Life* and *Look*, all-powerful magazines in the international press, related these historic moments with a sense of wonder and an evident enthusiasm. In 1960, at square Jasmin, Maïmé Arnodin encouraged Gérard Pipart to show his talent through her clients' brands. A year later, stylists were signing their models, or at least sharing in the collaboration, but it did not matter: even if it was two halves of a label, the event was an important one.

While Gérard Pipart learnt his profession with Fath and then Givenchy, Christiane Bailly and Emmanuelle Khanh, both models with Balenciaga and Givenchy, had lived alongside the work of the grand couturiers because of all the long hours of fittings they did. The ritual of the major houses fascinated them as did the dresses they showed daily to clients in the salons. But what they saw did not correspond to their idea of fashion and certainly did not match their lifestyle. In 1957, Ramón Esparza—Balenciaga's right hand man in charge of casting—chose Christiane Bailly and the painter Karel Appel's wife. It was clear that what Christiane Bailly was most interested in was gaining access to these demi-gods, Chanel and Balenciaga, and to share their skill in silence, immersing herself in their universe of shapes and refinement. And she did this despite the fact that while she was a student at the Beaux Arts, free and constantly on the verge of revolt, she threw herself heart and soul into the events of May 1968. She remained a grand bourgeois and she maintained a love-hate relationship with her own world. At that time, she was interested in only one thing: drawing. Thus an article on stylism that appeared in *Le Nouvel Observateur* piqued her curiosity. Unfortunately the fashion consultants of the time did not exercise the profession she dreamt of.

Andrée Putman, whom Bailly met during this period, strongly advised her to never admit she knew how to draw. Drawing, however, was something she had to do. Bailly's obstinacy helped her climb the ranks and become a top fashion stylist in the French fashion industry. She then tried to sell her drawings to the department stores' style offices, to Claude de Coux and Chloé de Bruneton along with a few mock-ups she placed with agents during the collection dates. After Emma-Christie, Claude Brouet, who had introduced Bailly to Denise Fayolle, advised her to join Chloé, which she did in 1963 when the team that was to replace Gérard Pipart was being put together.

At the same time, before going into an association with Christiane Bailly in Emma-Christie, Emmanuelle Khanh, a model with Givenchy, had designed her own fashion collection with the help of a third fittings assistant. One of her outfits was a small military jacket worn over a sailor skirt and it had had Hubert de Givenchy and Philippe Venet, his first cutter, in stitches of laughter when they unexpectedly entered the workshop at lunchtime. Their reaction did not seem to have discouraged her, and while she continued to create her dresses, she modeled free-lance for Prisunic and Galeries Lafayette; she also assisted Christiane Bailly, sketching models for Printemps or Dorothée, the Jacobson boutique. There was no doubt about it; she had a style that was soon recognized by Claude Brouet, who dedicated her first article to her.

At the end of 1962, the Emma-Christie adventure came to an end. In agreement with their respective husbands, Christiane and Emmanuelle decided to end their collaboration; in adversity, unselfish help from friends can allow one to overcome difficulties, but with the same unyielding logic, the nectar of success can undo a patiently woven relationship.

As a spectator, Alain Lalonde continued to believe that adventures like this could still exist. He did, however, acknowledge that distributing successfully both the Gil Coutin and Emma-Christie collections was challenging. Nonetheless, thanks to his perseverance, he soon launched a new association.

Daniel Hechter, a stylist with Pierre d'Alby, was also a regular at Lalonde's offices on rue Etienne Marcel. When Hechter decided to open an eponymous fashion house in 1962, Alain Lalonde financed his first fashion shows and lent Hecther his press attaché, as he had intuitively realized that the era of communication had dawned.

In 1967, he encouraged Christian Aujard, the sales director of Charles Maudret, to launch his own label. Lalonde supported him by advancing the necessary funds and offered him the top floor of his building for the new offices.

During this period, two boutiques had opened in Paris: Laura on avenue du Général Leclerc and Dorothée on rue de Sèvres. Their respective owners, Sam

Rykiel and Elie Jacobson, also had a professional and social relationship with Alain Lalonde. Elie Jacobson remembers the great attention Alain Lalonde paid to the most inventive and demanding stylists. Lalonde was particularly attentive to Elie's wife Jacqueline when she decided to develop her own collection.

It was a favorable period for the boutiques that put fashion in the forefront thanks to support generated in magazines such as *Le Jardin des Modes* and *Elle*. It was as if haute couture no longer existed. The fashion editors seemed to suffer from amnesia since they had only one thing that interested them: stylism! Everyone anxiously waited for magazines to hit the newsstands. The trends the whole profession were on the lookout for were immediately taken up and the models copied.

Once again, it was the ever-insightful Alain Lalonde who understood that business trends were going to be reversed. The boutiques created new management structures to organize their own fashion production. Lalonde was a pioneer when fashion retail changed its course and in 1964 he financed the opening of a boutique on place des Victoires, in the heart of Paris' Sentier neighborhood, an area he liked but which was totally foreign to fashion. Alain Lalonde's foresight was really impressive when one knows how well this area has done in retail. The boutique, under the management of Catherine Chaillet, was called Victoire and it showcased different fashion labels and products. She offered the first Loden coats; Donald Davies' Irish products; Marimekko's Finnish products; English products from Daks; along with jewelry, bags, and other accessories by Catherine Chaillet; and of course the Lalonde fabrics. In 1967 Alain Lalonde sold the shop to Antoine Riboud, and Françoise Chassagnac took over the management.

Like Dorothée Bis and Sonia Rykiel, Victoire offered a range that represented its original concept. The boutiques that were well established at the time included the oldest one, Marie-Martine. Marcel and Fred Salem, two cousins from Peru, opened the shop at the end of the 1950s on rue de Sèvres. This store was different from the others because it sold high-end products to a more bourgeois clientele. The Salems had a good reputation in fashion and bought grand couturiers' ready-to-wear from C. Mendès as well as the Trois Hirondelles collections on the specific condition that they would get good press reviews, which started to have an increasingly important[5] impact on consumers.

Michèle Rosier. In 1963 the trio consisting of Christiane Bailly, Emmanuelle Khanh, and Michèle Rosier—the most recent arrival—was nicknamed "the fashion terrorists." Rosier, who started her career in journalism, was different from the two other needle-and-scissor aficionados. She had been a reporter at *France Soir*, then editor-in-chief at *Nouveau Femina*. In the throes of a violent passion for a philosophy graduate—Jean-Pierre Bamberger, whose family business was in difficulty—she decided to abandon her pen for a pencil and sketched a fake-fur anorak for her friend. It was worn by slipping it over the head. It was a miracle! This item was a huge success and was immediately embraced by the press and the public. She then was practically obliged to start a company, for which she imagined a very short name, V de V, an abbreviation of "Vetêments de Vacances," a clever way to say "vacation wear." The business boomed ahead at top speed without her mother, Hélène Lazareff, knowing anything about it. When she found out, she was terribly upset that her daughter had gotten involved in fashion because of love! Very quickly her talent was recognized by *Life* magazine, to the great relief of *Elle* magazine because they could finally promote the owner's daughter. V de V set up a production unit at Roubaix that soon employed 100 workers. Michèle Rosier was the first to create active day wear. She particularly enjoyed manipulating fabrics: she invented stretch vinyl, consumed a vast quantity of parachute fabric, and used brightly colored nylon sail material.

While V de V was Rosier's main focus, she collaborated for several seasons with Chloé—where she replaced Christiane Bailly—alongside Karl Lagerfeld, Graziella Fontana, and Tan Giudicelli. At the same time, she was a designer for Pierre d'Alby and Monsieur Z, a manufacturer of "poor" fur (everyone remembers his multicolored rabbit). After 10 years of fashion, where she proved her great originality, she moved into the world of cinema in 1972 and directed her first feature film in 1973. Agnès B replaced her at V de V.

The 1965 fashion show organized by the Paris Fashion Group in Neuilly could have been called "Design versus Couture." On one side, Emmanuelle Khanh, Michèle Rosier, and Christiane Bailly had their clothes worn by "neurasthenic" looking models who wandered through the hall looking lost. On the other, Castillo, Jean Patou, Madeleine de Rauch, and Philippe Venet had their ready-to-wear worn by professional models that embodied the stereotype of Parisian chic. It was two irreconcilable visions of elegance.

Here are the trouble makers of French fashion: the stylists Graziella Fontana, Karl Lagerfeld, Emmanuelle Khanh, Jacques Delahaye, Michèle Rosier, Daniel Hechter, Christiane Bailly. *WWD*, 12 October 1966.
In 1963, Michèle Rosier created the brand V de V, an abbreviation of Vêtements de Vacances (vacation clothing), and invented extensible vinyl while continuing her collaboration with Chloé.
"Ready to wear defies haute couture," a Jacques Delahaye model was chosen for the cover of the magazine *Elle* in 1966.
3,000 units of Jacques Delahaye's leather trimmed, belted ratine coat were sold in 1967. Cover of the magazine *GAP*, 1967.
Christiane Bailly, 1962. Courtesy Antoine Stinco.

Everybody was instantly shocked. The divided audience was either enthusiastic or enraged, petrified by the outrage they felt they had been subjected to. In 1966 Hébé Dorsey invited the three heroines to New York for the "April in Paris Ball," accompanied by Paco Rabanne,[6] whose metallic dresses had made him famous. This time it was a total flop. The scandal became apparent from the caustic silence of the audience that filed out of the hall in dead quiet. Melka Treanton, who was a stringer at the time and Hébé Dorsey's assistant, has a shattering memory of the event.[7]

Jacques Delahaye. "Ready-to-wear is in the hands of women," read the headlines. It so happened that after having tasted the privilege of being the first, if not the only ones, in ready-to-wear, our three militants—Emmanuelle Khanh, Christiane Bailly, and Michèle Rosier—had to make room for a young man who, at the outset, introduced himself with a more classic but very innovative style. He was Jacques Delahaye. He fought on all fronts with the kind of audacity shy people sometimes have. He created coats for Dejac, dresses for Anne Marie, sportswear for Perrier, and leather for Mac Douglas—the best in leather at the time. The work Delahaye did for all these brands built his success that was unquestioned because his clothes were also solid commercial hits. His famous leather-trimmed and belted ratine coat sold 3,000 pieces in 1967.

Delahaye was originally from Cherbourg. At 30 years old, he had two little girls and, thanks to his talent, he was the first ready-to-wear designer that haute couture called upon for creative work.

In 1968, he signed a contract with the Jacques Heim company for two seasons, after its creator died. The contract was renewable if both parties were satisfied.

Although the corridors of fashion were impenetrable in 1968, Delahaye showed pantsuits and slinky, black silk dresses at the same time that Yves Saint Laurent did. His friend Juliette Gréco, whom he dressed, was a great inspiration. The collection was a brilliant demonstration of elegant virtuosity and balance, but the house's traditional clients—the most famous of whom was Yvonne de Gaulle, whom Simone Heim visited as a neighbor for the fittings—just did not understand. The contract was not renewed, and shortly afterwards Jacques Heim closed down.

Daniel Hechter and Jean Cacharel. Daniel Hechter and Cacharel were two famous fashion brands backed by two great entrepreneurs—Daniel Hechter and Jean Bousquet. At the age of 17 Daniel Hechter became a storekeeper at Max Mozès, a wholesale couture house where his father worked. Hechter was fascinated by the pattern designer's work in the office next to his. He desperately wanted to do the same, and registered at a cutting school on the avenue de l'Opéra where he studied part time. Did everything happen faster back then compared with today? At least things seemed to have been easier. A year later, he borrowed 2,000 francs and he rented a maid's room on avenue de l'Opéra where he made his sketches, and then went on to hire a cutter. In 1957, Louis Féraud and Jacques Esterel immediately bought his sketches. One of Hechter's designs, a turquoise suit, was chosen by Brigitte Bardot—whom Esterel dressed—for Michel Boisrond's film *La Parisienne.* Hechter also sold sketches to Pierre d'Alby, who hired him when he had completed his military service. He produced sketches that did not necessarily conform to d'Alby's taste, and for these he looked for additional clients. Daniel Hechter then thought of selling them himself for a sales representative's commission. He put them into a box and went to Laura, Dorothée, les Galeries Lafayette, and he was successful. Soon his commission plus his salary, as well as the royalties he received from Max Mozès, where he had become the stylist, raised his monthly income to 25,000 francs (about 10,000 euros).

In 1961, Hechter was 22 years old. With his savings as his capital, Lalonde's support, and a guarantee that Galeries Lafayette would place orders worth five million francs a year, he started his own company.

Jean Bousquet studied in a technical college, but he was first and foremost a self-made man. He loved soccer and women, and he loved the pleasure laborious laziness could procure. He started out as a trouser maker with his sister Marine, in a small workshop near rue Vieille du Temple, where he cut and gave everything to be stitched elsewhere. Elie Jacobson introduced him to Emmanuelle Khanh and for three years she designed his skirts, shirts, and sportswear.

It wasn't until 1970, however, that the Cacharel company began to reveal the full extent of its capacities. To start with, it developed a real image concept, thanks to the concerted help of its friends: Corrine Sarrut, a stylist who was married to the architect Gérard Grandval, and Robert Delpire, advertising executive, married to the photographer Sarah Moon.

After the men's line in 1969, the children's line appeared in 1972. The immense success of the perfumes that were licensed to L'Oréal contributed to the company's strength. Later, one could see Cacharel's influence on Naf Naf and Chevignon.

Jean Bousquet, known as Cacharel, c. 1965. Rights Reserved.

America rapidly became aware of the effervescence in French fashion and the 12 October 1966 edition of *Women's Wear Daily* declared its favorite talents: Christiane Bailly, Emmanuelle Khanh, Graziella Fontana, Michèle Rosier, Jacques Delahaye, Karl Lagerfeld, Daniel Hechter, and Jean Cacharel (illus. p. 279).

> This represents a considerable amount of talent. One thing is certain: they have made the French woman on the street more beautiful than ever. Gone are the days when secretaries, salesgirls or petites bourgeois wore pathetic imitations of elegant couture models. In addition, intelligent couturiers like Yves Saint Laurent, who have realised this, now lend their talent to ready-to-wear. A couture house has to slowly transform itself into a laboratory to test its ready-to-wear.

This was also the time when well-known boutiques decided to develop their own collections, thus placing themselves amongst the fashion designers.

The Fashionable Boutiques

Dorothée Bis. Starting in 1946, Elie Jacobson worked as a master furrier on rue d'Hauteville. He was an expert in his field, and in 1958 he opened the store Dorothée, rue de Sèvres. This unusual neighborhood was not totally foreign to fashion, as Marie-Martine had already aroused the curiosity of the elegant local population that was avid for novelty. The articles Dorothée sold were more avant-garde and more moderately priced. The boutique had the Parisian exclusivity for Cacharel. From Nale, they chose the pieces designed by Gérard Pipart, Christiane Bailly, and Emmanuelle Khanh; Michèle Rosier's fashions from V de V; and Jacques Delahaye's outfits from Dejac. They bought collections from Emma-Christie, Jane Lend, Renata, Jeanine de Poortère, Pierre d'Alby, I.D. Saint Clair. Jacqueline and Elie Jacobson made their fashion choices based on a mix of confidence and foresight.

Their immediate success put an end to their exclusivities. In 1962, they acquired the shop next door that they named Dorothée Bis, where Jacqueline Jacobson developed her own concept. Agnès B got her first job there, before Guy Paulin and Michel Klein.

Only time can determine the supremacy of a store. Every week, everyone who was anyone in the fashion press world, from Hélène Lazareff to Maïmé Arnodin, came to visit the shop looking for new ideas to fuel their columns.

Jacqueline Jacobson did not force herself to create a whole collection. She developed themes based on what the boutique needed and what her inspiration lead her to design. Other Dorothée Bis stores that became franchisees entrusted Elie Jacobson with their purchasing budget. To obtain commitments from the manufacturers who worked with his wife, or the weavers who executed his designs and colors, Elie Jacobson had to create his own network, just as Saint Laurent Rive Gauche had done before him.

However great its success, Jacobson's system had its limitations. He had serious problems like discovering at the last minute, during the show, that there were outfits shown that had no references or specification sheets. He encouraged his wife, who was not really trained for it, to design complete collections within a seasonal calendar.[8]

Sonia Rykiel. Like Jacqueline Jacobson, Sonia Rykiel helped her husband Sam Rykiel with his purchasing for the boutique Laura, avenue du Général-Leclerc. She was all the more indispensable to him, as he was color blind, while she, as we all know, has an innate sense of color.

Painting, literature, and boys fascinated Sonia Rykiel, and nothing had predestined her for couture. On a whim, she interrupted her studies to take sculpting classes at the Grande Chaumière, a famous art academy in Montparnasse where famous painters came to practice sketching, painting, and drawing. On the family pediatrician's advice, Rykiel's mother forced her, as a punishment, to do an internship at the Grande Maison de Blanc, a department store specializing in linens. She loved creating window displays until one day her boss, Mr. Bloch, requested her presence in his office where an old, bearded gentleman, elegantly dressed in a raincoat, was waiting for her. "Allow me Mademoiselle, to tell you how talented you are. I have just bought all the scarves that were decorating the window." It was Matisse.

Rykiel's fiancé was Sammy and Maurice Weinberg's cousin, whose parents had a boutique in the avenue du Général-Leclerc; why not ask Sonia to do the window displays? In 1956, pregnant with her daughter Nathalie, she went to the boutique one evening to do the windows while she was waiting for her husband. Tired of hiding her bulge under the eternal smock with a matching kangaroo skirt, she asked the alterations girl to make her a loose dress; she barely looked pregnant and wore it majestically, as she found it "sublime."

Sonia Rykiel, pullover and trousers for winter, 1986.
Photo Dominique Issermann.
Sonia Rykiel, 1971.
Courtesy Sonia Rykiel/Rights Reserved.

During one of her evening visits, she surprised her husband who was buying pullovers from an Italian knitwear representative. Why didn't he order one she liked but in her size?

The sweater crossed the Alps, between Paris and Venice, seven times before it found its final shape. The day it finally arrived in the boutique, Nina Dausset happened to be there:

"Is it a child's pullover?"

"No, it's my pullover."

The "poor boy sweater" made the cover of *Elle* and decided Sonia Rykiel's brilliant career.

Until 1965, she continued working on this poor pullover, perfecting it, modifying it, reworking it incessantly—and then she had fun turning it into a dress, again with the alteration girl's help. In 1968 she got divorced and consoled herself by buying an antique shop in rue de Grenelle. The interior was all teak wood; it was lined with books given to her by Christian Bourgois and furnished with two Breuer armchairs. The boutique opened in June and Sonia Rykiel's sister, ethnologist and sociologist at the Collège de France, was the manager.

Rykiel organized private showings there. When, for the first time in knitwear history, Rykiel dared to put the stitching on the outside, Karl Lagerfeld, who was filming her fashion show, sent her a message of encouragement: "Stay with it, I think you've got something there." Fame was on the horizon. Bloomingdale's, Henri Bendel's, and Galeries Lafayette placed their first orders.

Between 1968 and 1973, Rykiel designed for Timwear, Real, and Leonard Atkins in New York in addition to developing her own collection. She became the undisputed knitwear queen: 4,000 catalogued models, presented like an architect's drawings. The first Sonia Rykiel franchise stores began to appear. In exchange for exclusivity, Sonia Rykiel received royalties on the boutiques' turnover, as well as on the sales by licensed suppliers. The genius who had invented this system was none other then her ex-husband. Nobody before Sonia Rykiel had received royalties from both their clients and their suppliers.

Today, Sonia Rykiel and Kenzo are among the leading French ready-to-wear industrialists.

Kenzo. Born in Himeji, near Osaka, Kenzo Takada grew up in the teahouse owned by his father, a flutist and civil servant, surrounded by seven siblings. He graduated from Bunka College, the notable fashion school in Tokyo, and set out on a pilgrimage to Paris in 1965.

He began to look for a job in the city that had inspired him throughout his studies, and he showed his sketches to Louis Féraud. Zizi Féraud bought five of them. Then the staff at *Elle* magazine recognized the young Japanese man's talent, sent him to Jacques Delahaye, who was technical advisor at Bon Magique at the time. Delahaye bought 10 sketches at 130 francs each and generously opened his address book for Kenzo, a rare occurrence in this profession. The meeting was decisive for Kenzo's career. The following day, Soizic Carré, pattern manager at *Jardin des Modes* who went on to become fashion manager at *Elle*, also bought sketches from him, as did Dominique Peclers, the Printemps style office manager.

Jacques Delahaye also introduced him to Pisanti where he worked for six months; it was at this time that he met Tan Giudicelli.

In 1966 he left Pisanti for Relations Textile, the first major marketing, promotion, and image consultancy managed by Claude de Coux. She took a liking to him, lent him an apartment, and taught him to work with apparel manufacturers, whom he later constantly came into contact with. His path to success was opening up.

Kenzo's talent, backed by freshness and an unfailing kindness, made him the object of everyone's admiration. He responded to all these acts of kindness with Asian simplicity and elegance.

The years went by and in 1970 he stumbled upon a boutique in gallery Vivienne. He took the lease with two friends, Atsuko Kondo and Atsuko Ansaï; they repainted the shop with a jungle theme in the style of Douanier Rousseau, and Jungle Jap was born. The workshops were on the first floor. Kenzo got his fabrics from the Marché Saint Pierre in Montmartre and produced five collections a year, shown at Gallery Vivienne. This joyous, creative, self-sufficient organization soon reached its limits. The orders were pouring in while the crowd of admirers was growing. In 1971, he was forced to change his organization and join the official ready-to-wear calendar.

Jungle Jap was different from Dorothée and Laura, boutiques that had opened to sell other designer's collections. When Kenzo was confronted at the outset with growing industrial and commercial problems, he had to make his own way. He certainly attained fame more rapidly, but he had to resolve the increasingly pressing problems of a small industrial structure. Gilles Raysse[9] was

Kenzo Takada, 1973.
© Kenzo Takada/Photo Ulli Rose.

Kenzo Takada opens his first boutique—Jungle Jap, painted in a Douanier Rousseau style, in Galerie Vivienne in April 1970.
© Kenzo Takada/Rights Reserved.

Passage Choiseul, Kenzo Takada, and his team during renovation of the second boutique, September 1970.
© KenzoTakada/Rights Reserved.

the first to attempt to organize the growth before 1980 when François Baufumé joined Kenzo and turned it into a company everyone envied because of its strong image and financial success.

Kenzo was the first "star" designer. After a rapid and efficient professional training, his talent only served himself, unlike his predecessor stylists whose personality was erased by the brands who employed them. With Créateurs & Industriels, designers like Roland Chakkal or Jean-Charles de Castelbajac were able, like Kenzo, to gain almost immediate recognition.

Créateurs & Industriels

During the sixties, designers' notoriety grew at the same pace as couturier ready-to-wear developed. While these parallel activities met with identical enthusiasm from the public, there was a sense of ambiguity over certain collections. Emmanuelle Khanh and Christiane Bailly contributed to the success of the brands that employed them but nonetheless they remained in the shadows because their names did not appear on the labels of the collections they designed for. In addition, it was clear that couture would not renew itself. I was sorry to admit this as I had often wished and argued for the opposite in the catalogues C. Mendès distributed to journalists. In 1970, on a flight to Rome, I had an idea that I absolutely wanted turn into a reality. Ready-to-wear had conquered the public so successfully that couture seemed to have been temporarily buried. Fashion was in the street being led by a battalion of young stylists and they needed some business management. The first was the ability to put their names on their designs like the couturiers did. The second was to facilitate the growth of their labels by having them work with industrial apparel makers. The agreement in practice between the Yves Saint Laurent and C. Mendès companies seemed to me to be the best adapted to the situation as it had proved to be absolutely efficient until then.

Stylists would offer the use of their names, a label of creativity, to manufacturers of all kinds of products without having to create companies. The manufacturers would have free access to an external, multi-brand creative studio that would enable them to reach new markets that complemented their traditional business. Créateurs & Industriels would be the link between the two. The formula was a simple one.

The company Créateurs & Industriels would sign contracts with each stylist for an exclusive usage of the new label that they would commit to promoting against a guaranteed monthly payment of seven-twelfths of the fees allocated by the manufacturers. The manufacturers would enter them into a contractual agreement with Créateurs & Industriels that would provide the promotion costs and coordinate distribution. A new kind of retail space, to be defined, would showcase all the products.

Right or wrong, when one is 30 years old, one is convinced that ideas should not be given time to mature. By the time I returned from Rome, my mind was made up.

At the time, the idea of remaking fashion was shared by several of us in the industry. Quasar and Emmanuelle Khanh, to name one couple, had a house in Normandy, close to ours. One could say that Emmanuelle was highly experienced. After all, she had already presented numerous collections and worked with a large number of manufacturers. Her winter 1965 show at the Palais des Glaces—when models, wearing ice skates, showed sportswear, furs, ski clothes, knitwear, bags, and umbrellas, under a multitude of different labels—is still remembered today.[10]

"Fashion creators." Emmanuelle Khanh was the first to contest the title of stylist. In fact, the name implicitly expressed the fact that the manufacturer maintained control over the product. On the other hand, if the artist signed his work, he had the right to be considered the sole creator, or designer, of the model. The term "créateurs de mode" was thus acceptable to everyone. It was also accepted that while the manufacturer could influence his stylist, the fashion designer would be allowed to impose his decisions on the manufacturer. The association would be called Créateurs & Industriels.

Emmanuelle Khanh was the first to join, soon followed by Ossie Clark, the most famous London designer of the time, who was introduced to me by Lady Clare Rendlesham.[11] A Swedish accessory stylist, Gösta Claesson, who had been exercising his talents in the Givenchy studio, developed a line of accessories and jewelry under his own name. Denise Sarrault, who had been a model with Balenciaga and Givenchy at the same time as Christiane Bailly and Emmanuelle Khanh, declined my offer to manage the C & I artistic direction. A painter friend, Michel Warren, suggested

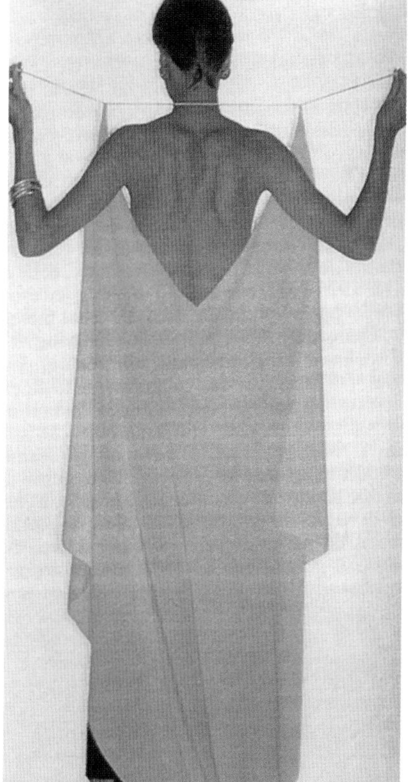

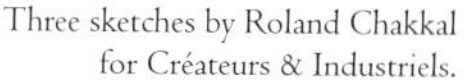

Three sketches by Roland Chakkal for Créateurs & Industriels.

Karl Lagerfeld at Chloé in 1978. Photo Guy Marineau.

Angelo Tarlazzi, models for Jean Patou, c. 1973. Photo V. Rochard for *Marie Claire*.

Angelo Tarlazzi and Sophie Xuereb at the Palace, c. 1980. Rights Reserved.

Andrée Putman. It was an excellent idea, but first she had to agree to leave MAFIA where she was doing a remarkable job for Prisunic.

Andrée Putman was undoubtedly the best choice; her looks alone were a guarantee of success. She was insatiably curious and she loved meeting people, as she was interested in everything that could affect creativity. Putman was modest. She knew how to listen to others and the work meetings with the designers soon came to resemble confession sessions. She made people perfectly comfortable with her warm attention, and whomever she was talking to opened up without hesitation, exalting their creative imagination. Andrée punctuated the conversation with allusive, poetic, or quite simply admiring remarks and had no fear of superlatives. The way she gave of herself, accompanied by her unflagging enthusiasm, had the power to put even the most introverted of creators at perfect ease. Putman was unwavering in her choices. Those who admired her heeded her authority in terms of taste; they were attentive and had constant demands. She enjoyed this reciprocity where admiration was at stake. She was truly dedicated, available at any time of day and night; one can easily imagine the extraordinary atmosphere that reigned at Créateurs & Industriels during the five years the adventure lasted.

March 1971: when the first fashion show was being prepared, I organized an initital meeting between designers and manufacturers at Faverolles in Normandy. The two days of spring sunshine and birdsong were omens of a good beginning. The guests took their places around the dining table: my sister, Sylvie; Michel Douard, manager with C. Mendès; a few major industrialists including Henri Zelnik, the director of Bidermann, men's ready-to-wear; Jean-Claude Weill, accompanied by his son Bernard, women's ready-to-wear; Dofan, leather; Lip, watches; Aiglon, belts; Barnasson and Adige, shoes; Superior, luggage; Chevalier, eyewear; creators like Olivier Mourgue, Quasar, Emmanuelle Khanh, Andrée Putman; and others. Madeleine de Rauch—brought by André Lévi, the director of Saint Laurent Rive Gauche—had come as a spectator. Hélène Lazareff herself, accompanied by Denise Dubois-Jallais, nobly represented the press.[12] In all there were about 50 people. All were surprised to suddenly realize that this country congress—far from Paris, and made up of complementary companies and individuals—could offer many more opportunities than meetings between colleagues in the context of union settings. This meeting had immediate consequences.

Fashion shows as events. In April, the first fashion show was inaugurated in the C. Mendès salons. The room was buzzing with excitement. Some were eagerly awaiting the event, convinced of its importance; others, worried or just curious, had already made up their minds to dislike it. Emmanuelle Khanh's models opened the ceremony, striding up and down the show rooms to the rhythm of inaudible messages, punctuated by music transmitted through transistors hanging from the hands of a group of nonchalant young women... The audience burst out laughing, then applauded. Then it was Ossie Clark's turn. The girls, who had come especially from London,[13] had been drunk since dawn. Dona Jordan and Donna Mitchell were among them. They stood in front of the spectators and insulted them in such vile cockney that soon Baroness Ordioni[14] from *Le Monde* and several of her colleagues could no longer pretend they didn't understand any English. Audiovisual presentations were trendy and Gösta's accessories were shown on a giant screen between the two collections. Madeleine de Rauch's collection, which was associated with the old system, was maintained in the program.

I had anticipated everything, including the scandal—how could I not have imagined it, knowing the composition of the audience and the incredible conservatism in force at the time? I had not, however, taken into account the gossip mongers' propensity to exaggerate the facts. What Madeleine de Rauch—for whom I had the greatest admiration—was told convinced her to abandon her usual reserve and terminate our association that had lasted over 15 years. I was even sadder, as my intention to show Madeleine de Rauch's collection with the two troublemakers was based only on the absolute rigor of her clothes—they were the only ones that could rival the two other creators' wild creativity. I had to face facts; a page had been irrevocably turned.

C. Mendès, Adige, Barnasson, Chevalier, Dofan, and Superior produced the collections. Emmanuelle Khanh labeled her products for the first time. Ossie Clark became the first foreign designer to be celebrated in Paris even though he had not set up a company there. The business that was now launched set up its offices on the sixth floor of C. Mendès' building.[15] The group soon acquired new members. In October 1971 Jean Muir, whom I had brought over from London, and Fernando Sanchez, who was personally accompanied by Pierre Bergé to prove his interest in the designers's talent, held fashion shows at rue Léopold-Bellan. In April 1972,

Thierry Mugler.
The house's 10th anniversary fashion show at the Zénith (1984).
6,000 people paid the entrance fee.
Rights Reserved.

Roland Chakkal, one of Yves Saint Laurent's assistants, brilliantly contributed to what *Women's Wear Daily* called "The Mendès Movement."

Starting in October 1971, the fashion shows that were held on two floors of the building attracted an incredible crowd of supporters who were ready to go to any length to attend the presentations. Some of the crowd went backstage, others took up space on the staircase, and the most daring sat on the window ledges. The models looked as if they had been parachuted in from Carnaby Street. They were like little sisters who had fallen out of bed, whom one spoke to in any and every language.

By winter 1971, the créateurs de mode were established. The Centre de création industrielle (CCI)—Center for Industrial Creation, part of the Musée des arts décoratifs—even planned an exhibition of their works, but the project was canceled because CCI could not raise the capital needed to stage a show.[16] The Salle Wagram hosted a friendly "fashion match" organized in partnership with Jungle Jap, Dorothée Bis, and Ter and Bantine. The event attracted a crowd of enthusiasts including models, journalists, and friends. Kenzo, Jacqueline Jacobson, and Chantal Thomass were at the brink of their international careers. Simultaneously, on Tan Giudicelli's initiative, Mic-Mac organized a show using transvestites instead of models, to the audience's amused stupefaction. Karl Lagerfeld invited journalists to a lunch at a club on rue Saint-Anne, to have them admire Mario Valentino's shoes worn by models perched on never-ending heels wobbling on the tables.

In October 1972, the Créateurs & Industriels' fashion shows took place on the work site of their future shops in rue de Rennes. It became clear that we had covered a huge distance over a few seasons, leaving the codified ritual of haute couture that had inspired couturier ready-to-wear far behind.

The brutal break with the established and regimented order of haute couture provoked inevitable waves of indignation. Evidently the deviation of the new kinds of fashion shows did not please everyone. Nonetheless, all this was nothing compared to the Créateurs & Industriels presentation of 1 April 1973 held at the Bourse du commerce.

For once the date was respected and kept all its promises, even the sunshine that brightened the beautiful spring Sunday. The Bourse du commerce, previously Catherine de Médicis' residence, had been chosen for the space. Its grand, translucent glass vault created an immediate aesthetic shock, making the venue a stronghold of pleasure and transgression. The previous year, Kenzo had also used the space for his show. Another of Andrée Putman's qualities was her sense of celebration, which she fully used for this occasion. The buffet tables ran along the rotunda, punctuating the space as if to better draw its contours. The podium was a clear line through the center of the circle while the chairs, placed in staggered rows like the Théatre au rond, awaited their occupants. The cupola was divided into two by a steel rope stretched 10 meters above the ground. The whispering was getting louder back stage, while disparate musical fragments, like an orchestra tuning up, disturbed the silence that reigned in the hall. The doors opened at 10:00 AM. The guests slowly took their places: the fashion editors in the first row competed with one another to be the most elegant. Has anyone forgotten how Peggy Roche was wrapped up in a big coat from Jacques Delahaye with large black and yellow squares? Or how Loulou la Falaise, seated between Karl Lagerfeld and Pierre Bergé, wore Yves Saint Laurent's black stirrup pants set off by a waterproof black jacket around which a double silver fox was wrapped? The pit was soon filled by the happy few, while the crowd standing near or behind the buffet tables struggled to recognize the chosen ones. Andrée Putman, the perfect hostess, officiated, going from one guest to the other. More dandyish than ever, she wore a Karl Lagerfeld navy blue men's indoor jacket, decorated with white and blue braid with a gigantic number on the pocket, over a pencil skirt.

The excitement was building and finally the microphone announced the first appearance with Christiane Bailly's collection. In 1972, Christiane was at the peak of her career. She developed Christian Aujard's collection as well as her "creators" collection that she had taken over from her previous assistant, Emmanuelle Khanh, who had just set up her own house. Bailly's collection resembled her: it was intransigent, melancholic, and idealistic.

People came and went; drinks flowed freely; the buffets were replenished at the rhythm of the buoyancy that gradually took over the audience.

The second appearance was Michèle Bruyère, a knitwear specialist of pastel colors and luxury sportswear. She had undoubtedly contributed to the success of Daniel Hechter, where she was a stylist.

Up above, a white bird fascinated the audience who, for the moment, raised their heads in its direction. Philippe Petit, the funambulist, made his appearance: he only came down from his nest at the end of the day.

It was Roland Chakkal's turn. I had miraculously woken him up in time for him to come and supervise his show. He rushed in, *in extremis,* holding a pair of scissors to cut the trousers on the models while they were wearing them as they came and went. Apparently, the proportions did not seem perfect to him. It was generally agreed that he made the most beautiful coats in the world: woolen, unlined, and smocked like shirts. Wide gathered or pleated trousers, short blazers, perfectly proportioned: only he knew the secret of his clothes. Unfortunately the huge success of his first collection made him forget about the second. It did not matter. The crowd was feverish with excitement; people who planned to stay until the end plotted to retain their seats. They took their turns to go to the buffets and returned with glasses and sandwiches to feed most of the row.

Then it was Jean-Jacques Martelli's turn. He was powdered like a Pierrot in a black suit and wore a black felt hat like an English military helmet on his head. His eyes were black and his hair extremely short; he was 21 and within a month, and for a year, he became the new genius of fashion. Ministers, models, actors, columnists, and other dandies looking for clothes flocked to his designer apartment for tea or dinner. His idol, Karl Lagerfeld, introduced him to Andrée Putman, who instantly succumbed to his seductiveness and offered to help him present his first collection. The models moved up on the podium to baroque music, their hands joined in front of them, ecstatic. There were long, structured black coats with padded shoulders, sometimes a white panel up the back, a pocket, or a collar. The statuesque models wore wide-brimmed, black felt hats and though they looked identical, each one was different. The audience fell silent before this pagan liturgy until these ecclesiastical ghosts of equivocal elegance left the podium to a storm of applause. Jean-Jacques Martelli existed! Colombe Pringle, a beginner, wore his clothes with rare elegance.

Sylvie Grumbach, another beginner, had also made up a perfect guest list. She was a talented press attaché and she had the genius that comes with panache. Was it because she was deeply iconoclastic, or because she nonchalantly cultivated paradox and derision to better twist the social hierarchy of the audience? Or was it the pure intelligence of her profession? Either way, the individuals she had gathered for the event were an absolute success. There was a measured proportion of foreign buyers; the top fashion editors; a good percentage of left and right wing intellectuals; a handful of artists; a cheeky, good natured bunch of crazy rockers; a few high ranking civil servants; the most dedicated fashion lovers, all of whom were watered with champagne, J & B, wine on tap, against a background of music, sometimes exalted, sometimes languid. This was her recipe.

Silence. It was Fernando Sanchez' turn. He was a fur stylist with Révillon but that day he showed his first collection of women's lingerie. It was immaterial and inalterable; it dressed more than it undressed.[17] Lys satin, lace, old-fashioned embroidery, eternal fluidity in pastel tones, with a predilection for flesh color. Pat Cleveland, who became the star we know, had come with Fernando from New York to present his collection. With each passage, she mimed a situation taken from daily life, appropriate to what she wore. For the last ensemble, she chose the theme of a gallant meeting that went wrong and defending herself from an imaginary importunate, she took off her shirt and ran off naked, to the audience's applause. Up in the sky, Philippe Petit crossed the cupola again.

Groups came together as if they were playing a board game, some flirted, others ate, and the ambiance was at its best when the Issey Miyake models entered. Issey Miyake had been represented in the United States since 1971 by Paris Collections Inc., a company managed by Jean Pierre and Sophie Xuereb—a connection that Kate Murphy, vice president of Bloomingdale's, had created. Paris Collections Inc. already distributed ready-to-wear by Yves Saint Laurent and Hubert de Givenchy; Issey Miyake had been his assistant before he went on to assist Geoffrey Beene in New York. I immediately offered to present Issey's collection in Paris and his first show was in 1973. For the first three years he showed in the context of Créateurs & Industriels, then with his own organization. From day one he was enthusiastically welcomed by everyone from Yvonne Deslandres, who offered him the Galleria Palace, to Maïmé Arnodin, Hélène de Turkeheim from the *Figaro*, Claude Brouet from *Marie Claire*... all of them warmly expressed their affection. In return, he took good care of his friends. His charm certainly contributed to the welcome Yohji Yamomoto and Rei Kawakubo received in Paris a few years later.

The party was coming to an end. After this intense day, weariness was setting in and Jean Muir surprised the gathering that was submerged in an atmosphere of semi-torpor, close to beatitude. Her jersey and crepe dresses, fluid, precise, and intangible, invaded the market within a year and were sold almost before they had been delivered. Her Paris shows made them internationally famous and they triumphantly brought the ceremony to a close. The hall emptied. I noticed Kuniko Tsutsumi, president of Seibu France, sitting alone amidst the overturned chairs, as if dazed by emotion.

The next show took place in the shop at 45 rue de Rennes. Although it was a huge space, it could not hold the hundreds of people who blocked the entry; they hurried over to boulevard Saint Germain, since they were not used to being refused access to a fashion show. Roland Chakkal irremediably created the incident of the evening. He thought his clothes deserved particular attention; concerned that each detail should be minutely prepared, he unfortunately asked his models to move at the same rhythm as the actors from Bob Wilson's play *Deafman Glance* that had just been immensely successful. After 20 minutes of suffering, the journalists, close to a nervous breakdown, protested and rushed out screaming as if they were suffocating. Roland Chakkal never got over it.

Rue de Rennes. Meanwhile, as new manufacturers came on board, Créateurs & Industriels' capital structure changed. In January 1973, Seibu, represented by Mrs. Kuniko Tsutsumi, sister of Seiji Tsutsumi; Richard Salomon, president of Charles of the Ritz;[18] and Balamundi, the leading European floor covering manufacturer of the time, presided over by Jacques Lannoye, all became equal associates with C. Mendès. These three new shareholders were to finance the shop located at 45 rue de Rennes, and to develop new licenses in their respective geographical areas of influence. At the same time, the manufacturers of women's ready-to-wear, Weill, Weinberg, Mendès, or Heko; the lingerie manufacturers, represented by BFT or Grimomprèz; and fur manufacturers, including Goldin and Feldman, were responsible for manufacturing the different collections.

These were the premises of market internationalization. These designers who had come from all over the world and became established in Paris could be produced in New York or in France.

In October 1973, the Créateurs & Industriels' shop opened its doors. This one-of-a-kind, 800 square meter space brought together objects, clothes, furniture, and jewelry imagined by a galaxy of new designers, just as it had been intended. After Andrée Putman had supervised the construction and interior design of the boutique, she then chose the hundreds of articles to fill it, thanks to her fun-loving[19] sense of style.

Exotic plants, elegant kitchen towels, old fashioned pens and watches, creative earthenware, porcelain, and ceramics cohabited with Elsa Peretti's precious jewelry, Agnès Comar's cushions, and Christiane Bailly's smocked dresses. You could have your pictures framed, or for 90 francs order 100 sheets of personal writing paper

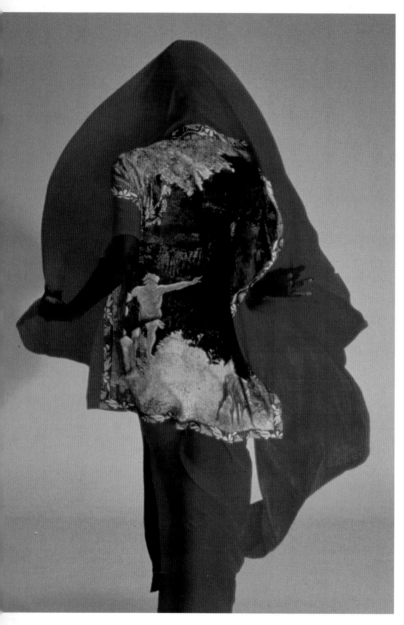

Issey Miyake, East Meets West, "Paradise Lost," 1976. Photo Noriaki Yokosuka.

Issey Miyake. Photo Tyen.

Facing page:
Issey Miyake, East Meets West, 1974. Photo Noriaki Yokosuka.

in an unimaginable choice of colors and fonts, to be delivered in 48 hours. An event related to gardening led to an exhibition of garden furniture and a choice of tulip bulbs that would have made Dutch botanists green with envy. For the art amateurs there were lithographs by great artists like Messagier, Bram van Velde, or Alechinski.

Items from the collections of Stephen Burrows, Georgio Sant'Angelo, and Betsey Johnson were exclusively imported from the United States. A pony auction was planned. The project did not stop there; the store broadened its offerings to include products from furniture designers. Pierre Paulin worked at C. Mendès on indoor clothing mock ups; Olivier Mourgue thought of a collection of felt chairs; Marc Held had a whole range of fiberglass furniture that had been perfected for Prisunic.

The space, originally an old SNCF bus station, was perfect for exhibiting the greatest variety of objects. Andrée Putman put forth two main ideas that determined the decoration of the shop was high-tech before its time: the glass roof was restored and the floors were covered entirely with Parisian cobblestones.

Sylvie Grumbach, the press service manager, also managed the purchasing and completed the offering of fashion lines. With her strong fashion sense she selected: Ko & Co by Castelbajac, Michel Costas by Claude Montana, Café de Paris by Thierry Mugler, and so many other young promising talents, exclusively for Créateurs & Industriels.

On the façade, around the C & I sign, the names of the designers connected to the company were written on vertical banners.

The shop had barely opened when a series of disturbing incidents curbed everyone's energy. The retailer C & A brought a summons against C & I demanding a change in the store's name. In fact, the avalanche of quotes in the press quite naturally aggravated the confusion in the client's minds. Thus, C & I became "Créateurs." Adidas attacked C & I—Emmanuelle Khanh and Barnasson—for having sold a shoe that was adorned with three parallel stripes, similar to those that typically distinguish Adidas goods. Due to a problem with molds, the non-viability of the furniture Marc Held had sold to C & I cruelly depleted the treasury.

More seriously, the aesthetic choices of the concept and the products sold were contested even amongst the shareholders despite the triumphant reception they had received. As soon as the work was finished, they decided to make certain changes and closed for three months. Nobody was really in control and there was discord about

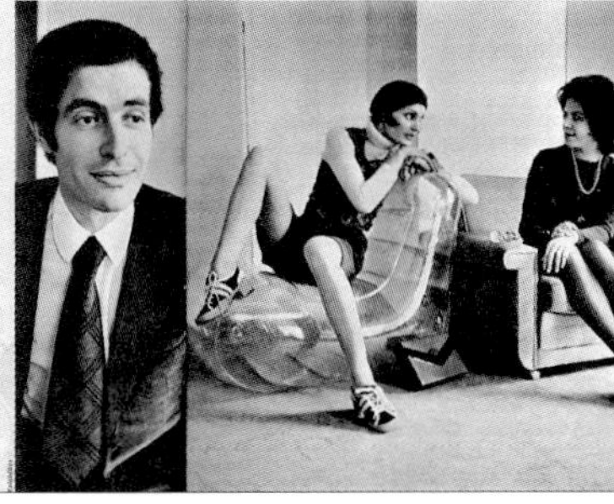

L'idée simple qui va démoder le luxe

par Denise Dubois-Jallais.

Trente-trois ans, visage de héros romantique, cerveau d'ordinateur, c'est l'homme du jour en Amérique. (« Women's wear » vient de lui consacrer une série d'articles.)

Fashion and design.
"One does not sit on an inflatable Quasar seat in the same way that one sits in a club chair," Denise Dubois-Jallais. "The simple idea that will outmode luxury," *Elle*, 24 May 1971.

Preparation for the Christiane Bailly fashion show for Créateurs & Industriels, 45 rue de Rennes, 1973.

Sylvie Grumbach, press attachée, and Issey Miyake at 45 rue de Rennes. 1973.

General view of the shop Créateurs & Industriels, 45 rue de Rennes. Andrée Putman, artistic director.

On the left: Didier Grumbach and the manager of Elsa Peretti.
On the right: Andrée Putman, artistic director of C & I, with the architect Reouven Vardy.

On the left: Yves Saint Laurent and Mme Mathieu Saint Laurent.
On the right: Gilles Néret, manager of the review *L'OEil*.

On the left: Yves Saint Laurent and Loulou de La Falaise.
On the right: Jacques Lannoye, president of Balamundi, and Pierre Bergé.

On the left: at the center of the group, Takada Kenzo and Hiroko Berghauer.
On the right: Quasar, Christiane Bailly, and Paco Rabanne.

On the left: Jean-Louis Scherrer.
On the right: Jacques de Beaumarchais, Karl Lagerfeld, and Jackie Iskander.

On the left: Olivier Mourgue and Paloma Picasso.
On the right: Clara Saint and Fernando Sanchez.

Above:
Inauguration of the Créateurs C & I shop
45 rue de Rennes.
From *Vogue*, November 1973.

Advertisement for Créateurs & Industriels in *WWD*, 4 March 1974.

everything. The shareholders were on the verge of a crisis every time a daring idea provoked a slight difference of opinion. By their very essence, precursors are in the wrong because they are ahead of their times. The first year, the shop lost one million francs, more than was expected. After two years, the project disintegrated and the building was sold. More generally, however, and despite constant support from Richard Salomon, president of Charles of the Ritz, I could not make my associates understand that designers' labels were an asset in and of themselves that deserved an investment. The idea was too revolutionary for the time, even more so because the designers loved flaunting their differences at every opportunity. Naturally, the couturiers acquired immediate notoriety by following the Chambre Syndicale calendar, while, in order to exist—and that was their role—designers had to affirm their non-conformism through excesses that condemned them in the eyes of the establishment. Noël Pouderoux, the charismatic president of CEGOS and administrator of Balamundi, came to visit me one day at rue d'Uzès in order to express his opinion. "I'm sure you're right," he said, "but today, what really goes against you is that your associates think you are mad."

Place du Marché Saint-Honoré. There was an amicable liquidation and everything could have stopped there, except for François Lévy's desire to continue. He had just left the position of president of Devanlay. Créateurs moved to 4 rue du Marché Saint-Honoré and the adventure took off again. Jean-Charles de Castelbajac joined C & I.

Issey Miyake, Jean-Charles de Castelbajac, and Roland Chakkal set up their boutiques at place du Marché Saint-Honoré, right next door to a boutique with a new concept—Toiles—that Michel Klein and Adeline André, in turn, used as their workshop.[20] The collection was designed and sewn in the shop itself, where women came to give their measurements and place their orders. Colombe Pringle managed it. At 4 rue du Marché Saint-Honoré, "Créateurs Grandes Ondes" presented knitwear collections by then-unknown créateurs like Jean Paul Gaultier Pablo & Delia, to name a few.

For the spring 1976 season, the same invitation announced several shows: Christiane Bailly, Roland Chakkal, Jean-Charles de Castelbajac, and Issey Miyake. On Saturday, 18 October 1975, the créateurs' calendar also included Claude Montana and Thierry Mugler, who settled respectively into the hotel Meurice and the Grand Hotel, while Michel Klein was showing his first collection at Angelina. Designed as a paper chase, the Créateurs invitation proposed a gastronomic itinerary that led buyers and journalists from hotels to tea rooms, to finish their walk at place du Marché-Saint-Honoré, where the high point of the day awaited them: an inflatable tent planted on the roof of the Marché-Saint-Honoré parking lot, which held 2,000 enthusiastic spectators.

The tent began to deflate imperceptibly and was about to sink down onto the worried audience, but there was no need to panic. The fire brigade arrived and with their usual efficiency they took up positions along the edges of the tent to hold it up and avoid the event ending up like a vast hairdressing session.

Two years later, in 1977, the project collapsed completely. The associates no longer shared the same vision of the enterprise. The principal reason though was that success drove the créateurs to establish their own companies. Emmanuelle Khanh and Christiane Bailly had set the example when they dissolved Emma-Christie. Andrée Putman founded Ecart and met with the success we know; in New York, Fernando Sanchez became the women's lingerie specialist. Christiane Bailly—still on the fringes—did not create her own brandand preferred to remain the independent stylist she had always been.

"Young Designers" and "Grands Couturiers"

It was a reality: designers, thanks to their ready-to-wear, had acquired notoriety equal to that of the couturiers. Nonetheless, some amongst the latter realized that the rules the profession imposed were not in tune with history, as they imagined it.

The designers' fashion shows provoked enthusiasm: Kenzo alone attracted crowds of fanatics. The progressive press was now only interested in stylists.

Who better than Pierre Bergé could know that the future of the profession lay in ready-to-wear? Saint Laurent Rive Gauche was an absolute success. Yves Saint Laurent took every opportunity to affirm that ready-to-wear was his passion. The 1971 Crédit national report was eloquent: four couturiers—Yves Saint Laurent,[21] Courrèges, Pierre Cardin, and Nina Ricci—planned to present a single winter collection in April 1972, grouping together couture and ready-to-wear.[22] This news could justifiably worry the majority of grands couturiers, who were frightened of no longer being different.

Yves Saint Laurent dropped out, leaving Robert Ricci and Pierre Cardin to go ahead with their project.

三宅一生●多摩美術大学卒業後、パリ留学。ジバンシー社などのアシスタントを経て、'70年東京にデザインスタジオを設立。ニューヨーク、東京、パリで年数回作品を発表している。その間、「三宅一生と12人の黒い女達」「一枚の布—ISSEY MIYAKE IN MUSEUM」「FLY WITH ISSEY MIYAKE」などのショーを開催。素材開発から製品に至る創作活動は、化学繊維の駆使から、日本の伝統を現代に蘇らせる仕事にまで及ぶ。'77年、衣服デザインを、ファッションの他領域にまで広げたとして、'76年度毎日デザイン賞を受賞。'78年には「EAST MEETS WEST—三宅一生の発想と展開」を出版。また、パリ秋の芸術祭の招待作家となっている。

ステファン・バロウズ●彼のデザイナーとしての経歴は、9年前、FIT（ファッション技術大学）を卒業してすぐ、シャツのデザインをした時に始まる。デザインを手がけた最初の頃から、ジグザグ・ステッチ、さざ波のように波うったヘムなどを考案し、トレード・マークになっている。かってなかった新しいアイデアを盛りこんだ服のデザイナーとして、'70年代にはアメリカのファッション界のスター的存在となった。みずから育った地域に近いハーレム街のスタイルをアメリカの服飾市場に普及させ、この個性的のファッションを創り出した。'77年、ヘンリ・ベンデルで開かれた秋冬コレクションで、'73年に次ぎ2度目のコティ賞を受賞。

ティエリー・ミュグレー●ストラスブールに生まれた。20歳の時、既成のモードの革新をめざしてパリへ。サン・ジェルマンにできたばかりのアバンギャルド傾向の店で働き始める。
さまざまなメゾンを経験後、'73年に自身のコレクションを「カフェ・ド・パリ」の商標で発表。プレスに認められ、翌年9月には「ティエリー・ミュグレー」の名で秋コレクション。この成功によって、ヨーロッパのみならず、アメリカや日本でも知られるようになった。自然素材を生かした美しく機能的な服のつくり手として評価が高い。

THE BEST SIX

ジャンニ・ベルサーチェ●カラブリア生まれ。若いころからファッションに強い興味を示し、デザイナーを志してミラノでひとり立ちし、数年のうちに大成功をおさめた。独特のバイタリティで世界の若者を魅了するイタリアン・ファッションの中でも、ひときわ注目される旗手。
さまざまなアイデアが林立するこの混迷の時代に、極端に走ることをきらい、知的で暖か味のある、きちんとした装いを創り出す。彼の仕事は、ファッションの歴史に新しい1ページを加えるものとの声価が高く、世界中が、彼の意表をつくインスピレーションに注目している。

ジーン・ミュアー●ロンドン・ファッションが世界を風びするようになった1950年代の末頃、「リバティ」にスケッチャーとして入社したのが出発。次に「イエーガー」社のデザイナーとして7年、後「ジェーン・アンド・ジェーン」で仕事を続け、1966年独立。「ジーン・ミュアー」の名で作品を発表し、ロンドンの実力派新星として注目される。70年代初めにパリ進出。パリ・モードにはない異色の魅力に人気が集まり、大成功を博した。以来毎シーズン、ロンドンだけでなく、パリでもコレクションを発表している。現在、ニューヨークの「ヘンリ・ベンデル」にブティックを持ち、ロンドン・ファッション界を代表する女性デザイナーとして確かな存在を誇る。

森　英恵●いま世界のハナエ・モリとして広く知られる彼女の存在は、東京・新宿に開いたブティック時代から際立っていた。プレタポルテ、映画衣裳など、日本のファッション界としては未踏の分野を次々に手がけ、デザイナーの仕事に対する一般の目をも開かせた。'65年、ニューヨークで作品発表。'70年にはニューヨーク店、'77年にはパリにクチュール・ハウス、今年6月には東京・表参道にハナエ・モリ・ビル（The Space の母体）をオープン、国際的な活躍を続けている。また今年、ヨーロッパ優秀品賞（フランス）、森田たまパイオニア賞（日本）、人間の尊厳賞（アメリカ・ミネソタ美術館）、パリ市の銀メダル（フランス）を受賞。

Invitation card for the fashion show *The Best Six*, 20 November 1978, organized in Tokyo by Hanae Mori
Issey Miyake, Stephen Burrows, Thierry Mugler, Gianni Versace, Jean Muir, and Hanae Mori.

1976: Chantal Thomass, Jean-Claude de Luca, Anne-Marie Beretta, Thierry Mugler, Jean-Charles de Castelbajac, France Andrevie, Claude Montana, and Issey Miyake. Hôtel St James & Albany.

Fashion creators journey to Tokyo, sponsored by Shiseido (president Mr. Onno) organized by Melka Treanton seconded by Jean-Jacques Picart. Thierry Mugler, Claude Montana, Jean-Claude de Luca, Anne-Marie Berreta, Jean-Charles de Castelbajac, and Dan Béranger. January 1976.

On 21 January Robert Ricci addressed a letter to all his clients:

> It is irrational and artificial that every three months, for every season, a modelist and his team have to create two different collections that cannot repeat themselves, nor become unfashionable. Thus on the dates below, we will present a unique, very important collection, that expresses the totality of our house's message. We will combine both the clothes intended for the future "Edition boutique" and those that by their nature and the way in which they are executed, remain specifically haute couture. Of course the latter activity will remain as brilliant as it always has been. In this manner, through a conscious modification of structures and habits, we are convinced we are contributing to a necessary change, and a standardisation, that is indispensable today.

In an interview he gave to *Elle*, on the same subject, Pierre Cardin spoke to Claude Berthod, who was known for the pertinence of his analyses:

> We refuse the tyranny of idiotic dates! Private clients? In January they are not thinking about summer. Manufacturers? For them, summer 1972 begins in October 1971. Now we have to think of next winter's fashion if we want to see it in the street. That is what I am working on at the moment. Haute couture or ready-to-wear? For me these are empty words. Creation, I hope. Ideas, dreams. To carry them out I need an elite work force. I will never be separated from my workshops. Tailors and workshop managers who know how to dress the most difficult women in the world... and who know, better than anyone else, how to adjust the basic mock ups we send to the factories...
>
> "Aren't you worried that this mixture of genres and dates will sound the death knell for haute couture?"
>
> "If it dies, it will be of pride. The pride of the designers, whom, each one of them draped in their 'exclusive' fabrics, cannot be bothered to descend from their towers and join the others to standardise the presentation dates and fight efficiently against counterfeit..."

The arguments put forward were as indisputable as those André Courrèges had expressed seven years earlier. This time, however, the comments came a little too late. The couturiers no longer had control over the ready-to-wear they had licensed out to third parties. In 1972, apart from Nina Ricci and André Courrèges, no haute couture company distributed or produced their models themselves if the production could be mechanized. This meant that the production profit margins went to the licensed manufacturers. Discouraged, Pierre Cardin and Nina Ricci decided to get in line. They had not been excluded, as nothing in the rules prohibited them from presenting haute couture and ready-to-wear together. As for the press release, everyone had forgotten about it!

Pierre Bergé and the Mode & Création (Fashion & Creation) Group. Pierre Bergé, in any event, considered this very radical approach to be premature. While he found it inadvisable to take the risk of depreciating haute couture by revealing it too early, he felt it was urgent to include the young designers whom the press extolled and were the object of all kinds of requests.

For their part, Bruno du Roselle, president of the Fédération du prêt-à-porter feminin, followed by William Lauriol,[23] were also interested in these talented newcomers. At 69 rue de Richelieu, Jeanine Belinsky played the same role as Denise Dubois, rue du Faubourg-Saint-Honoré. Season after season, she registered couturiers and creators in her industrial calendar.

Dorothée Bis also took part in the first ready-to-wear trade show, held at Porte de Versailles, in 1963.

Pierre Bergé gave Jacques Mouclier, who had been newly appointed to the Chambre Syndicale, the mission of imagining a way to bring couture and ready-to-wear closer together. It took shape under the initials GMC, Groupement Mode & Création, associating three couturiers and five designers: Yves Saint Laurent, Dior, Emanuel Ungaro, Chloé, Dorothée Bis, Sonia Rykiel, Kenzo, and Emmanuelle Khanh. The latter five were directors of autonomous companies. When she left C & I, Emmanuelle Khanh had created her own house with a new associate; Chloé, under Jacques Lenoir and Gaby Aghion's management, now had only one stylist, Karl Lagerfeld.

This group, constituted for the sake of convenience, was the beginning of the Chambre syndicale du prêt-à-porter des couturiers et des créateurs de mode, a trade association for couturiers' and fashion creative designers' ready-to-wear. Other couturiers that had ready-to-wear collections soon joined it. Pierre Bergé, who had been at the origin of the association, was naturally appointed president. The constitutive assembly of the new Chambre Syndicale officially gathered on 15 November 1973. It came under the new Fédération de la couture du prêt-à-porter des couturiers et des créateurs de mode. It was later, on 21 November 1973, that the Groupement Mode & Création was created, in the same offices at 100 rue du Faubourg-Saint-Honoré.

The following season Créateurs & Industriels was invited to participate as a group in the new Chambre Syndicale's fashion show calendar that for the first time included "foreign"[24] designers. On 21 November 1974, Pierre Bergé addressed Bruno du Roselle in these terms:

> As you know, we have joined the Chambre Syndicale du prêt-à-porter des couturiers et créateurs de mode, a new professional organisation that has the specific goal to preserve a common brand image for the press and the clientele. With this in mind, last season we published a calendar in which all our members were mentioned.
> Consequently, we would be grateful if you would not mention our house in the calendar of the Fédération française des industries du vêtement feminin.
> Nonetheless, it is understood that through the intermediary of our Chambre Syndicale we will draw up this calendar so as to avoid any clashes that would harm the houses' interests.
> Yours faithfully,

Pierre Bergé and Didier Grumbach at Roland Chakkal's fashion show at 45 rue de Rennes, 1973.

Once the Chambre Syndicale had received identical letters from all its members, they sent them on to Bruno du Roselle.

This implied that prêt-a-porter griffé, or "labeled" ready-to-wear, was now governed by the haute couture bodies, and had broken with the apparel industry. The bridges between designers and manufacturers had been burnt again, leaving the créateurs in the couturiers' camp.

The statutes of Groupement Mode & Création, ratified on 21 February 1974, planned for a very wide field of action that was paradoxically limiting.

> **Article 2**
> The aim of this association is:
> - Research in the area of fashion design.
> - Study and forecasting in the area of fashion.
> - Promotion of the brand.
>
> **Article 5**
> Any new membership has to be unanimously agreed on by the members in the group.

As it was closed in advance, this intermediary organization had little hope of admitting new members. In her letter of resignation, addressed to Pierre Bergé on 20 August 1976, Jacqueline Jacobson wrote: "These two years were not what I hoped they would be." As was the case in the past for Prêt-à-Porter Création, GMC lost its raison d'être when the Chambre Syndicale, which had been the motivating force behind the constitution of GMC, directly welcomed the next generation of designers. The logic was that everybody was for himself and in his own space should follow his or her own path. There were only a few common ad campaigns organized with two or three international newspapers. There was as much in common between a donkey and a sewing machine as there was between Dior and Dorothée Bis: it was hardly surprising that GMC did not survive its meetings.

Nonetheless, the Groupement Mode & Création had had the merit of being the first to bring down the barriers between the two kinds of corporations, each based on the designers' personalities. It required Pierre Bergé's strength of conviction to win this bet that everything indicated would fail. Henceforth, both the couture and the prêt-à-porter federations claimed the couture ready-to-wear sales in their statistics. The turnover generated by Courrèges, Saint Laurent Rive Gauche, and Chloé was reassuring for Jacques Mouclier's flow charts. When William Lauriol drew up the list of the 100 leading women's ready-to-wear companies in 1975, he was just as justified in including Courrèges, C. Mendès, and Chloé, as well as Cacharel, Hechter, Weill, and Weinberg.

A sparring match ensued, the result of which was a renewed competition between couture and ready-to-wear. In 1978, when Jacques Mouclier was looking for a place where his members could show their collections, he accepted William Lauriol's offer of a car park, Porte de Versailles. It was bad luck that an electrical problem occurred during Yves Saint Laurent's show. It was a memorable short circuit that set off another blaze. Finally in 1982, Jack Lang gave the Fédération de la Couture the Cour Carrée space in the Louvre. Who was going to complain? William Lauriol, who considered that his members belonged to the profession. Jacques Mouclier was summoned to Madame Rozès, the president of the tribunal's office, for urgent interlocutory proceedings: ready-to-wear was thrown out. Créateurs de mode and couturiers were the only ones allowed access to the central courtyard.

The designers' revolt. After Dorothée Bis resigned from the all-powerful Chambre Syndicale, there was another attempt to create a new designers' group.

Encouraged by William Lauriol, in 1977 Bruno du Roselle's successor, Elie Jacobson, outlined a meeting of the "diffusion" group that brought together Kenzo, Chantal Thomas, Daniel Hechter, Emmanuelle Khanh, Jean Charles de Castelbajac, and others.

In 1978, I suggested to Jacques Mouclier that he broaden the group of fashion designers associated with couture. He asked me to draw up a list and to take the time to organize the first two meetings that took place at 100 rue du Faubourg-Saint-Honoré. Angelo Tarlazzi, Chantal Thomass, Anne-Marie Beretta, Claude Montana, Thierry Mugler, Jean Paul Gaultier, Dorothée Bis, yet again joined Emmanuelle Khanh, Kenzo, Chloé, Jean-Charles de Castelbajac, Sonia Rykiel...

The cohabitation between these two newly associated groups did not occur without clashes. Scandalized by the créateurs' show events, the couturiers were the first to launch their attack on those who were only concerned with an image with no thought for sales, and threatened to exclude them. Exasperated, the designers circumspectly considered their position within an institutional group that relegated them to the second level. The most enraged of those in revolt was, with no doubt, Francis Menuge, president of Jean Paul Gaultier, who in 1983 led the opposition. The meeting was held at Kenzo, place des Victoires, where there were spacious and comfortable private salons. François Baufumé tried to calm the resistants' passions, reminding them that patience was a virtue.

After the fashion Oscars ceremony in February 1988, Pierre Bergé organized a lunch at Laurent with an aim to listen to the complaints voiced by the designers who had been left perplexed by the evening and the way it was organized. I took this opportunity to suggest to Pierre Bergé that the haute couture regulations be revised in order to allow fashion designers to be included as permanent members. The meeting began with Pierre Bergé's complaints about Jacques Mouclier's organization of the evening at the Opéra. This affair was not really worth going into.

Pierre Bergé then announced that I had a declaration to make: my short plea was met with a long silence. Francis Menuge, president of Jean Paul Gaultier, abandoned his usual reserve to catch the ball in mid-air and throw it further than I had hoped. "This Chambre Syndicale," he said with his habitual irony, "has never brought us anything in exchange for our active participation, why should we remain a part of it?" The discussion deteriorated. Facetious, Francis Menuge was evidently amused; the assembly grew more animated. An uncomfortable Pierre Bergé spoke again: "The grands couturiers are born grand couturiers. Fashion créateurs arrived much later. The statutes are what they are and I cannot do anything about it!" Glowering at me for my efficiency at creating confusion, he immediately left the hall. François Baufumé, generally an eloquent, even outspoken man, had remained silent during this exciting 15 minutes of oral jousting. "Ah! That's the way it is," he said. "They are nobility and we are the third estate! Well then, let's revolt!..."

As he saw his work being torn apart, Jacques Mouclier proposed that the fashion créateurs have their own statutes, which would still leave them associated with a recognized group. It was not the right time for division. A work group was set up and the first meeting was held on 8 March at the Chambre Syndicale. On the agenda, a decision had to be made as to whether fashion créateurs should be part of a new trade group and leave the existing Chambre syndicale du prêt à porter des couturiers et des créateurs de mode. They also had to define, and if necessary protect, the French designation "créateurs de mode."

For practical reasons, the following meetings were held in the conference rooms of the Institut français de la mode. As an introduction to the session of 29 March 1988, the president, Mouclier, read out the letters sent by the companies of Sonia Rykiel, Claude Montana, Karl Lagerfeld, and Jean-Charles de Castelbajac, reiterating their support for the existing agency. Although they considerably weakened their action, these defections did not really affect the conspirators' quest for reform. The companies now had to define the points on which common decisions could be made, like the dates for the fashion shows. While the sales periods continued to be on the traditional ready-to-wear dates of October and March each year, the press presentations could take place in January and July, in the week preceding the haute couture presentation. I was in favor of this, although several members of the group declared that they would find it difficult to convince their designers of these dates.

The meetings that took place on 26 April and 26 May dealt in turn with issues such as the designation "créateur de mode," the press release date, limiting the number of photographers, and discontinuing the practice of previews. Navigating these subjects made it clear that it would be difficult for companies with such different histories, structures, and creative concepts to agree on one strategic vision.

In a 10 point summary note dated 31 May 1988, Jacques Mouclier concluded by proposing a later meeting that never took place. Nothing changed. In fact, unlike the couturiers, whose methods of functioning were based on strict regulations established decades ago, the créateurs de mode found it impossible to fit into a predefined structure because their backgrounds were so diverse.

How the Créateurs de Mode Grew

In 1974 Melka Treanton, editor-in-chief of *Depêche Mode,* at the time considered the most avant-garde of the fashion magazines, was alone in her defense of the new generation of designers, just as *Elle* magazine had been 20 years earlier. In 1976, Shiseido wanted to organize a fashion show in Tokyo. After having already selected Jean-Charles de Castelbajac and Jean-Claude de Luca to participate, Shiseido asked Treanton to complete the list with her choice of designers. The chosen few were Claude Montana, Anne-Marie Beretta, Dan Béranger, and Thierry Mugler. Jean-Jacques Picart, a good press attaché, organized the journey. Ten years after the first designers' fashion show in New York, the journey to Tokyo represented a major event for the young designer brands. The show led to licensing contracts that also served to announce Japan's growing influence.

While the grands couturiers shared their haute couture management procedures, even if they were unprofitable, the ready-to-wear designers adopted the business practices their elders, the couturiers, had used: manufacturing and distribution licenses (Pierre Cardin system), manufacturing license (Yves Saint Laurent Rive Gauche system), integrated management (Chanel system). Of course, none of these policies were completely advantageous.

Manufacturing and distribution licenses. This solution meant that designers granted apparel manufacturers the use of their brand in exchange for the production and distribution of the models they created. Here, designers were psychologically closer to the grands couturiers for whom industry went beyond the artisanal framework of couture and was thus beyond their competencies. While the grands couturiers maintained control of haute couture, radiating their product diversifications downwards from the top of the pyramid, designers who opted to license out their ready-to-wear had little control over their brand image. Designers often pursued such licensing agreements because they had limited means to invest in their growth and the only advantage this formula provided was the low investment. The royalties the designers received, generally 10 per cent, provided the means to finance a small corporate structure that included design and communication.

This business model was used by many emerging designers and shot them into the spotlight. This was the case for Claude Montana and Jean Paul Gaultier, for

Claude Montana, spring–summer 1987. © Claude Montana/ Rights Reserved.

Claude Montana for Lanvin, wedding dress haute couture, spring–summer 1992. Photo Guy Marineau.

Claude Montana, winter collection end of the seventies. © Claude Montana/ Rights Reserved.

Claude Montana, autumn–winter 1985–1986. © Claude Montana/ Rights Reserved.

Claude Montana, spring–summer 1986. © Claude Montana/ Rights Reserved.

whom the adventure was a positive one. But such success was not always the case for scores of young designers and brands that hoped for that kind of miracle until they irremediably disappeared.

Licenses alone could not finance the growth of a designer's company because the remuneration percentage was not high enough. In addition, the lack of coherence between a product's image, its manufacturing, its distribution, and its communication implied a great risk for losing control over the brand, a situation that could be fatal for a company's survival. The combined energies of the different partners during the growth phase could not survive the slightest drop in turnover that would necessitate an injection of funds. At the same time, an apparel maker could not imagine financing or supporting a brand that he did not own. A designer with few management skills was often incapable of estimating his medium-term needs. Even if the designer's resources allowed him to invest in his company, the funds were rarely sufficient.

Montana and Gaultier showed that, despite everything, the traditional licensing system could still be useful in certain cases. In Claude Montana's case, he had been capable of changing licensees several times, without it damaging his reputation. Michel Costas, in France, preceded Ferrer and Sentis, a Spanish manufacturer (1975–1978), that was followed by three manufacturers: Gibo, for three years; Genny, between 1982 and 1987; and finally GFT. Every change corresponded to a new phase of growth. The latter two groups had an international distribution structure, something that was rare in our professions. However, today there is no company like GFT that can support a new brand of Montana's stature, and Montana would not be able to find a high quality company of GFT's size anywhere else.

As for Jean-Paul Gaultier, while his Italian licensees suffered a few financial problems, his Japanese licensee, Kashiyama, covered the interim period and took control of the Italian production units. The Japanese firm used the Italian facilities and handled distribution to the United States. In addition, Gaultier's energetic team that first Francis Menuge then Donald Potard had filled with enthusiasm took advantage of the handicaps within a system that had several weaknesses.

Jean Paul Gaultier. The trio comprised of Jean Paul Gaultier, Francis Menuge, and Donald Potard had been inseparable since their school days. The former two had already shared their drawings in elementary school while the latter two were students at the Lycée Lavoisier. Jean Paul Gaultier entered the fashion world at the age of 18. He first worked for Pierre Cardin then with Jacques Esterel and, between 1971 and 1973, he worked at Jean Patou alongside Michel Goma and Angelo Tarlazzi. In 1974, he returned to Pierre Cardin where, as a pattern designer at large in the Philippines, he designed his first signature collection. When he returned to Paris in 1975, he got together with his two accomplices because he had decided to throw himself into the adventure that turned into the indisputable success we know today. With Francis Menuge, who also had a passion for electronics, he presented a project for illuminated clothes and jewelry to Créateurs. The subversive androgynous creatures with shaved heads resulted in a collection of 15 knitwear models that were presented to journalists and clients at 4 rue du Marché Saint Honoré. Monique de Faucon wrote in the *New York Daily News*: "Jean Paul Gaultier, inventor of strobe flash cardigan buttons." Créateurs Grandes Ondes imploded. Barely a year later, Jean Paul Gaultier decided to finance his own collection.

Anna Pawlovski had become a star model after Gaultier had been instrumental in her being employed at Jean Patou. She lent her support to the trio for the first show that took place in October 1976 at the Grand Palais Planetarium. A loan he had taken to buy an apartment served to finance the collection. Donald Potard was responsible for the stage direction, the music, and the invitations. He was a professional stage manager and had a masters degree in theater studies. The fabric was bought at Marché Saint Pierre and the clothes stitched by his family and friends. The fashion professionals received the wonderfully scandalous collection he created with surprising indifference. Only one journalist from *Agence France Presse*, Jacqueline Claude, noticed his talent.[25] Jean Paul Gaultier bravely financed four consecutive shows that cost an astronomical sum, about 80,000 francs each (about 35,000 euros). His enthusiasm slowly turned to stress but miraculously he learnt that the Japanese were looking for a stylist. Melka Treanton recommended Gaultier to Dominique Emschwiller, manager of the boutique Bus-Stop-Kashiyama. Gaultier was hired as a stylist with Kashiyama, a job that gave him a structure to work in until the end of 1981.

At the end of this first period, he signed a licensing contract for Japan with Kashiyama Tokyo and replaced Claude Montana at Gibo. Starting with these agreements, Gaultier's distribution and production problems were resolved and

Jean Paul Gaultier, winter 1987. Photo Rights Reserved.

he was no longer limited by a lack of finances. This allowed Gaultier to concentrate on his communication concept. Until then the concept had been frozen: Gaultier grew himself, anticipating and adapting to the current trends. His exceptional talent is his ability to interpret the myths of his time. In 1982, Jean Paul Gaultier created a limited liability company, managed by Francis Menuge until his death, and then by Donald Potard. Jean Paul Gaultier's first perfume was launched in 1993.

Manufacturing licenses. Some designers developed licensing agreements for manufacturing only. They chose this method because perhaps they had not found manufacturers that could do international distribution, or because the designers simply wanted to retain better control over their distribution. Azzedine Alaïa was one designer who chose this solution, as did Angelo Tarlazzi for his first line. Azzedine Alaïa selected his clients and took their orders. Miles was chosen for knitwear, Chofflet for "warp and weft" paid for the raw materials, production, and billing, accepting the commercial and financial risk.

Alaïa and Tarlazzi received 10 per cent royalties, 10 per cent commission, and a share in advertising that was between 3 and 5 per cent that added up to a total fee of about 25 per cent. This business model could be successful as long as the company was a mid-size firm. It became more risky when the purchasing of raw materials implied a responsibility on the sales. It was a simple system, and although it worked earlier, as it did with the C. Mendès–Yves Saint Laurent association in 1966, it is less recommended today with the merciless competition that demands constant new product and great flexibility.

Angelo Tarlazzi. In 1960, Angelo Tarlazzi began his career in fashion as a designer with Carosa, a grand couturier based in Rome. He became Michel Goma's assistant at Jean Patou in 1965; he left Patou in 1968, but returned four years later as artistic director. In 1953, Marc Bohan was the first designer at Patou who had been promoted to the position of artistic director. In 1972, Angelo Tarlazzi was the first whose working contract mentioned the title of "artistic director."[26]

Between 1968 and 1972, Tarlazzi lived the typical life of freelance stylists of the time. He sometimes created nine collections a season, in ready-to-wear or couture, in France and abroad: Carosa in haute couture, Chombert for the furs in Paris,

Jerry Silverman in New York, to say nothing of all the Sentier houses that paid him well.

When Michel Goma established his ready-to-wear house, rue Montpensier, his previous assistant replaced him at Patou, but the soul of the legendary couture house had vanished since couture ready-to-wear had chased away the haute couture buyers. At rue Saint Florentin, there were only eight saleswomen and five workshop heads left in two ready-to-wear workshops and an adequate sales organization. In 1977, Tarlazzi left Jean Patou to create his own house, 5 rue du Louvre. In 1978 Gosset Champagne, former financial partners of Rochas perfumes, provided the capital necessary to set up an haute couture house at 7 avenue George V and to launch a perfume. Andrée Putman had been hired to do the interior design, her first big project. But Angelo Tarlazzi, despite the legal risks, suddenly backed out of what he considered a lost bet and soon the adventure was interrupted. The headquarters under construction was taken over by Saint Laurent Rive Gauche.

In 1980, the company moved to 29 rue du Faubourg-Saint-Honoré, and it was first financed by the payments from houses where he was again working as a stylist including Laura Biagiotti in Rome, and Alma or Basile in Milan. More funding came in the form of royalties and commissions for orders taken in his salons on behalf of his licensees. This was a clever way of controlling distribution without having to take on the responsibility for a production unit.

In 1989, Tarlazzi was chosen by Guy Laroche to succeed him. Tarlazzi decided to use his couture experience in the service of a company other than his own, while continuing to deign his signature ready-to-wear.[27] It is obvious that such a career course would not take place today.

Integrated management. The kind of financing this management imposed, until break-even was reached, was not higher than that required for the two previous examples, but it required a larger treasury.[28] In fact, the profit margin of about 40 per cent generated by the production easily compensated the expenses that a larger staff and the direct purchasing of raw materials implied. With integrated management, a company could better affirm its policy and impose its decisions because centralized decision-making enabled a coordination of creation, distribution, and production. The only drawback was that by renouncing the secure management model that a license contract guaranteed, a company, rather than its licensees, would be directly exposed to the hazards of the market and, most of all, currency fluctuations. The series of devaluations of the British pound, the Italian lira, and the Spanish peseta, prior to the introduction of the euro, put the French designer exporters in the same position that their predecessors had been in during the fifties.

Jean Charles de Castelbajac. He began as a stylist with Pierre d'Alby. While he was associated with Créateurs & Industriels, Jean-Charles de Castelbajac followed the integrated management model. De Castelbajac believed in the return to nature and the nation. He proposed modern, active, elegant, and playful clothes that, with their added creativity, could compete with Hermès. Against the background of French national heritage, he provided an alternative to Kenzo whose collections from 1970 onwards embraced Far Eastern folklore. With Castelbajac, the eternal values of French local culture were clearly evident, accompanying the amplitude of shapes, the sumptuous rigor of the materials, and the joyful harmony of the colors worn by a few legendary knights.

Although he had always actively chosen the licensing policy, he had the advantage of a family manufacturing structure in Ko & Co, previously the Valmont company. His mother, the marquise of Castelbajac, was both the owner and chief pattern maker of this company. The label was supported by the admirable technique this company provided. As soon as it came into existence, Ko & Co worked with other designers including Kenzo and Chantal Thomass.

In 1975, Jean-Charles de Castelbajac made quite an impact. He arrived in the fashion world as someone who could transcend French eternal values and resist métissage and Kenzo's strong influence.

Thierry Mugler. With the spontaneous proof that only belongs to true designers, Thierry Mugler established his universe for the long term within three decades.

In 1973, a young man with the air of a conqueror came up on the podium amidst the models just after showing his first signature collection called "Café de Paris." Prior to this, he had designed the clothes for the store Gudule. Starred letter paper, three-dimensional monuments covered in silver letters, and chiffon dresses with fox-fur trim for movie stars were already very much a part of his repertory.

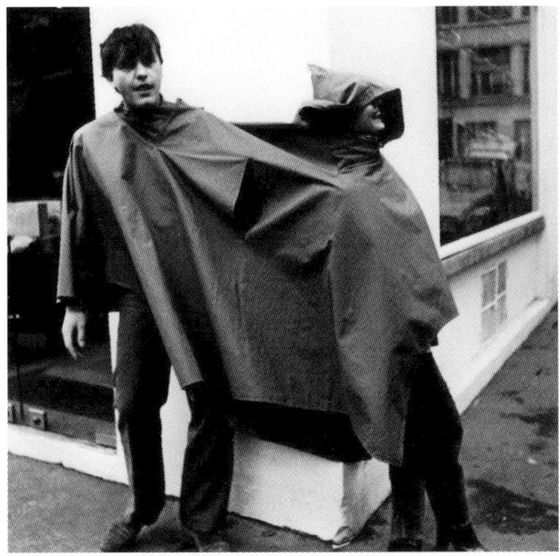

Jean-Charles de Castelbajac, c. 1978.
Photos Pierre Boulat,
courtesy Agence Cosmos.

Jean-Charles de Castelbajac,
Mickey dress, spring–summer 2002,
© Jean-Charles de Castelbajac/Rights Reserved.

Thierry Mugler, photographer.
The countryside around Volgograd,
July 1986. ©Thierry Mugler.

Angel by Thierry Mugler.
©Thierry Mugler.

In 1974, as an equal associate with Alain Caradeuc (a young HEC graduate), Mugler started his own company at 22 rue d'Hauteville. The collection he showed at the Grand Hotel in 1976 remains in my mind a prodigious revelation. When I came out of the show, I told him his talent would always keep him safe from problems. However, the problems soon arose in the form of a bill for 150,000 francs that endangered the company. Alain Caradeuc asked for C. Mendès' help, but despite my enthusiasm, the company refused to become associated with Thierry Mugler's destiny. A favorable analysis of the limited liability company's accounts—carried out by Michel Douard, manager with C. Mendès and Gérard Leplé, chartered accountant—did not suffice to convince my partners. Maybe I was not firm enough in explaining that it would be better to become associates in the design and production structure rather than continuing a contract that would have to be revised every three years, as had been the practice in our profession for the last 10 years. I also thought it was better for C. Mendès' survival to be a part owner of the label rather than an uncertain tenant. The situation was even more delicate as I was myself in the process of negotiating the sale of my own shares in C. Mendès. In 1977 salvation appeared, this time in the person of Alberto Beriro, a Spanish entrepreneur who wanted to invest in a fashion business. I advised him to lend the money to the limited liability company Thierry Mugler. Once he had seen the collection, he asked me to counter guarantee his loan. On 18 January 1978, as I had recovered my financial autonomy, I paid off my debt. In parallel, Umberto Ginochietti, the Italian industrialist who wanted to invest in a new label, joined Mugler, and I became the president.

Thierry Mugler, Alain Caradeuc, Umberto Ginochietti, and myself each owned one quarter of the shares.[29]

When Michel Douard joined the general management in November 1980, it was a big step for Mugler. Douard left C. Mendès and brought the skills and experience to Thierry Mugler that had ensured the success of Yves Saint Laurent Rive Gauche.[30]

Between traditional licensing policies and diversification, Thierry Mugler inaugurated a middle path that gave him control over all the elements of his label.

Apart from the central collection of women's ready-to-wear, manufactured in Thierry Mugler's French factory, the other collections were entrusted to industrialists who had a reputation for quality production of specialty products. They were able to guarantee consistent quality to Mugler and produce the goods at the right price. A common distribution network was available to the licensees who found it useful. In fact, the responsibility for sales was entrusted to agents that were recommended by the Mugler management. These agents chose the brand's authorized dealers to whom they offered a range of complementary and coherent products (in terms of style, range, and price) in exclusive showrooms, all within the respective territories for which they were responsible. This kind of showroom served as the label's ambassador and was set up in Milan, Madrid, Düsseldorf, and Brussels, as well as Paris and New York, where Thierry Mugler was his own agent. Japanese licenses operated via a specific contract signed with the Takashimaya group. This structure offered Mugler the advantage of growth without the risk of diluting the label's image.

In a fair deal for the perfume, Thierry Mugler acquired 34 per cent of the company Thierry Mugler Parfums, controlled by the Clarins group, which in turn bought one third of the shares of the couture company. The goal of both parties was to build a long-term association between both companies. *Angel* was launched in France in 1992.

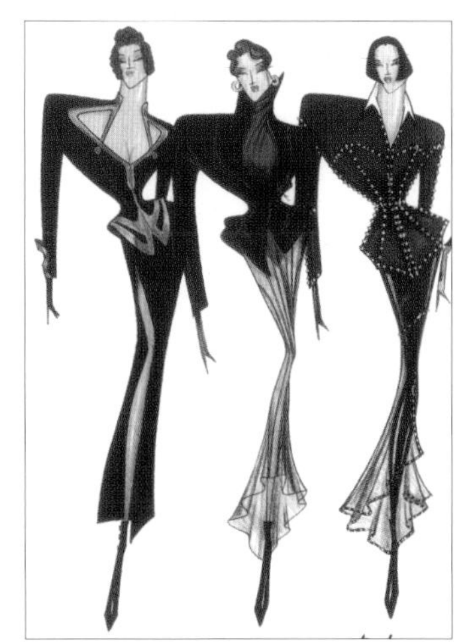

Sketch by Thierry Mugler for the haute couture collection autumn–winter 1992–1993.

The créateurs de mode attempted to broaden their scope of business as soon as they reached a desired level of success by introducing new products under their label. They did this by following the example set by the couturiers, their predecessors, and used various management models for this diversification.

Diffusion ready-to-wear, also called "second lines," was included in this strategy and the market got an injection of new lines, such as: Kenzo Studio, Beretta Médiane, Gaultier Junior, Inscription Rykiel, Tarlazzi II, Thierry Mugler Activ, State of Montana… following Miss Balmain, Miss Dior, Courrèges Hyperbole, Ungaro Solo Donna, or Yves Saint Laurent Variation. Once the designers chose to take advantage of their brand recognition, they also risked tarnishing their image. In theory, fame should allow a designer label to calmly participate in the price battle, on the condition that it remains

Janssens & Janssens
COLLECTION AUTOMNE-HIVER 92-93

LA VIE EN ÉTÉ

VENDREDI 31 JUILLET 1992

Janssens & Janssens
TISSUS HAUTE COUTURE
Tél. 42 65 04 00

PAR JANIE SAMET

Le journal des collections haute couture hiver 93 (5)

Face-à-face de dernière heure

Thierry Mugler : une haute couture qui déshabille

Toulouse Lautrec et Rita Hayworth

Givenchy : sa haute couture rassure

Jerry Hall and Thierry Mugler
at Studio, 1980.
Photo Pierre Boulat,
courtesy Agence Cosmos.

Work session at the workshop, Mirabelle, Marc, Martine, Thierry, Zuleïka, Chantal, Zaza, 1980. Photo Pierre Boulat, courtesy Agence Cosmos.

Thierry Mugler and Didier Grumbach. New York fashion show, on Bloomingdale's invitation, 1981. Photo Roxanne Lowit.

Le Figaro, 31 July 1992.
"The newspaper of the winter 93 haute couture collections." Janie Samet.
"Last minute meeting"
Thierry Mugler invited to participate in the haute couture calendar.
"Different but stunning!
The only criticism, in this collection there was a mixture of haute couture and ready to wear models and it was not easy to tell the two apart."

watchful over the integrity of its style and practices a distribution policy that is even more exclusive, while its new products make it more accessible.

Once the designers become institutionalized by the perfumes, their brand positioning changes, allowing for the emergence of a new generation of labels. Thus, those who assisted Karl Lagerfeld, Jean Paul Gaultier, Azzedine Alaïa, or Thierry Mugler as stylists move to the forefront and launch their own collections. Martin Margiela followed the Azzedine Alaïa model; Martine Sitbon and Sybilla worked like Jean Paul Gaultier; while Jean Colonna, Véronique Leroy, Ann Demeulemeester, Mariot Chanet, or APC integrated their production and sales services within their own company. However, in order to avoid under-performance that may have resulted from a dispersion of the decision-making poles, the designers, one after another, reverted to the industrial mode of management that couture had practiced when it was an industry.

Martine Sitbon, autumn–winter 2007–2008. Photo Stéphane Feugères, courtesy Martine Sitbon.

Notes

1. Thelma Sweetinburgh was a journalist with *Vogue* for seven years. She joined the International Wool Secretariat before she went on to manage *Women's Wear Daily*'s Paris office. She incarnated a power that was born of the pure elegance, warmth, and attention that she bestowed on the couturiers, enveloping this agitated period in seduction.
2. Head of the fashion section at *Figaro.*
3. Head of the fashion section at *Figaro,* a few decades after Marguerite de Souza.
4. Alain Lalonde was the father of Brice Lalonde, environment minister under François Mitterand.
5. His clientele was varied and prestigious: Mrs. Henry Ford II, Nicole Alphand, Hélène Rochas, Genviève Fath, Sophia Loren, Brigitte Bardot... His success was due to his skill in copying couture (his alteration workshop consisted of about a dozen workers, all from haute couture) until the stylist came onto the scene.
6. Until 1966, it had been the tradition to invite a French grand couturier.
7. Fortunately the insult was erased by the compliments Diana Vreeland, American *Vogue's* editor-in-chief, paid them. She visited the hotel the following day, accompanied by her whole team, to have a closer look at the collections.
8. Corrine Cobson, Jacqueline Jacobson's daughter, launched her own brand in 1986.
9. Martial Raysse's brother.
10. Chrome Cuir for leather, Neyrat for the umbrellas, Brezin for the bags, Cacharel for the sportswear, Bistrot du Tricot for knitwear, Rottenberg for furs, Skidress for the skiwear.
11. Lady Rendlesham, editor-in-chief of *Queen's* magazine. She later owned the Saint Laurent Rive Gauche boutiques and a Karl Lagerfeld boutique in London.
12. Denise Dubois-Jallais, "L'idée simple qui va démoder le luxe," *Elle,* 24 May 1971.
13. English *Vogue,* June 1971.
14. A highly respected columnist with *Le Monde* whose pen name was Nathalie Montservant.
15. Before occupying the printers at 4 rue d'Uzès, then occupied by the Sarfati establishment that is opposite the old Maria Carine offices.
16. *WWD,* 9 and 10 July 1971, and *Marie France,* October 1971.
17. Fernando Sanchez celebrated his house's twentieth birthday on Sunday 28 March 1993 in New York in his establishment at 5 W. 19th Street.
18. *WWD,* 16 January 1973.
19. French *Vogue,* November 1973.
20. Jean Charles de Castelbajac: 31 place du Marché-Saint-Honoré; Issey Miyake: 38 place du Marché-Saint-Honoré; Toiles: 30 place du Marché-Saint-Honoré; Roland Chakkal: 4 rue de Marché Saint Honoré.
21. Yves Saint Laurent, interviewed by Felicity Green: "What a relief; I have always suffered during the process of giving birth. I will only have to go through this agony twice a year, instead of four times." *Paris Fashion,* 1972.
22. Crédit national, *Influence de la haute couture sur l'industrie textile,* December 1971, p. 20.
23. Bruno du Roselle's assistant since 1969 who became president himself in 1974.
24. The same year Créateurs & Industriels invited Walter Albini, and the Mendès Valentino contract led the latter to present his ready-to-wear in Paris. Issey Miyake and Jean Muir were on the calendar for the first time as guests, citing C&I.
25. Marylène Delbourg-Delphis, *La Mode pour la vie,* Paris, Autrement, 1983, p. 110.
26. Interview with Jean de Mouy, CEO of Jean Patou.
27. Guy Douvier designed Guy Laroche's ready-to-wear.
28. "Stratétgies financière des jeunes marques," Denis Geffrault, Pernille, Ahlers, Vincent Boeri, Isabelle Foropont, *IFM,* July 1990.
29. Between 1980 and 1985, while I was in New York and president of Yves Saint Laurent Inc., Thierry Mugler's ownership fluctuated and Umberto Ginochietti sold his shares in 1986 to Mugler Triumvirat SA.
30. From this time on, Thierry Mugler produced his creations in a way that Yves Saint Laurent had refused to in the sixties and as Jean Patou had tried, unsuccessfully, to in the seventies. The company had industrialized and employed several senior managers from C. Mendès in management positions.

The creators of the year 2000, *Elle*, 6 December 1999. From left to right, bottom to top: Martin Margiela, Sonia Rykiel, Alexander McQueen, Véronique Leroy, Christian Lacroix, Valentino, Paco Rabanne, Loulou de La Falaise, Issey Miyake, Thierry Mugler, John Galliano, Ann Demeulemeester, Emanuel Ungaro, Olivier Theyskens, Martine Sitbon, Karl Lagerfeld, Jean Paul Gaultier, Jeremy Scott, Michael Kors, Claude Montana, Gilles Dufour, Eric Bergère, Kenzo Takada, Inès de La Fressange, Yves Saint Laurent, Yohji Yamamoto, Azzedine Alaïa, Vivienne Westwood, Jean-Charles de Castelbajac, Marc Jacobs, Zucca, Nino Cerruti, Peter Speliopoulos (Cerruti), Adeline André, Dries Van Noten, Cristina Ortiz (Lanvin), Isabelle Puech, Benoît Jamin, Junko Shimada, Isabel Marant, Nathalie Gervais (Nina Ricci), Alber Elbaz, Christian Louboutin, Renaud Pellegrino, Benoît Méléard, Philippe Model, Raymond Massaro, Marie Mercié, François Lesage, Peter O'Brien (Rochas), Dirk Van Saene, Rose-Marie Le Gallais (Daniel Swarovsky). © Photo 12. com/Photo Jean-Marie Périer.

Conclusion

The irreversible movement of democracy finds its expression in a common aesthetic and moral values, all of which indicate a mixing of cultures. In terms of the way people dress, social dissimilarities have gone from infinite to minimal.

In 1993, whatever its price, the kind of fashion design that replaced haute couture targeted the same "worlds" as couture or ready-to-wear. Thus the same brand can express two different concepts to the same person.

It took several decades for a handful of "precursors" to make themselves heard. Lucien Lelong, Jean Gaumont-Lanvin, Albert Lempereur, Cerf Mendès France, Jacques Heim, Alain Lalonde, Robert Ricci… wisely fought against a majority of deaf sceptics huddled behind their prerogatives. Little by little the pernicious effects of the 1910 break and the legislation of 1943 and 1945 were wiped away. When the latter legislation was formulated, ready-to-wear did not respect the quality criteria that couture demanded. As early as 1972, Hébé Dorsey predicted in *Paris Fashion:*

> It is clear that couture and ready-to-wear are increasingly alike. While the manufacturing techniques are being perfected, high quality ready-to-wear offers an elegance and refinement in its finishing that only haute couture could offer in the past. This does not mean the end of haute couture, which will simply become the most luxurious sector of ready-to-wear.

Effectively today, the work that can be better executed by machines is handled industrially while work that can only be done by hand remains exclusive to couture.

It only depended on the union authorities to ignore the strict regulations that had been elaborated during the last war for the traditional apprenticeship practices to be recreated. Jacques Mouclier could thus add Gaultier, Montana, or Mugler's ex-assistants to the fashion show calendar, as Daniel Gorin had done for Worth, Doucet, or Balenciaga's heirs: a mere return to the source, while taking new realities into account.

Paradoxically, those who had tried several times to establish a harmonious dialogue between couture and ready-to-wear had been cut off by the quasi unanimity of their colleagues. In 1961, Jacques Heim was the first to show great foresight, followed by Courrèges in 1965 and Pierre Cardin in 1972. In 1956 Raymond Barbas advised couturiers to modify their business if design ever entered the ready-to-wear field. And because they were not listened to, Jacques Heim,

André Courrèges, Pierre Cardin, and lastly Robert Ricci, retreated and went back into the established system.

Twenty years later, on 28 July 1992, Thierry Mugler played out the same scenario, changing the situation nonetheless: instead of presenting his couture and ready-to-wear collection in the March–October cycle, he found it more convenient to enter the haute couture calendar. The shows were broadcast live to New York and Tokyo and their timing coincided with deliveries to the retailers for the ready-to-wear as well as the placement of personal haute couture orders. The combined couture–ready-to-wear show was no longer only a prestige event but became a real support for the brand's dealers, while also increasing the potential clientele for made-to-measure orders.

Nothing has changed. As in the past, buyers and clients do not attend the same collections together. The private March and October showings are for the professionals and the July and January ones for the private clients. Is there any other industry in the world that takes the risk of exhibiting its discoveries, free, to the whole planet before having actually sold them?

François Baufumé ironically evoked this flaw in the system, in a note dated 26 January 1989:

> Tradition wants the collection release in October (or in March) to constitute an event. This event justifies everyone's passions and thus all the different excesses that surround the collection presentations. Passions, let us note in passing, that are not all related only to an admiration for the art, but more sordidly, to the good fortune that for some is to be found in the free access to the studios of Paris creative fashion.

With this kind of argument, Thierry Mugler's reasoning satisfied the requirements of logic; however, it required his colleague's approval. In order for the haute couture shows to regain their supremacy, they had to assemble the greatest number of talented creators. Emanuel Ungaro, who understood the logic of this decision, showed couture and ready-to-wear together on 20 July 1993; maybe he paved the way for other couturier-créateurs. The main issue, however, is no longer solely the survival of haute couture, but the emergence of new fashion brands. The fashion pendulum is constantly swinging from London to Milan, finding its balance in Paris. Worth, Redfern, Lucile, Mary Quant, Ossie Clark, Jean Muir, Zandra Rhodes, Vivienne Westwood, and John Galliano joyfully exult the transformations of fashion that Suzy

Menkès, a good analyst, had already predicted in the *New York Herald Tribune* of 13 March 1993: "Fashion is coming from the North: Helmut Lang from Austria, Marcel Marongiu, half Swedish; Ann Demeulemeester and Martin Margiela from Belgium are announcing a new era. Who knows where the wind will blow from and when it will change?"

One must know how to sail with the wind if one wants to be carried by it. Growth is occurring only from the margins; if there are no fringes, there will be no growth. The birth of a prestigious brand lies in a singular talent with an independent voice. This is not always compatible with the desires of a society that satisfies its inclinations more easily with the comfort of recognized values. Once a designer has attained success, even the liveliest talent succumbs to the parasites of ordinary fame. However, all the famous brands have begun as troublemakers, incapable of reaching a big audience. Their turnover is too small, their prices too high. Their clientele is too limited to start with and in addition, the fashion they develop takes too long to make its mark. What designers really need has little to do with their models produced through licensing, but rather to have financing for integrated industry. For this reason, the only recurring problem designers face today is one of finance. It is a fact that no couture house founded after 1965 has attained international fame while financially prospering, just as no fashion designer has been able to forcefully impose themselves over the last 20 years, and this, mainly for economic reasons.

How could one encourage a dialogue between a financial or textile group that represents an empire, and a young creator, whose main quality—his or her individuality—is also their vulnerability? Could there be harmony between computerized power on the one hand and picturesque sensitivity on the other? This antagonism can only be avoided if, right at the beginning of their career, the couturier-créateur was the major shareholder in his or her own company.

With this in mind, a project baptized "Mode & Finance" was established in 1990 that was piloted by a financial organization and supported by several textile groups. This project aimed to facilitate minority shareholding in fashion companies that had been in existence for more than three years and that had a responsible management system. The European textile mills and weavers, retailers looking for sources of inspiration, perfumers looking for new concepts, and financers looking for lucrative investments should be the first to support emerging brands. By allowing the twenty-first century to make room for new talent, all would ensure their future.

The creators seen by Steven Meisel and chosen by *Vogue* USA, July 2000. Left to right: Véronique Branquinho, Hedi Slimane, Hussein Chalayan, Filip Arickx, Nicolas Ghesquière, Ann Vandevorst, Lawrence Steele, Miguel Adrover, Viktor Horstling, Roberto Menichetti, Rolf Snoeren, Olivier Theyskens, Josephus Thimister, and Junya Watanabe.

Postscript

Twenty years have passed since the first edition of *Histoires de la Mode,* 20 turbulent years. The map of our trade has been transformed at the same frantic rhythm as the international economy. A number of "exotic" countries have become the dynamic actors of international commerce. During this period, the way the French percieve their situation has fluctuated. Europe still scares them, but they know it is inevitable. The new technologies they were convinced would destroy employment have in fact been a means for man to adapt to an exponential demographic growth.

As always, fashion, fortified by the economy and liberated by society, translates these upheavals in real time. Just as in the 1970s the Japanese economic upturn was visible in the west thanks to the emergence of brands like Kenzo or Issey Miyake, the Parisian fashion shows from Chapurin, Hussein Chalayan, Gustavo Lins, Exception, or Manish Arora have enriched the international community with the traditions of these designers' respective countries: Russia, Turkey, Brazil, China, and India.

Divisions in the world are disappearing; cultural mixes are replacing folklore and the resulting homogenization is a factor of harmony and not of impoverishment. Globalization upsets the way our industries work. In a world without borders, innovation is more effective than marketing and brands constitute powerful tools of differentiation. In parallel, national legislations dealing with the protection of brands and clothing that had remained disparate until now are finally beginning to work together towards the same goals.

In Europe, Paris and Milan are speaking the same language. Far from serving only the big companies, new technology gives emerging brands their chance and Internet applications, a determining factor in the area of fashion, give rise to great achievements. A drawing printed in Paris can be woven instantly in Sao Paulo; the Internet can be used to send a pattern and its graduations, made in London or Milan, to Peking. The fashion industry that France's *Grandes Ecoles*[1] had ignored because of its archaism has been so greatly transformed over the years that it has become a management model for other industries.

> Modernity went hand in hand with an important growth in fashion. The latter extended its role to a growing number of economic sectors. Companies need creativity to affirm their competitiveness; the life cycles of products are getting shorter, the current mood is omnipresent. To affirm that fashion is everywhere could lead one to think that it will become diluted. This is however unlikely, as fashion, in the strictest sense, clothing, continues to prosper as the collections are created, supported by the fashion creators and their brands' fame.
>
> Interview with Pascal Morand, 30 June 2007.
> Previously general manager of IFM.
> Since 2007, Pascal Morand has been general manager of ESCP-EAP.

I—FROM INTERNATIONALIZATION TO GLOBALIZATION

A single but authentic product for the world! This formula could summarize the effects of globalization today in terms of fashion, while internationalization, which characterized the 1970s, can be perfectly illustrated by the advertisement published in *Women's Wear Daily* (illus. p. 304) on 4 March 1974. After a century of unchallenged French domination, the Japanese designer Issey Miyake gained recognition in Paris the same year as New York's Oscar de la Renta. Créateurs & Industriels invited Walter Albini to Paris. Two American manufacturers, Goldin and Feldman Furs and Quote Me Inc., collaborated with Christiane Bailly. French collections remained preponderant,[2] but London, Milan, Tokyo, and New York made their differences known. On 20 November 1978 in Tokyo, on Hanae Mori's invitation, a significant event, "The Best Six," assembled Issey Miyake from Tokyo, Stephen Burrows from New York, Thierry Mugler from Paris, Gianni Versace from Milan, and Jean Muir from London. This broadening of horizons in a divided universe did not adversely affect the way that companies functioned.[3]

The way that globalization has developed during the twenty-first century represents a very deep and sudden change. With Japan, we have had the advantage of half a century of successive stages of adjustments, all of which happened in a protectionist world. The countries we are confronted with today, in a much freer world, have different traditions, different commercial habits, different training systems, and different laws. Practices are changing drastically. The international licensing of the past—that made the fortunes of houses like Dior, Cardin, or Yves Saint Laurent—no longer work. Today, the most prestigious brands are exporting a "made in France" product to China and India. Within companies, logistics managers have replaced licensing managers. And in this world without borders, an export manager no longer has the same job description as he once had. At the same time, young companies that distribute their products internationally are learning to handle their production all over the world, using a universally comprehensible computer language.

In this great upheaval, the state is no longer an adequate mediator, and professional trade federations have a central role to play: their intervention may be able to create harmony. Their relationships need to be peaceful. Now in all the countries where the garment industry is powerful (China, Italy, France, Brazil, etc.) professional organizations associating creative brands and industrial institutions coexist in a setting of armed peace. Their statutes, as well as their traditions, make them absolutely irreconcilable, and everywhere their relationships are marked by hypersensitivity.

In France in particular, the federations, heirs to a system established in 1945 at the Liberation (couture, women's clothing, knitwear, lingerie, leather, men's garments, leather goods, etc.), maintain a strong influence even though the industries they once represented no longer function under the same economic reality. Everywhere, transversal brands are doing better than single product brands. In the 1980s each federation had clearly demarcated members. Today's brands with their diversified product rosters depend on different and complementary organizations (couture, leather, shoes, etc.). Thus the industry that has largely de-specialized over 50 years is still represented by different categorical organizations.

The epistolary jousts between Jacques Heim and Albert Lempereur in 1959[4] and Pierre Bergé and Bruno du Roselle in 1974[5] were marvels of civility compared to the constant war of positioning that their successors now engage in. Their correspondence, less refined than that of their predecessors, is just as tasty.[6]

During the general assembly of the Fédération Française de la couture on 24 June 1997 Jacques Mouclier, at the head of the Federation since 1972, spoke of his departure and suggested forming a steering committee that, during this unstable period, would serve to redefine[7] the Federation's mission, as well as define the profile of the next president, depending on the mission itself.

After discussion, a committee was set up along the lines of the 1961 Jacques Heim commissions, and very similar to the one Dominique Strauss-Kahn had initiated at the Ministry of Industry in 1991.[8] Five areas of reflection were entrusted to five so-called "specialist" commissions. The latter were comprised of external experts and two members of the steering committee.[9] The strategic plan the committee elaborated was finally unanimously adopted:

- Reform the structures of the union organizations that were still very focused on the strict definition of the professions established in 1945;
- Internationalize the list of members;
- Change fashion education to include technological progress and the opening of markets;
- Continue the battle to protect brands and designs from being copied and encourage the emergence of new brands.

On 23 April 1998, the steering committee's executive commission decided to present me as a candidate for president of the Federation during the upcoming assembly to be held on 26 June.[10] The Federation statutes were then modified so that the rules that would apply during my succession would be clearly determined.[11]

Decompartmentalization

Since its creation in 1973[12] the Fédération Française de la couture had become more homogenous. The couture houses had diversified and regained control over their ready-to-wear that had been licensed out to external manufacturers. The ready-to-wear designers included made-to-measure pieces in their collections in order to enrich and complete them. Some of them—Alaïa, Gaultier, Mugler—even opened couture workshops...This amalgam of brands of diverse origins conformed to the way our professions had evolved. Wasn't Dior a manufacturer, créateur, and conceptor as much as he was a couturier? Until the 1970s Pierre Bergé welcomed advertising managers with a loud, "How much are you paying to mention my name?"

Things have changed completely. Over recent years, the financial groups LVMH, Richemont, and PPR have encouraged their subsidiaries to follow an industrial policy that generates margins and protects the companies' image. Thus the most prestigious haute couture houses, Chanel, Dior, Yves Saint Laurent... are today the biggest French exporters of ready-to-wear.

In this new context, the Federation organizes permanent study commissions which lead to virtualize the different unions it coordinates. Their existence is nonetheless justified, particularly with regard to the collection calendars they manage. The honorary presidents, presidents, and vice-presidents of the various Chambres Syndicales are entitled to sit on the Federation's managing committee, and the elected members of the same committee also belong to the Chambres Syndicales. An organization has been created that is stable, dynamic, and perfectly adapted to the current changes.[13] In fact, it was decided in 1998 that the Chambre syndicale du prêt-à-porter, as well as the corresponding men's wear organization, would be inclusive and international while the Chambre syndicale de la couture would remain exclusive and strictly Parisian.

This decision was concretized by the membership of foreign brands such as Rick Owens, Dries Van Noten, Zucca, Bernhard Willhelm, Akris, Loewe, Paul Smith, etc., while Issey Miyake was elected to the Fédération's executive committee. At the same time, after Agnès B became a member, other concept brands like Lacoste, Paule Ka, Façonnable, Cacharel, etc. joined. In addition, a number of new generation designer brands became members on the condition that they were large exporters and were sponsored and elected. Until the seventies, two or three brands set the tone for the Paris shows and others followed. The situation has changed now; Paris has never presented so many singular visions of fashion.

While the ready-to-wear was enriched by new participants haute couture, which had lived off a multiplication of licensing contracts on all the continents since the 1950s, was weakened by globalization that, by doing away with borders, ruined territorial contracts. In addition, the apprenticeship system that characterized the French industry had been wiped out;[14] the assistants did not succeed their masters anymore. In fact, within their federation, couturiers had long wanted to remain in a majority. Non-couture designers were of course aware that they were being used as promotion tools for haute couture that had lost its famous members over the years. Yet they were satisfied because, in turn, they benefited from the Malthusian policy their predecessors[15] had practiced by signing advantageous licenses.

The "Invited Members"

Nonetheless, during the 1990s, the system which had lost its dynamism wound down.[16] The international press orchestrated the death of haute couture. "Not so haute" was the title of the front page of the *Wall Street Journal* of 29 April 1995. "French fashion designers lose edge as Italians, Germans, Americans out-market them." "Good bye haute couture," added *Newsweek.*

In 1995, the Federation's management committee decided to make up a limited commission aimed at redefining the future of the profession.[17] In order to renew the couture brands in an organized manner, it was decided that new applications for membership from designers would be studied by the Federation's management committee and then ratified by the Chambre syndicale de la couture parisienne.[18] As a last resort, it would be the couturiers themselves who would elect the new "guests." Designers who were admitted would have to have couture skills, but they were free to mix original ready-to-wear models into their shows. They would not be permitted to use the appellation "haute couture" regulated by the decree of 1945, but they were authorized to use the term "couture."

Thierry Mugler and Jean Paul Gaultier were the first guests at the 1997[19] spring collections. The guest members could acquire member's status after five years of presence, a fresh vote, and an application to the Industry Ministry.[20] Up until now, couture houses had integrated their ready-to-wear, one after the other. Now, ready-to-wear houses began to establish their couture. This opportunity of once again associating the two skills in the context of a single event would put an end to the extremely perverse practice of entrusting the responsibility for couture and ready-to-wear collections to two different designers. In the latter case, couture that did not have industrial limitations, nor any real commercial future, devalued the ready-to-wear that financed its existence.

Thierry Mugler and Jean Paul Gaultier's entry into the calendar, John Galliano's storming of Dior, and Alexander McQueen's at Givenchy enthralled journalists from all over the world, beyond all expectations. The excitement provoked by the real demonstration of living art that each of their presentations showed was, and would always be, far more interesting than the most seductive advertising campaign.

After this, season after season Josephus Thimister, Adeline André, Viktor & Rolf, Felipe Oliveira Baptista, Anne-Valérie Hash... demonstrated their talent, "off calendar" first, before being invited by their couturier colleagues.[21] In a second step, after Jean Paul Gaultier, certain guest members became permanent members.[22] The last, in 2005 and 2006, Elie Saab, Martin Margiela, and Giorgio Armani[23] were definitively included in the first page of the calendar. Rather than being a fragile conservatory, haute couture was yet again the industry's observatory. It conjugated the twofold power of singling out and institutionalizing the brands it sponsored. In 2007, after participating in the couture calendar for five years, Maurizio Galante and Anne-Valérie Hash applied for permanent membership to the Chambre Syndicale.

In 2010 Julien Fournié, Maxime Simoens, and Alexandre Vauthier were elected "guest members" followed by Rabih Kayrouz, while Gustavo Lins and Christophe Josse—one year before Giambattista Valli—were awarded the haute couture label. In June 2011, Azzedine Alaïa presented to the press his couture and ready-to-wear collections in his own showroom and became a permanent member. In January 2012, Versace was readmitted in the first page of the calendar after eight years of being absent. Some brands which were discovered through haute couture, such as Viktor & Rolf and Felipe Oliveira Baptista, chose to revert to the ready-to-wear calendar but their followers, such as Vauthier, Bouchra Jarrar, and Yiqing Yin, have taken a positioning that clearly sets them apart from their competitors.

Thus, the opening up of markets, the growing importance of brands, the preponderance of design, and the urgent necessity to standardize the different legislations dealing with their protection create the necessity for cultural differences between communities to be known and understood, if possible, starting at school.

Education and Conviviality

Education is a vector of tolerance and conviviality. When fashion was strictly French, the Parisian schools were inevitable. Tokyo, New York, London, and Antwerp have also become fashion centers and they naturally have their own schools, some of which are excellent.

Fashion education had to be re-evaluated and the education commission, established within the framework of the steering committee, finally identified the conditions required for the successful creation of a training center of international proportions in Paris. The resulting project for the Cité de la mode[24] was the subject of a presentation for the minister on 23 July 1998 by Madame Marylise Lebranchu, who was then Secrétaire d'etat aux PME, au Commerce et à l'artisanat.[25] Thanks to Pascal Morand's[26] tenacity, under Pierre Bergé's presidency, the Cité de la mode was inaugurated in September 2008 at quai d'Austerlitz, on the banks of the Seine.

It has taken a bit more than 20 years, since the creation of the IFM in 1986, for a project perfectly adapted to the contemporary world to succeed. In fact, breaking down the barriers between managers and designers of all nationalities and uniting them under the same roof represented a huge accomplishment. The members of the couture federation that assemble internationally known or emerging brands, either industrial or artisanal, confidently recruit from within IFM. The new Cité de la mode et du design can only guarantee this position.

Education is a decisive issue and the rapprochement with China is an illustration of this. In 1987 Fang Min, a reputed stylist, was the first Chinese student to obtain the IFM diploma. She returned to China in 1991 and became director of the Xian Textile Institute while I was the director of studies at IFM. She invited me to spend a week in Xian[27] to give a series of classes. Zhang Zhe, her husband, devoted his career to establishing ties between the French and Chinese fashion industries. At the end of this first visit I met Mr. Du, China's textile minister[28] at the time, in Peking. Later Christine Zhao, who was from IFM's class of 1999, became the brilliant ambassador of French fashion in China.

Fashion had been a first meeting ground for the two countries when in 1989, on the instigation of the Chine Nouvelle agency, my predecessor Jacques Mouclier presented 12 haute couture collections in Peking. This event bore fruit when Sylvie Zawadzki, general secretary of the Federation, negotiated a partnership agreement in 1995 between the Chambre Syndicale schools and Dalian University to create a fashion department. Mr. Boxi Lai, future minister of commerce and vice prime minister, who was mayor of Dalian at the time, saw fashion as a major cultural subject. Exchanges between the schools, alternating with professional meetings, continued. In March 1999, Mr. Zheng, president of the company Firs and vice president of the Chinese federation, led a delegation of his colleagues to Paris for a program of meetings with people including the designer Thierry Mugler and Nelly Rodi, founder of the eponymous style bureau.[29] These actions were just like the French fashion missions that traveled to the United States after World War II, with alternating promotional events, fashion shows, visits to industrial units, press agencies, and education centers.

In March 2006, the Institut Français de la mode became a partner with the Tsinghua University of Peking. The exchanges and meetings multiplied. The last fashion show in Peking that year featuring young European designers[30] was essentially a repeat of what Melka Treanton had organized 30 years earlier in Tokyo for young French designers.[31]

The event which culminated this period of observation took place when my Chinese counterpart Du Yuhzu—the last Chinese textile minister, and artist painter, and photographer—was awarded the Officier des arts et lettres medal by French culture minister Frédéric Mitterrand.

The relations with the Indian fashion industry developed along the same lines as those with China's but they started a bit later. It was also thanks to student exchanges that India and France began to create industrial ties and that their respective brands became acquainted with each other. Ms. Rati Vinay Jha, the president of the FDCI, began coming regularly to Institut Français de la mode beginning in 1986, the year it opened at 33 rue Jean Goujon in Paris.

The Franco-Indian relationship continued to grow. A delegation of eight French students went to India between 30 April and 13 May 1987 with the blessing of Idris Latif, India's ambassador to France. Laurence Sudre, Hélène Kasimatis, Dominique Garretta, Marielle Belin, and the only man, Christophe Rouxel, were among these students, the majority of which, 25 years later, enjoy strong reputations in France and have a great memory of the welcome they enjoyed in India, especially from Manorama Sarabhai. The French students visited New Dehli, Jaïpur, Jodhpur, Ahmedabad, and Mumbai where they learned Indian traditions, visited museums, and learned about the structure of India's textile exports and the specific qualities of the country's unique handwork.

In 1989 France Grand and Stéphane Wargnier, professors at IFM, gave two weeks of lectures at India's National Institute of Fashion Technology (NIFT). The fashion show videos of contemporary designers had the same impact on Indian students as they would on the students of China's Textile Institute.

In 2006, Rati Vinay Jha invited me to Dehli's fashion week to give a lecture. At the end of the fashion week, I suggested that she come to the Festival d'Hyères à la Villa Noailles. Two weeks later, four Indian designers found themselves at the most celebrated fashion festival (see page 434).[32] That year, the Festival d'Hyères was presided over by Christine Lagarde, currently the director of the International Monetary Fund.

The next season, Manish Arora and Rajesh Pratap Singh showed their collections during Paris fashion week. Since then, Manish Arora continues to show his fashion in Paris and he became the first Indian member of the Fédération Française de la couture. Nearly 40 years after Issey Miyake became the first Japanese designer to gain international recognition, Manish Arora became the first Indian designer, and certainly not the last, to show his work on the Paris podiums. Arora's experience demonstrates how India's openness to the west and western fashion has accelerated over recent years. Manish, a graduate of NIFT 1994, never planned on having a career in fashion. When asked a question about his choice by *Prêt* magazine (Fall–Winter 2011), Arora answered: "A strong memory of fashion would be one of a Thierry Mugler show. It happened even before I was a student. I was also enthusiastic, later, about the Egyptian show by John Galliano Christian Dior for Spring 2004. However, Thierry Mugler remains the earliest and strongest memory in my mind."

The presentations of Manish Arora in Paris were immediately controversial and passionate, which is what Paris is good for. Admiration came gradually. When asked what Paris brought him in his life and in his work, Manish said: "I feel more confident as a person. I never was shy but it is easier to express myself here. In India, I had to control myself. Professionally, I am still learning. In France, you have to work on the silhouette in three dimensions, which is quite another technique; the French are more demanding on design and quality. In India, a fashion show is first a social event; in Paris, the competition is harder. It doesn't refer to any group or nationality and everybody must contribute. To understand this, you have to live here."[33] Like Issey Miyake, Manish now lives in Paris for part of the year. It is understandable as Marc Puig, president of the Puig Group, proposed him to be the artistic director for Paco Rabanne.

Manish is now a central figure of international fashion.[34] His accomplishment is quite a feat given that traditional Indian costume remains a strong force in Indian fashion in general. Ritu Kumar, the "dean" of Indian *créateurs de mode,* was the first to associate contemporary fashion and tradition.

After the Hyères 2006 event featuring Indian designers, Rohit Bal was proposed twice to show his line during Paris haute couture week. The splendor of his costumes should have brought a new facette to the event. It hasn't worked yet. In the meantime, Anamika showed her line in Paris with success. But her label needs a bigger team and time in order to become known worldwide, like any new fashion brand.

This year marks 25 years of the Indian fashion industry, and the FDCI will celebrate this anniversary. Some brands like Suneet Varma or Tarun Tahiliani have succeeded at establishing themselves. They, their colleagues, or successors will follow Manish Arora's example and will expand to Europe and the west.

There cannot be such a thing as French or Italian fashion anymore; there will be no such thing as Indian or Chinese fashion. The interpretations of Western dress reflected by Japan—and soon China and India—coexist with the resurgence of rich, hidden, cultural heritages like those of Flanders, Turkey, Serbia, etc. The list of winners at the Hyères[35] international fashion festival year after year includes a small minority of French, English, and Italians. This is due as much to the logic of numbers as the law of fashion. Our old countries have already said a lot. Design is what is unexplored. Fashion can no longer be an expression of power.

II—BRAND FRAGILITY AND DOMINATION

Couture or Ready-to-Wear

During couture's heyday, the capital required to put together a first collection was not exorbitant. The couturier worked directly for his clients, there was no multibrand intermediary, and often he was his own stylist and workshop manager. There was no intermediary between the artisan couturier and the consumer, no price limit, little investment, simple management. Wasn't Christian Dior the most efficient manager of the company that bore his name? However, the couture brands in the 1950s already found it difficult to finance their growth,[36] and without licensing, they would have disappeared a long time ago. Now the entry of designers into the industry under Maïmé Arnodin and other fashion advisors' impetus was going to further aggravate the situation.

In fact, ready-to-wear demands far more substantial financial and human resources than couture. The purchasing, production, sales, and communication services all require well-trained and, of course, well-paid specialists. The founding partners logically have to become financial partners. It's desirable that during the growth phase, the founders of young companies can freely write their story while remaining majority shareholders on the board. When they reach maturity it is just as desirable, unless they have natural heirs to take over, that they prepare themselves to give up their control in order for the brand to become depersonalized and get taken to another level. This remains the business model that prevails in almost all cases where fashion brands succeed in their growth and transformation, from Chanel to Yves Saint Laurent, from Kenzo to Thierry Mugler. This success was the finish line of a path full of obstacles.

Management and creation rarely work well together. Fashion is the most difficult of industries to manage because it is fueled with creativity. The balance between design and management that is needed within each company is a key element for success and understanding with the external world. In a company's initial phase, the design team must impose its repertory to then allow the management to express itself.

It is understandable that harmony is rare in the major fashion houses and that lasting success is something exceptional. A forceful manager in one company could be catastrophic for another. Of course there is no specific model growth plan. Each company has to imagine its own, depending on its strengths and weaknesses. Another hurdle is that fashion brands are not eternal and the founders have to take this temporality into account when they define their business strategies.

Brand Managers

> "To have the privilege of managing a company with creative teams requires a special gift. One has to fully accept, from within, to manage a process that does not follow the rules of management (...) Managers capable of fully living the latent internal chaos, implicit in the confrontation of these two worlds—management and design—will take their companies far beyond their competitors."
>
> François Cholle, *L'intelligence intuitive,* Eyrolles, Editions d'organisation, 2007.

In the 1920s, Lucien Lelong or Jacques Heim, just like Charles Frédéric Worth's or the Callot Sisters' successors, inherited companies from their ancestors. Heim and Lelong were both collection managers and managing directors of the companies that bore their names. Lucien Lelong's job, as judge and arbitrator of his workshop managers, (Pierre Balmain, Christian Dior, Hubert de Givenchy, etc.) and a sought-after personality in Parisian society, is not the same as the job his ready-to-wear counterparts perform today.

Sidney Toledano

> At the age of six or seven, I used to accompany my mother to Mme. Achille's; she was Dior's dealer in Casablanca, then later to Mme Henriette Ladreyt's. These salons were located in big apartments and followed the Dior codes: white boxes, tissue paper with more or fewer folds, a grey carpet, moldings. I grew up in this atmosphere. My father used to receive his tailor at home. I still remember exactly his gestures when he consulted the wad of samples, his pleasure in choosing fabrics. My adolescence was bathed in these colours, in the lights of a Morocco full of smells, flowers, sunshine. We had a taste for what we wore; we were very oriented towards the external world. Fashion was cashmere pullovers, Levi's jeans, loafers, Clarks. Appearance was important, certainly more so than culture.

In 1969, Sidney Toledano arrived in France to study science. He graduated from the Ecole centrale in 1982 and his first professional contact with a fashion stylist was at Kickers, a shoe company that was also making children's clothing. He learned about the industrial problems connected to the collection plans, cost prices, and specification sheets. Later, when he was manager at Lancel, he discovered the leather world; and in 1994 Bernard Arnault and François Baufumé came to convince him to move to Dior, where his mission would be to develop Dior's leather goods.

As soon as Dior terminated the worldwide leather goods license with Guéné, it was urgent to organize production. A first site was set up in Tuscany. The product had to contain all of the Dior brand's symbols. The Lady Dior bag became the Lady Di[37] bag. The sales of leather goods grew significantly between 1994 and 1997, and compensated for the company loss due the progressive phasing out of the licenses for other products. François Baufumé resigned in March 1998 and Sidney Toledano succeeded him. In 1994 the turnover, much of which came from licensed goods, was about 120 million euros. In 1998, it reached 200 million, with zero profit. Despite the rupture of the fabulous licensing contract with Kanebo in Japan, Dior returned to profitability in 1999 and has remained so ever since. In 2006, Dior announced 730 million euros of turnover and one billion euros in 2011.

The business model has changed; the image has been rejuvenated. John Galliano's first haute couture show with Dior, after Gianfranco Ferré's departure, took place in January 1997. Victoire de Castellane, a costume jewelry specialist, moved to Dior from Chanel in 1999. Her dream was to create high quality jewelry. For menswear, the first contacts with Hedi Slimane[38] materialized in 2001; three extremely talented designers with very strong visions—one dealing with men's fashion, the other with jewelry, and the third with women's fashion—gave an autonomous interpretation to the Dior universe. We gave them access to the archives, the Dior codes; of course, Dior only had 10 years to codify his brand, from 1947 to 1957. All the archives, all the shows, represent an important wealth of heritage, but there is still a certain freedom because Mr. Dior himself did not retain exactly the same codes from one show to the next; he reinvented everything each time. The couture look and spirit were present in men's fashion with Hedi as with his successor, who had been his assistant, Kris Van Assche.[39] For Victoire, the codes she more willingly used to interpret the Dior world were the flowery, animal, garden, or bee elements. For John, it was of course couture, the bar jacket, provocation, volumes. Each one worked on the values they codified in their own way; the common codes, of course, were not affected, and this allowed the Dior brand to run on three motors. Studies conducted by large consulting companies show that today the Dior brand has again found a place alongside Chanel, Hermès, and Vuitton, amongst the big powerful brands, and above certain Italian brands that have high revenues. As super premium brands, in France we have Vuitton, Dior, Chanel, and Hermès because these houses have a history and they knew which direction to take. We knew how to nourish these brands by creative work, by networks of boutiques that perfectly reproduce our universe, by marketing that is often at the service of design. I think this is what explains the strength of our [French] brands.

In the 1980s, Dior established itself directly in new markets like Japan, China, and eastern Europe. This had some far reaching effects on the cosmetic activities, creating synergies that did not exist. Designers today are involved in the image as well as the growth of cosmetic products and perfumes. There are strong relationships between the fashion and beauty teams that were not the case in the seventies or eighties. Dior has only one activity under license: eyewear. There is no longer a disparity between the couture house and the licensed products. In 2012, the arrival of Raf Simons to replace John Galliano allowed Dior to enter a new period and broaden its repertory.

Haute couture is a vast investment but its energy has a huge impact on the other activities and contributes to the brand's strength. It is the savoir-faire that creates the value; we have preserved this value thanks to haute couture, ready-to-wear, the workshops, and the artisans.

The manager of a fashion business today has to be very sensitive about design. Unlike other enterprises that revolve around marketing, with executive stylists and where the chief executive officer can concentrate on the product problems, we have to manage designers. The managers that existed during Jacques Rouët's time had precise and concrete notions of accounting, were not marketing theorists, and did not have as much money as is available today; they were economical. Today, our houses are permeated by the emotion that emanates from the studio; this is where the product comes from and creativity gives rise to emotion. The mood in the studio can be felt as far away as the house's reception area, among the hostesses. The designer may suddenly ask to see me. Sometimes one has to know how to bring down the pressure, improvise, and play with the rational and the irrational. We all have an asymmetrical brain. If one is too rigid in this profession, if you only know how to say no, history has proved that the company … and the brand can fail.

Ralph Toledano.[40] Ralph Toledano is not related to Sidney but they did attend the same schools in Casablanca, where they were born. He followed the same path as his classmate: same friends, same hobbies, same memories. An exceptional professional curriculum…Yves Saint Laurent, Lagerfeld, Guy Laroche, Chloé. However, his richest experience was a job in a group that was doing very badly called Boussac Saint Frères—his first job. "During those few years, I learned what a factory was, to what extent it was important to receive fabric in time, how to calculate prices. It was there that I learned the basics of the profession."

Ralph defines his profession as follows: "I could say I am a manager, an entrepreneur, a strategist, a builder... but all of that is only a partial vision of the reality. My real profession, my uniqueness, what I love and what has always fascinated me, is to manage creativity. It is not something one can learn; you have to have it in your blood. I think I know how to find the right words at the right time, and I understand people who design. In our industry we talk a lot about marketing, boutiques, advertising, celebrities, and yet... it all begins and ends with the product. The product is in the hands of people who create. My talent is certainly to be able to guide them and to help them give the best of themselves.

"It is a profession in which there is no negotiation, nor compromise. It demands total partnership. We both know that the only success stories in fashion history are those of a couple who succeeded. All over the world, success is based on a designer/manager duo, the greatest successes were in fact family histories as they convey the notions of respect, love and understanding."

Since Chloé was set up in 1952[41] under Gaby Aghion's management, creators like Gérard Pipart, Maxime de La Falaise, Christiane Bailly, Grazziella Fontana, Karl Lagerfeld, Tan Giudicelli, Guy Paulin, Philippe Guibourgé, then Martine Sitbon, and several others have added their bricks to the building. Stella McCartney's arrival rejuvenated the brand and made it more sexy. Phoebe Philo, in 2001, added sensuality and more sophistication, making it more offbeat.

In 1999, Chloé only had one asset: design. There was no communications budget, no direct distribution, and just barely a small wholesale network. It was mono-product, mono-network, almost mono-territory. Today it is a global enterprise in every sense, in terms of its products, geographical implantation, and distribution network. "The only way to make a brand survive is to give it the widest sustaining polygon possible, as there is no limit to the fields of activity a fashion house can enter."[42]

"Over two years, 2005–2006, we increased our turnover fourfold: it was both wonderful and exhausting. We couldn't integrate the reinforcements we needed quickly enough and we worked with almost the same structure. Paradoxically, from outside everyone thought we were the happiest people in the world. Imagine, quadrupling your weight in two years.... you would die! We survived this growth period because the team was just wonderful! We were working towards a new structure that could absorb this increased strength so that we can take our market forwards.

"It would, however, be a fundamental error to believe it is enough to sell bags and it doesn't really matter whether the ready-to-wear sells or not. We are a fashion company. Mme. Aghion started out by making five cotton shirts. If our ready-to-wear was not competitive, we could have the best handbags in the world, they still wouldn't sell."

The Richemont group that owns Chloé has 16 brands. Currently, Chloé is the youngest at 60 years old. The oldest, Vacheron Constantin, was created in 1755, and the majority of the others go back to the nineteenth century. What interests Richemont's president Johann Rupert the most is the DNA of the companies he controls; this is what determines their growth potential.

Nathalie Rykiel.[43] Respect, love, and understanding—the assets of family companies, according to Ralph Toledano's definition—are perfectly illustrated by Sonia Rykiel. Sam and Sonia Rykiel founded their brand in 1968 and Sonia was the president. The couple divorced and their daughter Nathalie and her husband, Simon Burstein—one in charge of artistic direction, the other, vice president, responsible for development—were the heart of the company for 20 years. Danièle Flis, Sonia Rykiel's sister, was the accessories director. Sonia's grandchildren were very involved and were always in the front row at the shows. Sonia was inseparable from her family. Nonetheless, even in this idyllic situation, with no one from outside owning shares in the family company, the question of succession was a sensitive issue.

In 1975, Nathalie Rykiel got involved in the brand by parading as a model for the Sonia Rykiel fashion shows. She then decided to plunge herself wholeheartedly into the company where she successively occupied the positions of sales director and artistic director for the shows.

To launch the brand into the future, Nathalie decided in 2000 to make herself known to the general public, lending her image to the international advertising campaign for *Rykiel Rose*, the new perfume she had created.

As her mother had often told her, "power is not something that is given to you, it is something you take..." Nathalie became managing director of Sonia Rykiel in

1998. Over several seasons, Sonia and Nathalie walked the podium together to the final applause of each collection. It is impossible, however, to imagine that this perfectly staged and, after all, perfectly natural moment, could be one of total harmony.[44] Successions in fashion are definitely problematic. In 2012, Nathalie Rykiel, with the full support of her collaborators and her mother's agreement, decided to open the capital and give the control of the company to a well-considered Chinese group presided over in Paris by Jean-Marc Loubier.

Yves Carcelle.[45] Born in Paris on the banks of the Seine, he was a graduate from the Ecole polytechnique, moderately fascinated by mathematics. At the end of the 1960s Yves Carcelle decided to make his career in a new area that some predicted would have a brilliant future: marketing. He discovered the creative and design professions during the five years he spent at the head of Absorba, a highly respected children's clothing brand. After this, he spent five years as president of Descamps, a fine household linens company. When Bernard Arnault bought the Boussac group, they became Carcelle's main competitors. In 1989, Boussac asked him to join his group. At the beginning of 1990, Bernard Arnault had won the difficult takeover battle for the Louis Vuitton Moët-Henessy group; at the age of 40, Yves Carcelle found himself suddenly propelled to the head of Louis Vuitton.

At this time, Vuitton's product range was strictly limited to travel goods, with a smattering of handbags. Ninety-seven per cent of the collection was based around the "LV" monogram fabric. Since Louis Vuitton's invention of the first modern trunk in 1854, the house was world famous, even amongst maharajas, but it was only known for its specialty of travel goods.

Between 1990 and 1997, while the use of the monogram toile continued to grow, Vuitton introduced new materials, leathers, checked patterns, and even fabrics into the collection. 1996 was the centennial anniversary of the monogram and its acceptance by the fashion world. Seven designers of different nationalities, including Azzedine AlaÏa,[46] Vivienne Westwood, and Isaac Mizrahi, created the object of their dreams out of this timeless material that has continued to maintain its incredible modernity. Louis Vuitton, trunk maker, became a leather goods maker. Bernard Arnault and Yves Carcelle then decided to push Vuitton into new territories, starting with ready-to-wear and shoes, and later on handbags, eyewear, fragrance, etc.

"The real strategic rupture for a brand like ours is that products designed for eternity are confronted with the notion of short-lived and seasonal renewal. This brutal culture shock was Bernard Arnault's decision and I put it into play; we recruited an American artistic director, Marc Jacobs, famous for his 'grunge' collections and he spent five months imbibing the Vuitton spirit, its history, and the vocabulary of the house. The first fashion show we held was in March 1998. Irony or provocation, only a single model of a bag was presented on the podium, to the general surprise of the audience. Louis Vuitton wants to become an essential ready-to-wear actor. Almost ten years later, I quite simply think that the Paris fashion week would not be quite the same if Louis Vuitton were not present. The perfectly harmonious cohabitation of the fashion collections near the same place as where the trunks are made, in Asnières, in the same manner as in the nineteenth century, this is the miracle of these last years!"

> The desire for luxury developed because, even if poverty was still very present in the world, the world was also getting richer. Quite honestly, I do not think there is a limit to the expansion, on condition that we do not infringe on our traditions and never lower the quality of our products to preserve profit margins, or compromise the quality of the service... If we do, we will be in danger. This is why no Louis Vuitton product is sold outside of our own shops. We want control over the atmosphere that surrounds the sales of our collections. The quality and the emotion of the service counts as much as the product.

"To look to the past without reinventing it is boring, but creating products that have no relationship to history is to be transient and purely in fashion... the synthesis is not easy to achieve."

Vuitton is a global brand firmly established in Europe, America, India, China,[47] and Russia. "In 2007, Vuitton opened shops in four new countries: Cyprus, Panama, Romania, Qatar. It was highly symbolic." In 2012,[48] Vuitton owned 461 boutiques in 54 countries. Its sales are estimated at 6.5 billion euros.

Yves Carcelle, as president, left Vuitton in 2012 and Marc Jacobs, as artistic director, resigned in 2013 after 16 years of success; however Vuitton will continue with a new phase.

Nicolas Topiol.[49] The last president of Christian Lacroix before the house closed followed an atypical professional path. Nicolas Topiol was born in Paris in 1964. In 1978, the very year Christian Lacroix opened, Nicolas chose haute couture as his final study subject. After his brilliant studies and obtaining an MBA from the Wharton

School in the United States, he chose to go into banking rather than fashion and he got a financial investment job with Société Générale then with Apax Partners. He moved to Florida with his family and worked at developing new companies in a variety of fields, or restructuring them.

This was how he met and advised the Falic brothers, who in 2001 had bought the American company World Duty Free, and renamed it Duty Free Americas. This business operated mainly in airports on the Canadian and Mexican borders. The Falic brothers asked him to negotiate for, and then directly manage, some of their acquisitions beginning with two very fashionable Californian cosmetic brands, Urban Decay and Hard Candy, which they had bought from LVMH. Because these acquisitions had proved themselves to be financially worthwhile, Topiol and the Falic brothers often asked the merger-acquisition manager at LVMH to let them know "if there was anything for sale." In October 2004, at the Cannes Duty Free show, they were offered the Christian Lacroix brand.

Christian Lacroix was a perfect business for the Falic brothers and Nicolas Topiol, even though the figures were depressing. They signed the sale agreement the day before the haute couture collection of January 2005 was presented, even though Christian Lacroix's contract was to end two months later.

Lacroix's contract was renegotiated. Production management was integrated into the company, although the house had never directly managed its production. The secondary ready-to-wear lines, a source of confusion, were abandoned and Lacroix's signature collection was expanded and strengthened at the same time. Christian Lacroix made up a duo with Nicolas Topiol and Topiol's observations follow: "When we began together in January 2005, I realized that the house was fragmented, but [Lacroix] was not. He proved that he had a capacity to renew himself and to question himself, which few people are capable of. At the time, the brand seemed to be split between haute couture, the lungs of the house, and a confused ready-to-wear. Today, everything fits together again... We are often idealistic and disappointed when we have expectations. Mine were high, but I would like to say to Christian that I have never been disappointed, in fact he has surprised me, by his humanity, his talent." [50]

Christian Lacroix's sentiments are quite similar:

> These people have been here for about two years, we are restructuring the house and I have the impression that the twenty years we are celebrating this year, are actually my

> first year... By "trimming" the house, cutting off all the branches that had been grafted on based on the pretext of profitability, the fairly useless products, all these ranges and sub ranges, by going back to something authentic, one realizes what the house really has in terms of individuality and if we allow it to grow in this direction, it will be profitable immediately.[51]

However, those sentiments did not last. The new partners fought and split. The house fell apart. The main cause of this failure is at the base of the construction; both Jean Jacques Picart, his partner, and Christian Lacroix should have been positioned in the organization chart in the heart of the brand and not out of it.

A Brand, an Autonomous Product

> "... It is the brand that is now the reality, while the product has become a sign. There is competition between Vuitton, Gucci, Dior, Armani, Hermès, Versace and a few others, and it is not about their products. Even less about their prices."
>
> Lucien Karpik, *L'Economie des singularités,* Editions Gallimard, March 2007.

Brands quickly become independent from the products from which they emanate. They are of such capital importance that the way designers position their brand when they start structuring their company is a strategic issue, and they situate it differently depending on their temperament and maybe also depending on their lawyers' more or less shrewd advice. Some protect it nervously in their own name, and concede it to one or several external entities; others bring it to the company for which they are artistic director and that bears their name. The former want to live off their talent and if possible get rich; the latter attempt to build a house that will survive them.

The first scenario has been used very frequently in France and it lends itself more easily to companies that follow a licensing strategy. The branded company creates the collections and receives royalties. The licensee that is dependent on the brand is responsible for manufacturing and distribution. Pierre Cardin, Yves Saint Laurent, Jean Paul Gaultier, and Claude Montana were examples of this kind of management for a long time. The second type of organization implies that the designer wants to create his own company and manage the manufacturing with industrial partners whose assets and skills are complementary to his own. The legal corporate structure the designer chooses implies certain consequences for his brand's life span. The brand is in fact by definition linked to a man's destiny; it is preferable to transform the physical person who owns the company into a moral entity as quickly as possible, as it generally undergoes less brutal transformations.

It was while taking all these factors into account that in 1999, in the context of the Federation steering committee, Caroline Joubin, administrator of the bank Natexis, presented a project for a European fashion investment fund to potential investors.[52] The fund would participate and invest in the mushrooming emergence of brands that were needed to renew the textile and garment industries.[53] This initiative came at just the right time. The international economic upswing was, as always, accompanied by the arrival of a number of new brands. As designers' talents are primarily subject to market demand, brands tend to emerge in clusters.[54] Paris benefited from this trend notably because, with its incomparable attraction, its position as fashion capital was no longer contested.[55]

The succession of the founding designer, a key element for a brand's perpetuity, is far more attractive to the media than the administrative birth of the company that bears the designer's name. The Chambre Syndicale regulations demanded that couture houses be managed by an exclusive designer. On Christian Dior's death, Marcel Boussac had hesitated a long time before keeping Dior alive. At the time it would not have been acceptable that Antonio del Castillo, Lanvin's artistic director, compete with Lanvin under his own brand or that Yves Saint Laurent, Dior's artistic director, could compete with Dior. Chanel upset the tradition in 1983 by working with Karl Lagerfeld, the polyvalent stylist who was also designing his own signature and other collections. His success encouraged others to do the same.

The Nature of Brands

Unlike luxury brands that gain in value over time (Révillon founded in 1723, Hermès in 1837, Vuitton in 1854), fashion brands age. A girl does not buy her clothes from the same place as her mother, and it is natural for each generation to identify with their own brands. A label that is as old as its designer finds it difficult to attract the next generation. Whatever the designers' ambitions with their second lines were—Miss Dior, Miss V. Yves Saint Laurent Variation,[56] Thierry Mugler Activ, Gaultier Junior—they were unable to attract their clients' children. It's for the same reason the labels Dior, Givenchy, and Balmain—all three of whom had been modelists together at Lucien Lelong—each had different destinies.

Christian Dior died young when his house had not even been in existence for 10 years. His successor Yves Saint Laurent, aged 20, took Dior beyond its designer and its time. Balmain and Givenchy aged and their labels had more difficulty surviving.

Over time, a succession of mortal designers constitutes a timeless brand. Chloé, Dior, and Chanel, coming from fashion, transformed themselves into luxury brands by following Poiret's example and by ensuring they retained control over their production and the management of their sales outlets.

At the other end of the fashion chessboard Kenzo, who never wanted to belong to haute couture, created a product-image-architecture concept that allowed him to progressively depersonalize his label, until he was detached from it. It could then be transformed successfully into an ageless "concept-brand" that was developed after him by Gilles Rosier and Antonio Marras, and in the context of the LVMH group. Finally, in 2011, under Pierre Yves Roussel's responsibility, Humberto Leon and Carol Lim were appointed artistic managers for Kenzo.

In 2000 Tom Ford, within the PPR group, carried out a similar exercise for Yves Saint Laurent, replicating the scenario Yves Saint Laurent himself had enacted at Dior in 1958. From 2004 onwards Stefano Pilati, under the president Valérie Hermann's management, shifted progressively away from Yves Saint Laurent's repertory—without destabilizing the brand's fans. At last, under Paul Denève's presidency in 2012, came Hedi Slimane to assure the artistic management of the brand.

Martin Margiela had a unique approach. He developed his brand in complete anonymity so that the product remained identifiable on its own. His refusal to be interviewed and photographed kept him out of the limelight and away from all the disturbances that generally accompany fame. On Jean-Marie Perier's "family photograph,"[57] showing all the great fashion creators of the year 2000, Margiela "occupies" the empty chair in the first row. People say he is handsome and intelligent. In such a context, fashion reviews can only talk about the collection and they ignore the designer.[58]

Thierry Mugler's situation is very different. He is, like Paul Poiret, the prototype of the star designer: his appearance attracted even more attention as he made it rare. His first show in New York in 1981 required the intervention of the mounted police! This effervescence intensified over the years and every inauguration, every media event (the launch of a perfume, for example) always provoked a frenzied crowd—such was the price of success.

One day in 2006, when he had retired from business, he asked me to help him become anonymous by writing a certificate for the French administration. "Having chosen to stop his activity after thirty years of success, and to live life at a different pace, his name has nonetheless continued to become increasingly famous, as he is no longer involved in the profession, and it would be fair not to disturb him"[59] and that he be allowed to change his first name.

As for Issey Miyake, in order to maintain his brand in the shifting fashion world and to prolong the growth phase, he used a tactic that is unusual in the west. Throughout his career, he financed his successive assistants; leaving his brand image in the hands of his last assistant, he dedicated himself to a futuristic line, APOC, that gave him room to express his talent.[60]

Masama Yamamoto, couturier, transmitted her passion for couture to her son, who in turn passed on to his daughter Limi. At Yohji Yamamoto, the company's perpetuity is a constant concern. This is often the case when the couturier is an artist (hadn't Balenciaga decided to shut down his house rather than pass it on?). "I think my destiny is marked by a fundamental contradiction... I am the head of a large family of four children and seven adults, including my son and my daughter who could be my heirs; this would reassure people about the future of my company. It would be an advantage at a practical level, but I have always wanted to avoid this situation, for example, by leaving behind a note: 'no activity post mortem.' It is as if the word 'family' is sacred to me in a way; I reject it and yet, I am proud of it. Until now, my collaborators, whether they wanted to or not, constituted the 'main capital' and if, for once, I wanted to clarify my thoughts, I would say I consider my team my own family. I am a man first and then a couturier..."[61]

It has been shown that disconnecting a brand from the person of the founder is a painful process. The orphan brand sometimes continues its path like a rocket that has been shot out of orbit. Thus, Jean-Louis Scherrer's[62] brand, which has already had a difficult time, has not completed its trajectory. In 1995 Kuniko Tsutsumi—manager of the company Ilona Gestion and sister of the president of Seibu Tokyo—sold Scherrer for her family company to a group run by the businessman François Barthes, in association with the special DGSE fund. In 2002, Mrs. Tsutsumi died at her lawyer's office while completing the annexes of the contract of sale. Scherrer's assets, along with Jacques Fath's, Emmanuelle Khanh's, Stéphane Kélian's, etc., were then sold to the financer, Alain Dumesnil, in the framework of EK-Finances. In five years the total loss for the DGSE amounted to 27 million euros.[63] In 2007 Stéphane Rolland, artistic director appointed by François Barthes, opened a couture house in his name at 10 avenue George V, financed by new investors. And in 2012, the name Jean-Louis Scherrer with no visible assets was sold to financers.

Emanuel Ungaro was wise enough to have dealt with his own succession and, to an extent, he did. After selling his company to the Ferragamo group, he started looking for a successor. Giambattista Valli was the lucky candidate. However, after a period of reciprocal enchantment, the relationship between the two designers—Ungaro in charge of couture and Valli responsible for ready-to-wear—could only deteriorate. Structures are always stronger than people. Emanuel Ungaro left the house of Ungaro a few months after Giambattista Valli, and Ferragamo sold the brand to Asin Abdullah, an American-Pakistani millionaire. In turn, Abdullah recruited the designer Peter Dundas. The Ungaro house continued to exist with a new president, Mounir Mouffarige, and a new creator, while in March 2005 Giambattista Valli presented his collection under his own name, supported by the Italian group Gilmar. In July 2007, Peter Dundas left Ungaro. In 2008, Ungaro was, however, still registered on the collection calendars. In 2012, Giambattista Valli was granted the haute couture status while Ungaro, for the first time in half a century, was absent of the couture agenda.

Artistic Directors and Founding Designers

Alber Elbaz was born in Casablanca in 1961. He arrived in New York in 1985, where he went through all the stages of the career of an accomplished stylist without ever having felt he was in a transition phase; at every stage, he committed himself fully. At Geoffrey Beene in New York, he worked in the shadows backstage, waiting. When Ralph Toledano hired him at Guy Laroche in 1995, he brought him into the light. He was appointed the artistic director for ready-to-wear at Yves Saint Laurent in 1999 where he spent weeks consulting the archives. "There is nothing we can add to perfection. I closed the door to the archives; I had understood and then forgotten them. I tried to do something imperfect."[64]

When he left Yves Saint Laurent, soon after it became a part of the Gucci group (a PPR subsidiary), Alber Elbaz took his time. He traveled in Africa, in India, and refused all the offers that were made to him. With whom could he do things differently? He was looking for the right formula and hoped he wouldn't find it.

Nonetheless, in 2002 it was he who took the initiative to contact Mrs. Wang, the owner of Lanvin. Paraphrasing Pierre Bergé, Alber said that "Chanel gave women freedom, Yves Saint Laurent made them powerful, and Lanvin gave them desire." In agreement with Mrs. Wang, he chose Paul Denève as his counterpart "an intelligent man, who had a new vision of the company," and later on, Thierry Andretta would develop the company with an amazing success.

Like his colleagues Nicolas Ghesquière at Balenciaga, Riccardo Tisci at Givenchy, and Olivier Theyskens then at Nina Ricci, Alber Elbaz is a veteran of the fashion industry and its related professions. Like them, instead of creating his own brand, he chose to incarnate a famous brand with which he felt a certain affinity.

Within the Chambre Syndicale old, regenerated brands have always coexisted alongside emerging brands that bring in a new energy. In the 1950s, the presidents of Worth and Paquin (nineteenth-century brands) participated in the same assemblies as young Dior, Carven, and Balmain. Among the newer arrivals, there always were a number that exploded at the wrong time in a morose market that had no time for them. Fortunately, in spite of the crisis, current international growth is encouraging the arrival of new brands and about 10 houses, of all different nationalities, are certainly destined to become the permanent pillars of the Parisian collections.

Since the Englishman Worth established haute couture, a number of foreign couturiers have followed him to Paris. The American Mainbocher; the English Redfern, Creed, Lucile, and Molyneux; the Spanish Balenciaga and Castillo; the Swiss Robert Piguet; the Italian Elsa Schiaparelli; the Greek Jean Dessès; the Belgian François Crahay; the Japanese Hanae Mori... all of them were enthusiastically adopted by haute couture, which in turn owes a large part of its fame to them.

Foreign fashion designers naturally followed their example. In 1974, without having to base themselves entirely in Paris, Jean Muir and Issey Miyake were included in the Chambre Syndicale's official calendar. They preceded a number of their fellow citizens including: Vivienne Westwood, John Galliano, Alexander McQueen, and Stella McCartney,[65] to name a few of the English; Yohji Yamamoto, Comme des Garçons, Junya Watanabe, followed by Undercover, among so many other Japanese.[66] The largest contingent came, however, from Belgium, propelled by two excellent fashion schools: l'Académie des beaux-arts d'Anvers and the La Cambre school. The "group of six" from the Antwerp academy, which Martin Margiela joined for a brief while, established Belgian conceptual fashion. It brought together Dirk Bikkemberg, Ann Demeulemeester,

Walter van Beirendonck, Dirk van Saene, Marian Yee, and Dries Van Noten, who were all from the same class of 1982. In the mid-eighties, once they had dispersed again, they presented their first collections in London, then Paris, while French creators Martine Sitbon, Jean Colonna, and Marc Audibet created their own brands.

Twenty years later, it is certain that a large number of European brands will survive their founders, and a new generation of French figurative designers who possess couture skills will in turn occupy center stage.

Fashion Brands and Luxury Brands

For the past few years we witnessed a new two-fold movement: while internationally famous fashion brands (Dior, Givenchy, and Yves Saint Laurent) have regained a new intensity by abandoning their licensing policies, the most prestigious luxury brands, timeless by their very nature (Vuitton, Hermès, Prada, Gucci...), are moving into the new territory of fashion in which they had only made tentative forays until now. They are invading the territory that overexploited fashion brands have slowly left to them. To ensure their success, they have a network of established, profitable, wholly owned boutiques that provides them with image and advertising budgets of a level that our professions in this quality range have never known. Most of all, they have the financial means at their disposal to allow them to acquire, or take control of, all kinds of internationally competing brands. These acquisitions provide them a potential for external growth that they will need when their own brands lose their powers of attraction. Fashion, however, remains marginal in their overall business, and it is better this way: fashion goes out of fashion and luxury is what remains when fashion passes.[67]

This new but transitory phenomenon that has marked the last decade of the twentieth century does not however change anything in the equation by which the brands create product line extensions from the main brand to the accessories. Boucheron or Charles Jourdan never had a vocation to become fashion brands, while Yves Saint Laurent or Chloé find immediate legitimacy in the jewelry or leather sectors. In this process, the product of reference—the one the brand was born from—remains a major element of its genetic code. A house does not have the same destiny, depending on whether its original specialty was harnesses for horses, luggage, furs, or fashion.

Unlike luxury brands that diversify over time, fashion brands are *de facto* transversal. Their life span is shorter but the territory they can exploit is very open.

These luxury brands that are of considerable value today and have become major financial players, are very careful to deactivate the link between the charismatic boss and the international clients, in order to protect themselves from the risks of succession .... The better known, more international and unattached the brand is, the easier it is to change. The more specific, personalized and linked to a family, a man, or a designer, the more difficult it is to pass on the flame.

Christian Blanckaert, *Luxe* 2007, Le Cherche Midi.

Fashion and Finance

The inevitable alliance between fashion and finance still encourages incessant comments about the guilty unawareness of one side and the inexcusable greed of the other. Yet... financial groups have always demanded returns on their investments from the brands they take over, however profitable they may be. Georges Aubert in the 1930s with Poiret,[68] Beer, Drecoll, Doeuillet, Doucet, Lenief; Marcel Boussac in the 1940s with Pierre Clarence, Philippe et Gaston, Christian Dior; Charles of the Ritz with Yves Saint Laurent and L'Oréal with Courrèges in the 1960s; Robert Kenmore[69] and the Kenton Corporation in the 1970s with Valentino, Cartier New York, Christofle, and the Ben Kahn and Kaplan furriers; and Bernard Arnault in the 1980s with Dior, Givenchy, Lacroix, and Kenzo: these investors always behaved like capitalists, while the couturiers have always been more or less justified in complaining about their associates' greed and roughness. In these instances, the press always takes the artist's side, even if they have sometimes become multimillionaires.

The Owners of Large Groups

"In competition, history is a doubly decisive asset; those who have it cannot lose it, those who do not have it, cannot acquire it."

Lucien Karpik, *L'Economie des singularités,*
Editions Gallimard, March 2007.

Company owners work differently based on their own family history.

Hermès

Thierry Hermès, a harness maker, set up his business in Paris[70] in 1837. Since then, five generations of his descendants have worked to build the company. In 1880, his son, Charles-Emile, transferred the family business to its current address at 24 Faubourg-Saint-Honoré and expanded the business into saddle making... In 1918, with the arrival of the motorcar, Emile Hermès, the founder's grandson, diversified his skills and started producing leather goods and luggage "stitched by saddle makers." The Hermès style was born and the brand developed new product ranges including couture, jewelry, silversmith's trade, agendas, and the famous silk scarves.[71]

In the fifties Robert Dumas and Jean René Guerrand, Emile Hermès' sons-in-law, continued the diversification while respecting the brand's heritage. From 1978 onwards, Jean-Louis Dumas gave Hermès a new boost by mastering and expanding into other professions[72] and by setting up an international network of wholly owned stores.[73] Twenty-eight years later, he gave up his position to Patrick Thomas, co-manager of Hermès since September 2004, while the overall artistic direction was entrusted to his son Pierre-Alexis Dumas and his niece Pascale Mussard, who represent the sixth generation of the Hermès family.

Jean-Louis Dumas.[74] "If fashion is what goes out of fashion, then luxury is what never goes out of fashion."[75] Hermès cannot go out of fashion. Why not? "A sense of family, duty and honour." Hermès is a luxury brand and family business. Like his predecessors since Hermès' creation, Jean-Louis Dumas was the president of the company and was responsible for the collections.[76] After he retired in 2006, the company's organizational chart changed, but the attitudes have not changed. The company's family values, handed down from one generation to the next, have forged deeply rooted habits. Will the Hermès House always remain a family business?

"Fortunately until now, the soul of Hermès has remained intact thanks to the deep friendship that links the seventeen members of my generation. We could imagine that this structure will continue into the future. It is true that the spirit of this house is rather like a principality. The people who work here appreciate the presence of a family member at the head of the company, as it is a symbol of solidity...."[77]

In the *Figaro* of 2 January 2000, Jean-Louis Dumas clearly expresses his credo:

> We need to be wary of the pollution of day to day living! I think that those who want to reach out to the new times have to do so with a long-term vision. Our house that draws its energy from a rich past, has always tried to see far ahead with a seven to ten year vision. Proud of our independence, we try to prune our rose bushes every morning, while planting trees that will grow tall over time.

> My second conviction is that of quality. I believe in well-made products, the intelligence of working with one's hands, the power of creation, constantly renewed. It is in fact quality, the result of a hundred processes, a thousand details, that the client identifies with our signature. To make quality evolve permanently is a challenge…
>
> Lastly and most of all, I think we must act for people. For their dignity, a shared pride and not only for money which of course is indispensable but making it cannot be the only goal. Many will remember these words by Henry Ford: 'A company that only earns money is very poor'. In addition to paying attention to management ratios, our company wants to successfully cultivate its identity through the strength of our employees. ... For a company that wants to extend its field of action throughout the world, placing the accent on the human element also implies a respect for cultural differences. We can be international by being multi-local and not uniform, from one end of the planet to the other. Asia, Europe, Latin America want to be recognised. The Americans are more inclined to adopt this approach than one might think. Hermès aims to continue to develop its alchemy of instinct, imagination, listening and rigour…
>
> 27 per cent of actions are held publicly and I think that the listing was a factor that helped consolidate family support for the company, because I think there is no better support than when it is given freely.

In 2006, the turnover of the Hermès group reached 1.515 billion euros, its consolidated net result was 268 million euros, with 6,825 employees. Hermès products are distributed through 246 exclusive shops worldwide, 136 of which are subsidiaries.[78] All Hermès' product ranges, or trades, are growing. Even if some shareholders decide one day to leave the ship, others will remain out of interest, of course, but also to preserve a tradition, just as some families remain attached to their castle.[79] In 2011, Hermès' success was sensational: with 334 shops, the turnover grows to 2.840 billion euros with a historical result of 885 million euros, and to everyone's surprise, it appears that Bernard Arnault has patiently acquired 22 per cent of the company.

PPR

François-Henri Pinault. In 2003, François Pinault symbolically transferred his power over the group he had developed to his son François-Henri: "Here are the keys. You have just turned 40; it's time for you to take over… at 50 it will be too late." He handed over the keys to his office on a specially designed key chain made up of three rings. On one, his own name was engraved; on another François-Henri; and the third was bare, intended for the following generation. This spirit of principality that Jean-Louis Dumas evoked was already growing at Pinault Printemps Redoute (PPR). The son's admiration for his father, the father's constant desire to remain unobtrusive in order not to bother his successor, François-Henri's pleasure in magnifying the group's founder "who wants to take his revenge on life," his will "to continue developing the company and to do as well as him": this family piety exists at Hermès. However, there is a major difference between the two companies: when Hermès took over John Lobb, Puiforcat, the Cristalleries de Saint-Louis, or bought shares in Perrin or Vacher, it was primarily to acquire highly qualified skills in the fields of men's shoes, table arts, silk, or watch making, in order to benefit Hermès as a whole. "Hermès' entire growth program is focused on Hermès."[80]

PPR has not grown out of traditional skills. One cannot decide to create a luxury brand because by definition it is constituted over time. When the Pinault group was listed on the Paris stock exchange in 1988, its turnover was less than one billion euros from international commerce and the wood industry. Luxury had no place in its history nor among its projects.

François-Henri Pinault graduated from the Ecole des hautes etudes commerciales (HEC) and joined the group in 1987, first with Pinault Distribution, a subsidiary specializing in the import and distribution of wood, then as a managing director of France Bois Industries, the company that headed all the companies' industrial activities. For the first 10 years, he managed the different branches of the group. When he was appointed chief executive officer of the Fnac in 1997, he joined the group's executive committee and contributed specifically to strategic choices. "In 1998, we realized that the only options for growth in the area of electrical equipment distribution lay in acquisitions. We very actively studied the do-it-yourself sector, and focused on a very large company. It did not work out.

"At the beginning of 1999, the Gucci file came up. By coincidence, we had set aside certain reserves, but there were other, more pressing considerations, in particular, we were highly focused on the French market, at the level of our retail stores rather than the brand level. It is difficult to communicate through companies outside of their main market. To introduce the Fnac in Italy, for example, we had to start from nothing. A brand, however, on the contrary is visible in stores, present in cosmetics, etc. Ideally, we were looking for professions with high international growth rates than retail, and, if possible, based on a brand."

Thus, that same year PPR acquired 42 per cent of the Gucci Group, presided over by Domenico De Sole. In May 2004, a takeover bid gave them control over the remaining capital. This was the first step in the growth of a new and very important luxury group under the Gucci banner. In 1999, the Gucci Group bought Yves Saint Laurent, YSL Beauté, and Sergio Rossi; in 2000 Boucheron and Bédat & Co.; and in 2001 Bottega

Veneta and Balenciaga. Also in 2001, the Alexander McQueen and Stella McCartney companies were set up in partnership with each of the designers who had a specific role in the structure: the financial balance between the partners encouraged the pursuit of common interests that were a guarantee of harmony within the companies.

The events of 11 September 2001 nonetheless disturbed this well-balanced organization. Since then François-Henri Pinault has analyzed both the heritage of the group's brands as well as the performance of its stores. "I believe in this plural structure, with the luxury activities[81] on the one hand, and general public[82] activities on the other. It is a logic of balance, performance and the group's strength and the fact of having both these types of businesses has never been an obstacle for one or the other. If I feel that one of the distribution activities does not have the required growth potential, I can decide to sell it and with the money from the sale, enter another profession that offers better development options."

In 2006, PPR, with about 80,000 employees, had a turnover of about 18 billion euros. Luxury represented 17 per cent. The current operating profits were nearly 1.3 billion euros, 43 per cent of which came from luxury activities. This shows that the margins generated by the Gucci Group, presided over by Robert Polet, are far superior to those that the distribution. Gucci and Bottega Veneta are currently the Gucci Group's gold nuggets. At the end of 2006, Gucci owned 217 shops they managed themselves, with a turnover of 2.101 billion euros. Bottega Veneta owns 97 shops themselves, with a turnover of 267 million euros. Gucci employs 6,059 collaborators, Bottega Veneta, 926. Frida Giannini is creation manager with Gucci, and Tomas Maier is creative director with Bottega Veneta. Each of them has adapted their universe to the brand they personify and this exercise demands as much talent and certainly more rigor than intuitive and liberating design. Gradually, in the following years, François-Henri Pinault would concentrate the activities of the group on world brands, luxe, or sports and eliminate its original activities. In 2011, Brioni was acquired by his group, and in 2012 Hedi Slimane joined Yves Saint Laurent.

Prada

Patrizio Bertelli. In 1913, Mario Prada founded a company specializing in leather goods, accessories, and shoes in Milan. In 1978 it was his granddaughter, Miuccia, with her husband Patrizio Bertelli, who launched the company into ready-to-wear. She held a doctorate in political sciences and was a member of the Communist party. Her education had not prepared her for the fashion world, but over the years it became evident that she had an intuitive vision and a great talent as a collection manager. This capacity to guide stylists without involving herself in design allowed her to split her activity and to create a second brand, Miu Miu. Patrizio Bertelli[83] considers this to be another expression of his wife's talent with products that correspond to a different clientele than Prada's; he does not consider it a "second line" of Prada. The first Prada show took place in Milan in 1988, the first Miu Miu show in New York, in September 1992. The Miu Miu show then moved to London in February 1997, before being held in Paris in March 2006. Both brands however, are not positioned in the same territory because Prada was born out of accessories while Miu Miu started off and grew as a fashion brand.

At the end of the nineties, Prada adopted a brand acquisition policy. Apart from Prada and Miu Miu, Prada SpA includes Church's, Car Shoe, and Azzedine Alaïa. In 2005, the overall turnover was 1.33 billion euros,[84] over 80 per cent under the Prada brand. Prada's receipts alone reached 1.128 billion euros. The Miu Miu brand's total receipts were 126 million euros in 2005. The Prada group has over 6,000 employees, it manages 237 mono brand boutiques and 30 franchise boutiques. It is present in 65 countries all over the world. In 2012, after having successfully raised 2.46 billion dollars at the Hong Kong stock exchange market, Prada's revenues and results exploded. Their first market is China (22 per cent of sales; before Italy, 18 per cent). Revenues increased by 26.4 per cent by reaching 2.56 billion euros. The number of boutiques rose to 388 and the brand expected to open 160 more before the end of 2013.[85]

The Jil Sander and Helmut Lang companies were acquired by the Prada group in 1999 and then were sold in 2006 to the British investment fund Change Capital Partners for Jil Sander, and the Japanese group Link Theory Holdings Co. Ltd for Helmut Lang. Under Raf Simons' artistic direction, Jil Sander[86] continued to develop. The designer who has had the greatest influence on men's fashion continued Jil Sander's work in both men's and women's wear, while continuing to operate his signature label. The Helmut Lang brand has been revamped by Michael and Nicole Colovos, creators of a Los Angeles sportswear brand, without Helmut Lang's involvement.[87] At times like this, Patrizio Bertelli realized the difficulty of integrating labels led by their founders once they have sold their shares into a single management structure. The reforms necessary for a brand's expansion rarely correspond with the ways of operating that designers remain attached to. According to Bertelli, a company's survival is not compatible with a sense of ownership. A peaceful cohabitation between the founding designer and the new owner is impracticable. Maybe he is right. In 2007, he sold Prada's shares in Azzedine Alaïa and Richemont is Alaïa's new partner.

Chanel

Alain Wertheimer.[88] Ultimately, Chanel belongs to the Wertheimer family. Alain Wertheimer was appointed president because he was the oldest. As a private company, Chanel has neither a reason nor an obligation to publish its financial information, especially since discretion is an integral part of its business. Apart from Karl Lagerfeld, who freely expresses his opinion on every subject, the general staff remain obstinately hostile to communication. Alain Wertheimer himself is as invisible as Martin Margiela. His absence does not imply that he delegates his power to his managers: the international board of directors over which he presides allows Wertheimer to coordinate the brand's policy on all the continents without revealing himself.

Chanel's shareholdings are very diverse. Some of the acquired companies serve to ensure the brand's predominance, preserving skills that are in danger of disappearing, for the company's benefit. The acquisition of Lesage embroideries, Michel hats, Lemarié feathers, Goossens jewelry, and Massaro shoes were all done with an aim to optimize Chanel's fields of expertise.[89]

Other family acquisitions. Alain and Gérard Wertheimer inherited a love for contemporary art from their grandfather Pierre, a great Douanier Rousseau fan. Race horses were a weak spot for Pierre and his brother Paul—after all, they met Gabrielle Chanel at the Longchamp race course[90] in 1924—and Jacques Wertheimer, Pierre's son, followed their example. Alain and Gérard thus received a great love for stud farms as part of their family inheritance; they own one in Normandy and another one in Kentucky. Like their half-brother, Charles Heilbronn, they devoured books, and their taste for reading was expressed in the acquisition of the Abrams and La Martinière publishing companies. Well informed oenologists, their meticulous knowledge of the best vintages was translated into the ownership of two Bordeaux vineyards. These shareholdings were not at all strategic and the profit lies in the pleasure they procure.

Luxury and creativity have always been the spearheads of our industries. Even in 1939, France's main exports were luxury and creation while prêt-à-porter apparel was only distributed in the colonies.[91] Today, can creativity compete with luxury? In fact, independent designer brands encounter two major obstacles: insufficient capital and the risk of their inventions being counterfeited. Luxury, by definition, only incidentally lends itself to marketing, while fashion often takes marketing into account.

Fashion and Marketing

Schematically, there are two broad categories of fashion brands: those that conform to trends to ensure their sales and to reassure their clients, and those that do not concern themselves with the public's expectations and instead propose their artistic director's intuitive vision. The former rely on marketing, the latter on innovation. The former adapt their propositions to a given market; the others, by definition, break with trends, constitute a niche market, and target a selective and international clientele. It is the latter, regardless of their nationality, which mainly comprise the Parisian fashion show calendar and make Paris the capital of fashion design.

Some of these labels, to overcome the mysteries of globalization, can be inspired by the original Saint Laurent Rive Gauche model. In the 1960s and 1970s Anne Marie Munoz—Yves Saint Laurent's studio director and, historically, the first product manager—gave the prototypes that came out of the workshop to various manufacturing partners, according to their speciality and their rates. The sahara jackets went to Innoval active sportswear manufacturer; the cheap little summer dresses to Indreco; the couture models to C. Mendès; sportswear to Marty; shirts to Halm; and knitwear to Michel Paris or sometimes even to a Spanish manufacturer. Today the couture models are still made in France. The other pieces, thanks to the Internet, can be produced in Brazil, China, India, Romania, or Morocco. While the new designer fashion brands have an international vocation, they can also be produced anywhere in the world. There is no need to multiply the product lines because it is sufficient to rationalize the offer in the context of a single collection, as Anne-Marie Munoz did the same year that Courrèges amalgamated his different collections. It still remains however, that the overwhelming power of the groups is an imposing reality for young companies to face, despite the new perspectives for growth.

Another non-negligible reason for the fragility of independent brands is the growing efficiency of copies and their instant use, notably by fast-fashion retailers.

Omnipresent Competition

First View is more competitive than Milton; Internet is infinitely faster than the Belinograph.[92] Fashion is the only industry that puts its new, not-yet-at-retail[93] innovations at the disposal of the whole planet, at no cost, so that counterfeiters can deliver their clients' orders before the designers, who are no longer even given the credit for their inventions.[94] At least until the 1990s they were mentioned by the press, who attended their collections, and in this way they could be identified by the multi-brand retailers looking for media conscious suppliers. Castelbajac, Mugler, and Montana were never advertisers, but were nonetheless the "darlings" of the international press[95] for decades. Unfortunately, this is no longer an option: the battle between Jean-Claude Weill and Ginette Sainderichin in 1968 will never happen again the same way. Today, Jean-Claude Weill will be gratified[96] by the magazines in which he places paid advertisements. The publisher now intervenes in editorial decisions and advertisers fight bitterly over the editorial section of the magazine; this happens all over the world. In its 12 September 2002 issue, *Women's Wear Daily* amused itself by estimating the cost of the editorial coverage for the main advertisers in five American magazines surveyed: *In Style, Vogue, W, Elle,* and *Harper's Bazar* for their September 2002 issue.

Prada	58 credits[97]	US$ 3.4 million*
Chanel	47	US$ 2.4 million
Dior	50	US$ 1.9 million
Gucci	43	US$ 2.3 million
YSL	46	US$ 1.86 million

**A three-page article on Muccia Prada in* In Style *accounts for Prada's advantages.*

Consequently, in their current form, what purpose do fashion shows actually serve? The advertisers do not really need them, as they negotiate their editorial space in their target media, and the less well-off designers must do without them as the press[98] only mentions them anecdotally.

In the television world, the situation is no less confused. For decades, TV channels respected the Chambre Syndicale's instructions. The agreed upon maximum number of models that could be shown was seven, and it was not to be exceeded. Beyond this number, the fashion pieces were no longer strictly in the area of news and designers could claim their rights. They actually had no interest in promoting their creations in the media several months before they could be delivered to their sales outlets. In 1995, at the Cirque d'Hiver to celebrate his house's 20th birthday, Thierry Mugler staged a memorable epic as a kind of pre-farewell. This was no longer just a fashion show, but a work in itself. In order to justify this abyssal cost overrun, the event was broadcast live, in its entirety, on Paris Première and all the international channels—a first. The editorial and television impact was fantastic. It was a huge success, and live became the rule, a habit, albeit a bad habit. In fact, what could be an accidental advantage for one or two brands cannot be considered the best option for the whole community. If everyone in the profession does big expensive shows, who are these brands and designers targeting? The clients? No, of course not! As Pierre Cardin used to say: "In March, they are not interested in the winter collections and in October they don't care about the summer presentations." Buyers? They prefer to place their orders in the calm of a showroom. These huge media circuses do not interest them.

The Internet has made this situation even more critical because fashion designers have no one to appeal to when their creations are broadcast on the Web. In the United States in particular, the applied arts in general, and particularly the drawings and models of functional objects, have no legal protection. This is a perverse consequence of the sacrosanct principle of free trade. Since the arrival of the digital era, this ultra liberal system has created chaos. It is clear that China, in particular, where the reproduction of ancient works represents the zenith of art, has no reason to apply a regulation that the United States also refuses to implement. In this time of globalization, it is vital that Europe, Asia, and the United States introduce compatible laws on such a sensitive subject, particularly since China is progressively developing a legal arsenal with an aim to protecting intangible components—design and brands—in order to put a stop to counterfeiting and in turn to enter into an industrial logic of design and creation.[99]

Since Madeleine Vionnet obtained a legal judgement in 1921 for fashion to be qualified as a major art, the cultural differences between Paris and New York are at the origin of the practices that both sides consider scandalous. A reform of American legislation in the domain of fashion will be a huge legal event. The United States is the only western country that has not protected its designers' rights in the field of the applied arts. A reform in this area could, in the long term, have positive repercussions on fashion, as well as other industries.

III—LAW AND FASHION

On 26 June 2000, the Camera Nazionale della Moda Italiana—represented by its president, Mario Boselli and the Federation I am president of—signed a five-point agreement at Bercy, in the presence of our respective ministers of external commerce.[100] One of the points was the development of a common action regarding the respect of intellectual property and control over the broadcasting of fashion images.

On 21 October 2004, the first Franco-Italian meeting on these questions was held in Paris at the hotel Bristol. The meeting was attended by Mario Boselli; Jean François Boittin, plenipotentiary minister and France's trade advisor to the United States; Paul Benyamine, general manager of Défi; different representatives from the Industry Ministry; Patrick Thomas, co-manager of Hermès; Alain Coblence, a lawyer who had offices in New York and Paris; and the corporate attorneys of the Vuitton, Dior, Yves Saint Laurent, Chanel, Hermès, and Jean Paul Gaultier companies who were all members of the *ad hoc* committee coordinated by Sylvie Zawadzki.[101]

Italy is a country where counterfeiting is common, and the Italian designers and brands are the first victims of this practice. The members of the Camera wanted legislation adopted at a European level that would reiterate the protective clauses of the French law and regulations regarding drawings and models. They were, of course, in favor of a modification of American copyright legislation, but were reserved on the specific theme of broadcasting images of the fashion shows, considering that in the digital era, this was almost impossible to control.

Intellectual Property

The Federation and the Camera started lobbying in the United States in order to get Congress to adopt a law that would protect fashion renderings and actual prototypes. The two federations mandated Alain Coblence to carry out a detailed study on the situation of American law and jurisprudence to gain the support of American designers represented by CFDA, and also to convince the different political, media, and professional actors of the advantages of introducing new legislation. On 23 February 2006, during a heated meeting, Alain Coblence convinced the CFDA's executive committee to take charge of this campaign and to give him responsibility for the mission. It was in this context that the presidents and artistic directors of the American, Italian, and French creative brands took part in making a 15-minute video presenting their different arguments in favor of a legislation that would protect drawings and models. In the documentary, the United States was represented by the creators Stan Herman, Diane von Furstenberg, Zac Posen, Jeffrey Banks, and by Bertrand Stalla Bourdillon, president of Marc Jacobs; Italy by Robert Triefus, Armani's executive vice president and Giovanna Gentile Ferragamo, president of Ferragamo; France by Arie Kopelman, president of Chanel, Inc., Sidney Toledano, president of Dior, and Patrick Thomas, co-manager of Hermès.

A reception was organized in Washington on 14 March 2006 for the screening of the film; the American representatives and senators were invited, and the French, Italian, and European Union ambassadors were to attend as well as the presidents of the three federations. During the day, a delegation of participants met the relevant American congress members. When Diane von Furstenberg became president of the CFDA in 2006, it was an added asset for the action initiated by the French and the Italians.

On 25 April 2007, a bill was introduced by Democrat Bill Delahunt, and Republican Robert Goodlatte. The project was sponsored in the senate by New York state senator Chuck Schumer, a democrat, and Republican Senator Kay Bailey Hutchinson. The bill was also supported by the candidates for the upcoming presidential election, Hilary Clinton and John McCain: the procedure had truly begun.[102] The action, which was first considered at the Hyères Festival in the presence of Mrs. Christine Lagarde in 2004, will come to a positive conclusion one day or another thanks to Alain Coblence's energy, Diane von Furstenberg's support, and the Défi's contribution.

Once the fashion designers' rights are recognized and established, would photographers have the right to sell the photographs they took during the collection presentations without prior authorization? Are the designers really the only owners of the images of their shows?

Image Broadcasting Rights

In a legal action that began in 2003, almost half a century after the Milton affair that had occupied the Chambre Syndicale's legal services for years, 10 major Parisian couture houses—including Dior, Chanel, Hermès, Vuitton, Givenchy, Yves-Saint Laurent, and Jean Paul Gaultier—won a legal victory on 17 January 2007 before the 13th criminal division of the Paris appeal court.

The plaintiffs accused three photographers of broadcasting images of their fashion shows on the photographers' websites without prior authorization. These images were accessible for a fee on an American website that two of the photographers had shares in.[103] In addition, the photographers considered themselves artists and claimed competing rights over their photographs. Their lawyers considered that the appeal court should adapt the law to current technological means. The federation and its member's lawyers, on the contrary, defended the position that: "at a time when new technologies encourage an anarchic distribution of fashion images, the use of new channels such as mobile phones, portable digital equipment, etc, should remain subject to a legal judicial framework."

The appeal court pronounced that couture houses were the only owners of the rights over the designs and the fashion shows. Consequently, they had the right to restrict the distribution of their images and to authorize, or not, the reproduction or the distribution of their creations. However, what was the use of being owner of one's rights if it was impossible to ensure they were respected?[104] In the 1930s eradicating copying in a profession whose vocation was to sell copies was rather like Penelope's work. In the 2000s, despite the existence of a restrictive legislation, there is a strong temptation for certain medias to distribute fashion images for a fee because distribution is so easy and the exploitation of these images is highly profitable. There are many who cannot resist. When an industry is innovative, it can be considerably weakened. This fact was taken into account in the five-point agreement signed at Bercy on 26 June 2000 by French and Italian professional organizations:

> IV—Paris and Milan share the same viewpoint on information and the television broadcasting of their collections. It would be fitting to use new technology in the interest of both the industry and the media: encouraging live information that is controlled, encouraging programmes that are broadcast at a later date to coincide with the availability of the fashion products on the market, favouring the medias that respect this policy.

The "invited members" procedure was the first application of this commitment. In this case, sales of collections preceded the broadcast of the images as Balenciaga had wanted. He presented his collections to professionals (B2B) several months before the public presentations (B2C). As Lady Duff Gordon had desired, fashion shows became a commercial event for clients. The invited members—Alexander Vauthier, Anne-Valérie Hash, Bouchra Jarrar, Felipe Oliveira Baptista, Yiqing Yin, etc.—received, just like Viktor & Rolf did before them, substantial media coverage that encouraged the distribution of their collections at the right time.[105]

In the same way, Pamela Parmal, curator of the Boston Fine Arts Museum, in a superb exhibition dedicated to contemporary haute couture held in November 2006, quite rightly associated 10 brands of different origins: Azzedine Alaïa, Hussein Chalayan, Chanel, Christian Dior, Christian Lacroix, Martin Margiela, Rochas, Valentino, Viktor & Rolf, and Yohji Yamamoto. Her choice was solely motivated by creativity and skill.[106] The public had no objection, nor did the grands couturiers and journalists. The same year, a retrospective at the Musée des arts décoratifs associated Cristobal Balenciaga's haute couture models with the ready-to-wear of his current successor, Nicolas Ghesquière. Ready-to-wear and couture, as Hébé Dorsey had predicted in 1972, had been reconciled. The brands that had renounced haute couture could yet again be included in its calendar. It will take time and tenacity for my successors to once again fulfill the mission of copyright guardian that Madeleine Vionnet had attributed haute couture. Nonetheless, there are a number of publications that continue to predict its inevitable decline. They have been doing so consistently since the 1930s.

Nevertheless, on 7 July 2011, to celebrate the 100th year of its existence, the Chambre Syndicale gave a ball in Versailles at the Grand Trianon. It had a double purpose: to re-establish the tradition and to show its absolute confidence in the future.

This book is dedicated to the graduates of fashion schools, particularly those from IFM and the Chambre Syndicale school. Some of them have brought glory to our profession[107] while others are in the process of writing its history. I have had the great fortune of having accompanied them and to be able, for the length of this book, pay them the homage they deserve.

NOTES

1. Top universities and graduate schools.
2. In 1979, ABC showed a 52 minute program on their top 10 creators for the end of the century. They were Karl Lagerfeld, France Andrevie, Claude Montana, Kenzo, Angelo Tarlazzi, Thierry Mugler, Issey Miyake, Marithé and François Girbaud, Jean Paul Gaultier, and Tan Giudicelli. The program, rediscovered by the journalist Florence de Monza in 2004, shows the joy and the freedom that reigned in the fashion world at the time.
3. The American manufacturers, who did not have the need or the ambition to export to Europe, asked C & I to pay them an advance. Those who granted licenses imposed their perpetual standard contracts, inspired by the one Jacques Rouët had drawn up for Dior.
4. See text pages 80–81.
5. See text page 310.
6. "Comma letter" from J.P. Mocho dated 2 October 2001, letter from D. Grumbach dated 12 April 2006. *Exploit d'huissier October* 2001. Chambre Syndicale archives.
7. Minutes of the General Assembly of 24 June 1997.
8. Under Didier Grumbach's presidency (Thierry Mugler), the committee assembled the following presidents or general managers: François Baufumé (Christian Dior), Simon Burstein (Sonia Rykiel), Jean-Charles de Castelbajac, Jean-Louis Dumas (Hermès), Christophe Girard (Yves Saint Laurent), Françoise Montenay (Chanel), Donald Potard (Jean Paul Gaultier), Carlo Valerio (Emanuel Ungaro), Denis Vignal (Nina Ricci); the meetings were held at the Couture Federation on the fourth Thursday of each month, at 4:00 PM
9. The themes were: a reform of the professional structure, harmonization of training programs, mediatization of the collections, new technologies, and the emergence of new brands. The work groups were temporary and were designed to function for a year. Three structures were, however, maintained. The first dealt with training, the second fashion show organization, and the third legal questions. The commission's conclusions, approved by the committee, led to the execution of projects that had or could have positive repercussions on the globalization that was taking place.
10. Report by Jacques Mouclier on 28 April 1998. The *New Yorker* of 21 September 1998, "The Crash of Parisian Haute Couture."
11. In 2001, a study group led by Simon Burstein suggested that if a president delegué was nominated, a professionally active president could be elected for two years, renewable only once, following the model that already existed for the Chambre Syndicale presidents.
12. Press communication of 8 October 1973: " . . . Two new union organisations have just been added to the current Chambre Syndicale de la Couture parisienne, they are: la Chambre Syndicale du Prêt-à-porter des Couturiers et des créateurs de Mode and la Chambre Syndicale de la Mode Masculine. . . Everybody will realise how important this reorganisation is and the determining role the Fédération française de la Couture will now have to play."
13. French fashion's top governing body said it would create an executive committee to bolster its independence and speed decision-making in a fast-moving industry. Among the committee's first orders of business: to propose to the board a candidate for the Federation's next president. Didier Grumbach, president of the Fédération Française de la couture, du prêt-à-porter des couturiers et des créateurs de mode since 1998, said he would consider running for another two-year term. "If they all ask me to do it, I will" he said. Grumbach explained that adding an executive committee would inject "dynamism" to an organization charged with preserving Paris' reputation as the world capital of fashion design. The new executive committee is to have a maximum of five members, each charged with a specific mission, among them emerging brands, international outreach and the fashion show calendars. *WWD*, 2 April 2012. The first executive committee had been elected on 23 May 2012 and regrouped Bruno Pavlovsky for Chanel, Sidney Toledano for Dior, Guillaume de Seynes for Hermès, Ralph Toledano for Jean Paul Gaultier, and Paul Denève for Yves Saint Laurent.
14. Didier Grumbach, *Evolution des structures professionnelles et devenir des marques. Repères Mode & Textile IFM*, 1996. Margiela was Gaultier's assistant; Gaultier was himself Cardin's assistant; Cardin was Dior's assistant; Dior, Piguet's assistant; Piguet, Poiret's assistant; Poiret, Doucet's assistant. . .
15. See texts pages 311–312.
16. See text page 42.
17. Françoise Montenay (Chanel), François Baufumé (Christian Dior), Patrick Thomas (Hermès), Jacques Mouclier, Didier Grumbach (Thierry Mugler) took part.
18. On Sidney Toledano's proposal, in 2001, the Chambre syndicale de la couture parisienne (Parisian Couture Union) became the Chambre syndicale de la haute couture (Haute Couture Union).
19. Minutes of the Couture Federation management committee meeting of 1 October 1996. Thierry

Mugler had however taken part in the 1992 couture calendar with his ready-to-wear. "Conclusion," first edition.

20. This new procedure, initiated in 1996, which made it possible to include ready-to-wear brands in the couture calendar, was reworked in 1998 by the executive committee that functioned in the same manner as the limited organization constituted in 1995.

21. Thus, 100 years after Raudnitz—the couturier who had taken the initiative to assemble his most prestigious colleagues in 1897 (Cheruit, Lanvin, Doucet...) with the idea of establishing a coordinated, later, delivery calendar, that would block the copies made by Viennese manufacturers (a first attempt to structure couture)—the couturiers slightly opened their doors to the industry.

22. Members or correspondents "...The modifications made to the text that founded haute couture, were mainly designed to allow new houses to benefit from this designation and also to structure the granting of the legally protected label with the procedure for invited members, set up by the Couture Chambre Syndicale in 1997, in order to open the collection calendars to young creation companies..." Press release of 1 October 2001. Chambre Syndicale archives.

23. Fax from Robert Triefus, executive vice president of Armani, 30 November 2004. Chambre Syndicale archives.

24. Concluding report of the study committee on the standardization of training in fashion professions in France, written by Bruno Remaury and Carlo Valerio. Led by Bruno Remaury, head of the creation department at the French Fashion Institute at the time, it included: Simon Burstein (Sonia Rykiel); Carlo Valerio (Emanuel Ungaro); Véronique Delignette Schilling (IFM); two human resource managers, Sylvie Boissière (Chanel) and Philippe Grigaut (Indreco); Olga Saurat from the Saint Roch school; Sylvie Zawadzki, general secretary of the Couture Federation; and in a second stage, Chantal Baudron. The report was amended the following year by François Baufumé.

25. "Mr Didier Grumbach has created an association to set up a Cité de la Mode... The complex that would combine the Saint Roch school and the IFM could constitute the backbone of this centre. It will also include a research and information centre, a documentation centre, a museum... it is a wonderful project that we must carry out." Photo p. 432.

26. He was the patient project manager and general manager of IFM. In 2007, Dominique Jacomet, seconded by Sylvie Ebel, took over from Pascal Morand.

27. On 3 April 1991, I sent the following message to Zhang Zhé, a marketing graduate from the Paris Dauphine University, and his wife Fang Min: "I am sending you my project for a programme: History of the economy of fashion in France: The internationalisation of markets; image, the driving element of the garment industry; the sources of creation, the trends. I will bring several SECAM videos, some books and slides. Would you be kind enough to let me know what the weather is like in Xian?"

28. This trip was the beginning of a number of meetings in Paris and Beijing. After the cooperation agreement was signed between the Chinese Designers Federation, presided over by Wang Quing, and the French Couture Federation in 2001, a new agreement was signed on 29 August 2005 by Mr. Jiang Heng Jie, president of the Industry Federation, who was succeeded by Mr. Chen Dapent who, amongst other things, instituted the bi-annual study committee meeting. (*Journal du Textile*, 15 September 2005).

29. The announcement of their budget allowed us to book rooms at the Hotel Ibis, avenue de Suffren. I was amazed to find them housed at the Hotel Ritz the next day. Mr. Du signed the preface to the Chinese edition of *Histoires de mode* in 2007.

30. In October 2006: Anne-Valérie Hash, Sharon Wauchob, Adam Jones, A.F. Vandevorst, Felipe Oliveira Baptista, Lutz.

31. In 1976: J. C. de Castelbajac, J.C. de Luca, Claude Montana, Tan Giudicelli, Dan Beranger, A.M. Beretta, and Thierry Mugler.

32. In 2012 Mrs. Jha's successor, Mr. Sunil Sethi, renewed his invitation to Mr. Grumbach to participate to the Dehli Fashion Week on the occasion of the present book publication.

33. Interview by Didier Grumbach on 11 March 2011.

34. "I do a small collection just for the Indian market. It's a lot more traditional." Manish Arora's interview, *Crash*, October 2011.

35. Jean-Pierre Blanc created the Hyères international fashion and photography festival in 1986. A number of the winners of the festival took part in the French couture, men's fashion, and women's ready-to-wear fashion show calendars: (for winter 2007) Gaspard Yurkievich, Viktor & Rolf, Romain Kremer, Ute Ploier, Wendy and Jim, Jeroen Van Tuyl, Henrik Vibskow, Felipe Oliveira Baptista, On aura tout vu, Marc Le Bihan, Richard René.

36. See text page 75.

37. Lady Diana.

38. Hedi Slimane left Dior in 2007 and joinded Yves Saint Laurent in 2012.
39. Kris Van Assche succeeded Hedi Slimane in 2007.
40. Interview with Ralph Toledano (20 February 2007). In 2012, Ralph Toledano was named president of Jean Paul Gaultier, and Geoffroy de la Bourdonnaye became president of Chloé. Phoebe Philo is Céline's designer and Clare Waight-Keller is Chloé's new voice.
41. Chloé, 60 years of fashion. Palais de Tokyo, October 2012.
42. It is the vision André Courrèges expressed, interview with Didier Grumbach. See text page 133.
43. Interview with Nathalie Rykiel (20 March 2007).
44. In 2012, Nathalie Rykiel decide to sell 80 per cent of the shares of the company to the Chinese group Fung Brands from Hong Kong, presided over by Jean-Marc Loubier, formerly general manager of Louis Vuitton and president of Céline. *Le Figaro*, 26 January 2012—*Journal du Textile*, 31 January 2012.
45. Interview with Yves Carcelle (1 June 2007).
46. See photo page 403.
47. Sixteen shops in China, the first in 1992.
48. *Les Echos*, 14 May 2012.
49. Interview with Nicolas Topiol (2 April 2007).
50. *Le Figaro*, 5 and 6 May 2007.
51. Round table "You said profitable?" Hyères Festival, international meetings (27–30 May 2007).
52. They were LVMH, the Caisse des dépôts et consignations, GFT, Lucien Deveaux, Médéric, Natexis, and later le Défi. Paul Benyamine, general manager of Le Défi, was on the administrative board of Mode et finance. Le Défi also decided to buy 20 per cent shares in its capital, estimated at a sum of one hundred million francs. Today, Caroline Joubin, Natexis, manages the investment fund management group. Sylvie Coumau, an IFM graduate, assisted her devotedly and efficiently from 1999 until 2006. Delphine Le Mintier replaced her in 2007. Caroline Joubin died in 2008 and the fund, in 2009, came under management of Isabelle Ginestet from the Caisse des Dépôts.
53. Conclusion of the 1993 edition.
54. 1962: P. Venet, Yves Saint Laurent, Courrèges, Scherrer, Emmanuelle Khanh, Christiane Bailly, Cacharel, Daniel Hechter… 1973–1974: Montana, Mugler, Castelbajac, Miyake, Beretta, Michel Klein, Angelo Tarlazzi, Adeline André…
55. In fact, "Paris remains the place where fashion movements are organised. By showing their collections there, Jean Muir in 1972, Issey Miyake in 1973, Valentino in 1975, initiated an irreversible movement that motivated creators whose style was sufficiently individual to retain the interest of an international market, to leave their national showrooms. Milan and London were not worried by this trend. What is important, in terms of economics, is where the production takes place, not where the fashion shows are held, which only immediately affects the hotel industry. As this is a natural movement to everyone's benefit, it was hoped that our federal representatives would come together to participate in the Paris bi-annual event, that the 1993 deadline makes even more inevitable." (Didier Grumbach, *Mondo Economico*, June 1990).
56. Here we could also cite Saint Laurent Rive Gauche, because he targeted his couture clients' daughters in a similar manner in 1966. Idem for Carven Junior in 1955. Miss V was a Valentino second line.
57. *Elle*, 6 December 1999, photo page 328.
58. In association with Mode & Finance, Martin Margiela and Jenny Meyrens, his associate, sold the majority of their capital to Diesel in July 2002, in order to ensure the durability of their company and its continued development. Renzo Rosso, the new majority shareholder, and Martin Margiela, artistic director, finally separated.
59. Excerpt of the certificate Didier Grumbach provided Thierry Mugler with in 2006.
60. Letters from Naoki Takizawa dated 4 November 2002 and 3 November 2006. Zucca, Naoki Takizawa, and Tsumori Chisato were, in turn, members of the Federation. Federation archives.
61. Interview with Yohji Yamamoto (15 March 2007).
62. See texts pages 167–169.
63. *Paris Match*, 16 November 2006: "Quand la DGSE perd sa chemise dans le luxe et la haute couture." (DGSE are the French Secret Services).
64. Interview with Alber Elbaz (10 April 2007).
65. The latter were trained at Central Saint Martins College.
66. Y. Yamamoto 1980, Comme des Garçons 1981, J. Watanabe 1991.
67. Gucci 12.5 per cent, Bottega Veneta 7.1 per cent.
68. *Art et Phynance*, Paul Poiret, Paris, Lutetia, 1934.
69. Robert Kenmore continued his career as a political economy teacher at Fontainebleau. Mrs. Kenmore became the owner of 7, a famous bar-restaurant in rue Sainte-Anne.
70. 2005 annual report, group presentation.
71. Hermès created their first silk scarves in 1936.
72. Hermès works in 14 areas: leather goods, scarves, ties, men's and women's garments, perfume, watch making, diaries, hats, shoes, gloves, enamel, lifestyle, table arts, and jewelry.

73. Since 1976 his wife, Rena Dumas, has been responsible for their architecture.
74. Jean-Louis Dumas' quotes are taken from different interviews he gave over the last few years, to Michèle Champenois of the *Monde,* Catherine Schwab of *Paris Match,* Pascale Renaux of *Numéro,* Philippe Trétiak for *Magazine Air France.*
75. *Magazine Air France,* February 2004.
76. Interview with Rena Dumas (12 April 2007).
77. *Numéro,* 23 October 2003.
78. Financial report, 2006.
79. Interview with Patrick Thomas (12 April 2007).
80. *Ibid.*
81. Luxury: Gucci, Bottega Veneta, Yves Saint Laurent, YSL Beauté, Balenciaga, Boucheron, Sergio Rossi, Bedat & Cie, Alexander McQueen, Stella McCartney.
82. Distribution: Redcats, Fnac, Conforama, CFAO.
83. Interview with Patrizio Bertelli (5 March 2007).
84. The receipts for the Church's brand are not included.
85. *Le Figaro,* 30 March 2012.
86. In 2012, Raf Simons left Jil Sander and Jil Sander herself became again artistic manager of the company she created.
87. *Herald Tribune,* 7 November 2006.
88. Interview with Alain Wertheimer (6 June 2007).
89. Montex embroideries acquired in 2012.
90. Coco (Gabrielle) Chanel owned horses herself and was a splendid horsewoman.
91. See text page 188.
92. See text page 101.
93. "In terms of fashion, it is a question of reconciling form and content (...) Seasonal collections–presented a year in advance—no longer correspond to anything, as everything is on the Web seconds later. As fashion cannot adapt its logistics, fashion has to chase fashion, and suddenly has to defend itself by presenting pre-collections and post-collections. All that used to make sense, but no longer does. For me, the real question is one of how a brand can be redeveloped in the future." Hedi Slimane, *Le Monde,* 23–24 September 2007. Same point of view developed by *WWD* on 22 May 2012.
94. Reuteurs dispatch, Didier Grumbach (14 January 2004).
95. Claude Brouet, *Magazine* n° 38, February–March 2007: "I am interested in Richard René's work, he was one of Jean Paul Gaultier's assistant's, whom I knew at Hermès. He makes beautiful clothes, with real skill and true elegance. Have you read anything about his work? I don't know how long he will be able to hold out... Rather than supporting new names, financers prefer the immediate profitability of old houses that have been renewed by puffy bags or grotesque glasses. Young talents like Richard René will always exist but the current system does not allow them to flower. I remember a time when we stuck together, when the press tried to help. This does not really seem to be the case today."
96. See text page 201.
97. Credit = mention.
98. Debate in the *Figaro,* 1 October 1999. "Wasted innovation," Pierre Bergé, Isabel Marant, Didier Grumbach.
99. *Mode recherche n°* 5—IFM. "Panorama de la Propriété intellectuelle en Chine," Marie-Pierre Gendarme, January 2006.
100. M. Letta and Huwart. Photo page 432.
101. Minutes of the meeting of 21 October 2004.
102. *Washington Post, Fashion Wear Daily...*
103. *Les Echos,* 8 February 2007.
104. "One reaches a point where you ask yourself what purpose author's rights serve, if technique reigns supreme." Pierre Sirnelli, round table "Culture de la protection et protection de la culture." International textile and garment meetings, 20 April 2007.
105. "Le rythme des saisons remis en question," Frédéric Martin-Bernard, *Le Figaro,* 7 October 2006.
106. *Fashion Show: Paris style,* MFA Publications, 2006.
107. Yves Saint Laurent, Issey Miyake, Valentino, *et al.*

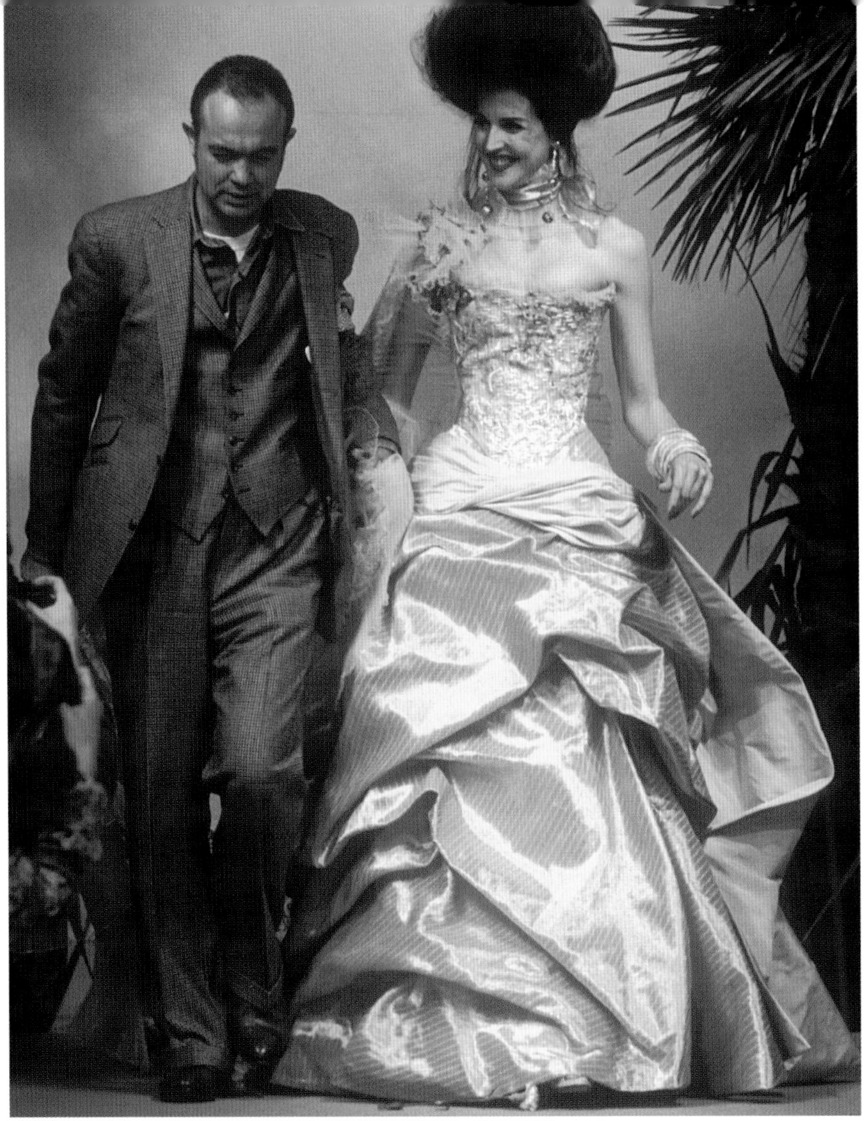

Christian Lacroix, haute couture spring–summer 1993. Photo Guy Marineau.
Christian Lacroix and Marie Seznec, haute couture autumn–winter 1989–1990. Photo Guy Marineau.

Christian Lacroix, haute couture autumn–winter 1998–1999. Photo Guy Marineau.

Dries Van Noten, spring–summer 2007. Photo Vincent Lappartient.
Dries Van Noten, autumn–winter 2004–2005. The finale. Photo Etienne Tordoir/Catwalkpictures.
Facing page: Dries Van Noten, finale of the spring–summer 2007 fashion show. © Dries Van Noten/DR.
Dries Van Noten, 20th collection for the show celebrating 10 years of existence. A banquet table transformed into a podium for 450 guests. © Dries Van Noten/Rights Reserved.

Azzedine Alaïa retrospective at the villa Noailles, April 2005. Photos Juliette Ruggieri.

Azzedine Alaïa and Pat Cleveland, 1981. *Stern*.

Fashion Show. Museum of Fine Arts, Boston, 2006. Rights Reserved.

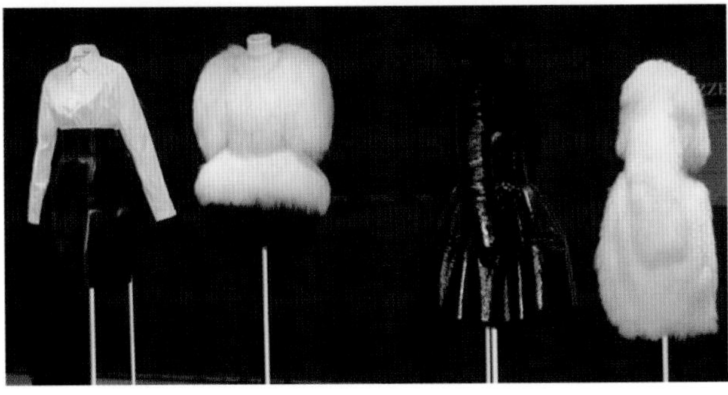

Yohji Yamamoto,
autumn–winter 2006–2007.
Photo Vincent Lappartient.

Yohji Yamamoto,
autumn–winter 2007–2008.
Courtesy Yohji Yamamoto.
Photo Monica Fendi.

Yohji Yamamoto,
spring–summer 1998.
Rights Reserved.

Opposite:
Yohji Yamamoto.
Courtesy Yohji Yamamoto.
Photo Kazumi Kurigami.

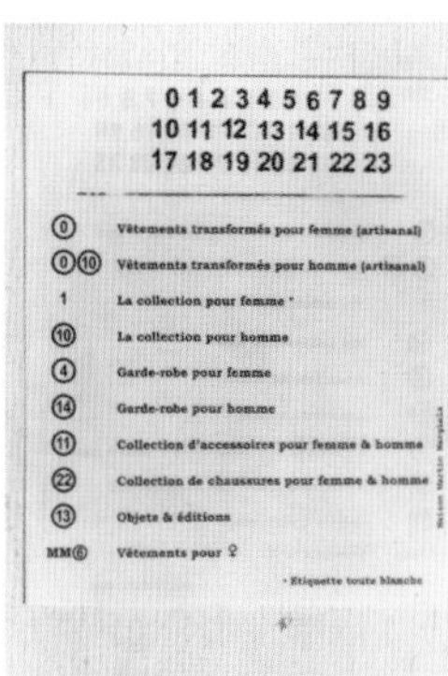

Maison Martin Margiela, Mars. Trenchcoat, hand-crafted range, autumn–winter 2007–2008. © Maison Martin Margiela/ Rights Reserved.

Maison Martin Margiela, 11 Range. © Maison Martin Margiela/Rights Reserved.

Label, Maison Martin Margiela. © Maison Martin Margiela/ Rights Reserved.

Opposite:
Maison Martin Margiela, hand-crafted range, January 2006, spring–summer 2006. © Maison Martin Margiela/ Rights Reserved.

Maison Martin Margiela, spring–summer 2006. Photo by 2/Catwalkpictures.

Ann Demeulemeester, spring–summer 2007. Photo Etienne Tordoir/ Catwalkpictures.

Ann Demeulemeester, 1989. Photo Willy Vanderperre.

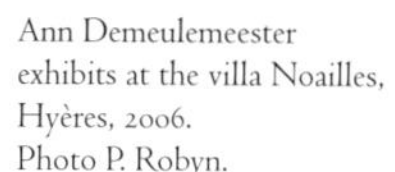

Ann Demeulemeester exhibits at the villa Noailles, Hyères, 2006. Photo P. Robyn.

"This woman was once a punk,"
Vivienne Westwood made up as
Margaret Thatcher
on the cover of *Tatler*, 1989.
Photo Michael Roberts.

Vivienne Westwood,
Anglomania collection,
autumn–winter 1993. Rights Reserved.

Opposite: Vivienne Westwood,
Erotic Zones collection,
spring–summer 1995. Rights Reserved.

Cover of *Le Monde* 2
"John Galliano:
my profession as a couturier,"
6 January 2007.
Photo Paolo Roversi.

John Galliano,
spring–summer 1994.
Courtesy John Galliano.
Photo Patrice Stable.

Opposite:
John Galliano,
autumn–winter 1999.
Photo Guy Marineau.

Chloé,
autumn–winter 2005–2006.
Photo Inez Van Lansweerde
and Vinoodh Matadin.

Chloé,
spring–summer 2005.
Photo Inez Van Lansweerde
and Vinoodh Matadin.

Chloé,
spring–summer 2004.
Photo Mustafa Hulusi.

Chloé, spring–summer 2007.
Photo Vincent Lappartient.

Chloé bags,
campaign spring–summer 2006.
Photo Inez Van Lansweerde
and Vinoodh Matadin

Armani haute couture
spring–summer 2007.
Photo Thibaut de Saint-Chamas.

Giorgio Armani, 2007.
Photo Thibaut de Saint-Chamas.

Opposite:
Giorgio Armani, a photograph of his associate Sergio Galleotti on the desk, who seems to be watching over the sketches, 1979. Photo Armani/DR.

Facing page:
Armani haute couture
spring–summer 2007.
Photo Thibaut de Saint-Chamas.

Chanel fashion show, Grand Palais, haute couture spring–summer 2006. Photo Simon Procter.

Finale of the Chanel ready-to-wear collection, 2004. Karl Lagerfeld and his models. Photo Etienne Tordoir.

Autoportrait, Karl Lagerfeld, 2007. © Karl Lagerfeld

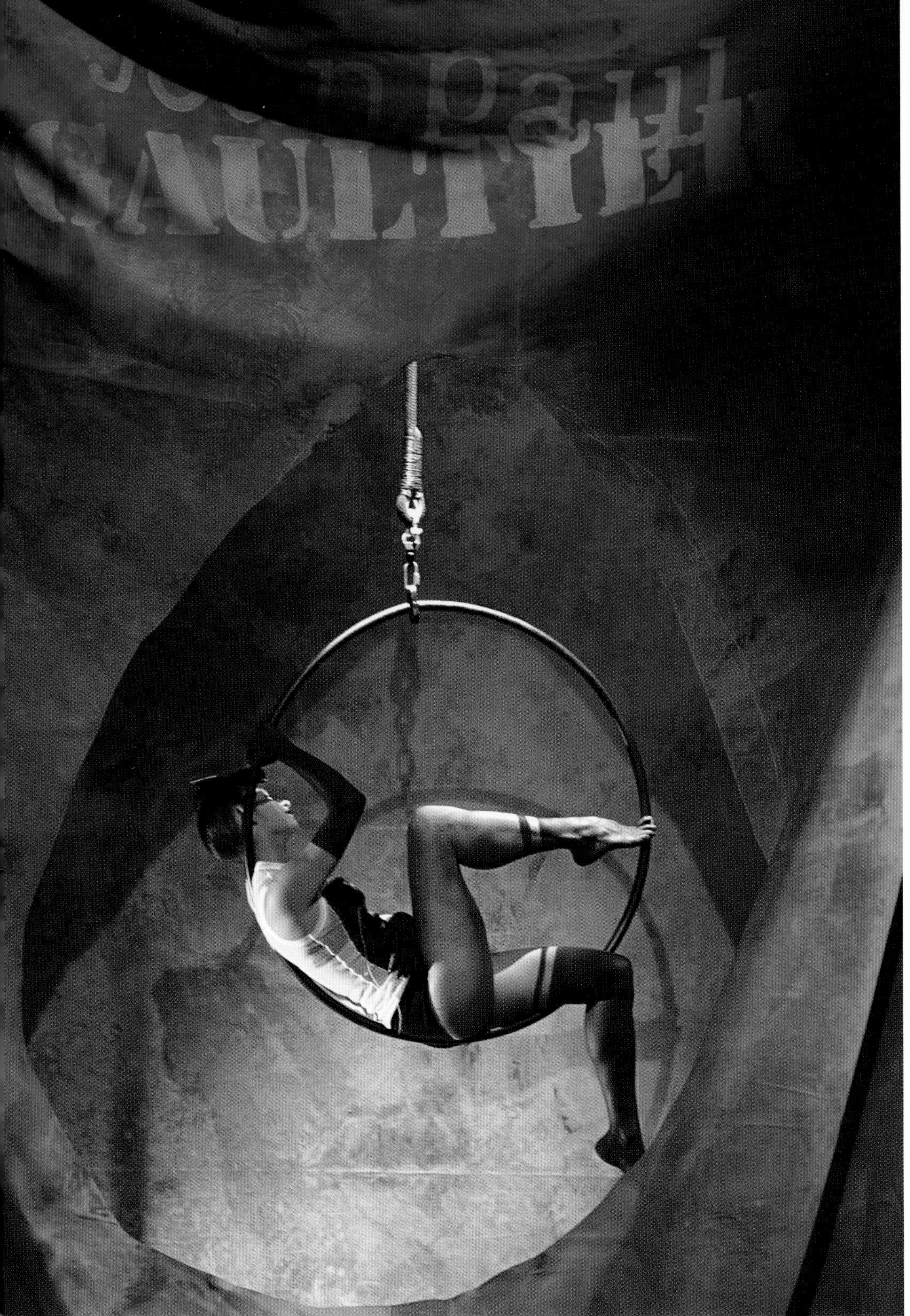

Jean Paul Gaultier, spring–summer 2003 collection. Photo Etienne Tordoir/Catwalkpictures.

Madonna models for Jean Paul Gaultier,
autumn–winter 1995–1996.
Photo Etienne Tordoir/Catwalkpictures.

Jean Paul Gaultier, spring–summer 2007.
Photo Etienne Tordoir/Catwalkpictures.

Jean Paul Gaultier,
haute couture spring–summer 1999.
Photo Guy Marineau.

Dior, finale of the haute couture spring–summer 1998 collection. Photo Guy Marineau.

Dior, ready-to-wear spring–summer 2007. Photo Vincent Lappartient.

Facing page:
Dior haute couture autumn–winter 2007. © Dior/Rights Reserved.

Dior

Kenzo,
spring–summer 2006.

Kenzo,
spring–summer 2007.
Photos Etienne Tordoir/
Catwalkpictures.

The Louis Vuitton monogram fabric centenary. Azzedine Alaïa photographed by Jean Paul Goude. © Louis Vuitton/Jean Paul Goude.

Louis Vuitton autumn–winter 1998–1999 collection. © Louis Vuitton Malletier. All rights reserved.

Façade of the Louis Vuitton shop in Omotesando in Tokyo, architect Jun Aoki. Photo Ano, Daici pour Nacasa &Partners Inc. © Louis Vuitton/Nacasa&Partners Inc.

Marc Jacobs. Photo Vincent Lappartient.

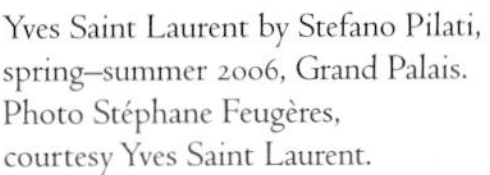

Yves Saint Laurent by Stefano Pilati, spring–summer 2006, Grand Palais. Photo Stéphane Feugères, courtesy Yves Saint Laurent.

Yves Saint Laurent by Stefano Pilati, autumn–winter 2007–2008. Photos Stéphane Feugères, courtesy Yves Saint Laurent.

Yves Saint Laurent,
spring–summer 2008.
Photo But-Sou Laï
for *Stiletto*.

Stefano Pilati.
Photo Willy Vanderperre,
courtesy Yves Saint Laurent.

Miu Miu, spring–summer 2007.
Photo by 2/Catwalkpictures.

Patrizio Bertelli and Miuccia Prada.
© Prada/Rights Reserved.

Fratelli Truck Prada, delivery truck.
© Prada/Rights Reserved.

Letter from the Queen of Italy to the Prada house, 1918. © Prada/Rights Reserved.

Prada Epicentre in Tokyo, Aoyama
created by the Herzog et De Meuron firm, 2003.
© Prada/Rights Reserved.

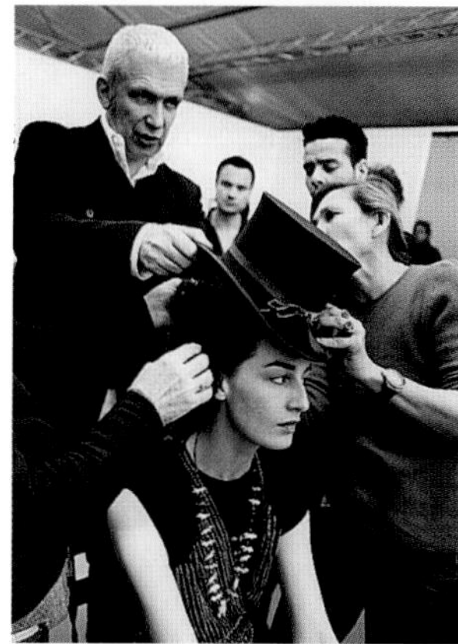

Jean-Louis and Rena Dumas.
Courtesy Rena Dumas.

The sixth generation,
Pierre Alexis Dumas and Pascale Mussard.
Photo Quentin Bertoux.

Jean Paul Gaultier
at his first fashion show for Hermès,
autumn–winter 2004–2005.
Photo Gérard Uféras.

Hermès collection by Jean Paul Gaultier, autumn–winter 2004–2005.
Photos Etienne Tordoir/Catwalkpictures.

Sonia Rykiel,
finale of the
spring–summer 2008 fashion show.
Photo Vincent Lappartient.

Sonia Rykiel, finale of the
spring–summer 2005 fashion show.
© Sonia Rykiel/Photo Rights Reserved.

Sonia Rykiel
and Nathalie Rykiel.
Photo Vincent Lappartient.

Emanuel Ungaro,
haute couture
autumn–winter 2003–2004.
Photo Rights Reserved.

Emanuel Ungaro,
haute couture
spring–summer 1990.
Photo Rights Reserved.

Above:
Alexander McQueen,
Rights Reserved.

Opposite:
Alexander McQueen,
spring–summer 2004.
Photo Etienne Tordoir/
Catwalkpictures.

Alexander McQueen,
autumn–winter 2004.
Photo Etienne Tordoir/
Catwalkpictures.

Rick Owens backstage, spring–summer 2007. Photo Vincent Lappartient.
Rick Owens, spring–summer 2006. © Rick Owens/Photo R. Castro.
Rick Owens, spring–summer 2008. Photo Asha Mines.

Lanvin, spring–summer 2007. Photo by2/Catwalkpictures.

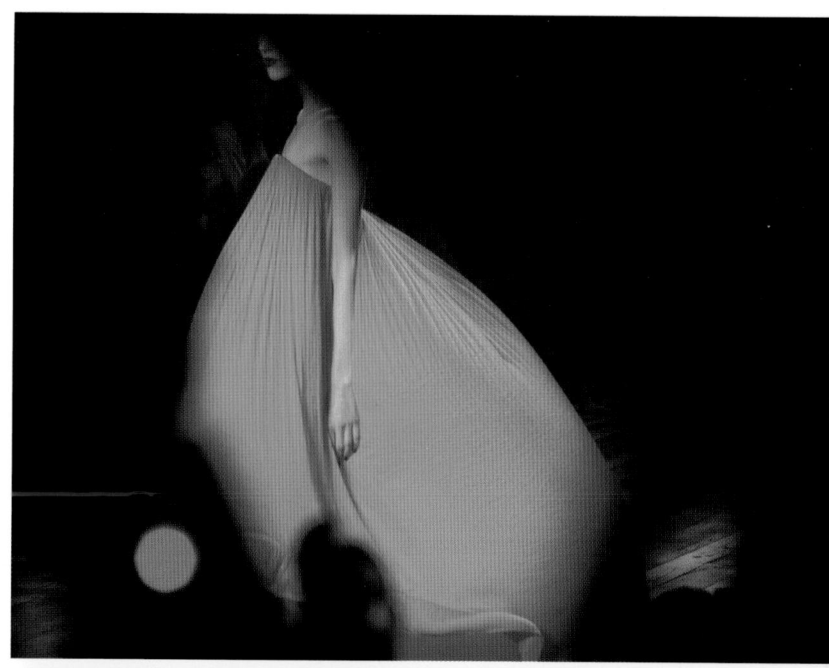

Lanvin,
spring–summer 2008.
Photos But-Sou Laï
for *Stiletto*.

Alber Elbaz
during the
autumn–winter 2003–2004 fashion show.
Photo Vincent Lappartient.

Nicolas Ghesquière.
Photo David Sims.

Balenciaga,
spring–summer 2008.
Photo But–Sou Laï
for *Stiletto*.

Balenciaga, autumn–winter 2007–2008 and spring–summer 2007.
Photos Etienne Tordoir/Catwalkpictures.

Ricardo Tisci.
Photo Rights Reserved.

Opposite:
Givenchy, ready-to-wear spring–summer 2006.
Photo Etienne Tordoir/ Catwalkpictures.

Givenchy,
haute couture
spring–summer 2007.
Photo Etienne Tordoir/ Catwalkpictures.

Rochas by Olivier Theyskens,
spring–summer 2005.
Photo Vincent Lappartient.

Nina Ricci by Olivier Theyskens,
autumn–winter 2007–2008.
Photo Julien Claessens.

Opposite:
Olivier Teyskens.
Photo Nico.

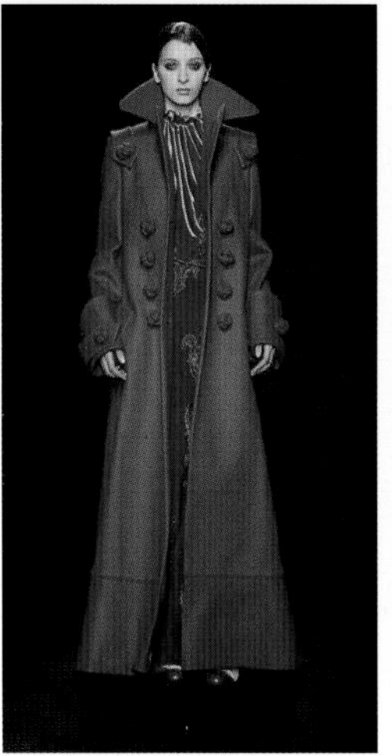

Viktor & Rolf, spring–summer 2005. Photos Etienne Tordoir/ Catwalkpictures.

Opposite:
Viktor & Rolf, autumn–winter 2002–2003. Photos Etienne Tordoir/ Catwalkpictures.

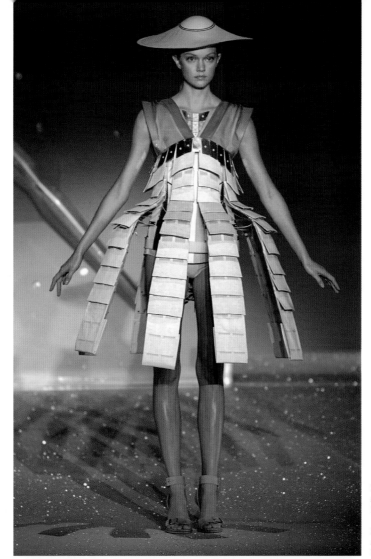

Hussein Chalayan, spring–summer 2007. Photo Chris Moore.

Hussein Chalayan, autumn–winter 2007–2008. Photo Chris Moore.

Stella McCartney,
spring–summer 2003.
Photo Etienne Tordoir/
Catwalkpictures.

Stella McCartney.
Photo Rights Reserved.

Stella McCartney,
spring–summer 2006 collection.
Fashion show at the Grand Hotel.
Photo Simon Procter.

Véronique Branquinho, autumn–winter 2002–2003. Photo Etienne Tordoir/ Catwalkpictures.

Véronique Branquinho, autumn–winter 2004–2005. Photo Etienne Tordoir/ Catwalkpictures.

Bruno Pieters,
autumn–winter 2004–2005.
Photo Etienne Tordoir/
Catwalkpictures.

Bruno Pieters,
spring–summer 2004.
Photo Etienne Tordoir/
Catwalkpictures.

Raf Simons, fashion show at the Géode, spring–summer 1999. Photo Etienne Tordoir/ Catwalkpictures.

Raf Simons, spring–summer 2000. Photo Etienne Tordoir/ Catwalkpictures.

A. F. Vandevorst,
spring–summer 2007.
Photo Vincent Lappartient.

A. F. Vandervorst,
spring–summer 2004.
Photo Etienne Tordoir/Catwalkpictures.

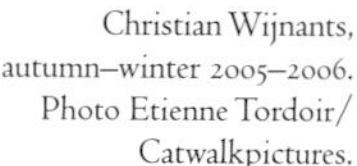

Christian Wijnants,
autumn–winter 2005–2006.
Photo Etienne Tordoir/
Catwalkpictures.

Bernhard Willhelm,
autumn–winter 2003–2004.
Photo Etienne Tordoir/
Catwalkpictures.

Anne-Valérie Hash, couture autumn–summer 2007–2008.
Anne-Valérie Hash, couture spring–summer 2006. Photos Bettina Rheims.

Maurizio Galante
"Galanterie" at the Fondation Cartier,
couture spring–summer 2004.
© Maurizio Galante.

Maurizio Galante,
spring–summer 2006.
Photo Vincent Lappartient.

Julie Gayet wearing Richard René, *happening* "Hyères Encore" at Galeries Lafayette, 19 November 2007. Photo Rights Reserved.

Vanessa Paradis wearing Richard René, video-clip "Dès que je te vois" "As soon as I see you" by John Nollet. Photo Emanuele Scorcelletti.

Monica Bellucci wearing Richard René, 2006. Photo Simon Hawk for *Elle*.

Felipe Oliveira Baptista, drawings exhibited at an exhibition at the MUDAM in Luxembourg, December 2007.

Marc Le Bihan,
couture autumn–winter 2007–2008.
Photo Cécile Guyenne.

Ralph Rucci and Deeda Blair.
Courtesy Ralph Rucci.

Cathy Pill, couture autumn–winter 2006–2007. Photo Etienne Tordoir/Catwalkpictures.
On Aura Tout Vu, couture spring–summer 2006. Photo Vincent Lappartient.

"The Magnificent Seven," the creators seen by Steven Meisel and chosen by *Vogue* USA, September 2006. From left to right: Stefano Pilati, Marc Jacobs, Olivier Theyskens, Narciso Rodriguez, Miuccia Prada, Nicolas Ghesquière, Alber Elbaz.

Facing page: Exception, Wu-Yong, autumn–winter 2007–2008 collection. Photos Enrico Dagnino.

Bercy agreements, 26 June 2000. MM. Mario Boselli and Didier Grumbach with their respective ministers for foreign trade, Enrico Letta and François Huwart. | François Loos, minister for foreign trade, Hyères, Sunday 2 May 2004. Euromediterreanean round table attended by Pascal Morand (IFM), Mario Boselli (Italy), Mario Ferrera (Portugal), Salah-Eddine Mezouar (Morroco), Ali Nakaï (Tunisia), Umut Oran (Turkey), Guilaume Sarkozy (Textile Industries Union), Claude Tétard (French Garment Industry Union). | Marylise Lebranchu, minister for trade and crafts and Didier Grumbach, 23 January 1998. | Christine Lagarde, minister for foreign trade and maître Alain Coblence. Villa Noailles, Hyères, 30 April 2006. Round table on intellectual property. | Indian delegation at the Hyères Festival 2006. Around Mrs. Rathi Jha (president of the FDCI), the creators Manish Arora, Rajesh Pratap Singh, Rohit Bal, and Anju Modi. | Andrée Putman interviewed by Michèle Champenois, *Le Monde 2*, during the "Design Parade" of July 2006, at the villa Noailles.

The exchange years France–Chine 2003–2004. | The exchange years France–Chine. The Great Wall. Adam Jones, Anne-Valérie Hash, Lutz, Felipe Oliveira Baptista. | Finale of the Peking Fashion show. A. F. Vandevorst. | Meeting of the Franco-Chinese committee in Peking, 29 March 2006. | Didier Grumbach, 27 March 2006, during the 3rd Chinese textile economic forum, presided over by Mr. Bauxi Lai, Chinese minister for trade. | Conference on the world of brands. Audiovisual presentation by Thierry Dreyfus. Beijing, 29 March 2006. | Meeting of the Franco-Chinese committee in Beijing, 29 March 2006. In the first row, François Steiner (president of Kenzo), Perrine Houdoux (president of Thierry Mugler), Didier Grumbach (French Couture Federation), Hengjie Jiang (president of the Chinese Garment Federation), Chen Dapeng (general delegate).

Frédéric Mitterrand, French minister of culture, presenting Yuzhou Du with the Arts et lettres officer's decoration on 19 September 2011. (Copyright: Pascal Montary) | Manish Arora, SS 2008 Show (Reserved Rights) | Manish Arora, *Crash* magazine, October 2011 (Reserved Rights).

INDIA'S BREAKOUT FASHION EXPORT DEMONSTRATES THAT GOOD THINGS OFTEN COME IN SMALL, SPARKLING, RELENTLESSLY SMILING PACKAGES

– TEXT –
ISAAC LOCK

MANISH ARORA

anish Arora is perky, incredibly so. Incorrigibly upbeat. When we meet he has just spent the best part of an hour lying on a damp concrete floor covered in petals to be photographed. 'The floor was fine,' he says; 'the petals were quite cold. I got on the crack-of-dawn Eurostar to come to London and be covered in petals in a damp cemetery. This day is so much fun!' There's not a hint of irony. Jollity is the cornerstone of Manish Arora's personality, which in turn is the cornerstone of his business.

'The basic idea behind my brand is happiness,' he continues, when we sit down in a pub near to the scene of the petalling. (His choice. He orders a pint, even though it's midday. 'Why not? I'm in London!') 'I imagine that someone who's wearing my clothes will have a smile on their face, and people who look at people wearing my clothes will have smiles on their faces too. There's nothing deeper than that to look at.' See, for example, Rossy de Palma opening his spring/summer 2012 show in a sculptural holographic dress, or a girl with a life-sized toucan on her head. 'India is a country of 1.3 billion people and I'm the only designer from there who is showing internationally, doing my own line and working for another house. I don't need to complain.'

His positivity, he suggests, is what saw him accepted to India's first fashion school in Delhi with no experience, or 'really any fashion leanings whatsoever', celebrated in India when he launched his own line in 1997, ushered onto the catwalks of London then Paris, and finally, last year, appointed as creative director of Paco Rabanne. 'The idea behind my brand is that life is beautiful. I tell that to myself every morning and it actually works. There are enough designers making dark, dull, depressing clothes; I don't need to do that. I'm a very happy person, and that's what I like to show in my work. Why not? It sells!'

And there's the surprise. Manish's clothes – painstakingly crafted, but ultimately, by his own admission, 'a bit insane' – make money. Not as in just enough money for him to keep churning out collections for the love of it, but as in, enough money for him to employ 250 full-time staff in his Delhi studio alone.

There is, Manish concedes, 'probably complicated analysis' that could be done to explain his phenomenon, but it's not something he's interesting in doing. 'The story of my success is simple,' he chirps. 'All you have to do to make it work is really believe in what you do, and people will accept it. You don't have to complicate your life. You just have to do something that you think is good. If you believe in it, soon enough you find that other people do too.' ●

FASHION EDITOR SALLY LYNDLEY

Chinese and French delegations at the French Ministry of Culture on 19 September 2011 (Copyright: Pascal Montary) | Didier Grumbach and Yuzhou Du presenting designer Yutao Wang with the Beijing Fashion Week Grand Prix Award on 1 November 2011 (Reserved Rights).

Bibliography

Allilaire, Jean, *Les Industries de l'habillement et du travail des étoffes,* Paris, Société d'éditions françaises et internationales, 1947.

Andia, Béatrice de, *Paris, Lieux de pouvoir et de citoyenneté,* AAVP (Action artistique de la Ville de Paris), Collection Paris et son patrimoine, Paris, September 2006.

Assouly, Olivier, *Goûts à vendre: Essais sur la captation esthétique,* Institut français de la mode, Regard, 2007.

Assouly, Olivier, *Le Luxe: Essais sur la fabrique de l'ostentation,* Institut français de la mode, Regard, 2000.

Blanckaert, Christian, *Luxe,* Le Cherche Midi, 2007.

Boucher, François, *Histoire du costume en Occident,* Paris, Flammarion, 1965.

Bourdieu, Pierre, "Le couturier et sa griffe: contribution à une théorie de la magie," Paris, *Actes de la recherche en science sociale,* n° 1, September 1974.

Braudel, Fernand, *Les Structures du quotidien,* Paris, Armand Colin, 1979.

Bromberger, Merry, *Comment ils ont fait fortune,* Paris, Plon, 1954.

Carlier, Jean, *Freddy—Souvenir d'un mannequin vedette. Dans la coulisse de la haute couture parisienne,* Paris, Flammarion, 1956.

Chapon, François, *Mystère et Splendeurs de Jacques Doucet,* Paris, Jean-Claude Lattès, 1984.

Cholle, Francis, *L'Intelligence intuitive: pour réussir autrement,* Eyrolles, Editions d'Organisation, March 2007.

Delbourg-Delphis, Marylène, *La Mode pour la vie,* Paris, Autrement, 1983.

Demornex, Jacqueline, *Madeleine Vionnet,* Paris, Editions du Regard, 1991.

Demornex, Jacqueline, *Lucien Lelong. L'Intemporel,* Editions Gallimard, 2007.

Deschamps, Germaine, *La Crise dans les industries du vêtement et de la mode à Paris pendant la période de 1930 à 1937,* Paris, Librairie technique et économique, 1938.

Deslandres, Yvonne, *Le Costume image de l'homme,* Paris, Albin Michel, 1976.

Deslandres, Yvonne, *Paul Poiret,* Paris, Editions du Regard, 1986.

Deslandres, Yvonne, et Müller Florence, *Histoire de la mode au XXe siècle,* Paris, Somogy, 1986.

Dior, Christian, *Christian Dior et Moi,* Paris, Bibliothèque internationale des nouveautés, 1956.

François, Lucien, *Comment un nom devient une griffe,* Paris, Gallimard, 1962.

Franklin, Alfred, *Dictionnaire historique des arts, métiers et professions exercés dans Paris depuis le XIIIe siècle,* Paris, Jeanne Laffite, 1906.

Garnier, Guillaume, 40 *années de création, Pierre Balmain,* Paris, Musée de la mode et du costume, 1985.

Garnier, Guillaume, *Paris-Couture années 30,* Paris, Musée de la mode et du costume, 1987.

Garnier, Guillaume, *Balenciaga,* Paris, musée de la Mode et du Costume, 1987.

Gendarme, Marie-Pierre, "Panorama de la propriété intellectuelle en Chine," *Mode Recherche* n° 5, Institut français de la mode, January 2006.

Giroud, Françoise, *Christian Dior,* Paris, Editions du Regard, 1987.

Glynn, Prudence, *In Fashion,* Londres, George Allen, 1978.

Grumbach, Didier, *Evolution des structures professionnelles et devenir des marques,* Repères mode & textile, Institut français de la mode, 1996.

Grumbach Didier, Parmal Pamela A.,

Fashion Show—Paris Style, Museum of Fine Arts, Boston Publications, 12 January 2006.
GUILLAUME, Valérie, *Jacques Fath*, Paris, Adam Biro, 1993.
HEILBRONN, Max, *Galeries Lafayette, Buchenwald*, Paris, Economica, 1989.
HERNDON, Booten, *Bergdorf's on the Plaza*, New York, A. Knopf, 1956.
JACOMET, Dominique, *Mode, Textile et Mondialisation*, Economica, 2007.
JOUVE, Marie-Andrée et DEMORNEX, Jacqueline, *Balenciaga*, Paris, Editions du Regard, 1988.
KAMITSIS, Lydia, *Dress Code—Tenue de cocktail*, Catalogue de l'exposition du musée de la mode à Marseille, Editions Musées de Marseille, 19 May–10 September 2006.
KARPIK, Lucien, *L'Economie des singularités*, Editions Gallimard, March 2007.
LANZMANN, Jacques et RIPERT, Pierre, *Cent Ans de prêt-à-porter*, Weill, Paris, PAU, 1992.
LIPOVETSKI, Gilles, "La mode de cent ans," *Le Débat*, n° 31, September 1984.
LYNAM, Ruth, *Paris Fashion*, Londres, Michael Joseph, 1972.
MANUSARDI, Jean, *Dix Ans avec Pierre Cardin*, Paris, Fanval, 1986.
DE MARLY, Diane, *The History of Haute Couture*, 1850-1950, Londres, Batsford, 1980.
MERCERON, Dean, ELBAZ, Alber, KODA, Harold, *Lanvin*, Rizzoli International Publications, 18 October 2007.
MORAIS, Richard, *Pierre Cardin, the Man Who Became a Label*, Londres, Bantam Press, 1991.
PALMER WHITE, Jack, *Poiret le Magnifique: le couturier de la Belle Epoque*, Paris, Payot, 1986.
POCHNA, Marie-France, *Boussac*, Paris, Laffont, 1981.
POCHNA, Marie-France, *Nina Ricci*, Paris, Editions du Regard, 1992.
POIRET, Paul, *En habillant l'époque*, Paris, Grasset, 1930.
POIRET, Paul, *Art et Phynance*, Paris, Lutétia, 1934.
QUESSADA, Dominique, *La Société de consommation de soi*, Verticales, November 1999.
REMAURY, Bruno, *Marques et récits*, Institut français de la mode, Regard, 1998.
ROCHE, Daniel, *La Culture des apparences*, Paris, Fayard, 1989, et coll. "Points Histoire," Editions du Seuil, 1992.
DU ROSELLE, Bruno, *La Mode*, Paris, Imprimerie nationale, 1980.
RUCCI Ralph, *The Art of Weightlessness*, Yale University Press, in association with the Fashion Institute of Technology, New York, 2 February 2007.
SAINDERICHIN, Ginette, *Kenzo*, Paris, Editions du May, 1989.
SIMON, Philippe, *La Haute couture, monographie d'une industrie de luxe*, Paris, 1931.
VEILLON, Dominique, *La Mode sous l'occupation*, Paris, Payot, 1990.
VITTU, Françoise, *Au paradis des dames. Nouveautés, modes et confection*. 1810–1870, Paris-Musées, 1993.
WORTH, Gaston, *La Couture et la confection des vêtements de femmes*, Paris, Chaix, 1895.

Chronology

1675 • Louis XIV hands down an order, albeit with a few restrictions, granting master seamstresses the right to dress women

1791 • Suppression of guilds and masterships

1824 • La Belle Jardinière, the first Parisian department store, opens

1830 • The sewing machine is invented by Barthélémy Thimonnier

1858 • Charles Frédéric Worth, considered to be the first grand couturier, opens a "special fashion house" in partnership with Otto Gustav Bobergh at 7 rue de la Paix

1868 • The Chambre syndicale de la couture et de la confection pour dames trade association is founded

1910 • The Chambre syndicale de la couture, des confectionneurs et des tailleurs pour dames trade association is dissolved

1911 • The Chambre syndicale de la couture parisienne is founded at 6 rue d'Aboukir and is presided over by Léon Réverdot • Paul Poiret is the first couturier to manufacture his own fragrances and he names them after his eldest daughter, *Rosine*

1920 • The French edition of *Vogue* debuts under the editorial leadership of Michel de Brunhoff

1929 • The Chambre syndicale de la confection en gros pour dames et fillettes becomes the Chambre syndicale de la confection et de la couture en gros

1934 • Lucien Lelong creates the "Edition" division at his company, marking the first time a couturier introduces a second line

1937 • *Marie Claire* is launched as a weekly magazine and is financed by Jean Prouvost. The title is a mix of luxury and mass market and is largely inspired by American media

1943 • The V3A7 decision puts laws into place that regulate the use of the terms "couture" and "couturiere," "haute couture," and "grand couturier" • On the same day, the V3A8 decision creates the statute "maisons de couture en gros" in the arena of women's apparel manufacturing • The Association de protection des industries artistiques saisonnières (PAIS) becomes part of the Chambre syndicale de la couture parisienne

1944 • Madame Carven moves her headquarters on rue des Pyramides to the Rond-Point des Champs-Elysées • The house of Rochas launches the perfume *Femme* • The Trois Hirondelles label is launched by the Association des maisons de couture en gros • Hubert de Givenchy joins the house of Lucien Lelong • Pierre Cardin joins the house of Paquin • Robert Weill regains possession of his company; he was forced to give up the management of his company during World War II

1945 • Pierre Balmain opens his own house • Hubert de Givenchy joins Schiaparelli • Nina Ricci launches its first fragrance, *Coeur Joie* • Jean Gaumont-Lanvin, the head of Lanvin, replaces Lucien Lelong as president of the Chambre syndicale de la couture • The founding of the Fédération nationale de la couture • Hélène Lazareff launches the weekly *Elle* magazine

1946 • Jeanne Lanvin dies • Marcel Boussac decides to finance Christian Dior • Pierre Balmain launches the *Elysées 64-83* perfume • Jacques Heim signs a licensing agreement with the American company Junior League for a ready-to-wear collection called Heim Jeunes Filles • The Fédération française du vêtement feminine takes the term "confection"—or "manufacturing"—out of its official name

1947 • Christian Dior opens his own house and shows his debut New Look collection. He creates a fragrance subsidiary and launches Miss Dior • The first convention for the Industries du vêtement feminine takes place in Lyon under the direction of Albert Lempereur

1948 • Jacques Fath creates his perfume company • Nina Ricci launches the *L'Air du temps* perfume • Christion Dior opens Christian Dior, Inc., a luxury ready-to-wear company in New York City at 745 Fifth Avenue • Jacques Fath signs a ready-to-wear license with the American firm Joseph Halpert • Albert Lempereur spearheads a French mission to the US under the Marshall Plan with the goal of studying American apparel manufacturing

1949 • Christian Dior signs his first two licensing agreements with American companies for hosiery and ties • Jacques Heim and Marcel Rochas choose to work with C. Mendès to produce a selection of coats and jackets to be sold exclusively in their Paris stores, as well as shops in the French provinces • Pierre Cardin leaves Christian Dior and opens his own company to make theatrical costumes at 10 rue de Richepanse

1950 • André Courrèges joins Balenciaga • Antonio Canovas del Castillo becomes the artistic director of Lanvin-Castillo • Jacques Rouët creates a wholesale division at Christian Dior to sell accessories • Weill and Lempereur launch their own brands and use advertising, which associates their brand name with the term "ready-to-wear" • Jacques Heim establishes the Marina Carine company to make ready-to-wear dresses • Jean Gaumont-Lanvin and Marcel Dhorme become joint partners in Les Couturiers Associés, the first company to specialize in distributing couture ready-to-wear under license

1951 • Raymond Barbas, the president of the Chambre syndicale de la couture, asks the government for a subsidy to support Parisian haute couture • A group of Italian couturiers stage a fashion show in Florence • Zyga Pianko, better known as Pierre d'Alby, founds his first company in Paris called Piantex

1952 • Hubert de Givenchy shows his first collection • Ghislaine de Polignac becomes the first "stylist" of French fashion at Galeries Lafayette • *Elle* publishes its first dossier on ready-to-wear entitled: "Would you like to be able to find ready-made dresses?" • Lucien Vogel assigns Maïmé Arnodin the new ready-to-wear column in *Jardin des Modes* • The "findings for youth" column in *Vogue* is renamed "Everything about ready-to-wear" • A vote is held for taking legal action against copyright infringement in the apparel and finery industries • The French government subsidy for haute couture, L'Aide Textile, is enacted • Christian Dior creates an autonomous licensing subsidiary and names the first ever "Directeur des Licences"

1953 • Pierre Cardin sets up his own company at 118 rue du Faubourg-Saint-Honoré • After one season of business, Marc Bohan closes his company and joins Jean Patou • Callot Soeurs' business is shuttered • Marcel Rochas closes his couture business • Gaby Aghion, in partnership with Jacques Lenoir, opens the house of Chloé • Jacques Fath registers the brand Fath Université. The first collection made under this label by the Groupe Provoust is shown the following year • The new ready-to-wear section in *Elle* magazine is assigned to Claude Brouet • Denise Fayolle establishes and manages the trend office of Prisunic • The Trois Hirondelles group organizes a fashion show in New York

1954 • Chanel shows its first collection after a 15 year absence • Les Parfums Chanel buys the Chanel couture house and the company is renamed Chanel SA • Karl Lagerfeld and Yves Saint Laurent win a fashion contest organized by Thelma Sweetinburgh for the International Wool Secretariat • The houses of Paquin and Worth merge • Schiaparelli closes • Jacques Fath dies • Jules-François Crahay joins Nina Ricci

1955 • Lanvin, Patou, Dior, and Fath sue Frédéric Milton before the US Supreme Court for selling books filled with sketches of couture models • Albert Lempereur becomes president of the Maisons de couture en gros • Albert Lempereur is invited by the American Secretary of Trade to come to the US on a trade mission to learn about the American apparel industry. Lempereur assembles a group of French manufacturers, advertising managers, fashion journalists, and a representative of the French government. French journalists discover American ready-to-wear • The Givenchy Université label, a ready-to-wear license of the Prouvost group, is launched • Léon Cligman takes over the management of Indreco • Albert Lempereur heads up the formation of the Comité de coordination des industries de la mode (CIM) • *Jardin des Modes* magazine launches its first special edition dedicated to ready-to-wear. A suit from the brand Wébé is featured on the cover and the magazine announces that information about ready-to-wear will be covered twice yearly, in February and in August

1956 • Jean Dessès is the first couturier to open a boutique at Galeries Lafayette • The first trade show for women's wear is held at the Théatre des ambassadeurs, currently the Espace Cardin. The trade show would be held every year from 1957–1962 at the former Réamur department stores • *Vogue* launches its first special edition for ready-to-wear and an outfit from Lempereur is featured on the cover

1957 • Christian Dior dies • Guy Laroche opens his couture house • Pierre Cardin joins the Chambre syndicale de la couture • The Prêt-à-porter création group is formed within the Chambre syndicale de la couture under the auspices of Jacques Heim. This group's goal is to defend and coordinate the interests of its members, which included Carven, Grès, Madeleine de Rauch, Nina Ricci, Maggy Rouff, Lanvin, Jean Dessès, Jacques Griffe, Jacques Heim, and Guy Laroche • Weill inaugurates its first factory in Lens

1958 • Yves Saint Laurent shows his first collection for Christian Dior • Jacques Heim becomes president of the Chambre syndicale de la couture • The Printemps department store creates its own trend forecasting office under the direction of Jacqueline Bénard • Elie Jacobson opens the Dorothée store on rue de Sèvres

1959 • L'Aide Textile, the French government subsidy for haute couture, is suspended • An agreement is signed between Berlin-based apparel makers represented by IMOS and the Chambre syndicale de la couture parisienne: 15 couturiers accept to participate in pre-season fashion shows in Berlin and Dusseldorf

1960 • Pierre Balmain sells his fragrance company to Charles Revson, the president of Revlon • The Société parisienne de la confection, a manufacturing subsidiary of Galeries Lafayette, closes • Maimé Arnodin opens her trend forecasting office • Pierre Belleteste buys the Isadore Dumail (I.D.) company and Maimé Arnodin becomes its artistic director • Jacques Esterel joins the Chambre syndicale de la couture

1961 • Pierre Cardin signs a licensing deal with Georges Bril for men's suits • The Trois Hirondelles group discontinues operations

1962 • Louis Féraud joins the Chambre syndicale de la couture • Michel Goma replaces Karl Lagerfeld at Jean Patou • Jean-Louis Scherrer, Yves Saint Laurent, Oonoag Ferreras, Philippe Venet, and André Courrèges open their own couture houses • Jacqueline Jacobson shows her first collection and the Dorothée Bis store opens • Daniel Hechter opens his own fashion company • Sammy and Maurice Weinberg inaugurate an ultra-modern production facility at Bourges • The Groupement de Paris du prêt-à-porter de luxe, a luxury ready-to-wear group, is created under the impetus of Jacques Dransard • The first Emma-Christie collection is shown, designed by Emmanuelle Khanh and Christiane Bailly, styled by Gil Coutin, and financed by Alain Lalonde • Michèle Rosier launches V de V, a name which is the abbreviation for Vêtements de vacances, or vacation-wear

1963 • Christiane Bailly and Maxime de La Falaise join Chloé • Marcel Boussac consolidates his corporate holdings into one company, the Comptoir de l'industrie textile de France (CITF) • Lempereur opens a factory in Bressuire, in the Deux-Sèvres region • Didier Grumbach takes over the management of C. Mendès • The first Salon international du prêt-à-porter opens at the Porte de Versailles convention center • Cacharel becomes famous after one of its shirts, photographed by Peter Knapp, is featured on the cover of *Elle*. The shirt sold for 55 old francs at Dorothée • Gérard Pipart joins Nina Ricci

1964 • Antonio Caonvas del Castillo opens his couture house • *Y*, the first perfume from Yves Saint Laurent, is launched • The Victoire store opens at Place de Victoires. The store is financed by Alain Lalonde and managed by Catherine Chaillet • Lucien Abra launches the *Journal du Textile*, a weekly trade newspaper

1965 • Angelo Tarlazzi joins Jean Patou as a design assistant • L'Oréal acquires a stake in Courrèges and the couture house moves to 40 rue François Premier • For spring 1966, Courrèges shows three collections in one fashion show: Prototype for haute couture, Couture Future for ready-to-wear, and Hyperbole, a diffusion line with knitwear • Françoise Vincent-Ricard opens the Promostyl trend-forecasting office • Emanuel Ungaro opens his couture house on avenue Mac-Mahon

1966 • Balmain launches *Miss Balmain*, the first fragrance produced by Revlon • CIRIT, the Comité interprofessionel de renovation des structures industrielles et commerciales de l'industrie de textile, is founded • Courrèges opens its first boutique dedicated to ready-to-wear • C. Mendès opens its first factory in Chalonnes-sur-Loire • The Yves Saint Laurent Rive Gauche ready-to-wear collection is launched by four partners with equal shares: C. Mendès, Didier Grumbach, Pierre Bergé, and Yves Saint Laurent

1967 • Christian Aujard launches his signature label • The first collection of Ungaro Parallèle is launched by C. Mendès • Miss Dior, the first diffusion ready-to-wear collection from Christian Dior, debuts • C. Mendès acquires Maria Carine and establishes a subsidiary, Paris Collections Inc., in New York • Antoine Riboud buys the Victoire boutique and Françoise Chassagnac becomes its new manager

1968 • The house of Balenciaga closes • Indreco buys Newman and Seiligmann • Sonia Rykiel debuts her first collection and opens her shop on rue de Grenelle • The Spanish group Puig buys the Paco Rabanne name and registers it under perfumes for 20 years • C. Mendès buys the Cotariel d'Angers factory with 450 sewers • C. Mendès and Givenchy join forces to launch Givenchy Nouvelle Boutique • Maïmé Arnodin and Denise Fayolle found MAFIA (Mäimé Arnodin Fayolle International Associates) as an advertising and trend forecasting company

1969 • A new recovery plan for fabric creation and couture is established and it allows couturiers to use French fabrics for free in their collections • Chantal et Bruce Thomass open the Ter et Bantine store on rue Dauphine • The fashion trade magazine *GAP* (*Groupe Avant Première*) is launched by Ginette Sainderichin

1970 • Emanuel Ungaro signs a ready-to-wear contract with CIDAT, a subsidiary of Turin-based GFT • The Chambre syndicale des tissus spéciaux à la haute couture is renamed Chambre syndicale des maisons de tissus de création • John Kornblith, the American licensee of Cardin's men's suits, subcontracts his production to Bidermann in France • Raymond Barbas opens a factory in Angers whose production is exclusively for Jean Patou ready-to-wear • Dominique Peclers opens the Peclers Paris trend forecasting office • Kenzo opens his Jungle Jap store in the Galerie Vivienne • Jean Paul Gaultier joins Pierre Cardin as a design assistant

1971 • Paco Rabanne joins the Chambre syndicale de la couture • Jean-Louis Scherrer sells his name to Orlane • Didier Grumbach creates the Créateurs & Industriels company within C. Mendès; Emmanuelle Khanh and Ossie Clark participate in the new group's first fashion show • Andrée Putman leaves Mafia to take over the artistic direction of Créateurs & Industriels

1972 • Angelo Tarlazzi replaces Michel Goma as artistic director of Jean Patou • Pierre Cardin and Nina Ricci regroup haute couture and ready-to-wear in a single fashion show • Courrèges opens a ready-to-wear factory in Pau • Emmanuelle Khanh opens her own company • Jacques Mouclier is named acting president delegate of the Chambre syndicale de la couture

1973 • Five American designers (Bill Blass, Oscar de la Renta, Anne Klein, Halston, and Stephen Burrows) show their collections for the first time in France alongside five French designers (Pierre Cardin, Givenchy, Christian Dior, Yves Saint Laurent, and Ungaro) at the Théâtre Royal of the Chateau of Versailles • Issey Miyake stages his first fashion show at the Bourse de Commerce as part of the Créateurs & Industriels design initiative • Claude Montana signs a licensing agreement with Michel Costas • Thierry Mugler presents his first collection under the Café de Paris label • The I.D. company is sold to Prouvost • Yves Saint Laurent sells his shares in Rive Gauche to C. Mendès • The Groupement Mode & Création (GMC) is formed by Pierre Bergé, the president of Yves Saint Laurent, bringing together Yves Saint Laurent, Christian Dior, Emanuel Ungaro Chloé, Dorothée Bis, Sonia Rykiel, Kenzo, and Emmanuelle Khanh • Créateurs & Industriels opens a retail shop at 45 rue de Rennes • Yves Saint Laurent and Pierre Bergé buy Yves Saint Laurent Couture back from Squibb and Squibb's Charles of the Ritz subsidiary • The Première Vision fabric trade show is launched in Lyon

1974 • Anne-Marie Baretta holds a fashion show for her first signature collection and opens her first store • Thierry Mugler opens his own company on rue Hauteville in a 50/50 partnership with Alain Caradeuc • C. Mendès signs a worldwide licensing agreement with Valentino for luxury ready-to-wear • Jean-Charles de Castelbajac joins the Créateurs

1975 • Christian Dior New York Inc. is closed

1976 • Yves Saint Laurent launches the *Opium* fragrance • Chanel signs a ready-to-wear license agreement with C. Mendès. Philippe Guibourgé is the artistic manager • Jean Paul Gaultier holds his first fashion show at Palais de la Découverte • Jean-Louis Scherrer buys his company back from Morton-Norwich, the parent company of Orlane • Agnès Bourgois opens her first store under the name of Agnès B at 3 rue du Jour • The Groupement de Paris du prêt-à-porter de luxe association closes down • The Shiseido cosmetics company and Melka Treanton invite Claude Montana, Anne-Marie Baretta, Dan Béranger, Thierry Mugler, Jean-Charles de Castelbajac, and Jean-Claude de Luca to show their collections in Tokyo • Adeline André shows her first signature collection at the Angelina tea salon

1977 • Léo Gros, the president of Montagut, buys the Pierre Balmain company • Maïme Arnodin and Denise Fayolle introduce Sonia Rykiel to the 3 Suisses catalog with a double-page

1978 • Cacharel launches the *Anaïs, Anaïs* fragrance

1979 • Valentino discontinues its ready-to-wear contract with C. Mendès and signs with Italy's GFT • The Aide à la création textile et couture subsidy is discontinued • Pierre Bergé buys C. Mendès in partnership with Léon Cligman, the president of Indreco

1980 • The Ter et Bantine label becomes Chantal Thomass • Yohji Yamamoto holds his first Paris fashion show

1981 • Chanel discontinues its ready-to-wear licensing agreement with C. Mendès and takes direct control over this collection's production • Comme des Garçons (Rei Kawakubo) has its first fashion show in Paris • Chevignon opens its first store on rue du Four in Paris • Giorgio Armani launches the Emporio Armani diffusion line

1982 • Jean Paul Gaultier creates his eponymous company and François Menuge becomes its manager • French culture minister Jack Lang allows the Chambre syndicale du prêt-à-porter des couturiers et des créateurs de mode a hold its fashion shows at the Cour Carrée du Louvre • Azzedine Alaïa holds a fashion show for his first signature collection at 60 rue de Bellechasse

1983 • Chanel names Karl Lagerfeld the artistic director of its collections • Vivienne Westwood holds her first fashion show in Paris at Angelina • Sybilla opens her fashion house in Spain while Franco Moschino and Romeo Gigli open their own companies in Italy

1984 • The CIRIT becomes the Défi • Sylvie Grumbach opens 2e Bureau, an event and publicity company for fashion companies, notably new labels, including Jean Colonna, Vivienne Westwood, John Galliano, Hervé Léger, Matsuda, and Koji Tatsuno • Thierry Mugler holds a fashion show for paying ticket holders at the Zénith theater and 6,000 people attend • Naf Naf launches its first ad campaign, "Le Grand Méchant Look" • The Ferinel company controlled by Bernard Arnault acquires Boussac, the parent company of Christian Dior

1985 • The Chambre syndicale des maisons de tissus de création association is dissolved • World, the third largest Japanese textile company, acquires 66 per cent of Chantal Thomass • Hervé Léger launches his signature label • Benetton and its French advertising company, Eldorado, launch the worldwide slogan: "United Colors of Benetton" • Martine Sitbon holds her first fashion show at the Pavillon Gabriel and Jean Colonna stages his first fashion show at the Musée d'art moderne

1986 • Pierre Bergé and Yves Saint Laurent buy Charles of the Ritz, the company that holds the license for Yves Saint Laurent fragrances, from Squibb • Germaine Monteil launches Claude Montana's first fragrance • The Institut Français de la mode opens • Helmut Lang holds his first fashion show at the Centre Georges Pompidou • Marc Audibet shows his first signature collection

1987 • Bernard Arnault launches and finances the house of Christian Lacroix • Spanish group Puig buys Paco Rabanne • Kookaï creates a groundbreaking black and white ad campaign with CLM/BDDO which puts the brand on the fashion map

1988 • Robert Ricci allows Elf-Sanofi to buy shares in his company • Kenzo diversifies into fragrances • John Galliano holds his first fashion show in Paris • Olivier Guillemin, Mariot Chanet, Martin Margiela, and APC are launched

1989 • Bernard Arnault takes over the majority of shares of Louis Vuitton Moet Hennessy (LVMH) and thus gains control of Christian Dior, Givenchy, Christian Lacroix, and Céline • Lanvin is sold to L'Oréal and Orcofi • Angelo Tarlazzi succeeds Guy Laroche for haute couture while continuing to design his own ready-to-wear • Romeo Gigli holds his first fashion show in Paris • Donna Karan launches DKNY and Jean Paul Gaultier launches Junior Gaultier

1990 • The house of Balmain is sold to a banking pool organized by Alain Chevalier, former president of LVMH • Jean-Louis Scherrer sells the majority of his company to Ilona Gestion, a company in which Seibu held a 65 per cent stake and Hermès a 35 per cent stake • Esprit opens its first boutique in Paris at Place des Victoires and it is run by Alain Caradeuc • Versace shows his first haute couture collection in Paris

1991 • France's industry minister Dominique Strauss-Kahn nominates a commission whose goal is to update the norms of haute couture and the haute couture appellation • Ann Demeulemeester, Véronique Leroy, and Marcel Marongiu show their collections for the first time in Paris • Pierre Barberis succeeds Christian Derveloy as the head of group VEV, a company comprised of the former Prouvost and Boussac groups

1992 • Issey Miyake launches the *L'Eau d'Issey* perfume • Thierry Mugler launches the *Angel* fragrance • Erik Mortensen replaces Jean-Louis Scherrer at the house of Scherrer • Oscar de la Renta is named artistic director of Pierre Balmain • Pierre d'Alby sells his company • The first A/X Armani Exchange boutique opens in Soho in New York • Courrèges Parfums Investissements S.A. acquires 100 per cent of Courrèges Parfums from L'Oréal

1993 • Elf-Sanofi gains control of Yves Saint Laurent • Jean Paul Gaultier launches his fragrance • La Société de bâtiments et de participations (SEBP) owned by Bernard Arnault acquires control of Kenzo • Chargeurs Textiles, the world's largest weaver of wool textiles, organizes a fashion cruise in the fjords of Norway to encourage networking between European designers, manufacturers, and weavers • Viktor & Rolf win the grand prize at the Festival international de la mode d'hyères

1994 • Tom Ford is named creative director of Gucci • Rick Owens launches a signature label in Los Angeles

1995 • Thierry Mugler celebrates the 20th anniversary of his label at the Cirque d'Hiver • A study group is created within the Fédération de la couture • John Galliano is named creative director of Givenchy

1996 • Alexander McQueen replaces John Galliano as creative director at Givenchy • Ralph Toledano, president of Guy Laroche, recruits Alber Elbaz as creative director

1997 • New steering committee within the Federation presided over by Didier Grumbach • Thierry Mugler and Jean Paul Gaultier are the first "invited" members to the haute couture calendar • Clarins acquires control of Thierry Mugler • The Colette store in Paris opens • Nicolas Ghesquiere shows his first collection for Balenciaga • John Galliano presents his first collection for Christian Dior • Stella McCartney is named artistic director of Chloé • Michael Kors becomes artistic director of Céline • Gaspard Yurkievitch wins the grand prize of the Festival international de mode d'hyères • Helmut Lang sets up his business in New York and presents his collections there • Hedi Slimane is named creative director of Yves Saint Laurent Homme

1998 • Marc Jacobs designs Louis Vuitton's ready-to-wear • Didier Grumbach is elected president of the Fédération de la couture and the Chambre syndicale de la haute couture • Alber Elbaz becomes creative director of the Yves Saint Laurent Rive Gauche women's wear collection • Hermès appoints Martin Margiela artistic director of women's ready-to-wear

1999 • PPR buys 42 per cent of the Gucci Group • Gucci Group acquires Yves Saint Laurent, YSL Beauté, and Sergio Rossi • Prada acquires control of Jil Sander and Helmut Lang

2000 • Hedi Slimane leaves Yves Saint Laurent to become artistic director of Dior Homme men's wear • PPR buys Boucheron and Bedat & Cie • Mario Boselli, president of Italy's Camera nazionale della moda, and Didier Grumbach sign a five-point agreement at Bercy in the presence of each country's foreign trade ministers

2001 • Helmut Lang moves back to Paris • An agreement is signed between the Fédération de la couture and the Chinese association of stylists represented by Wang Qing • L'Oréal sells its shares in Lanvin to Mrs. Shaw Lan Wang of Taiwan • Julien Macdonald is named artistic director of Givenchy • Stella McCartney leaves Chloé and signs an agreement with the Gucci Group to launch her own collection • Phoebe Philo shows her first collection for Chloé • PPR buys 51 per cent of Alexander McQueen's company • PPR buys Balenciaga and Bottega Veneta • The rules governing the appellation "haute couture" are reviewed and reformed

2002 • Yves Saint Laurent stops designing haute couture and a retrospective fashion show is held at the Centre Pompidou • Alber Elbaz shows his first collection for Lanvin • The Diesel Group, presided over by Renzo Rossi, acquires control of Martin Margiela

2003 • Jean Paul Gaultier replaces Martin Margiela as head designer of Hermès women's ready-to-wear • François Pinault hands his power over the group he created to his son François-

Henri • Olivier Theyskens becomes artistic director of Rochas • Rick Owens leaves Los Angeles and sets up shop in Paris

2004 • Karl Lagerfeld creates a collection of 30 pieces for H & M • Antonio Marras shows his first collection for Kenzo • Jean Paul Gaultier shows his first collection for Hermès • Tom Ford and Domenico de Sole leave the Gucci Group • Stefano Pilati shows his first collection for Yves Saint Laurent • A Franco-Italian ad campaign about intellectual property rights is launched by Didier Grumbach and Mario Boselli

2005 • Adam Jones, Felipe Oliveira Baptista, and Nicolas Andreas Taralis create collections of about 10 pieces each for Uniqlo • Armani shows his Armani Privé couture collection in Paris and is elected a member of the Chambre syndicale de la haute couture • Valérie Hermann becomes president of Yves Saint Laurent • Helmut Lang leaves the company he founded • An agreement is signed between the Fédération de la couture and the Chinese fashion industry federation, presided by Mr. Jiang • Ricardo Tisci replaces Julien Macdonald as artistic director of Givenchy • Frida Giannini, originally accessories designer at Gucci, becomes the brand's artistic director under the watchful eye of president Mark Lee • Russian designers Chapurin and Alena Akhmadullina join the Paris ready-to-wear calendar • Ivana Omazic shows her first collection for Céline • The Falic brothers buy control of Christian Lacroix from LVMH • Giambattista Valli holds the first fashion show for his new signature label

2006 • Jean Louis Dumas steps down as president of Hermès • Christophe Decarnin shows his first collection for Balmain • Peter Dundas shows his first collection for Ungaro • The Miu Miu fashion show is held for the first time in Paris • Rochas discontinues its fashion business • Prada sells its shares of Helmut Lang and Jil Sander • Two Chinese brands, Jeffen and Wu Yong, join the Paris ready-to-wear calendar • Phoebe Philo leaves Chloé • Raf Simons' holds his first fashion show for Jil Sander • The house of Martin Margiela joins the haute couture fashion show calendar • Dai Fujiwara succeeds Naoki Takizawa as artistic director of Issey Miyake • Elie Saab is elected to join the Chambre syndicale de la haute couture

2007 • Italian department store Rinascente buys the Paris-based Printemps department store chain • Anne-Valérie Hash and Maurizio Galante join the Chambre syndicale de la haute couture • Prada sells its shares in Azzedine Alaïa • Esteban Cortazar replaces Peter Dundas as women's wear designer at Ungaro • The Eley-Keshimoto design team take over the artistic direction of Cacharel • Azzedine Alaïa partners with the Richemont group • Olivier Theyskens shows his first collection for Nina Ricci • Indian designers Manish Arora, Anu Mika, and Rajesh Pratap Singh join Paris' ready-to-wear calendar • Valentino Garavani holds the final fashion show for the house he created • The first fashion show for Limi Feu in Paris • Paul & Joe stage their first fashion show • Fendi presents a dramatic fashion show on the Great Wall of China • Alexis Mabille and Stéphane Rolland are invited to participate in the haute couture fashion show calendar

2008 • Yves Saint Laurent dies • Estaban Cortazar presents his first fashion show for the house of Emanuel Ungaro • Ma Ke, the Chinese designer behind the Wu Yong couture collection (and Exception), is invited to show during haute couture week • Collette Dinnigan, Escada, Giambattista Valli, Jeremy Scott, Jose Castro, and Miu Miu are elected members to the Chambre syndicale du prêt à porter des couturiers • Ann Demeulemeester, Cerruti, Dries Van Noten, John Galliano, Kris Van Assche, Raf Simons, and Valentino are elected members to the Chambre syndicale de la mode masculine • Gareth Pugh holds his first fashion show in Paris • The Stéphane Rolland collection is officially recognized as haute couture • Ted Lapidus dies

2009 • Kris Van Assche, Manish Arora, and Peachoo Krejberg are elected members of the Chambre syndicale du prêt à porter des couturiers • Alexandre Matthieu and Rabih Kayrouz are invited to show during Haute Couture week • The house of Loulou de la Falaise becomes part of the Accessories group within the Chambre syndicale de la haute couture • Peter Copping is named artistic director of Nina Ricci • The house of Christian Lacroix is placed under judicial regulation • Phoebe Philo joins Céline as artistic director • Rochas, Roland Mouret, Shiatzy Chen, and Vanessa Bruno become new members of the Chambre syndicale du prêt-à-porter des couturiers

2010 • A group of six Place Vendôme high jewelry houses—Chaumet, Mellerio, Van Cleef & Arpels, Boucheron, Chanel Joaillerie, Dior Joaillerie—become part of the haute couture calendar • Alexander McQueen dies • Jean-Louis Dumas dies • Designer Akiza Onozucca leaves the house of Zucca • Carine Roitfeld leaves *Vogue France* as editor-in-chief • Bouchra Jarrar is invited to show during haute couture week • Sarah Burton becomes the artistic director of Alexander McQueen • Ralph Toledano steps down as president of Chloé; Geoffroy de la Bourdonnaye becomes new Chloé president • Felipe Oliveira Baptista is named artistic director of Lacoste following the departure of Christophe Lemaire • Nicolas Formichetti joins the artistic direction of Thierry Mugler (Sébastien Peigné is in the women's wear studio and Romain Kremer is with the men's wear) • Adam Kimmel, Arnys, Damir Doma, Franck Boclet, and Zilli are elected members of the Chambre syndicale de la mode masculine • American designer Zac Posen shows his collection in Paris • Jean Paul Gaultier holds his last fashion show for Hermès • Julien Fournié, Maxime Simoëns, and Alexandre Vauthier are invited to join the haute couture fashion calendar

2011 • François-Henri Pinault becomes head of the luxury division within PPR • Christophe Josse and Gustavo Lins are officially classified as couturiers • Manish Arora is named artistic director of Paco Rabanne • The house of Azzaro and Vanessa Seward part ways • Christophe Decarnin leaves the house of Pierre Balmain • Cédric Charlier leaves Cacharel • Christian Dior lets go of John Galliano • Hermès sells its stake in Jean Paul Gaultier and the Spanish group Puig takes control • Christophe Lemaire's first fashion show for Hermès • LVMH buys Italian jeweler Bulgari • Michael Kors opens a 650 square meter store on rue Saint-Honoré in Paris • Julien David joins the ready-to-wear fashion week • PPR buys American skate brand Volcom • PPR buys Brioni for 300 million euros • Clare Waight is named artistic director of Chloé • Giambattista Valli and Iris Van Herpen are invited to join haute couture fashion week • Marie-Claire Pauwels dies • Azzaro, Carven, Damir Doma, Felipe Oliveira Baptista, Thimister, Véronique Leroy, and Zac Posen become new members of the Chambre syndicale du prêt-à-porter • Olivier Rousteing's first fashion show for Balmain • Guillaume Henry holds his first fashion show for Carven • Dawei Sun and Ling Liu present their first show for Cacharel • Manish Aroras holds his first fashion show for Paco Rabanne • Design team Humberto Leon and Carol Lim present their first fashion show for Kenzo • Yoshiyuki Miyame's first fashion show for Issey Miyake • François Lesage is given the Maître d'art award by Frédéric Mitterrand • François Lesage dies • Loulou de la Falaise dies • Yiqing Yin is a new invited member to the haute couture calendar • The house of Versace returns to haute couture after an eight-year absence • Chanel buys the Montex embroidery house

2012 • Raf Simons leaves Jil Sander; Jil Sander returns as artistic director to the label she founded • Stefano Pilati leaves Yves Saint Laurent, where he was artistic director since 2004 • The first and last fashion show of Maxime Simoëns for Léonard • LVMH acquires a stake in Maxime Simoëns • Chinese designer Masha Ma joins the official ready-to-wear calendar • Sacaï joins the official ready-to-wear calendar • Richemont announces that Stanislas de Quercize, formerly president of Van Cleef & Arpels, is the new president of Cartier, taking over from Bernard Fornas • Extraordinary meeting of the Fédération de la couture on 30 March and creation of a five-member executive committee • Yohji Yamamoto is jury president of the Festival de la mode d'hyères • Annual meeting of the Fédération de la couture on 11 June and confirmation of new form of governance. The five members of the new executive committee are: Paul Denève, Yves Saint Laurent; Bruno Pavlovksy, Chanel; Guillaume de Seynes, Hermès; Ralph Toledano, Jean Paul Gaultier; and Sidney Toledano, Christian Dior. Didier Grumbach is reelected president of the Fédération de la couture • Hedi Slimane becomes new artistic director of Yves Saint Laurent • Raf Simons named artistic director of Dior women's collections

INDEX

Page numbers in italics refer to illustrations

D

G

H

Q

R

ACKNOWLEDGEMENTS

I would like to express my great friendship for José Alvarez; without his encouragement this book would never have been written.

I am also grateful to all those who expressed their trust in me by sharing their memories: Gaby Aghion, Adeline André, Maïmé Arnodin, Manish Arora, Christiane Bailly, François Baufumé, Denis Belleteste, Jacqueline Bénard, Françoise Benhamou, Renata Bénichou, Pierre Bergé, Henry Berghauer, Patrizio Bertelli, Albert Blin, Marc Bohan, Primrose Bordier, Maryse Boxer, Claude Brouet, Chloé de Bruneton, Marion de Brunhoff, Yves Carcelle, Marie-Louise Carven, Léon Cligman, Alain Coblence, André Courrèges, Nina Dausset, Christian Delahaigue, Jacques Delahaye, Jean Dieudonné, Michel Douard, Jacques Dransard, Denise Dubois, Rena Dumas, Alber Elbaz, Maxime de La Falaise, Giancarlo Fare, John Fairchild, Louis Féraud, Armand Fouks, François Gaumont, Ginette Germond, Françoise Giroud, Hubert de Givenchy, Madeleine Godeau, Michel Goma, Andrew Goodman, Jacques Gourbaud, Antoine Gridel, Léo Gros, Sylvie Grumbach, Valérie Guillaume, Daniel Hechter, Max Heilbronn, Philippe Heim, Elie Jacobson, Emmanuelle Khanh, Peter Knapp, Wladimir de Kousmine, Caroline Lalonde, Valérie Lalonde, William Lauriol, Christian Legrez, Bernard Lehman, Pierre Lempereur, Marie-José Lepicard, André Lévi, Francine Lonnet-Lalonde, Manolita Lopez, Jean Manusardi, Simone Marbrier, Rosette Mett, Daniel Monsénégo, Pascal Morand, Erik Mortensen, Jacques Mouclier, Jean de Mouy, Helmut Newton, Jack Oppenheim, Gilbert Personeni, Zyga Pianko, François-Henri Pinault, Gérard Pipart, Ghislaine de Polignac, Carmine Porcelli, Donald Potard, Claude Potier, Andrée Putman, Annie Rivemale, Philippe Rolloy, Jacques Rouët, Nathalie Rykiel, Sonia Rykiel, Ginette Sainderichin, Richard Salomon, Robert Sakowitz, Jean-Louis Scherrer, Robert Schoettl, Marie-Hélène Serreules, Alice Springs, Antoine Stinco, Laurence Sudre, Thelma Sweetinburgh, Jean-Sébastien Szwarc, Angelo Tarlazzi, Patrick Thomas, Bruce Thomass, Ralph Toledano, Sidney Toledano, Nicolas Topiol, Melka Treanton, Emanuel Ungaro, Marie-Claude Vaillant-Couturier, Philippe Venet, Jean-Claude Weill, Katie Weisman, Maurice Weinberg, Sammy Weinberg, Alain Wertheimer, Yohji Yamamoto, Sylvie Zawadzki.

I thank the photographers who were kind enough to allow me to use their photographs: Pierre Boulat, Patricia Canino, Julien Claessens, Enrico Dagnino, Jean Paul Goude, Cécile Guyenne, Mustafa Hulusi, Christophe Jouin, Nick Knight, Karl Lagerfeld, Vincent Lappartient, Roxane Lowit, Guy Marineau, Chris Moore, Thierry Mugler, Simon Procter, Bettina Rheims, Michael Roberts, Patrick Robyn, Juliette Ruggieri, Thibaut de Saint-Chamas, Patrice Stable, Ronald Stoops, Etienne Tordoir, Gérard Uféras, Inez VanLamsweerde and Vinoodh Matadin, Willy Vanderperre.

Nathalie Bailleux, Louis-René Béziers, Laurent Buhler, and Marie Weigel helped with the research.

Isabelle d'Hauteville was the wonderful iconographer, with Jimmy Pihet's collaboration.

Lastly, I thank Stéphane Wargnier whose care and attention were very precious.

D.G.